D1613003

Indo-European Linguistics

The Indo-European language family comprises several hundred languages and dialects, including most of those spoken in Europe, and south, south-west and central Asia. Spoken by an estimated 3 billion people, it has the largest number of native speakers in the world today. This textbook provides an accessible introduction to the study of the Indo-European proto-language. It clearly sets out the methods for relating the languages to one another, presents an engaging discussion of the current debates and controversies concerning their classification, and offers sample problems and suggestions for how to solve them. Complete with a comprehensive glossary, almost 100 tables in which language data and examples are clearly laid out, suggestions for further reading, discussion points and a range of exercises, this text will be an essential toolkit for all those studying historical linguistics, language typology and the Indo-European proto-language for the first time.

JAMES CLACKSON is Senior Lecturer in the Faculty of Classics, University of Cambridge, and is Fellow and Director of Studies, Jesus College, University of Cambridge. His previous books include *The Linguistic Relationship between Armenian and Greek* (1994) and *Indo-European Word Formation* (co-edited with Birgit Anette Olson, 2004).

WITHDRAWN FROM
THE LIBRARY OF
UNIVERSITY OF
WINCHESTER

KA 0422902 9

CAMBRIDGE TEXTBOOKS IN LINGUISTICS

General editors: P. AUSTIN, J. BRESNAN, B. COMRIE, S. CRAIN,
W. DRESSLER, C. EWEN, R. LASS, D. LIGHTFOOT, K. RICE,
I. ROBERTS, S. ROMAINE, N. V. SMITH

Indo-European Linguistics

An Introduction

In this series:

Indo-European Linguistics
An Introduction

JAMES CLACKSON

University of Cambridge

CAMBRIDGE
UNIVERSITY PRESS

UNIVERSITY OF WINCHESTER
LIBRARY

CAMBRIDGE
UNIVERSITY PRESS

University Printing House, Cambridge CB2 8BS, United Kingdom

Cambridge University Press is part of the University of Cambridge.

It furthers the University's mission by disseminating knowledge in the pursuit of education, learning and research at the highest international levels of excellence.

www.cambridge.org
Information on this title: www.cambridge.org/9780521653671

© James Clackson 2007

This publication is in copyright. Subject to statutory exception
and to the provisions of relevant collective licensing agreements,
no reproduction of any part may take place without the written
permission of Cambridge University Press.

First published 2007
5th printing 2013

A catalogue record for this publication is available from the British Library

ISBN 978-0-521-65367-1 Paperback

Cambridge University Press has no responsibility for the persistence or accuracy
of URLs for external or third-party internet websites referred to in this publication,
and does not guarantee that any content on such websites is, or will remain,
accurate or appropriate.

UNIVERSITY OF WINCHESTER

04229029 | 410
CVA

Contents

Figures

Tables

Preface

Do we need another introduction to Indo-European linguistics? Since 1995 four have been published in English (Beekes 1995, Szemerényi 1996, Meier-Brügger 2003, Fortson 2004) and the ground seems to be pretty well covered. This book, however, aims to be an introduction of a different sort. Whereas the works mentioned give up-to-date and (usually) reliable information on the current thinking on what is known in Indo-European studies, here the aim is to present rather areas where there currently is, or ought to be, debate and uncertainty. Whereas previous introductions have aimed for the status of handbooks, reliable guides to the terrain presented in detail, this one aspires more to the status of a toolkit, offering up sample problems and suggesting ways of solving them. The reader who wants to know the details of how labio-velar consonants developed in Indo-European languages or the basis for the reconstruction of the locative plural case ending will not find them here; instead they will be able to review in detail arguments about the categories of the Indo-European verb or the syntax of relative clauses. The result is that this book has shorter chapters on areas such as phonology, where there is now more general agreement in the field, and correspondingly longer sections on areas which are passed by more summarily in other introductions. Memory athletes may be disappointed by the reduction in data, but I hope that others will welcome the increase in argumentation.

This book contains a number of exercises and discussion questions within and at the end of each chapter, designed to help readers get to grips with some of the issues in Indo-European linguistics and prompt further discussion. Answers to some of the exercises, hints and tips for others can be found at www.classics.cam.ac.uk/clacksonindoeuropean.

This book originates in the suggestion made some years ago by Geoff Horrocks, Professor of Comparative Philology at the University of Cambridge, to the two young (then) lecturers in his department that they should write a book which concentrated on explaining some of the issues of Indo-European linguistics. Torsten Meißner and I embarked together on the project with enthusiasm, and the framework of the book, and an early draft of Chapter 3 and parts of Chapters 1 and 2 were originally written in collaboration. Other duties and commitments delayed the completion of the work, however, and after a lapse of a few years I took up the project again on my own, partly through freedom allowed me by the generous award of a Philip Leverhulme Prize. Throughout the whole writing process Torsten has been an invaluable colleague and friend, he has commented on drafts of the entire work at various stages and I have learnt from him more than it is possible to express about all aspects of Indo-European. Without his input, this book would be half of what it is now. He is of course, like all the others mentioned here, exculpated of any responsibility for my own errors or misjudgements.

I have also benefited greatly from the help of many other colleagues and students. Parts of the work in draft were read by Andreas Bartholomä, Dr Michael Clarke, Dr Coulter George, Dr Antonia Ruppell and Dr Sheila Watts. I owe particular gratitude to Alex Mullen, who worked as research assistant and as an exacting copy-editor over one summer and saved me from innumerable errors and anacolutha. Professor Peter Matthews, one of the series editors for the CUP Textbooks in Linguistics, read and commented on the work in draft and Andrew Winnard, the CUP linguistics editor, was always ready to offer help and advice. Chris Jackson acted as an assiduous and attentive copy-editor for CUP and plugged many gaps in my knowledge. Sarah Clackson gave love and support in the initial stages of writing. Véronique Mottier enabled me to continue and complete the manuscript.

Finally, my first teacher in Indo-European linguistics was the late and much missed Bob Coleman, sometime Professor of Comparative Philology at the University of Cambridge. This book is dedicated to his memory.

Transliteration conventions

Words and texts cited in this book generally follow established conventions of transliteration or citation and are not given in IPA transcription. The following notes are intended to guide the reader to the pronunciation of forms cited in this book. Since in many cases the languages are no longer spoken, there is often uncertainty about the precise realisation of certain sounds, and the pronunciations given here can only at best be approximate. It should be noted that we have not attempted to give comprehensive accounts of the phonologies of the languages concerned, but merely to aid readers to understand how a particular sign is used. In general we have avoided giving details of signs which are not used in this book. Where no information is given on the pronunciation of a sign, the reader can assume that it has a value approximately equivalent to its IPA equivalent. In all cases we have tried to follow the standard orthography used in the scholarly literature, except in the case of Greek, for which we have not used the Greek alphabet, but a transliteration which should make it accessible to all and enable readers who know Greek to recognise the original words.

Albanian

Albanian is written in the Latin alphabet.

c ç q gj x xh represent affricates or palatals: *c* = [ts] *ç* = [tʃ] *q* = [c] *gj* = [ɟ] *x* = [dz] *xh* = [dʒ]
dh th sh zh represent fricatives: *dh* = [ð], *th* = [θ] *sh* = [ʃ] *zh* = [ʒ]
ë is the central unrounded mid vowel [ə]

Armenian

Armenian is written in its own alphabet. The transliteration here follows that used in most modern scholarly accounts of the language, for example Schmitt (1981).

c j č ǰ represent affricates: *c* = [ts] *j* = [dz] *č* = [tʃ] *ǰ* = [dʒ] *š ž* represent postalveolar sibilants: *š* = [ʃ] *ž* = [ʒ]

p' t' c' č' k' represent aspirates: *p'* = [pʰ] etc.

ł represents a velarised lateral [ɫ]

r̄ represents a trilled [r], whereas *r* represents the approximant [ɹ]

y represents the palatal approximant [j]

ê represents a close-mid unrounded front vowel, *e* an open-mid unrounded front vowel.

Avestan

Forms cited are transliterated from the Avestan alphabet, following the practice of Hoffmann and Forssman (1996: 41).

Vowels written with a macron, such as *ā*, are conventionally pronounced long.

ą represents a nasalised vowel.

å represents a vowel in between [a] and [o], probably the unrounded low back vowel [ɑ].

c j represent affricates: *c* = [tʃ] *j* = [dʒ]

š ž represent post-alveolar sibilants: *š* = [ʃ] *ž* = [ʒ]

n̥ represents an unreleased nasal.

y represents the palatal approximant [j] in word initial position; the same sound is generally represented by *ii* within a word.

v represents the labio-velar approximant [w] in word-initial position; the same sound is generally represented by *uu* within a word.

Palatalised consonants are denoted with a superscript acute accent, for example *ń* represents a palatalised *n*.

Labialised consonants are written with following superscript *v*, for example *xᵛ* represents a labialised velar fricative.

Etruscan

Etruscan is written in an alphabet adapted from the Greek alphabet. The transliteration follows standard scholarly practice.

c represents an unvoiced velar plosive.

z probably represents an affricate [ts]

θ represents an unvoiced dental consonant, distinguished in some way from the unvoiced plosive *t*.

χ represents an unvoiced velar consonant, distinguished in some way from the unvoiced plosive *c*.

Gothic

The Gothic alphabet is an adaptation of the Greek alphabet, with reuse of some letters to correspond to sounds present in Gothic but not in Greek. The transcription here follows the standard scholarly conventions, as given, for example, in Rauch (2003: 6).

There is dispute about what sounds the digraphs *ai au* represent. Etymologically, and in transcriptions of foreign words into Gothic, these digraphs correspond both to short and long vowels and diphthongs; *ai* thus appears to represent all of [ɛ], [ɛː] and [ai] and *au* appears to represent all of [ɔ], [ɔː] and [au]. We have not used here the convention of using the notation *aí* for [ɛ] and *ái* for [ai], since this corresponds to no difference in the actual written texts.

Long vowels are not marked separately to short vowels except in the case of a long *i*, which is written with a digraph *ei*. The vowels *e* and *o* are only used to represent the long close-mid front and back vowels [eː] and [oː], for which there are no short counterparts.

g written before another velar consonant represents the velar nasal.
q represents a voiceless glottal stop with simultaneous lip-rounding [kʷ]
hw represents the glottal fricative with simultaneous lip-rounding [hʷ]
þ represents the voiceless dental fricative [θ]

Greek

Mycenaean Greek is originally written in a syllabic script. In the transcription, syllabic signs are identified through writing hyphens between them (= is used to indicate a syllabic boundary which is also a clitic boundary). The syllabic script does not represent voiced stops other than [d], or aspirated stops, and *r* represents both [r] and [l]. The syllabary only has signs for open syllables, and frequently sounds which occur in the coda of syllables are omitted in the script.

q represents a voiceless stop, a voiced stop and an aspirated stop which have various outcomes in later Greek, and are usually understood to be [kʷ], [gʷ] and [kʷʰ].

Alphabetic Greek is written in the Greek alphabet, which has many different local variants. Forms cited are generally taken from the Attic dialect. The transliteration used here transliterates Greek letters by single letters, except in the cases of the so-called double consonants, where *zd* represents Greek ζ, *ps* represents Greek ψ and *ks* represents Greek ξ.

ph th kh represent aspirated consonants, so that *ph* = [pʰ] etc.
Vowels written with a macron, such as *ā*, are long.

ei and *ou* in Attic Greek represent front and back long close-mid vowels, but in other dialects and earlier Greek these are front and back rising diphthongs.

u and *ū* in Attic Greek represent close front rounded vowels, but in other dialects and in earlier Greek these are close back rounded vowels.

Three accent marks are used. The acute is reckoned to indicate a rising pitch on the vowel, the circumflex a rise and fall in pitch on a long vowel or diphthong, and the grave is a modification of the acute accent when it stands before another accented word.

Hittite

Hittite is written in a form of the cuneiform syllabic script employed also for the Semitic language Akkadian. As well as using signs to represent syllables, the script also employs various conventional ideograms and classificatory signs, and sometimes scribes use Akkadian words in place of Hittite ones. We have followed the conventional means of transcribing these, which sometimes gives the text a confusing appearance, with capital and superscript letters alongside lower-case. For our purposes it may suffice to state here that only the text in lower-case reproduces Hittite words and endings. The reader who wishes to know more is advised to consult Friedrich (1960: 21–5).

In our transcription of Hittite we have followed current scholarly practice in using a broad transcription which reproduces the likely shape of the Hittite word. We have avoided using diacritics in the transcription as far as possible (thus we write *s* and *h*, not *š* and *ḫ*, in line with current practice).

ku before a following vowel probably indicates a labialised velar plosive [k^w]
z probably represents an affricate [ts]

Vowels written with a macron, such as *ā*, represent the combination of two syllabic signs, and are usually reckoned to have been long vowels.

= is used to indicate a clitic boundary.

Latin

i represents both the vowel [i] and the consonant [j].
u represents both the vowel [u] and the consonant [w]. By convention when in upper case this sign is written *V*.
qu represents a combination of [k] and [w].

Vowels written with a macron, such as *ā*, are pronounced long.

Lithuanian

Lithuanian is written in the Latin alphabet, with some extra characters.

č represents an affricate, [tʃ]
š ž represent post-alveolar sibilants: *š* = [ʃ] *ž* = [ʒ]
ė represents a long close-mid front vowel; *e* represents an open-mid front vowel.
y represents a long unrounded high front vowel.
ą ę į ų represent vowels which were orignally nasalised, but which have
   now lost their nasalisation and are pronounced long.

Accented short vowels are marked with a grave accent. On accented long vowels
or diphthongs (which include combinations of vowel and *l, m, n, r*) two signs
are used to represent different pitch contours: the acute accent signifies a falling
pitch, the circumflex a rising pitch.

Luwian

Luwian is written either in the cuneiform syllabary employed for Hittite (see above) or in a hieroglyphic syllabic script. We here follow the transcription
of the hieroglyphic script as employed in Hawkins (2000 and 2003).

Lycian

Lycian is written in its own alphabet, adapted from the Greek. The
transcription of the Lycian alphabet here follows that used in Melchert (2004).

ã and *ẽ* are nasalised vowels.
m̃ and *ñ* may represent unreleased nasals.
q represents some sort of voiceless velar consonant.
x represents some sort of voiceless velar consonant; it is transcribed as χ in earlier
   works.
z can represent the affricate [ts]

Old Church Slavonic

Old Church Slavonic is written in the Cyrillic and Glagolitic alphabets.
There are many competing systems of transliteration of the Cyrillic alphabet; the
one we use here follows Comrie and Corbett (1993), except in the use of the signs
ĭ and *ŭ*.

c č represent affricates: *c* = [ts] *č* = [tʃ]

š ž represent post-alveolar sibilants: *š* = [ʃ] *ž* = [ʒ]

ě represents an open-mid unrounded front vowel (*e* is a close-mid unrounded front vowel).

y represents a close unrounded back vowel.

ĭ represents a mid central unrounded vowel.

ŭ represents a mid central rounded vowel.

ę and *ǫ* are nasalised vowels.

Old English

Old English is written in the Latin alphabet (see above) with additional letters.

þ and *ð* are used to represent voiceless and voiced interdental fricatives [θ] and [ð].

æ represents an open unrounded front vowel, *a* an open unrounded back vowel.

y and *œ* represent rounded close and mid front vowels.

Old High German

Old High German is written in the Latin alphabet. Long vowels are denoted with a macron.

ch represents the voiceless velar fricative [x]

Old Irish

Old Irish is written in the Latin alphabet (see above) with a number of orthographic innovations.

Long vowels are indicated by an acute accent, for example *á*.

Palatalisation of syllable-final consonants is indicated by writing *i* before the consonant.

p t c represent voiceless stops word-initially; elsewhere they stand for voiced stops.

pp tt cc represent voiceless stops word-medially or word-finally.

b d g represent voiced stops word-initially; elsewhere they stand for voiced fricatives [β] [ð] [ɣ]

ph th ch represent voiceless fricatives, [f] [θ] [x] respectively.

= is used to indicate a clitic boundary.

Old Norse

The Old Norse cited in this book is taken from texts originally written in a form of the Latin alphabet, with added letters, diacritics and digraphs. Long vowels are denoted with the acute accent: for example, *á* and *é* are the lengthened counterparts to *a* and *e*.

þ represents the voiceless dental fricative [θ]

Old Persian

Old Persian is written in a syllabic script. The transcription used here follows Brandenstein and Mayrhofer (1964: 17–24). Vowels written with a macron, such as *ā*, represent the combination of two syllabic signs and are pronounced long.

y represents the palatal approximant [j]
= is used to indicate a clitic boundary.

Oscan

Oscan is written both in the Latin alphabet and a native alphabet. We have not followed the standard practice of differentiating between the two alphabets through the use of bold script, since all the forms in this work are originally written in the native script.
    Any doubled vowel, such as *aa* and *ii*, represents a long vowel.

Palaic

The very small corpus of the Anatolian language Palaic is written in the same cuneiform script as Hittite.

Russian

Russian is written in the same Cyrillic script as is used for Old Church Slavonic (with the abandonment of a few signs). The transcription here used is the same as for Old Church Slavonic, except for the use of the soft sign '.

c č represent affricates: *c* = [ts] *č* = [tʃ]
š ž represent post-alveolar sibilants: *š* = [ʃ] *ž* = [ʒ]

y represents a close unrounded back vowel.
' written after a consonant denotes that the consonant is palatalised.

Sanskrit

Sanskrit forms are generally cited from the earliest texts, the Vedic hymns and associated texts, the language of which is sometimes called Vedic. The transliteration of the devanagari script adopted here is the one used in modern scholarly treatments of the language, (for example, Mayrhofer 1986–2001).

ph th ṭh ch kh represent aspirated consonants, so that *ph* = [pʰ] etc.
bh dh ḍh jh gh represent consonants traditionally described as voiced and aspirated.
c ch j jh represent palatal stops, so that *c* = [c] *j* = [ɟ]
ṭ ṭh ḍ ḍh ṣ ṇ represent retroflex consonants, so that *ḍ* = [ɖ] *ṇ* = [ɳ] etc.
ś represents the palatal fricative [ç]
h represents the voiced glottal fricative [ɦ]
ñ represents the palatal nasal [ɲ]
y represents the palatal approximant [j]
ṛ represents a syllabic *r* [r̩]

Vowels written with a macron, such as *ā*, are pronounced long.
The acute accent indicates a rise in pitch on the syllable.

Serbian

Serbian is written in the Cyrillic alphabet, and the transcription used here is the same as that for Russian.

Tocharian

Tocharian uses a version of the same script as Sanskrit (see above). It also has an additional vowel sign transcribed *ä* which is taken to represent a mid central unrounded vowel [ə]. In Tocharian *ts* represents an affricate [ts].

Umbrian

Umbrian is written both in the Latin alphabet and a native alphabet. We have not followed the standard practice of differentiating between the two alphabets through the use of bold script, since all the forms cited in this work are originally written in the Latin alphabet, except for one, *utur*, written in the native script. In the word *utur*, *t* may represent a voiced dental stop, since the Umbrian alphabet has no separate sign for this sound. For the other forms, see the notes for the Latin alphabet given above.

Welsh

Welsh is written in the Latin alphabet, and the forms cited here are in the modern orthography.

ch th represent the unvoiced fricatives [x] and [θ] respectively.
dd represents the voiced dental fricative [ð]
f represents the voiced labio-dental fricative [v], *ff* its unvoiced counterpart [f].
u represents the close unrounded central vowel [i].
w represents either the close rounded back vowel [u] or the consonant [w].
y represents an unrounded central vowel, either [ə] or [i].

1   The Indo-European language family

1.1   Introduction

Indo-European (IE) is the best-studied language family in the world. For much of the past 200 years more scholars have worked on the comparative philology of IE than on all the other areas of linguistics put together. We know more about the history and relationships of the IE languages than about any other group of languages. For some branches of IE – Greek, Sanskrit and Indic, Latin and Romance, Germanic, Celtic – we are fortunate to have records extending over two or more millennia, and excellent scholarly resources such as grammars, dictionaries and text editions that surpass those available for nearly all non-IE languages. The reconstruction of Proto-Indo-European (PIE) and the historical developments of the IE languages have consequently provided the framework for much research on other language families and on historical linguistics in general. Some of the leading figures in modern linguistics, including Saussure, Bloomfield, Trubetzkoy and Jakobson, were Indo-Europeanists by training, as were many of those who taught in newly founded university departments of linguistics in the second half of the twentieth century. Despite this pedigree, IE studies are now marginalised within most university linguistics courses and departments. In most US and European institutions, Indo-Europeanists with university posts do not teach in linguistics departments but in classics, oriental studies, celtic studies or the like. Historical linguistics courses may include a section on PIE, or Saussure's work on laryngeals as an example of internal reconstruction, but few students will engage in any current work on IE in any depth.

The intention of this book is not to convert general linguists to IE studies, or to restore the discipline to the central position in linguistics that it had a hundred years ago. Rather it aims to set forth some of the areas of debate in IE studies. In recent years a number of grammars and handbooks of PIE have been published in English (Gamkrelidze and Ivanov 1984 (English translation 1995), Sihler 1995, Beekes 1995, Szemerényi 1996, Meier-Brügger 2000 (English translation 2003), Fortson 2004). Most of these works are excellent, but sometimes the apodeictic style of the presentation leaves the reader uncertain about whether what is presented is actually hypothesis or 'fact'. One explanation for a historical change may be preferred over another, but the author may not make clear what is at stake in the choice between the alternatives. This book takes a different approach. It is

1

deliberately not intended to be a grammar of IE, or a survey of the developments that have taken place between PIE and the daughter IE languages, but rather to be a survey of some current debates and topics of more general interest in the reconstruction of PIE, and a guide to the ways in which some of these issues have been addressed. The material throughout the book is selective and illustrative, and the reader who wants to find out more will be advised to follow the further reading sections at the end of each chapter.

1.2   The IE languages

The IE language family is extensive in time and space. The earliest attested IE language, Hittite, is attested nearly 4,000 years ago, written on clay tablets in cuneiform script in central Anatolia from the early second millennium BC. We have extensive textual remains, including native-speaker accounts of three more IE languages from 2,000 years ago: Ancient Greek, Latin and Sanskrit. Also from the beginning of the Christian Era we have much more limited corpora of many more IE languages. The stock of recorded IE languages further increases as we move forward in time. In 2003, over 2.5 billion people spoke an IE language as their first language, and there were at least seventy codified varieties, each spoken by a million or more native speakers. Four hundred years ago nearly all speakers of IE lived in Europe, Iran, Turkey, Western Asia and the Indian sub-continent, but migrations have now spread speakers to every part of the world. The wealth of historical material makes IE the best-documented language family in the world.

What is it that makes an IE language IE? What does it mean to be classed as an IE language? It is usual at the opening of books on IE to repeat the famous words of Sir William Jones in 1786 which are traditionally taken to have inaugurated the discipline. Jones remarked on the similarity of Sanskrit to Latin and Greek, stating that they all bore 'a stronger affinity, both in the roots of verbs and in the forms of grammar, than could possibly have been produced by accident; so strong, indeed, that no philologer could examine them all three, without believing them to be sprung from some common source, which, perhaps, no longer exists'. Jones also noted that Gothic, Celtic and Persian could be added to the same family. Since 1786, a considerable methodology has been established to qualify and quantify Jones' notion of 'affinity' between the grammars and lexicons of the IE languages, and to work out a hypothetical model of the 'common source', PIE. But there has been no advance on Jones' criterion for relatedness between languages of the family: greater similarity in verbal roots and morphological paradigms than might be expected by chance. Languages which belong to the IE family do so either because the similarity between them and other IE languages is so strong as to be self-evident, or because they can be clearly related to languages which do obviously belong to the family. For a language which has textual remains sufficient for the linguist to extract lexical and grammatical information, it is possible to apply the techniques of reconstruction, such as the comparative method, to build a picture of its development from PIE. However, the operation of the comparative method does not guarantee a language's place in the family; only the initial recognition that two or more languages are related can do that. (We shall return to examine the implications of this point more fully in section 1.6.)

When does a linguist decide that there is enough material to relate a language to the IE family? There is no absolute set of criteria beyond the general rule that the evidence must convince both the individual linguist and the majority of the scholarly community. A language which only survives in a very limited corpus may contain sufficient IE features to be generally agreed to be IE. As an example, take the case of Lusitanian. Lusitanian is known from a handful of inscriptions from the west of the Iberian peninsular, written in the Latin alphabet around the first century of the Christian Era. One of these inscriptions, from Lamas de Moledo in Portugal, reads as follows (the slash / signals the end of the line in the original inscription):

RVFINVS. ET
TIRO SCRIP/SERVNT
VEAMINICORI
DOENTI
ANGOM
LAMATICOM
CROVCEAIMAGA
REAICOI. PETRANIOI. T
ADOM. PORGOM IOVEAI
CAELOBRIGOI

The first four words are Latin: 'Rufus and Tiro wrote (this).' But the remainder of the inscription is not Latin. The inscription is taken to refer to the sacrifice of animals by a people called the *Veaminicori* to gods who are also addressed with their cult titles. Not all the words are understood, although the structure is clear: *Veaminicori* is nominative plural, *doenti* is a verb meaning 'they give'. The rest of the inscription has nouns in the accusative singular, denoting what is given: *angom lamaticom*, *tadom porgom*; and the names of the recipients in the dative singular: *petranioi, caelobrigoi*. This is not much, but enough that no Indo-Europeanist doubts that Lusitanian is a member of the IE family. Several of the word-forms are very similar to Latin. For example, the dedicated item *porgom* is very likely to mean 'pig' (Latin accusative singular *porcum* 'pig'), and *angom* to mean 'lamb' (Latin accusative singular *agnum* 'lamb'). The verb-form *doenti* 'they give' contains the root *do-* 'give', familiar from the equivalent forms in Greek (*dō-*), Latin (*da-*) and Sanskrit (*dā-* / *d-*). More importantly, it shows a third person plural ending *-enti* which is also found in these languages (dialectal Greek *-enti*, Archaic Latin *-nti* and Sanskrit *-anti*). Furthermore, the ending *-oi* coincides with a dative singular marker elsewhere (Greek *-ōi*, Archaic Latin *-oi* and Sanskrit -*ai*), and the nominative plural ending -*i* accords with the nominative plural -*i* of one Latin noun declension. The interpretation of this inscription rests entirely on the identification of its language as IE, but most scholars have found it hard to believe all these similarities are entirely due to chance.

Compare with Lusitanian the case of Tartessian, another language from Ancient Spain which is known only from short inscriptions. Tartessian is better attested than Lusitanian, and from a period 600–800 years earlier. Unfortunately, we are not confident about our reading of the Tartessian script, and we do not have the helpful marks which are usually present in the Lusitanian inscriptions indicating where words begin or end. We consequently do not know a lot about the morphology of the language. However, some scholars have identified in Tartessian repeated patterns of (what they take to be) verbal endings. Consider the following inscription, reproduced in its entirety:

botieanakertorobatebarebanarkenti

The final nine letters, *narkenti*, occur elsewhere in the inscriptional corpus, as do the similar forms *narken*, *narkenii*, *narke*, *narkenai*. Here again we see a final element -*nti* that could represent the third person plural of a verbal ending in an IE language, just as in Lusitanian above. However, there is no obvious connection in the older IE languages to what would appear to be the verbal 'stem' *nark*-. Moreover, if we try to use what we know of IE morphology and vocabulary to interpret the rest of the inscription, we do not get very far. In Lusitanian, the assumption that the language was IE yielded vocabulary and morphology. In Tartessian, we have nothing more than the ending -*enti*. We do not even know enough about the morphological structure of the language to be confident that *narkenti* should be analysed as stem *nark*- + affix -*enti*. Accordingly, the general consensus is that Tartessian should not be included among the IE family.

The status of languages as IE or not may change in the light of an increase in our knowledge of the family. This is the case with the languages Lydian and Lycian, spoken in Anatolia in the first millennium BC, and known from inscriptions written in modified forms of the Greek alphabet. Before the discovery and accurate description of older IE languages in the Anatolian family, Hittite and Luwian, written in cuneiform and hieroglyphic scripts hundreds of years earlier, Lydian and Lycian could not be securely included in the IE family. However, their affinity to the earlier Anatolian languages is now patent, and since these show clear morphological and vocabulary similarities with the rest of IE, there is no doubt that Lydian and Lycian belong in the family as well. If we did not have any Anatolian languages other than Lydian and Lycian, we would not now be so certain of their ancestry. Indeed, we would not be able to make much sense of them at all, since it is only through the knowledge of how Anatolian languages are structured that headway has been made with the interpretation of the surviving inscriptions. It is, consequently, conceivable that a language such as Tartessian could come into the IE fold, if we were to have some intermediate steps to show the link between the rest of the family and the inscriptional remains that we have.

1.3   The branches of the IE tree

It follows from the remarks about Lydian and Lycian that the sub-families of IE are vitally important in determining the membership of the family. Whereas the affinity of the oldest IE languages declares itself as stronger than could be produced by chance (to most of those who study them), the affinity of languages attested more recently is sometimes only discernible through first relating them to sub-families of IE. Thus, to take an example of two languages at the far ends of the historical IE speech area, Modern Irish and Sinhala would not strike a linguist who was fluent in each, but unacquainted with their history, as *necessarily* related. It is only through relating Modern Irish to Old Irish, and Sinhala to Sanskrit, that the connection between the two languages becomes clear.

The majority of IE languages currently spoken belong to six large sub-groups of IE. Modern Irish and Old Irish are members of the Celtic sub-group, which also includes Welsh, Scots Gaelic, Breton, Cornish and Manx. Sinhala is part of the large Indic family, comprising most of the languages currently spoken in North India and Pakistan, Sanskrit and the Middle Indian Prakrits. English is a member of the Germanic branch; this includes Dutch, German and the Scandinavian languages among living languages, as well as earlier stages of these languages, such as Old English, Old High German and Old Norse, and other extinct varieties such as Gothic, once spoken in south-east Europe and southern Russia. The other large sub-groups are Romance and Slavic in Europe, and Iranian in Asia. All of these sub-groups of IE were themselves recognised as linguistic families before Jones' identification of the larger IE family cited above. The traditional criterion for grouping these languages was, in general terms, analogous to the criterion Jones used for IE. The members of a sub-group are so much more similar to each other than they are to other IE languages that the similarity cannot be put down to chance. Now, however, there are firmer criteria for membership of a sub-group. Two languages grouped together in a sub-group are assumed to have derived from a language, the 'sub-group parent language', which is chronologically earlier than either of the grouped languages, but which was spoken after PIE. The relationship can be represented diagrammatically as a family tree, with the historically prior languages situated at higher nodes in the tree. In figure 1.1, languages A and B constitute a sub-group, since they derive from a single language intermediate between them and the parent. Languages C and D do not constitute a sub-group between each other or with either A or B.

The family tree model has been very influential in IE studies, and we shall consider it in more detail below. In some cases, as in the Romance language sub-group of IE or the Indic sub-group, we have records of an early language variety which either can be identified with the sub-group parent, or which is very close to the sub-group parent (Latin and Sanskrit in the two cases respectively). But for some other sub-groups we do not have an attested parent, and it has to be reconstructed using the comparative method. It is now generally agreed among

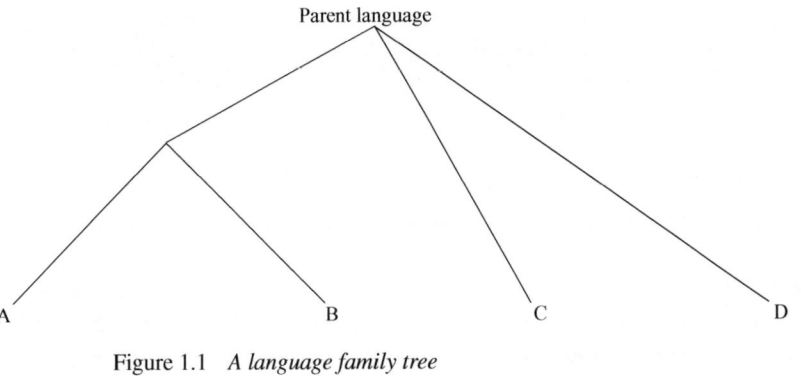

Figure 1.1   *A language family tree*

linguists that the most certain sub-groups are constructed on the basis of unique shared morphological innovations. That is, where there is no attested parent for a group of languages, they may be reckoned to belong to the same sub-group if they share a significant number of new developments in their morphology, particularly inflectional morphology. If, for example, two languages have constructed a new morphological category with a new morphological marker, and the marker is not found in other IE languages, this is reckoned to be a significant morphological innovation. It is only through morphological changes of this sort that we can be sure that there is a reconstructed sub-group parent: lexical and phonological developments are too easily shared through linguistic convergence, and we do not generally have enough information about reconstructed syntax to be certain that syntactic changes are innovations.

Using this methodology of sub-grouping it is possible to identify further sub-groups of Indo-European beyond the six large sub-groups identified above. Lithuanian and Latvian are only attested from the Early Modern period, and together with the now extinct Old Prussian they form the Baltic sub-group. Two sub-groups are no longer extant: Anatolian, mentioned in section 1.2 above, which was widespread in central and western Anatolia before the Christian Era, and Tocharian, known from the textual remains of two separate languages (now known as Tocharian A and Tocharian B) spoken in central Asia in the sixth to eighth centuries A D. Sub-grouping methodology also makes it clear that the Indic branch and the Iranian branch are more closely related to each other than to any other branch, and they are now recognised as an Indo-Iranian sub-group. Baltic and Slavic are usually also assumed to stem from a single Balto-Slavic branch, but in this case we cannot be so sure, since the languages are attested so much later.

A few IE varieties still spoken are not allocated to sub-groups, but are usually represented as separate 'branches' of the IE family tree. The languages in question are all spoken around the Eastern Mediterranean: Greek, Albanian and Armenian. Greek, as we have seen, has a long history, but the other two languages are more recent: Armenian dates from the middle of the first millennium, Albanian from the second millennium of the Christian Era. Greek, Albanian and Armenian are thought by some scholars to comprise a 'Balkan IE' sub-group, but this hypothesis is disputed, since Albanian and Armenian have undergone so much linguistic change that their morphological developments are difficult to identify with confidence. Finally, there are varieties of IE no longer spoken which are not securely allocated to sub-groups. These are sometimes called 'fragmentary IE languages', since most are known from only a small corpus of material. Lusitanian, discussed in section 1.2 above, is an example of such a language.

It is a curious paradox of IE linguistics that the languages which are attested earliest are often the most difficult to assign to any sub-group. Of the IE languages spoken today, only Greek, Armenian and Albanian do not have close relatives in the same way that English compares to Dutch and German, or French to Italian and Spanish. Two thousand years ago, the linguistic map was different. Many of the languages spoken around the Mediterranean in 500 BC were superseded by Latin and its descendants following the Roman Conquest. As far as we can tell from the scanty textual remains of these languages, most were independent branches of IE, and not part of a sub-group. Lusitanian is one example of such a language, and Messapic provides another. Messapic is the name given to the language of around 300 short inscriptions from the heel of Italy, which were written in the Greek alphabet between the fifth and second century BC. Like Lusitanian, it is generally recognised to be IE, but it is not securely associated with any other IE language. The difficulty of assigning Messapic to any branch of IE is not just a problem of interpretation of a scanty corpus; the language shows significant divergences from the IE branches which are attested closest to it: Greek, Latin and the Sabellian languages of Italy, and Albanian. Other scantily attested Mediterranean languages which do not fit into a sub-group include: Phrygian, attested in central Asia Minor in two different varieties (Old Phrygian, from the eighth to the fourth century BC, and New Phrygian, from the second and third century AD); Venetic, attested in north-east Italy in nearly 300 short inscriptions from around the sixth to the second century BC; Thracian, the name given to the language of a text of sixty-one letters inscribed on a gold ring found at Ezerovo in Bulgaria and some short inscriptions on coins. Of the languages attested in the last 200 years, the only good candidates for a new branch of IE are the Nuristani languages spoken in remote valleys in eastern Afghanistan, which are thought to represent a third branch of the Indo-Iranian sub-group beside Indic and Iranian.

Table 1.1 is intended to illustrate the point about sub-groups; it shows first attestations of language and language groups by date and place, dividing the IE speech area into four different zones. Northern Europe comprises the area north of the Alps stretching from Ireland in the west to the Urals. The western Mediterranean comprises Spain, southern France and Italy. The eastern Mediterranean comprises Greece, Anatolia and the Black Sea area. The fourth zone includes Asia east of the Urals, the Indian sub-continent, and Iran and neighbouring countries to the east. The table gives the first appearance of languages in lower case and IE sub-groups or languages which represent independent branches of IE in

Table 1.1 *IE languages by date and place of first attestation.*

Date	Northern Europe	Western Mediterranean	Eastern Mediterranean	Iran / Central Asia / India
1800 BC			Old Hittite (ANATOLIAN)	
1400 BC			Mycenaean Greek (GREEK) Mittani (INDIC)	
500 BC		Latin (ROMANCE) South Picene (SABELLIAN) VENETIC Lepontic (CELTIC) MESSAPIC	PHRYGIAN THRACIAN MACEDONIAN	Old Persian (IRANIAN)
1 AD	LUSITANIAN			
500 AD	Rune inscriptions (GERMANIC)		ARMENIAN	
1000 AD	Old Church Slavonic (SLAVIC)			TOCHARIAN
1500 AD	Old Prussian (BALTIC)	ALBANIAN		
2000 AD	NURISTANI			

SMALL CAPS. The information in the table relies on dated texts, which means that the Indic family is attested first through the existence of some personal names and words relating to horse-training which occur in Hittite, Hurrian and Babylonian records from 1400 BC on, and not through the orally transmitted Vedic hymns. A similar problem surrounds the dating of the Iranian languages: Gathic Avestan, the language of the central portion of the sacred books of the Zoroastrians, certainly reflects an earlier stage of Iranian than the Old Persian inscriptions, but its transmission history does not allow us to date it securely. In the table, once one member of a sub-group is attested the sub-group is not recorded again, even when later representatives of the family occur in a different zone.

The order of attestation of different languages is reliant on the transmission of scripts and literacy. Unfortunately, the social and cultural changes which brought about an increase in literacy in much of the area where IE varieties are spoken also led to the spread of a few dominant languages at the expense of others. Table 1.1 shows the effect this has on the attestation of different languages. In the western and eastern Mediterranean zones at the onset of literacy in the first millennium BC a number of different languages are attested. In the early centuries of the Christian Era most of these languages were replaced by Latin and Greek and their descendants. The spread of these languages, and of the other large sub-groups, is not surprising. Most of the area where the IE languages are spoken are classic 'spread zones' in the terminology of Nichols (1992). That is to say, they are areas where large-scale population movement is possible, and where one social group may readily achieve dominance over its neighbours. The IE languages for which we have fairly extensive records from before 1000 AD – Latin, Greek, Germanic, Iranian and Indic – have been the carriers of cultures which have in time predominated over other indigenous groups, with resultant language shift. Populations which once spoke Messapic, Venetic and Lusitanian eventually shifted to speaking Latin, Phrygians adopted Greek and Thracian lost out to overlapping waves of Greek, Latin, Germanic (Gothic) and Slavic. In the Mediterranean area, the early adoption of literacy allows us to know of a range of IE varieties. In northern and eastern Europe, where the first written records appear considerably later, we do not know whether there was a similar diversity in the territories later occupied by speakers of Celtic, Germanic, Slavic and Baltic languages. We shall consider further the question of how we can assess the evidence for the early relationship of the IE family, considering what we have lost, in the next section.

1.4   Cladistics: constructing family trees

The family tree model of IE is over 150 years old. The model was first put forward in the nineteenth century, and the first tree diagram was produced by the German Indo-Europeanist August Schleicher (reproduced in figure 1.2). Schleicher's tree does not include Armenian, which was not then recognised as a separate branch of IE, nor Anatolian or Tocharian, which were not then known. As our understanding of the IE languages has increased and changed, so also the tree has changed. In Schleicher's tree, the first split is made between Germanic, Baltic and Slavic and the other language groups. This split reflects the fact that the three sub-groups spoken in the north of the IE area form dative-ablative and instrumental plural cases in some noun paradigms with a marker involving the original phoneme *m, whereas the other languages use a marker with *b^h, as shown in table 1.2, which gives the instrumental plural markers in various IE languages (note that all reconstructed, as opposed to attested, sounds, morphs and words are preceded by * throughout this book and in most works on PIE).

This divergence between the languages is still unexplained – it may be that the two plural cases which use *m or *b^h, the dative-ablative and instrumental, originally took separate markers, but some languages generalised *m to both of them, others *b^h. Modern scholars do not see the distinction between the use of *b^h and *m in these cases as sufficient evidence for a fundamental split between two parts of the IE language family. Furthermore, there are other features which unite the languages of the western IE zone: Celtic, Germanic and Latin and the Sabellian languages. In constructing a family tree, the shape of the tree depends on what the linguist sees as important.

Table 1.2 *Instrumental plural markers in various IE languages.*

PIE *-*mis*	Germanic: Gothic -*m*
	Slavic: Old Church Slavonic -*mi*
	Baltic: Lithuanian -*mis*
PIE *-*bʰis*	Indo-Iranian: Sanskrit -*bhis*
	Greek: Mycenaean Greek -*pi* (/-pʰi/)
	Celtic: Old Irish -ⁱ*b*

In recent years, the advance of statistical techniques and the use of computers to process very large amounts of data have allowed the construction of family trees from a much wider data set and a resurgence in interest in drawing a family tree for IE. Since computer analysis allows for such a large amount of discrete data to be handled, trees can be constructed using hundreds of different features. The new technology brings with it a new terminology, and now linguists are beginning to talk not of family trees, but *phylogenies*, and to use the term *cladistics* for referring to the techniques of constructing family trees. Two recent phylogenies of PIE are given in figure 1.3 (the 'New Zealand' tree constructed by Gray and Atkinson 2003: 437) and figure 1.4 (the 'Pennsylvania tree' taken from Ringe, Warnow and Taylor 2002: 90). The two phylogenies use different features in order to rank languages against one another.

The New Zealand tree, figure 1.3, relies upon vocabulary items only, following in a long tradition of language surveys which rely upon word lists or 'basic

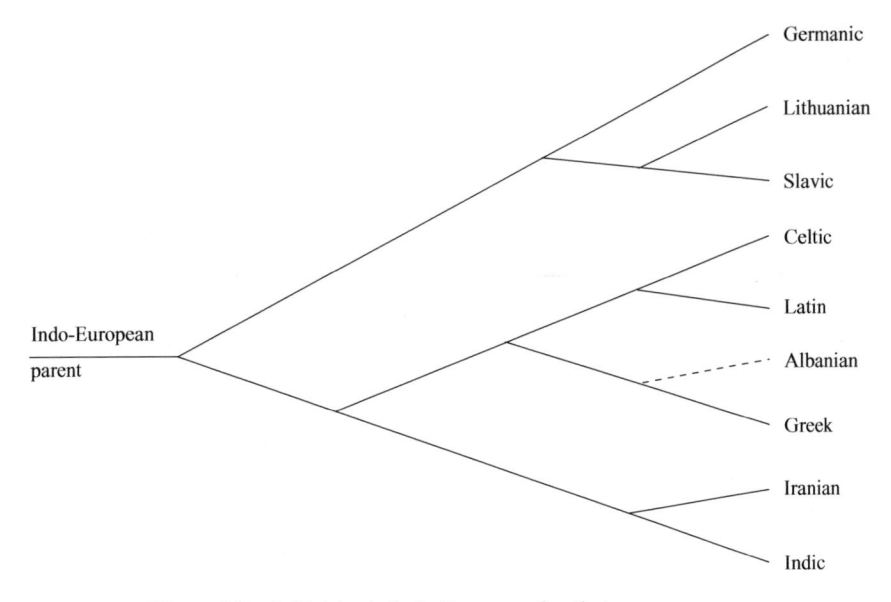

Figure 1.2   *Schleicher's Indo-European family tree*

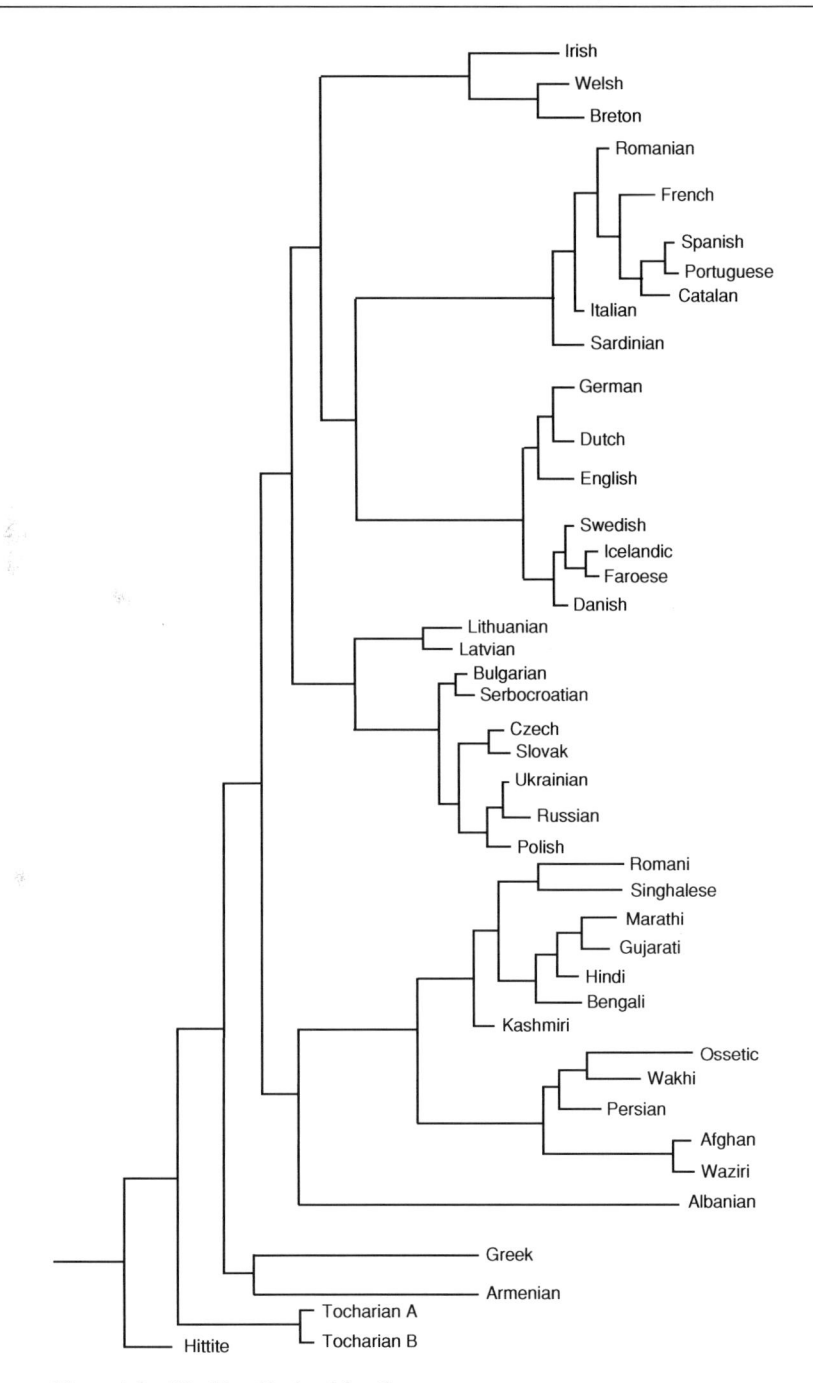

Figure 1.3 *The New Zealand family tree*
Adapted by permission from Macmillan Publishers Ltd: *Nature* 426 (2003)

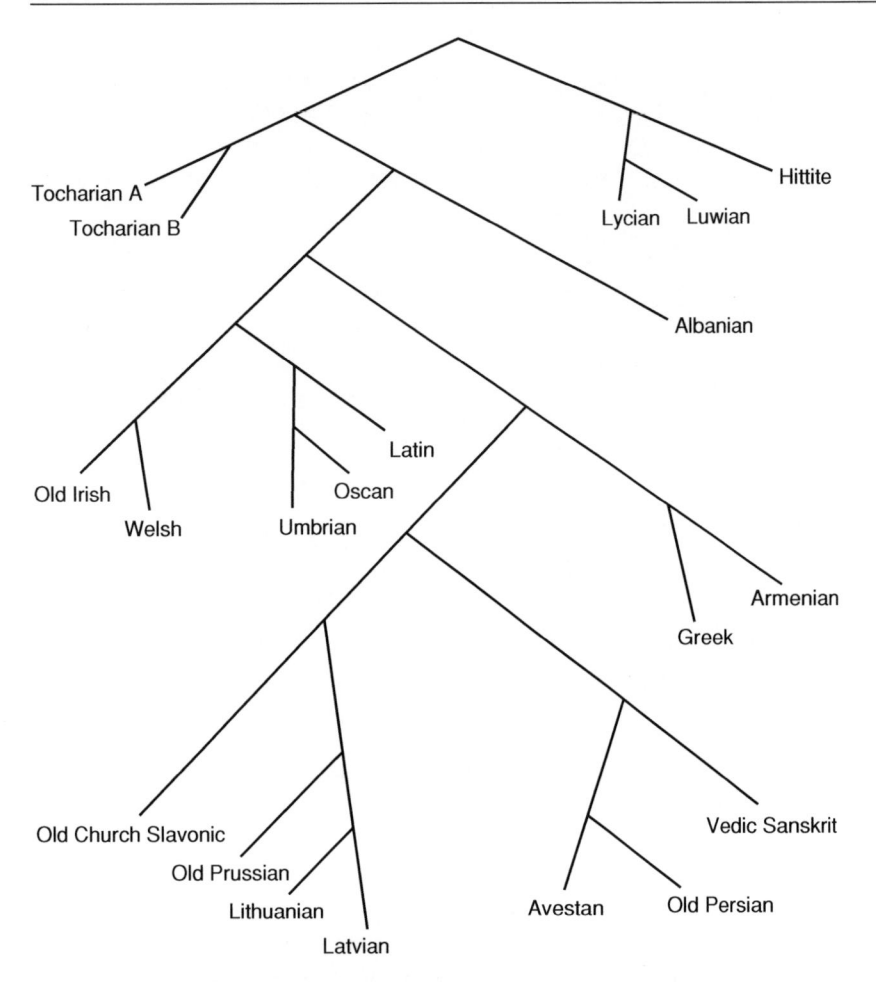

Figure 1.4 *The Pennsylvania family tree*
Reprinted by permission of Blackwell Publishing Ltd: *Transactions of the
Philological Society* 100 (2002)

vocabulary' lists. As we have discussed in section 1.2 above, vocabulary alone
has not generally been considered as sufficient for constructing sub-groups of
languages. However, the ease with which the vocabulary data can be recovered
and used in computer analysis makes it a very amenable data set. The use of the
'basic vocabulary list' originally compiled by Swadesh without the IE language
family specifically in mind means that the selection of data is neutral: the New
Zealand team cannot be accused of pre-selecting the data with a certain outcome
in mind. Gray and Atkinson's tree also applies techniques first used by geneticists
working on the cladistics of DNA sequences to assign dates to the divisions in the
family. Their dating is still controversial, and we shall discuss the dating issue in
more detail in the next section.

The 'Pennsylvania tree', figure 1.4, is constructed on the basis of compared
features over a much larger range. Languages are compared not just through

vocabulary items, but also phonological and morphological features. While the New Zealand tree takes lexical data principally from the modern spoken forms of the languages, the Pennsylvania tree uses the earliest attested languages for information. Ringe has used his own extensive knowledge of the IE family to select items which have already been reckoned to be diagnostic for sub-grouping, and features can be marked as innovations in the computer sorting process. Furthermore, some features, such as morphological innovations, can be given extra weight, whereas others, such as lexical agreements, carry less weight in the tree. The Pennsylvania tree is made utlising the scholarship on the IE languages, the New Zealand tree is not.

If we compare the New Zealand tree of IE with the Pennsylvania tree, we see that they share some fundamentals on the interrelationship of the IE languages. In both models, the first split in the tree is between the Anatolian group of languages and all the others, and the second is between Tocharian and the rest of the family. This is in accordance with the views of the majority of Indo-Europeanists at present. Anatolian is radically different from the rest of the family in many respects, and much of the rest of this book will be concerned with looking for an explanation of these differences. However, once we proceed beyond the first splits in the tree, there appear to be striking differences between the trees; note in particular the position of Albanian and the Germanic group. In the New Zealand tree, Albanian is grouped closest to the Indo-Iranian languages, forming a separate branch with them. Germanic forms a branch with the Romance languages, with Celtic as an outlier group. The Pennsylvania tree sees no close connection between Albanian and Indo-Iranian. Germanic is omitted from the tree, since there is no best-fit tree with Germanic, but Italic and Celtic are closely linked on the tree.

The existence of these discrepancies is not in itself reason to cast doubt on the exercise of drawing up trees through phylogenetic techniques. The New Zealand tree and the Pennsylvania tree actually assess different things: the first is a measure of the affinity of lexicons, not of grammatical systems, and the second tracks a range of innovations and changes across families. It is perfectly possible for both phylogenies to be correct. The relationship of vocabularies may not be the same as the participation in linguistic changes. The modern Germanic languages have vocabularies which have been influenced by and which have influenced the modern Romance languages, and this is reflected in the closeness of the languages on the New Zealand tree. The difficulties that arose in the construction of the trees are themselves instructive. As already mentioned, for the construction of the Pennsylvania tree, Germanic was removed from the analysis in order to provide a 'best fit'. This may point to unusual changes in the prehistory of Germanic, and possible convergence with other IE varieties. Comparing the cladistics in this way may alert researchers to potentially problematic or interesting areas of linguistic development and allow the construction of hypotheses to account for why the divergences exist.

However, we have seen in the preceding section that many of the scantily attested IE varieties which appear early in the historical record, languages such as

Lusitanian and Messapic, do not fit well into the language sub-group and family tree model. Often we do not know enough about these languages to include them in the phylogenetic analyses. We cannot draw up a basic vocabulary list or know for certain which innovations they have or have not undergone. Yet these fragmentary languages may be representative of a much wider range of IE varieties which have been lost beneath the spread of the big IE sub-groups. Is there any way we can include these languages in the model of PIE?

Recent work by Andrew Garrett (Garrett 1999 and 2006) has used the fragmentary languages of the Mediterranean area to rethink the validity of the family tree model for the early stages of the IE language family. Furthermore, Garrett's work calls into question the reconstruction of sub-groups in the west of the IE speech area. Take the example of Celtic. We have so far discussed the Celtic languages as a unit, with Lepontic, recorded in inscriptions in northern Italy from around 600 BC, as the earliest branch of the language to be attested. Other members of the sub-group attested before the Christian Era include Gaulish, known from texts in France, and Celtiberian, known from a few inscriptions in central Spain written in a modified form of the Iberian script. These languages share some characteristic lexical features with the other members of the Celtic group, principally Irish and Welsh, and the loss of the sound *p, generally assumed for all the Celtic languages. However, the number of morphological innovations which are shared by all the Celtic languages is extremely small, and if we use the strictest criteria for reconstructing sub-groups, the Celtic languages do not qualify. Even the loss of *p seems only to be underway in the Lepontic inscriptions and may have spread across the whole language area from language to language, rather than being a feature of a sub-group parent from which they all descended. It is therefore possible that other sub-group parents as such do not exist, but that sub-groups actually represent later convergence of closely related languages.

Garrett further underlines his doubt of the existence of sub-group parents by detailed consideration of the history of the Greek language. Greek is first attested from 1400 BC in the Linear B texts, in a phase of the language termed 'Mycenaean Greek'. After the collapse of Mycenaean society at around 1200 BC, there is no direct evidence for the Greek language until around 800 BC, when the first inscriptions written in the Greek alphabet appear (this stage is sometimes called 'alphabetic Greek'). The Greek we have preserved from Mycenaean times is largely uniform, but the later Greek texts show considerable dialectal variety by region and also by literary genre. Although we do not have clear evidence for different dialects attested within Mycenaean Greek, we know that there must have been other dialects spoken, although not written down. This is because Mycenaean Greek has undergone some changes, such as the phonological change of original *-ti to -si, which are shared with some later Greek dialects but which did not take place in others.

By the family tree model, all of the different varieties of Greek, including Mycenaean, would appear as branches off a single node, the sub-group parent, which is usually called Proto-Greek or Common Greek. In his most recent paper,

Garrett draws up a set of features which could be assumed for Proto-Greek on the basis of the alphabetic Greek varieties. In doing this, Garrett performs the same exercise for the Greek sub-group that other scholars have attempted for other sub-groups, such as the Sabellian languages of central Italy, where the very earliest texts are attested at around the same date. However, for Greek there is the advantage that the features assumed for Proto-Greek can actually be compared with a language of the second millennium BC, Mycenaean Greek. We know that Mycenaean cannot be equated with Proto-Greek, since it has undergone some changes shared only with some later Greek dialects, and so it must be later. Yet all of the distinctive morphological features, and many of the distinctive phonological features, which are assumed to be distinctive for Proto-Greek can be shown not to have taken place at the time of Mycenaean. Wherever the later Greek dialects have made innovations in morphology from PIE, Mycenaean Greek appears not to have participated in that innovation. In other words, the distinctive aspects of the later Greek dialects (which they all share) arose across a number of varieties which already were distinguished one from another. It is not possible, using the shared morphological innovation criterion, to construct a unified invariant entity such as 'Proto-Greek' which is distinguishable from PIE. Certainly, Mycenaean Greek shares many specific lexical features with the later varieties, and a few phonological changes which are distinctively Greek must predate Mycenaean. But if we had more evidence for other IE languages other than Anatolian contemporary with Mycenaean, we might not be able to separate out what was 'Greek' about Mycenaean from its neighbours. The Greek sub-group was only truly formed in the period after Mycenaean, when convergence between the different dialects of Greek took place, in part related to social changes coupled with a strong sense of Greek ethnic identity. It is worth quoting Garrett's conclusion about sub-grouping of the IE languages in full, with the caveat that he is discussing IE languages apart from the Anatolian sub-group, which he accepts has branched off earlier from the rest of the languages:

> If this framework is appropriate for IE branches generally, we cannot regard IE 'sub-groups' as sub-groups in a classical sense. Rather, the loss or 'pruning' of intermediate dialects, together with convergence *in situ* among the dialects that were to become Greek, Italic, Celtic and so on, have in tandem created the appearance of a tree with discrete branches. But the true historical filiation of the IE family is unknown and perhaps unknowable.   (Garrett 2006)

1.5   The time and place of PIE

The existence of the IE language family presupposes a parent to the family, as William Jones realised in the quotation given in section 1.2. The similarities between IE languages cannot be explained through convergence or borrowing from one language to another. The parent language, PIE, can be reconstructed through the comparative method, as we shall see in the rest of this book. But the existence of a language implies speakers. Where did they come from, and when did they exist? These two questions are entirely natural, and the answer to them has been sought by linguists, archaeologists and others for the last two hundred years. Since this book is primarily concerned with linguistic rather than archaeological material, we shall not attempt to give an answer to these questions here (but see further section 7.5). It is, however, worth examining some of the linguistic assumptions which feature in the debate.

Firstly, it is useful to distinguish between the hypothetical, reconstructed 'language' which is the result of the operation of the comparative method on the IE languages, what we shall call 'reconstructed PIE', and the unattested spoken language from which we presume all the IE languages derived, which we shall refer to as 'the spoken IE parent language'. Reconstructed PIE may have some features in common with the spoken IE parent language, but it is not the same as it, and is not a real language. Reconstructed PIE is a construct which does not have an existence at a particular time and place (other than in books such as this one), and is unlike a real language in that it contains data which may belong to different stages of its linguistic history. The most helpful metaphor to explain this is the 'constellation' analogy. Constellations of stars in the night sky, such as The Plough or Orion, make sense to the observer as points on a sphere of a fixed radius around the earth. We see the constellations as two-dimensional, dot-to-dot pictures, on a curved plane. But in fact, the stars are not all equidistant from the earth: some lie much further away than others. Constellations are an illusion and have no existence in reality. In the same way, the asterisk-heavy 'star-spangled grammar' of reconstructed PIE may unite reconstructions which go back to different stages of the language. Some reconstructed forms may be much older than others, and the reconstruction of a datable lexical item for PIE does not mean that the spoken IE parent language must be as old (or as young) as the lexical form.

Indo-Europeanists have attempted to construct models for PIE which bring the language into a closer approximation with the spoken parent language. The most influential model of this type is the 'Space-Time' model originally drawn up by Meid (1975). According to Meid's model, the spoken IE parent language existed over time and space. As time progresses, the number of speakers increases and the language spreads over a larger area. Hence one can draw a triangular representation of the language, as in figure 1.5, with the dispersal of the language over space plotted as the horizontal axis, and the time-scale plotted on a vertical axis.

Meid originally plotted reconstructed PIE onto this model, dividing up the language into three stages (Early, Middle and Late), and attempted to assign features and relative chronologies to different stages, and indeed to plot real dates on the time-line. There are two problems with this. Firstly, the technique of comparative reconstruction has the aim of reducing variation, by giving a single ancestor to phonemes, morphemes or words which differ in daughter languages. The method favours the reconstruction of everything to a single point, and it is not always clear on what grounds the linguist can separate out different features into

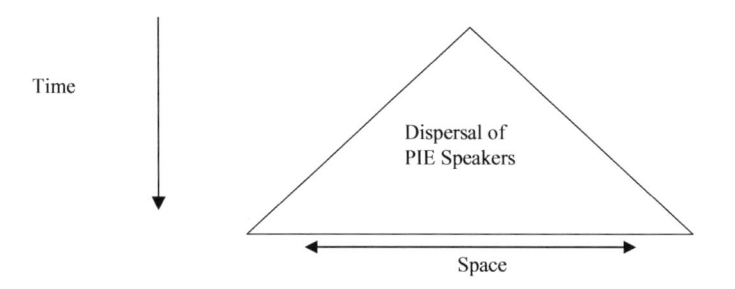

Figure 1.5   *Meid's Space-Time model*

different stages. Secondly, dating the model in real time is obviously problematic, since it is not clear how one can date a feature such as a reconstructed case marker or verbal paradigm, although it may be possible to assign some absolute dates to items of material culture, such as wheels or the terminology for spinning wool.

Meid's model also relies on various underlying assumptions about the expansion of the speakers of IE. They are thought to have spread over ever greater space and to have come into existence in a vacuum. Indeed, Meid explicitly states that at the earliest stage of IE there would have been no dialectal variation, because the speakers were most probably a very small, tight-knit band. The Space-Time model is extrapolating backwards from the spread of IE speakers in historical times and in recent prehistory, and assuming that since they expanded, they can be projected back to a single point. There is also an attempt to conflate reconstructed PIE, which is reduced to an invariant linguistic system as a consequence of the comparative method, and the spoken IE parent language, which is made to go back to a dialect-free stage in order to comply with the reconstructed language.

The Space-Time model is now looking distinctly unstable, and the idea that the spoken IE parent language was once invariant and spoken in a single place and time is far from certain. The assumption that in linguistic prehistory individual languages spread by fanning out over a wide area has been challenged by work on Australian and other areas, where there have been long periods of linguistic convergence, and it can no longer be assumed that there was a prehistoric rapid expansion of speakers of IE languages. The Space-Time model is also under attack from the renewed interest in cladistics discussed in the preceding section. As most scholars now believe there was an early split between the Anatolian languages and the other IE languages, we can no longer so easily bundle all the languages together, but we must rather reconstruct two separate stages, a pre-Anatolian PIE and a post-Anatolian PIE. All this makes discussion of the location in time and space of the speakers of the IE parent language rather more complex than has been reckoned in some previous accounts.

We saw in section 1.4 that the New Zealand team which reconstructed an IE phylogeny from a comparison of word-lists of living IE languages incorporated dates into their family tree. The attempt to use the changes in the lexicon to calculate the age of language families and sub-groups is not new. Lexical change was first used as a clock to measure the age of languages by American scholars working on basic vocabulary lists in the 1950s, in an enterprise that became known as 'glottochronology'. However, the first wave of glottochronological research has become largely discredited, since there was a simple reliance on a constant rate of linguistic change. It was easy for other scholars to demonstrate that in documented language history lexical replacement takes place at wildly differing rates across different languages and in different periods of a single language's history (as shown by Bergsland and Vogt 1962). The New Zealand team do not make the same mistakes as the glottochronologists do. They use models which were originally designed to build phylogenies based on DNA and other genetic information, which do not assume a constant rate of change. Instead, their model accepts that the rate of change varies, but it constrains the variation within limits that coincide with attested linguistic sub-groups. For example, it is known that the Romance languages all derive from Latin, and we know that Latin was spoken 2,000 years ago. The rates of lexical change in the Romance family can therefore be calculated in absolute terms. These different possible rates of change are then projected back into prehistory, and the age of the parent can be ascertained within a range of dates depending on the highest and lowest rates of change attested in the daughter languages. More recently (Atkinson *et al.* 2005), they have used data based not just on lexical characters, but on morphological and phonological information as well (reproduced here in figure 1.6). In this figure, two competing archaeological models for the spread of speakers of the IE languages are indicated on the family tree. One theory, first put forward by Colin Renfrew in 1987, relates the spread of languages to the spread of farming from the Ancient Near East. By the New Zealand team's hypothesis the likely dates for the spread of farming would relate to the split of the Anatolian sub-group from the rest of the IE family. The alternative theory, labelled the Kurgan theory, follows the work of Gimbutas and others (and is most conveniently summarised in Mallory 1989). This links the speakers of IE to nomads on the steppes of southern Russia who gain a technological advantage over other societies through the use of wheeled transport. As the figure shows, the dispersal of the IE languages, apart from Anatolian, could be made to fit with this model.

However, the findings of the New Zealand team must be used with caution. Although the use of advanced statistical techniques and complex mathematical models enables them to come up with real numbers, there is currently controversy over whether the dating given to the family should be accepted. Although the mistakes of the glottochronologists have been avoided, the correct use of different statistical models is still hotly debated, with members of the Pennsylvania team uncertain that the models used by the New Zealand team are in fact appropriate for what they want to do, and others questioning their use of data. Furthermore, the use of language changes in historical time to project back into language change in prehistorical time is itself questionable. Language change, and vocabulary change in particular, may be affected by the size of the population speaking the language and the level of shared literacy. Large literate populations may retain words better than small illiterate populations. A linguistic innovation does not need so long to take hold in a small population, especially if there is no retarding influence from

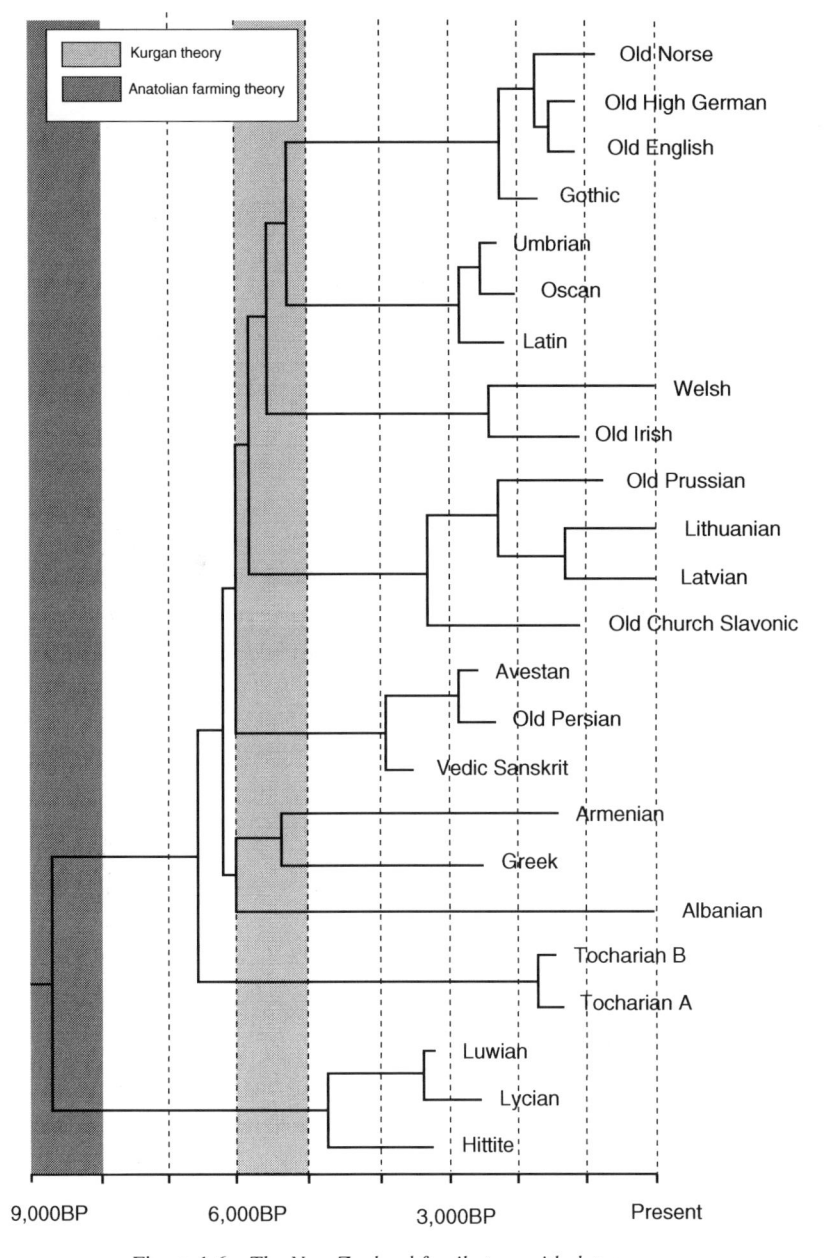

Figure 1.6   *The New Zealand family tree with dates*
Reprinted by permission of Blackwell Publishing Ltd: *Transactions of the Philological Society* 103 (2005)

the written word and education. This may have the effect of making linguistic change slower in modern languages than in languages spoken in prehistoric times, and therefore skewing the rates of linguistic change that are projected back into prehistory. For the moment, then, the jury is still out on whether phylogenetic dating can help solve the problem of how old the IE language family is.

1.6   Nostratic and other supergroups

In the history of IE studies there have been many attempts to link IE and other language families together into larger genetic groupings, which can be called language *phyla* (singular *phylum*). At the very beginning of IE studies, in the early nineteenth century, the German Indo-Europeanist Franz Bopp had attempted to connect IE with 'Malayo-Polynesian', and over the following two hundred years claims were made for links with Uralic, Afro-Asiatic, Kartvelian, Eskimo-Aleut, Ainu, Etruscan and practically every other language in the Old World, and some in the New. In recent years, the phylum known as 'Nostratic', first proposed by Holger Pedersen, has received much discussion after the reconstruction of Proto-Nostratic attempted (originally independently) by two linguists working in Soviet Russia, Illič-Svityč and Dolgopolsky, and the revised reconstruction attempted by the American Bomhard. Nostratic is generally thought to comprise the language families of IE, Uralic, Kartvelian, Afro-Asiatic, Dravidian and 'Altaic' (or, according to some, the individual groups of Turkic, Tungus and Mongolian), and some scholars include other languages from among Korean, Japanese, Ainu, Sumerian, Etruscan, Chukchi-Kamchatkan, Nilo-Saharan, Eskimo-Aleut and Gilyak (also known as Nivkh). There have also been suggestions that Nostratic is itself related to other hypothetical large language phyla such as Greenberg's Amerind or Sino-Caucasian, and there have been a few brave attempts to reconstruct some lexemes in 'Proto-World', the hypothetical ancestor of all human languages. It is beyond the scope of this book to consider all these claims in detail, but we shall briefly examine the methodological basis upon which the reconstruction of Proto-Nostratic (and, by extension, such families as Greenberg's 'Eurasiatic') is based. It is not possible to disprove the premise that IE is distantly related to language X or belongs to language phylum Y, and no one would deny that IE did not arise *in vacuo*. However, by briefly looking at the case for Nostratic, it will be seen why the reconstruction of groupings at a higher level than PIE is not very plausible given our current state of knowledge. Furthermore, even if the Nostratic hypothesis were correct, it is unlikely to be fruitful for IE studies.

It has been claimed that the methodology for reconstructing Nostratic is exactly the same as the methodology for reconstructing Germanic or IE or any language family: the comparative method. Items in different languages are compared, correspondence sets between sounds are established and the parent language is thus reconstructed. The frustration evident in many of the statements of Nostraticists is clear: they are using the same methods as IE linguists, yet their results are not accepted by most IE linguists for reasons which are seldom clearly articulated. This confusion arises from a misunderstanding about the comparative method. The (partly) successful operation of the comparative method over a non-restricted field of (open-class) vocabulary does not furnish proof that two languages are genetically related, rather the comparative method is used to reconstruct the parent language of any two languages which are already hypothesised to be related. The hypothesis that the IE languages are related is, as we have already seen in section 1.2 above, based upon a self-evident affinity between languages. This affinity is manifested in the obvious similarity between inflectional morphemes and vocabulary in restricted semantic sets (kinship terms and numerals are two standard examples; note that these vocabulary sets are not reconstructable for Nostratic). Operation of the comparative method may elucidate the relationships between languages, but it does not 'prove' the hypothesis of relationship.

An advocate of Nostratic might object that when dealing with a language family of the time depth of Nostratic, it is unrealistic to look for the same sort of evidence as we have for IE in order to construct a hypothesis of language relationship; furthermore, it might be inappropriate to seek out the sort of morphological agreement we find in IE in a language without inflectional morphology, as Nostratic is hypothesised to have been. The Indo-Europeanist, our advocate of Nostratic might add, is in the fortunate position of having well-documented histories of most of the languages in the family. Let us consider again the example of Modern Irish and Sinhala (see section 1.2 above). If we were to attempt to compare them without any access to their history, the Nostraticist would argue that their relationship could only be unearthed through vocabulary comparison. The Indo-Europeanist might counter that, without our historical knowledge of the two languages, they cannot be shown to be related beyond reasonable doubt. The debate only serves to illustrate the gulf between the two sides.

The most effective counterblast to Illič-Svityč and Dolgopolsky's Nostratic has come from the Indo-Europeanist Ringe (see Ringe 1995 and 1999), who has claimed that the large number of vocabulary comparisons amassed by Illič-Svityč in support of Nostratic is not indicative of a genetic relationship, but in fact is equally likely to be the result of chance similarity between very broadly similar phonetic forms and (usually rather vague) meanings. Ringe plots the number of roots which are attested in the Nostratic family. In most cases, a Nostratic root appears in two separate branches of the family. A smaller number of roots appear in three branches, and the number diminishes up to a very small number of roots that appear in all six branches of the family. Ringe shows that the spread of roots across the number of language families closely parallels the expected statistical distribution if any single root from one language family has a 40 per cent probability of being matched to another root in another branch. One way of understanding this is to imagine the six language families as if they were six bags of differently coloured marbles. Finding matches for roots across the Nostratic family is analogous to finding marbles of the same colour in different bags. If the chance of finding a matching marble is 40 per cent, the distribution of the number of marbles of the same colour found in two bags, three bags, etc. approximates the distribution of roots in the Nostratic languages. Ringe also examines the distribution of vocabulary correspondences over the IE family, and here the distribution is not the same. There are more roots shared across a number of languages than would be found if there were just a 40 per cent chance of

Table 1.3 *Nostratic and PIE stop comparisons.*

PN	PIE (Moscow)	PIE (Bomhard)
**d	*dh	*d^h (= 'traditional' *dh)
**t´	*t	*t´ (= 'traditional' *d)
**t	*d	*t^h (= 'traditional' *t)

finding a match between two languages, which implies that there is a better basis for reconstructing a family.

Ringe's arguments assume that there is a 40 per cent chance of finding a parallel root somewhere else in the Nostratic phylum to a root chosen at random. This may seem a high probability if there is no genetic relationship between the languages, but if one considers the comparisons offered in dictionaries of Nostratic, it does not look so unlikely. Root morphemes are generally short (roots are monosyllabic in PIE), and many reconstructed roots have a wide semantic range. In large language families such as IE, Uralic and Afro-Asiatic there is a huge body of data from which to draw vocabulary, and there may be a number of roots reconstructed for these families which are themselves the result of chance similarities. Furthermore, Nostraticists have tended to be lenient to some inexactitude in the phonological and semantic correspondences between roots.

The sheer weight of evidence produced in support of Nostratic has normally been the biggest argument in favour of the hypothesis. Although it may be possible to find coincidental matches for some roots, is there really a 40 per cent chance of finding a cognate to so many vocabulary items across so many language families? Strong corroborative evidence for Ringe's position comes, however, from the work of the Nostraticists themselves. There are two leading schools of Nostratic reconstruction. The reconstruction of Nostratic put forward by Illič-Svityč and Dolgopolsky and followed by the Moscow school has been revised by Bomhard in the light of a different reconstruction of PIE stops. Table 1.3 gives a comparison of the equivalences between Proto-Nostratic (PN) and PIE in the two systems (note that PIE reconstructed forms are denoted by an *, Proto-Nostratic forms by a double asterisk preceding them).

As table 1.3 shows, the PIE correspondences to PN **t´ and **t are reversed in the Moscow and Bomhard versions of Nostratic. The same reversal affects the other stop series, **p´ and **p, **k´ and **k. However, many of the same PIE roots containing the disputed sounds are given Nostratic etymologies by both the Moscow school and Bomhard; clearly, they cannot both be right. This demonstrates that, even if Nostratic is indeed a valid language phylum, it is possible to find a considerable number of false positives – i.e. matches for PIE roots which are invalid. There has not yet been any rebuttal of Ringe's claim about the distribution of Nostratic roots across language families, and if Nostratic is to gain more credence among the wider academic community, the number of convincing etymologies across languages must be increased.

The verdict given by one leading Indo-Europeanist (Watkins) that the results of Nostratic research 'even if true, are not very interesting' provoked an outraged response from a number of scholars. For the purpose of IE studies, there is a kernel of truth about Watkins' remark. The reconstruction of Nostratic at present adds nothing to our understanding of PIE, and it is difficult to see how further Nostratic research can improve this situation. Some scholars have argued that the reconstruction of Nostratic can help settle many of the existing uncertainties over the phonology of PIE, including debates concerning the number and nature of laryngeals; the reconstruction of glottalic consonants in PIE; the reconstruction of two or three velar series; and the reconstruction of voiced aspirates. However, closer examination shows that the Nostratic contribution to these debates consists only of ambiguous and doubtful data which do not add to our existing knowledge.

It may be instructive to conclude this section with a consideration of one of the most widespread and semantically plausible Nostratic roots, and its pay-off for IE studies. The Nostratic reconstruction is **$k\ddot{a}lU$ meaning 'female relation of the opposite moiety', and this is held to be the direct ancestor of PIE *$gl\bar{o}$- 'husband's sister' (Latin $gl\bar{o}s$, Greek $g\acute{a}l(o)\bar{o}s$, Late Church Slavonic $z\breve{u}l\breve{u}va$, Armenian tal, all meaning 'husband's sister', and the recently added (and unknown to the proponents of Nostratic) Sanskrit cognate $giri$- 'sister-in-law'). For the Indo-Europeanist, the formal reconstruction of this word is problematic for two reasons: the original inflectional pattern is difficult to reconstruct, and the word appears to contain two vowels side by side with no intervening consonant – vocalic *l and *$\bar{o}$. The Nostratic reconstruction helps with neither of these problems: the vocalism is deemed to be an entirely IE development (vowels are often particularly problematic in Nostratic etymologies), and there is as yet no comparative morphology for this word. Furthermore, the Sanskrit cognate shows that the word must be reconstructed with initial *g- (as opposed to *g'-, see section 2.4 for the significance), which cannot derive directly from **$k\ddot{a}lU$ according to current theory. The Nostratic comparison is no more helpful when it comes to semantics: the exact meaning of the PIE form (which is opposed to terms for 'husband's brother', 'husband's mother', 'husband's father' and 'husband's brother's wife', see section 7.4) is replaced by a catch-all term 'female-in-law'. Considering the present state of research in Nostratic, the Indo-Europeanist can afford to limit the time and space devoted to its study.

Further reading

General

There are numerous surveys of the IE language family, the reconstruction of PIE and of the individual languages in the family. Among recent studies Fortson (2004) gives a reader-friendly overview of much of the current work on reconstruction and also includes chapters on the individual branches of

UNIVERSITY OF WINCHESTER
LIBRARY

the family, with sketches of their diachronic development from PIE and indications of reliable editions of texts, grammars and lexica. Meier-Brügger (2003) is also excellent for bibliographical surveys of the field and indications for further reading on current debates. Further useful surveys of the family and the major IE languages and language groups may be found in Bader (1997), Ramat and Ramat (1997) and Woodard (2004). Lusitanian and Tartessian are two of the languages of Spain for which information has been made more widely available recently thanks to the work of Untermann (see Untermann 1997 for a survey and texts in Lusitanian and Tartessian).

Work on reconstructing the IE family tree and cladistics has recently received an upsurge of interest, with scholars from genetics and computer science joining with linguists to work out the best phylogeny for the IE family. Two volumes of papers, McMahon (2005) and Forster and Renfrew (2006), offer the most recent reconstructed trees and discussion of the most appropriate methods of computer-based quantative comparison. Many earlier scholars had proposed that Anatolian and Tocharian had broken off earlier from the PIE family than the other language branches on the basis of phonological, morphological and lexical features (see, for example, Klingenschmitt 1994 (for Anatolian) and Ringe 1988–90 (for Tocharian)).

There has been much debate about the location of the speakers of PIE in time and space since the publication of Renfrew (1987). Much of the discussion is centred around archaeological, rather than linguistic, data; Mallory (1989) and Mallory and Adams (2006) present alternative theories to Renfrew. The edited volumes by Blench and Spriggs (1997–9) and McMahon et al. (2000) include articles by historical linguists and Indo-Europeanists addressing the methodological problems of connecting archaeological and linguistic data, and assigning a time-depth to a reconstructed proto-language.

A very good introductory account of long-range comparison in general is given by Trask (1996, Chapter 13). Much of the Russian work on Nostratic is untranslated, including the still incomplete, posthumously published work of Illič-Svityč (1971–84), although some of the key Russian articles are translated in Shevoroshkin and Markey (1986). In English, Manaster Ramer (1993) gives a sympathetic overview of Illič-Svityč's work and the history of Nostratic studies after Illič-Svityč, and presentations of reconstructed Nostratic are given by Kaiser and Shevoroshkin (1988) and Dolgopolsky (1998 and 1999). A very brief sketch, together with putative connections between Nostratic and other language groups and the reasons why the Nostratic hypothesis is 'plausible and fruitful', is found in Shevoroshkin and Manaster Ramer (1991). Bomhard and Kerns (1994) reconstruct their own brand of Nostratic, with which Greenberg's 'Eurasiatic' (Greenberg 2000) is in close accord (Eurasiatic is Nostratic without Afro-Asiatic or Dravidian, or Kartvelian, but with Eskimo-Aleut, Gilyak, Chukotian and Japanese-Korean-Ainu). The argument against the misuse of the comparative method is well put by Nichols (1996). Ringe's (1992) work dealing with the mathematics of comparing Nostratic correspondences with pure chance is superseded by Ringe (1995 and 1999). Critical comments on the Nostratic theory are also found in many of the papers in Joseph and Salmons (1998), and Ringe (2002) is a devastating review of Greenberg's work on Eurasiatic. Watkins' verdict on the uninteresting nature of Nostratic, followed by comments from various linguists, is found in Rowenchuk (1992). For Sanskrit *giri-*, and literature on the word for 'husband's wife' in IE, see Mayrhofer (1986–2001: I 487f.).

Discussion points

1. Why study Indo-European rather than another large language family?
2. Why are morphological correspondences taken to be crucial as an indication of language relatedness?
3. In a famous article (Trubetzkoy 1939), the linguist Trubetzkoy stated that it was not possible to isolate a series of lexical and morphological elements which were present in all IE languages and absent from all non-IE languages. He proposed instead that languages could be classed as IE on the basis of the presence of the following six structural features: i) absence of vowel harmony; ii) absence of any restriction on which consonants could stand at the beginning of a word; iii) possibility to derive new words through prefixation (e.g. English *unkind*, derived from *kind*); iv) use of vocalic alternations within the lexical stem in morphology (e.g. English *ride*, *rode*, *ridden*); v) use of alternations of consonants within morphology (e.g. English plural morpheme has form /s/ in *cats* but /z/ in *dogs*); vi) the subject of a transitive verb having the same form as the subject of an intransitive verb. How well do Trubetzkoy's structural criteria apply to any IE languages you know? Are structural features a better way of grouping the IE languages together than lexical and morphological elements?
4. The Etruscan language is increasingly better understood. Some features of Etruscan grammar and morphology are given below:

Pronouns: *mi* 'I' *mini* 'me' (accusative)
           ita 'this' *itan* / *itun* / *itn* this (accusative)
Nouns: Case and number marking
           nominative / accusative – no affix
           genitive *-s* or *-l*
           locative *-i*
           plural (human) *-r*
           plural (non-human) *-χva*

Affixation is basically agglutinative, so, for example, *clan* 'son' has a plural *clenar*, and the genitive plural is *clinii-ar-as* (the vowel changes in the stem are the result of particular sound changes which affect this stem and are not general).

Verbs: Tense and mood marking
           -ke past active
           -χe past passive

Verbs seem not to change for singular and plural, or for different persons.

Numbers

θu 'one'	*θunz* 'once'	*θunur* 'single'	*θusna* 'first'
zal 'two'	*eslz* 'twice'	*zalar* 'double'	
ci 'three'	*ciz* 'three times'	*ciar* 'treble'	
zaθrum 'twenty'			*zaθrumsna* 'twentieth'
cialχ 'thirty'			

Vocabulary

clan 'son', *seχ* 'daughter', *apa* 'father', *api* 'mother', *ruva* 'brother', *puia* 'wife', *nefts* 'nephew', *am-* 'be', *tur-* 'give', *ar-* 'make, put', *lup-* 'die', *θi* 'water', *vinum* 'wine', *-c* 'and', *sval* 'alive'.

Sample texts

ein θui ara enan
not here put anything-ACC
'don't put anything here'

itun turuce venel atelinas tinas cliniiaras

this gave Venel Atelina Zeus-GEN sons-PL.GEN
'Venel Atelina (a name) gave this to the sons of Zeus'

Arguing from the basis of any IE languages which you know, what arguments can be constructed a) for the inclusion of Etruscan in the language family; and b) against the inclusion of Etruscan in the IE language family? What do we need to know to make the argument conclusive in either direction? (You may wish to return to this question after reading later chapters.)

2   Phonology

2.1   Reconstruction and the comparative method

Current research into the Indo-European language family largely involves linguistic reconstruction. Reconstructing aspects of the parent language is both an end in itself and an aid to understanding the links between the languages in the family and explaining their historical development. In Indo-European studies, reconstruction has enabled linguists to interpret texts in languages which have left only scanty linguistic remains and which would be otherwise largely obscure (as in the case of Lusitanian discussed in section 1.2). It is possible to reconstruct any aspect of the parent language, but the crowning achievement of comparative linguistics is phonological reconstruction. There is a broad consensus among scholars that the phonemic inventory of PIE can be reconstructed fairly accurately, although there is still debate about the phonetic realisation of the phonemes. Most Indo-Europeanists would place greater confidence in the reconstructed phonemic system than in many of the reconstructions of individual lexemes or morphological or syntactic phenomena.

How does this confidence in reconstructed phonemes come about? As an example, let us consider the comparison of English, Dutch and German, which are all members of the Germanic branch of Indo-European. Any speaker of one of these languages will see similarities in the vocabulary and grammar of the other two. An English speaker learning Dutch and German, for example, cannot fail to notice that the words for 'bread' and 'water' in the two languages (*brood* and *water* in Dutch, *Brot* and *Wasser* in German) are extremely close. The words for 'but' and 'onion', on the other hand, are dissimilar in the three languages (*maar* and *ui* in Dutch and *aber* and *Zwiebel* in German). Then there are some words which are alike in two of the languages but different in the third, such as 'bird' in English but Dutch *vogel* and German *Vogel*. Among the similar words there are some which are similar in many other languages too, such as terms for 'tea', 'chocolate' and 'music' (Dutch *thee*, *chocola* and *muziek*, German *Thee*, *Schokolade* and *Musik*), but these mostly reveal themselves as recent imports into the languages. In contrast, words such as 'bread' and 'water' and terms for members of the family (English *mother, father, brother, sister*, Dutch *moeder, vader, broer, zuster*, German *Mutter, Vater, Bruder, Schwester*) seem to be more integral to the languages, and we can hypothesise that these words stem directly from the parent of the sub-group; they are 'inherited' rather than 'borrowed'.

We find an exactly comparable situation in the other sub-groups of Indo-European. In the Romance languages, for example, the words for 'bread' and 'water', for 'mother' and 'father', and many other lexemes are similar. In the case of the Romance languages, we have the bonus of having records of Classical Latin, which is close enough to the spoken variety from which the Romance group evolves to be considered the sub-group parent. We can see in Latin the word-forms which will eventually evolve to become the shared vocabulary of Romance: *aqua* 'water' can be considered the earlier form ancestral to Italian *acqua* and Spanish *agua*; *pater* 'father' develops into Italian *padre* and Spanish *padre*. For the Romance group, we can unearth the phonological changes which words have undergone in the centuries between Roman times and the present. We can identify which words are borrowings and which stem from Latin. We can see which languages have replaced an inherited word and where the meaning has changed between the ancient and modern language.

For the Germanic group, we have no attested sub-group parent, but we hypothesise that there must have been such a language. We can further hypothesise what the vocabulary of the sub-group parent must have been: from the English, Dutch and German words for 'bread', for example, we might guess that the original word was **brod* or something like it, and **water* the original word for 'water'. (The * before the word highlights the fact that the word is a hypothetical item, and not directly attested.) Yet our reconstructed items here are mere guesswork, worked out on a principle that the form which was found in two languages won out over a variant found in the other. Thus in reconstructing **brod* for 'bread' we take the vowel from the Dutch and German words, and the final consonant from English. In Dutch, final consonants written voiced are standardly devoiced, but we can assume that the spelling with *-d* represents an earlier stage of the language where final consonants could be voiced. In reconstructing **water* for 'water' we took the medial consonant from Dutch and English as against the German form.

If we followed this word-by-word reconstruction procedure further, we would soon run into difficulties. Consider the words for 'father' and 'sister': English *father, sister*, Dutch *vader, zuster*, German *Vater, Schwester*. No two languages agree about the medial consonant of the word for 'father', and it is not possible to say which of the three alternative consonants on offer would be the original. In the word for 'sister', only German has fricative *w* [v] after the initial sibilant, and yet it is more likely that a fricative has been lost historically than that speakers of German have added a sound to the word. Furthermore, if we reconstruct word by word, how can we be sure that we are not including words which are in fact unrelated, but just happen to look the same? And would we be able to capture words which were related, but where the sounds have changed more radically? The French words which stem from the same origin as Italian *padre* and *acqua* are barely recognisable as such: *père* 'father' and *eau* 'water'.

In order to avoid the pit-falls of reconstructing word by word, historical linguists use a reconstruction process known as the *comparative method* (CM). For

Table 2.1 *A correspondence set for English* t *and German* ss.

English	German
foot	Fuss
nut	Nuss
nit	Niss
white	weiss
great	gross
eat	essen
hate	Hass
bite	beissen
forget	vergessen
grit	Griess
gate	Gasse

the operation of the CM, a single example is not enough, and rather than comparing single words, the aim is to compare sets of words. Therefore, rather than seeing a similarity between the English and German words for 'water', the linguist using the CM would attempt to draw up a correspondence set of words which had *t* in English but *ss* in German. Such a set is given in table 2.1 (for convenience German *ß* is here written *ss*, but both are pronounced identically as [s]; the German orthography is based on the principle that *ß* is written following a long vowel).

Now, rather than one comparison, we have a set of ten comparisons between English and German. We may feel uncertain about a particular item in the set: perhaps the vowel difference between *great* and *gross* seems too much, for example, or perhaps the difference in sense between *gate* and *Gasse*, which means 'lane' or 'alley', is unacceptable, despite the existence of English street names such as *Micklegate* in York (in fact, this is a separate word from *gate* meaning 'opening'). However, there is strength in numbers. If two words from different languages sound similar, they may be related, but the similarity may just be chance or the result of earlier language contact. But if ten inherited words in one language can be matched to ten inherited words in a second language with the same correspondence of sound, then the likelihood is that the sound correspondence results from changes to an original sound. The correspondence between English medial *t* and German *ss* is more secure than the comparison of any pair in the set. The correspondence set can be further increased by taking in further languages or earlier stages of languages; we also know the word for 'water' and many of these other words in Old English, Old High German, Gothic and Old Norse (not to mention Friesian and Old Friesian, Old Saxon, Norwegian, Swedish, Danish and Icelandic). We can thus extend the correspondence set in table 2.2.

The correspondence set in table 2.2 has some gaps in it, where we do not have words attested in one language, but there is enough information there to

Table 2.2 *Extended correspondence set for medial* *t *in Germanic.*

English	German	Dutch	Old English	Old High German	Gothic	Old Norse
water	Wasser	water	wæter	wazzar	wato	vatn
foot	Fuss	voet	fōt	fuoz	fotus	fótr
nut	Nuss	noot	hnutu	nuz		hnot
nit	Niss	neet	hnitu	niz		gnit
white	weiss	wit	hwīt	wīz	hweits	hvítr
great	gross	groot	grēat	grōz		
eat	essen	eten	etan	ezzan	itan	eta
hate	Hass	haat	hete	haz	hatis	hatr
bite	beissen	bijten	bītan	bīzan	beitan	bíta
forget	vergessen	vergeten	forgitan	firgezzan		
grit	Griess		grēot	grioz		grjót
gate	Gasse			gazza	gatwo	gata

show that the English and German words fit into a much larger picture. In all the languages except Old High German and Modern German we further see that there is a regular correspondence between medial or final *t*. If we were to assign a value to the sound in the parent language from which all these sounds derive, it would make sense to set this sound as *t*. This is the most economical explanation, since we do not have to reconstruct any intermediary changes between the sound in the parent language and in the attested languages except for German. The CM is basically a two-fold process: the first task is to match recurrent patterns across different languages, the second, to find a value for the reconstructed sound which gives the best explanation for the correspondences.

Reconstruction of a sound may not always be so easy, particularly when we compare more language groups and attempt to go back further in the family tree. For example, we can look at the correspondences between some of the words featured in table 2.2 over a wider set of languages:

water   Hittite *widār*
              Umbrian (Sabellian language) *utur*
              Sanskrit *udan-*
              Greek *húdōr*
              Armenian *get* (Armenian *g-* corresponds to *w-* in other languages)
              Old Church Slavonic *voda*
foot   Old Hittite *pad-*
              Latin *ped-*
              Sanskrit *pad-*
              Greek *pod-*
              Armenian *ot-*
              Tocharian A *pe*

eat	Hittite *ed-* (*edmi* 'I eat')
	Latin *ed-* (*edō* 'I eat')
	Sanskrit *ad-* (*adánti* 'they eat')
	Greek *ed-* (*édomai* 'I shall eat')
	Armenian *ut-* (*utem* 'I eat')
	Lithuanian *ėd-* (*ė́du* 'I eat')
	Old Church Slavonic *jad-* (*jadętĭ* 'they eat')

In these three comparisons it is clear that where the Germanic languages have medial or final -*t*, other Indo-European branches generally have -*d*, except Armenian, which agrees with Germanic in having *t. On the majority rule principle, it has been usual to reconstruct *d for this sound in PIE. However, as we shall see at section 2.3 below, there is uncertainty about the actual phonetic value of this sound.

Exercise 2.1

The following set of words contains correspondence sets for two different IE consonants, in both the initial and medial / final position of the word. Sort out the material into the two different sets and speculate on likely reconstructions for the two sounds.

Sanskrit	Latin	Greek	English	Meaning
bhár-	*ferō*	*phérō*	*bear*	'carry'
mádhya-	*medius*	*mésos*	*middle*	'middle'
	forēs	*thurā́*	*door*	'door'
dhūmá-	*fūmus*	*thūmós*		'breath'
bhrā́tar-	*frāter*	*phrā́tēr*	*brother*	'brother'
nabh-	*nebula*	*nephelḗ*		'cloud'
	flōs		*blossom*	'flower'
édhā-	*aedēs*	*aíthō*		'burn' / 'house'
dhā́-	*faciō, fēcī*	*títhēmi*	*do, deed*	'do'
bhrū́-		*ophrū̂s*	*brow*	'eyebrow'
rudhirá-	*ruber*	*eruthrós*	*red*	'red'
bhū́-	*fu-*	*phúomai*	*be*	'become'
dhā́-	*fēlō*	*thēlús*		'suck'
vábh- / ubh-		*huphaínō*	*web*	'weave'

Phonological change provides the best field for the operation of the CM, for a number of reasons. The object of our reconstruction, the phonemic system of the parent language, forms a discrete, well-ordered and finite set. Attested histories of a number of different languages provide examples of possible sound-changes, with which hypothetical developments in prehistory may be compared. And finally, sound-change tends to be largely regular over time. Sounds in the same phonetic environment will undergo the same change, irrespective of other factors. It is this regularity which led scholars in the nineteenth century to class

Table 2.3 *Six sound-laws and a rule of Indo-European.*

Name	Language(s) affected	Effect
BRUGMANN's Law	Indo-Iranian	$*o > \bar{a}$ in open syllables
GRASSMANN's Law	Greek and Indic (separately)	$C^h VC^h > CVC^h$ affects voiceless aspirates in Greek: *títhēmi* < earlier **thith*; voiced aspirates in Indic: *dádhāmi* < earlier **dhadh-*
GRIMM's Law	Germanic	$*b^h > \beta, *b > p, *p > f$ $*d^h > \eth, *d > t, *t > \theta$ $*g^h > x *g > k, *k > h$, etc. often called 'the (first) consonant shift'
OSTHOFF's Law	Greek and possibly other languages	$\bar{v}RC > vRC$ (long vowel before $*i *u *r *l *m *n$ and consonant is shortened) e.g. $*luk^w\bar{o}is$ > Greek *lúkois*
Law of the PALATALS	Indo-Iranian	Describes a series of changes of dorsal consonants before front vowels $*k^we > ca, *g^we > ja, *g^{wh}e > jha$ (or *ha*) but $*k^wo > ka, *g^wo > ga, *g^{wh}o > gha$ (or *ha*)
RUKI Rule	Indo-Iranian, Slavic *et al.* (?)	Describes a conditioned change of $*s$ when it follows $*r, *u, *k, *i$ Outcomes differ: in Sanskrit 'ruki' $*s > \d{s}$
VERNER's Law	Germanic	Intervocalic voiceless fricatives become voiced unless preceded by the accent (a corollary to Grimm's Law) e.g. Old English *broþer* < **bhrā́ter, fæder* < **pǝtér*

sound-changes as 'sound-laws' by analogy with the laws of natural scientists. 'Sound-laws' named after their discoverers are still frequently encountered in IE studies (see table 2.3 for some famous laws). The regularity of sound-change is not an essential factor to ensure the success of the CM, although it has been championed as such since the late nineteenth century. Since the method operates on a majority rule basis, it is possible to reconstruct sounds as long as *most* (if not all) of the sounds in a language change in the same way.

With the benefit of sociolinguistic studies on language variation and change, we now have a better understanding of sound-change than the nineteenth-century promulgators of sound-laws. The 'laws' of phonological change are more analogous to the laws of economics or other social sciences rather than the absolute entities of the natural sciences. We now know, from the pioneering studies by Labov and others in the last few decades, that sound-change does not happen overnight, but spreads gradually through a community of speakers, borne along by factors such as sociolinguistic prestige. These modern studies have shown that sound-changes are not 'exceptionless': some changes may not spread to all words in the lexicon, and indeed some sound-changes may remain restricted to certain groups in a speech community. For the historical linguist, however, the regularity of sound-change is a convenient fiction, which gives a close approximation to actual phonological developments in real languages. Inevitably, when one undertakes detailed studies of sound-changes in progress the picture is much messier.

2.2   The sounds of PIE

The reconstructed phonemic inventory of PIE is displayed in table 2.4. It is important to stress that the reconstructed phonemes are slightly different entities from phonemes of attested languages, since we do not always have a clear idea of how they were realised in speech. As we shall see later in the chapter, in some cases it is possible to argue for widely divergent phonetic realisations of a PIE phoneme. Certain items within this table are also controversial. The reconstructed sound *b, for example, is only rarely attested from correspondence sets across the IE languages, and the sound may have been absent from the language (hence it is enclosed within brackets in the table).

The PIE phonemes of table 2.4 are grouped into three different classes: consonants, resonants and vowels. The term *resonant* is used in a particular way in IE comparative philology to describe elements which can be realised as vowels, i.e. *syllabic resonants*, or as consonants, i.e. *non-syllabic resonants*. For these phonemes alone we can therefore reconstruct allophonic variation; in contrast, members of the consonant class can never function as a syllabic peak, and members of the vowel class can only function as such. Whereas the consonant sounds of PIE can be arrived at directly from the operation of the CM through the construction of correspondence sets, the reconstruction of the resonant class takes the results of the CM one step further. The reconstruction of one resonant, with consonantal allophone *w, and vocalic allophone *u, (and given as *w in table 2.4) can serve to illustrate the process. Consider the following correspondences sets:

A. 'settlement': Sanskrit *viś-*, Mycenaean Greek *wo-ko*, Latin *uīcus*, Old Church Slavonic *vĭsĭ*, Gothic *weihs*, English *-wick* (in place-names)

'know': Sanskrit *véda*, Greek *(w)oîda*, Old Church Slavonic *vědě*, Armenian *gitem*, Gothic *wait*, English *wit*

'see, find': Sanskrit *vindáti*, Greek *(w)eîdon*, Latin *uideo*, Old Church Slavonic *videtĭ*, Lithuanian *véizdeti*, Armenian *gtanem*

'year': Hittite *witi*, Sanskrit *vát-*, Mycenaean Greek *we-to*, Latin *uetus* 'old', Old Church Slavonic *vetŭxŭ* 'old', Lithuanian *vētušas* 'old'

'water': Hittite *widār*, Old Church Slavonic *voda*, Armenian *get* 'river', Gothic *wato*, English *water*

B. 'yoke': Hittite *iukan*, Greek *zdugón*, Sanskrit *yugá-*, Latin *iugum*, Gothic *juk*

Table 2.4 *Phonological inventory of PIE.*

Consonants

Stops

Labial	Dental	Palatal	Velar	Labio-velar
*p	*t	*k´	*k	*kʷ
(*b)	*d	*g´	*g	*gʷ
*bʰ	*dʰ	*g´ʰ	*gʰ	*gʷʰ

Fricatives

*s

'Laryngeals'

$*h_1$, $*h_2$, $*h_3$

Resonants

Nasals

*m	*n

Continuants

*r, *l, *y, *w

Vowels

short	*e, *o, (*a)
long	*ē, *ō, (*ā)

'red': Sanskrit *rudhira-*, Greek *eruthrós*, Latin *ruber*, Lithuanian *raũdas*, Old English *rudian* 'be red'

'stock animinal': Sanskrit *páśu*, Latin *pecū*, Umbrian *pequo*, Old Lithuanian *pēkus*, Gothic *faihu*

'last year': Sanskrit *parút*, Greek *pérusi*, Armenian *heru*

'water': Sanskrit *udan-*, Greek *húdōr*, Umbrian *utur*

Correspondence set A can lead to the establishment of a consonant *w, and correspondence set B of a vowel *u. But the last two correspondences in sets A and B can be compared to each other. Sanskrit *parút* appears to be a compound, with final element *ut* comparable to the words relating to the meaning 'year' in set A, and the same form appears to lie behind the words in Greek and Armenian (in the Greek dialect where *pérusi* is attested, the combination *ti* develops to *si*, in Armenian *t* is regularly dropped in this position). The words for 'water' in the two correspondence sets share similar endings and declension patterns, and only disagree on the initial syllable.

We could reconcile the two different forms in which the words for 'year' and 'water' occur if we assume that *w and *u were originally allophones of the same phoneme and the different forms of the words are morphologically conditioned. We shall see in section 2.5 and in later chapters that our understanding of the morphology of PIE is reliant on a theory that the presence or absence of the reconstructed vowels *e, *o, *ē and *ō in different positions of a word is governed by morphological criteria. In support of this hypothesis, consider the reconstructed paradigm of the PIE word for 'dog':

	PIE	Sanskrit	Greek
Nominative	*kʹwōn	śvā́	kúōn
Genitive	*kʹun-es	śúnas	kunós

Once we allow that the *ō of the nominative singular is a morphological device for indicating the nominative case, just as the affix *es (with a variant *os which survives in Greek) encodes the genitive case marking, then it becomes clear that the lexical root meaning 'dog' has the form *kʹwn-. In the sequence *kʹwn-es, the resonant *w is realised as the vowel *u, but it is non-syllabic in the nominative *kʹw-ō-n. In the same way we can explain that the different forms for 'year' and 'water' by hypothesising skeletons *wt- and *wd- with vowels inserted within these skeletons in some morphological environments. It follows from this that in all cases where we have reconstructed *w or *u we can posit a single phoneme with two allophones.

Exactly similar considerations apply to the reconstruction of other members of the resonant class, *n, *m, *r, *l and *y, which have vocalic allophones conventionally written *n̥, *m̥, *r̥, *l̥ and *i. Compare the following parallel examples to the behaviour of *w for *y and *r in the reconstructed paradigms of *dyew- 'sky, sky-god' and *ph₂ter- 'father' (fuller paradigms are given at section 4.2):

nominative singular *dy-e-w-s: Sanskrit dyáus, Greek Zdeús
genitive singular *dyw-és (/*diwes/): Sanskrit divás, Greek Di(w)ós
dative singular *ph₂tr-éy: Sanskrit pitré, Greek patrí
locative plural *ph₂tr-su (/*ph₂tr̥su/): Sanskrit pitŕ̥ṣu, Greek patrási.

An example of a syllabic realisation of the resonant *n is found in the paradigm of PIE 'dog' discussed above. As we have seen, in this word *n functions as a consonant in the nominative and accusative cases; but in other parts of this paradigm *n may be realised as a vowel. For example, the instrumental case in the plural is reconstructed as *kʹwn-bʰis (realised as /*kʹwn̥bʰis/), a form from which the Sanskrit instrumental plural śvábhis directly derives (Sanskrit a is the regular outcome of *n̥). The syllabification /*kʹwn̥bʰis/, rather than /*kʹunbʰis/, is accounted for by a rule for the distribution of the vocalic and consonantal allophones formulated by Schindler (1977b): the vocalic allophone is found between two non-syllabic elements, and the consonantal allophone occurs next to a syllabic peak; where two or more resonants are situated alongside each other, the rightmost is syllabified first (thus /*kʹwn̥bʰ-/ rather than /*kʹunbʰ-/). It would be completely consistent to follow a notation for the PIE resonants in which the allophonic variants are not indicated, but in the rest of this book the distinction between the consonantal and vocalic realisations of the semivowels will always be indicated (i.e. the symbols *w and *u, *y and *i will be used), but for the other resonants the symbols *r, *l, *m and *n will serve to indicate both syllabic and non-syllabic allophones.

The existence of this large set of resonants sets PIE apart from its daughter languages; in all IE languages the nasals *n and *m have lost their original vocalic allophones, and vocalic *r is preserved only in Indic. Although, as we have already seen, there are examples of the high vowels i and u alternating with non-syllabic y and w, no attested IE language treats i / y and u / w as allophones of single phonemes. This 'drift' away from the reconstructed picture is remarkable, and it is possible that the reconstructed phonology is not adequately described in terms of 'phonemes' and 'allophones'.

The reconstruction of a set of resonants has led to a paucity of true vowels in PIE, since *i and *u are covered in the resonant class, rather than among the vowels. We shall see later in this chapter (section 2.5) that the loss of the laryngeals in most of the PIE languages also had concomitant effects on the vowel system, and there is still debate about whether the reconstructed system really needs the vowels *a and *$\bar{a}$, which accordingly have been bracketed in the phoneme inventory given in table 2.4. Over the last fifty years the scholarly consensus has swayed between accepting these vowels in the parent language and rejecting them. Some Indo-Europeanists have gone even further and reconstructed an original vowel system with only one vowel, *e. At present, the balance of opinion has settled in favour of reconstructing *a and *$\bar{a}$, principally supported by correspondence sets such as the word for 'nose', which in different IE languages derives from a stem *nas- or *$n\bar{a}s$-:

*nas- / *$n\bar{a}s$- 'nose': Sanskrit nominative dual $n\acute{a}s$-$\bar{a}$, genitive dual $nas\acute{o}s$ 'nostrils', Latin $n\bar{a}r\bar{e}s$ 'nostrils', Old High German $nasa$, English $nose$

If these a vowels were attested in PIE, they were certainly not widespread: their occurrence is restricted mainly to a few nominal roots, and they were not used in inflection or derivational affixes.

The other category of sounds which appears to be underrepresented in PIE is fricatives. Only one fricative, the sibilant *s, is reconstructed, although this does have an allophone z when it stands before a voiced plosive. A separate fricative, *$þ$, used to be reconstructed from the correspondence of a dental in Greek (and Irish) with a sibilant elsewhere, as in the words for 'bear' and 'earth':

*$h_2rkþo$- 'bear': Sanskrit $\acute{r}k\d{s}a$-, Greek $\acute{a}rktos$, Latin $ursus$, Middle Irish art
*$g^hþom$- 'earth': Sanskrit $k\d{s}\acute{a}m$-, Greek $khth\acute{o}n$, Lithuanian $\check{z}\dot{e}m\dot{e}$, Old Irish $d\acute{u}$

However, the elucidation of Anatolian and Tocharian has provided further cognates to words in this set, and the reconstruction now looks much less straightforward. Both languages show sequences with dental before velar in these words. The word for 'bear' in Hittite is normally written $hartagga$- in the cuneiform syllabary, but represents spoken /hartka-/; the word for 'earth' in Hittite is $tekan$, in Tocharian A $tkam$. The agreement between Tocharian and Hittite here seems significant, and it is now thought that these clusters with *$þ$ are the end-result of a metathesis of clusters with dental and dorsal stop which may have taken place in the parent language after the Anatolian and Tocharian branches split off. The words for 'bear' and 'earth' are therefore now reconstructed as *$h_2rtk'o$- and

Table 2.5a *Comparative IE phonology: stops.*

PIE	Hittite	Sanskrit	Avestan	Greek	Latin	Gothic	Old Church Slavonic	Lithuanian	Old Irish	Armenian	Tocharian
*p	p	p	p f	p	p	f b	p	p	Ø	h w ø	p
*b	b p	b	b β	b	b	p	b	b	b	p	p
*bʰ	b p	bh	b β	ph	f b	b	b	b	b	b	p
*t	t	t	t θ	t	t	þ d	t	t	t	t' y	t c
*d	d t	d t	d δ	d	d	t	d	d	d	t	ts ś
*dʰ	d t	dh h	d δ	th	f d b	d	d	d	d	d	t c
*ḱ	k	ś	s	k	c	h g	s	š	c	s	k ś
*ǵ	g k	j	z	g	g	k	z	ž	g	c	k ś
*ǵʰ	g k	h	z	kh	h g	g	z	ž	g	j z	k ś
*k	k	k c	k c	k	c	h g	k č	k	c	k'	k ś
*g	g k	g j	g j	g	g	k	g ž z	g	g	k	k ś
*gʰ	g k	gh h	g j	kh	h g f	g	g ž z	g	g	g	k ś
*kʷ	k	k c	k c	p t k	qu	hw g	k č	k	c	k' č'	k ś
*gʷ	ku	g j	g j	b d g	gu u	q	g ž z	g	b	k	k ś
*gʷʰ	ku gu	gh h	g j	ph th kh	f gu u	g b	g ž z	g	g	g j	k ś

Table 2.5b *Comparative IE phonology: other consonants and consonantal resonants.*

PIE	Hittite	Sanskrit	Avestan	Greek	Latin	Gothic	Old Church Slavonic	Lithuanian	Old Irish	Armenian	Tocharian
*s	s	s ṣ	s š h	s h- ø	s r	s z	s x	s š	s ø	s ø	s š
*l	l	r l	r	l	l	l	l	l	l	l	l
*r	r	r	r	r	r	r	r	r	r	r	r
*m	m -n	m	m	m -n	m	m	m	m	m -n	m -n	m
*n	n	n	n	n	n	n	n	n	n	n	n
*w	w	v	v uu	ø	u	w	v	v	f b	g w v	w
*y	y	y	y	h zd ø	i ø	j ø	j	j	ø	ø	y
*h₁	ø	ø	ø	ø	ø	ø	ø	ø	ø	ø	ø
*h₂	h-	ø	ø	ø	ø	ø	ø	ø	ø	ø	ø
*h₃	h- ø	ø	ø	ø	ø	ø	ø	ø	ø	ø	ø

The sign ø is used to indicate loss of a sound in the relevant language.

Table 2.5c *Comparative IE phonology: vowels, vocalic resonants and diphthongs.*

PIE	Hittite	Sanskrit	Avestan	Greek	Latin	Gothic	Old Church Slavonic	Lithuanian	Old Irish	Armenian	Tocharian
*e	e	a	a	e	e	ai	e	e	e i	e i	ä a ø
*o	a	a ā	a ā	o	o	a	o	a	o	o u	e a
*a	ha a	a	a	a	a	a	o	a	a	a	ā ā
*ē	i e	ā	ā	ē	ē	e	ě	ė	í	i	e a
*ō	a	ā	ā	ō	ō	o	a	o uo	á	u	a o
*ā	a ahh	ā	ā	ē ā	ā	o	a	o	á	a	a o
*i	i	i	i	i	i	i ai	ĭ	i	i e	i ø	ä a ø
*u	u	u	u	u	u	u au	ŭ	u	u o	u ø	ä a ø
*ī	i ihh	ī	ī	ī	ī	ei	i	y	í	i	i
*ū	u uhh	ū	ū	ū	ū	u	y	ū	ú	u	u
*l̥	al	r̥	ərə	la al	ul	ul	lŭ lĭ lī lũ	il	li al	ał al	äl al
*r̥	ar	r̥	ərə	ra ar	or	aur	ĭr ŭr rĭ rũ	ir	ri ar	ar	är ar
*m̥	am	a	a	a	em	um	ę	im in	é im	am	än am
*n̥	an	a	a	a	en	un	ę̆	in	é in	an	än an
*ei	ie	e	e	ei	ī		i	ei ie	é ia	ê i	i
*oi	e	e	e	oi	ī ū oe	ai		ai ie	oi ai	ê i	i e ai
*eu	e	o	ao	eu	ū	iu	u	au	ó ua	oy u	u
*ou	u	o	ao	ou	ū	au	u	au	ó ua	oy u	o au

*d^hg^hom-. This leaves PIE again with only one fricative, although it is possible that all or some of the consonants reconstructed as 'laryngeals' may in fact have been fricatives of one kind or another (section 2.5).

We have already given some indications of the comparative material on which the reconstruction of some sounds is based. For the other phonemes listed in table 2.4 we shall only present a summary of the correspondence sets in table 2.5. It should be stressed that the data given in table 2.5 has been established gradually over the last two hundred years, and we ask the reader to take the equivalences on trust. It is true that some uncertainties in the IE correspondence sets remain, particularly for sounds in languages which are not well-attested or for which written records do not go back very far, but for the most part the work of finding which sounds are cognate in different languages has been done. Some of the detailed comparative evidence in support of the correspondences given in table 2.5 is presented in other handbooks and specialist works, and the recommended reading at the end of the chapter should be consulted for further details if necessary. (Note that where the table gives more than one equivalence in a particular language for a reconstructed sound, the reader should assume that a phoneme split has occurred. Full details of the factors affecting these splits have not been provided. Note also that table 2.5 gives the evidence for the vocalic and consonantal allophones of the resonant series separately, and includes the development of the diphthongs *ei, *eu, *oi, *ou for reference.)

An adequate description of the phonology of a language should also include details of the distribution of phonemes. In the case of a reconstructed language, this is clearly impossible, owing to the absence of any complete texts. However, an idea of the relative frequency of different reconstructed phonemes may be gained by a survey of reconstructed roots. Table 2.6 gives frequency counts for the frequency of initial segments of roots in the *Lexikon der Indogermanischen Verben* (Rix *et al.* 1998), or *LIV*. There are drawbacks to calculating phoneme frequency in this way: sounds which are widely used in inflectional and derivational affixes (such as *t, *n and *m) are liable to be underrepresented in the sample, and the calculation relies on the judgement of Rix *et al.* Note in particular that the number of plain velars *k etc. is high, since in many cases Rix *et al.* reconstruct a plain velar where other scholars would reconstruct a palatal *k´. However, some things emerge clearly from the table, particularly the relative infrequency of the phoneme *b compared with the other labials, and the uneven frequency of the dorsal consonants, with the labio-velar series underrepresented.

2.3   The realisation of PIE phonemes: the glottalic model

The traditional values assigned to the three separate stop series of PIE, and the notation used for them, reflect the history of work in comparative reconstruction. In the nineteenth century *four* separate stop series were reconstructed:

Table 2.6 *Frequency of reconstructed phonemes in PIE roots in LIV.*

	*p	*b	*bʰ	*t	*d	*dʰ	*ḱ	*ǵ	*ǵʰ	*k	*g	*gʰ	*kʷ	*gʷ	*gʷʰ	*s	*h₁	*h₂	*h₃	*m	*n	*r	*l	*y	*w
Frequency – total number	139	14	119	168	139	104	91	40	45	192	93	57	29	30	17	312	129	212	50	108	142	315	205	225	351
Frequency – percentage	4.2	0.4	3.6	5.1	4.2	3.1	2.7	1.2	1.4	5.8	2.8	1.7	0.9	0.9	0.5	9.4	3.9	6.4	1.5	3.2	4.3	9.5	6.2	6.8	10.6
Rank	10	25	13	8	10	15	17	21	20	7	16	18	23	22	24	3	12	5	19	14	9	2	6	4	1

Exercise 2.2

The following correspondence set gives Latin, Greek and English words which contain PIE *t. In one language a phoneme split has occurred. Identify it and speculate on what phonological factors may have led to the split.

Latin	Greek	English	Meaning
trēs	treis	three	'three'
stella	astér	star	'star'
tenuis	tanu-	thin	'thin'
stāre	hístēmi	stand	'stand'
-to- (in iste)	to-	the	pronominal stem
tū	tú	thy	'you'
torreō	térsomai	thirst	'dry'
tegō	stégō	thatch	'cover'
stultus	stéllō	stall	'set'

Exercise 2.3

Re-examine the data given in exercise 2.1. In which language has a phoneme split taken place, and what factors govern the split?

Exercise 2.4

Use the following words to work out the phonetic environments in which original *s develops to a retroflex sibilant, transcribed ṣ, in Sanskrit:

varṣá- 'rain'   ṛṣi- 'seer'
uṣā́s 'dawn'   duṣ-'ill-'
vákṣati 'let him come' mátsya- 'fish'
ádikṣam 'he showed'   íṣu- 'arrow'
vasná- 'price'   ásu- 'breath'
ásmi 'I am'   pā́rṣṇi- 'heel'
ási 'you are'   māmsá- 'flesh'
ásti 'he is'

Hint: if you are stuck, one of the laws in table 2.3 will help.

voiceless (for example, *t), voiceless aspirate (*tʰ), voiced (*d) and voiced aspirate (*dʰ). Only one of the daughter languages has such a four-way contrast, Sanskrit. However, Sanskrit was viewed as the most conservative IE language, and correspondence sets could be set up to support a four-way division of stops, as in

Table 2.7 *Reconstructed four-way stop system of PIE.*

	Greek	Skt	Latin	Gothic	O.C.S.	Lith.	Arm.	O.Irish
*t	*t*	*t*	*t*	*þ*	*t*	*t*	*t'* / *ø*	*t*
*$treyes$	*treis*	*tráyas*	*trēs*	*þrija*	*trije*	*trȳs*	*erek'*	*tri*
'three'								
*t^h	*t* / *th*	*th*	*t*	*þ*	*t*	*t*	*t'*	*t*
*-$t^h a$	*-tha*	*-tha*	*-tī*	*-þ*				
Verbal morph								
*d	*d*	*d*	*d*	*t*	*d*	*d*	*t*	*d*
*$dek'm$	*déka*	*dáśa*	*decem*	*taihun*	*deseţĭ*	*dẽšimt*	*tasn*	*deich*[N]
'ten'								
*d^h	*th*	*dh*	*f/b/d*	*d*	*d*	*d*	*d*	*d*
*$d^h ē-$	*éthēka*	*ádhāt*	*fēcī*		*-dĕ*	*démi*	*edi*	
'put, do'								

table 2.7 (for reasons which will become clear, laryngeals are not used in this table).

Cognates from the Anatolian languages and Tocharian are not included in table 2.7 (they were not known to the nineteenth-century scholars who reconstructed the stop-system with four different manners of articulation). In these branches, the reflexes of reconstructed *t, *d and *d^h are reasonably clear. All Anatolian languages merge the reflexes of *d and *d^h, but maintain *t distinct. In Tocharian the reflexes of *t and *d^h appear to be merged as *t* or *c* (an affricate); but *d develops differently, to *ts* or *ś*. Neither Anatolian nor Tocharian shows evidence for a reconstructed *t^h differing from *t; the second person singular marker cognate to Sanskrit *-tha* takes the form *-ti* in Hittite, and this may also be the origin of the second singular marker *-t* in Tocharian.

In the four-way reconstructed stop system the position of the voiceless aspirate series is anomalous. There are few words or morphological items which necessitate the reconstruction of *t^h, or any other voiceless aspirated consonant. In contrast, there are many cognate sets which necessitate the reconstruction of the voiced aspirates including *d^h. Furthermore, it is only in Indo-Iranian and Greek that the outcome of a voiceless aspirate is regularly distinct from the outcome of a plain voiceless stop.

The eventual acceptance of the laryngeal theory (detailed in section 2.5) led to a radical revision of the stop system. Nearly all cases of the PIE voiceless aspirates could be explained through the combination of voiceless stop and the laryngeal consonant *h_2. Indeed, in Indo-Iranian any voiceless or voiced stop is aspirated when followed by *h_2. The evidence in support of this development is overwhelming and includes the celebrated reconstruction of the paradigm of the word for 'path'. This word has an irregular declension in both Sanskrit and Avestan. From comparison of the two it is possible to reconstruct the Proto-Indo-Iranian paradigm as follows:

	Proto-Indo-Iranian	Vedic Sanskrit	Avestan
nom. sing.	*pántās	pánthās	pantā̊
gen./abl. sing.	*pathás	pathás	paθō

The reconstructed paradigm is very anomalous. There is variation between an unaspirated and an aspirated consonant at the end of the stem, which is not found in other words (leading to the levelling of the paradigm in Sanskrit). Furthermore, there is a complementary distribution between aspiration and length: the nominative has unaspirated *t but a long vowel in the final syllable, the genitive has a short vowel but aspirated *th. We know that the laryngeal *h_2 causes lengthening of a preceding vowel, and if we suppose that it can also lead to the aspiration of a preceding consonant, we can reconstruct a paradigm that would be regular in PIE, and which explains the anomalies of Sanskrit and Avestan:

	PIE	Proto-Indo-Iranian
nom. sing.	*pént-oh_2-s	*pántās
gen./abl. sing.	*p$n̥$t-h_2-és	*pathás

Nearly all voiceless aspirates in Indo-Iranian can therefore be explained through a combination of voiceless stop and *h_2. For Greek, the picture is not so clear-cut, and there is a very small number of forms which cannot be explained by the combination of a voiceless stop and a laryngeal, and which appear to support the reconstruction of voiceless aspirates. For the voiceless aspirated *t^h the evidence comprises the following correspondences:

*k^went^h- 'suffer': Greek épathon 'I suffered', Lithuanian kentù 'I suffer', Old Irish cesaid 'suffers'
*skeh₁t^h- 'injure': Greek a-skēthḗs 'unharmed', Gothic skaþis 'harm', Old Irish scís 'tiredness'

There is too slender a correspondence set from which to reconstruct a PIE phoneme, and accordingly in current IE studies the voiceless aspirate series is not now reconstructed, and most scholars now reconstruct three separate stop series for PIE, in line with the three different series which survive in Greek, Armenian, Proto-Italic and Proto-Germanic.

However, the reconstruction of a three-way, rather than a four-way, division of stops brings with it new problems for the reconstruction. Do we need to change the description of the stops now that we have only three series? The course of least effort for the Indo-Europeanist is to retain the earlier reconstruction intact, and still talk of 'voiceless', 'voiced' and 'voiced aspirate' stop series, and still retain the asterisked forms *t, *d and *d^h, and indeed, in most handbooks (including this one) these symbols are retained. However, the reconstruction of a three-way voiceless, voiced and voiced aspirate stop series does not correspond to

Table 2.8 *Glottalic and traditional PIE reconstructed stop system.*

Glottalic PIE	Traditional PIE	Greek	Sanskrit	Latin	Gothic
*t[h]	*t	t	t	t	þ
	*treyes	treis	tráyas	trēs	þrija
	'three'				
*t'	*d	d	d	d	t
	*dek´m	déka	dáśa	decem	taihun
	'ten'				
*d[h]	*dʰ	th	dh	f/b/d	d
	*dʰeh₁-	éthēka	ádhāt	fēcī	
	'put, do'				

the phonology of any early IE language. Moreover, voiced aspirate consonants without a corresponding voiceless aspirate series is unusual not only in IE, but also among all the languages of the world, as Jakobson pointed out fifty years ago (Jakobson 1958). The course of least effort results in a reconstructed stop system with barely a good parallel anywhere, and this has seemed unsatisfactory to many scholars.

Typological considerations have consequently led to attempts to reassign phonetic values to the three series. Among several different proposals the one that has won most adherents is the *glottalic model*. The correspondences set up in table 2.7 (except for the 'voiceless aspirate series') are maintained in the glottalic model, although the reconstructions arrived at differ, as seen in table 2.8, where we have also included the values in the so-called 'traditional model'.

The glottalic reconstruction replaces the traditional voiceless and voiced aspirate series with voiceless and voiced series, where aspiration is seen as allophonic. The voiced series in the traditional model is replaced by a *glottalic* series, that is, plosives using airflow generated by closing and raising the glottis, rather than the airstream from the lungs. When discussing the glottalic model we shall continue to use the notation of the traditional model, i.e. *t, *d and *dʰ. We shall further use the same notation to refer to the stops which share the same manner of articulation; for instance, we shall term *p, *t, *k´, *k and *kʷ the *t series, and refer to the other two stop series as the *d series, and the *dʰ series.

The revised system proposed under the glottalic model may at first seem counter-intuitive. The typologically unusual plosive series in the traditional model are the voiced aspirates. The PIE *dʰ series develop to voiced aspirates only in Indic and in some Modern Armenian dialects (see Vaux 1998), and in both cases they exist alongside a voiceless aspirate series. In all other language branches they have developed differently. They become voiced stops in Iranian, Baltic, Slavic and Celtic, where they merge with the *d series; voiceless aspirate stops in Greek; voiceless or voiced fricatives in Latin and Sabellian and Germanic (with some subsequent development to voiced stops). Yet in the glottalic reconstruction these typologically marked voiced aspirates are left virtually intact. To be fair, the glottalic model sees the voiced aspirates as allophonic variants of plain voiced stops, but in practice the aspirated allophone appears to have occurred in most environments. It is, however, the traditional voiced consonants, the *d series, which are reconstructed as glottalic stops, even though these consonants develop to voiced stops in most of the IE language branches.

The rationale behind this reconstruction lies in the odd behaviour of the *d series, which is more highly marked than either of the other two series. This marking is shown not only by the rarity of the labial voiced stop (there are no secure reconstructions which have an initial *b-, and only very few with medial *-b- – see the frequency distribution in table 2.6), but also by the avoidance of the *d series in inflexional affixes. The consonants *b^h, *t, *d^h and *k' are all widely used in inflectional or derivational affixes, but *b, *d, *g', *g and *g^w are only rarely employed. (Note that, although the ablative singular case marker of one nominal declension is sometimes reconstructed *-$\bar{o}d$, with *d in final position, this is not significant, since at word-end the opposition between *d, *t and *d^h is neutralised.) Other evidence to support the marked nature of the *d series comes from phontotactics: there is no cluster *dg reconstructed for PIE, although the clusters *tk' and *$d^h g^h$ can be reconstructed (see section 2.2 for the reconstructions *$h_2 rtk'os$ 'bear' and *$d^h g^h om$- 'earth'). Furthermore, there is no reconstructed PIE root with two consonants of the *d series, such as *deg- or *$g^w eid$-, a restriction which does not affect the other series (for example, *tep- 'be warm' reconstructed from comparison of Latin $tepe\bar{o}$ 'I am warm' and Sanskrit $tápati$ 'be hot'; *$d^h eg^{wh}$- 'burn' with reflexes including Latin $foue\bar{o}$ 'I heat' and Sanskrit $dáhati$ 'burn'). Proponents of the glottalic model argue that the markedness of the *d series supports their view that these consonants were produced with glottal, rather than pulmonic, airstream. To speakers of languages without glottalic consonants, this may seem a strong point in its favour, but it should be noted that in languages which do have such sounds constraints of this type are not typical (see the discussion of Job 1995). Indeed, Allen reports how non-literate native informants of both the North West Caucasian language Abaza and the Indic language Marwari perceive a glottalised series to be unmarked against other phonation types (Allen 1976: 239).

The glottalic model is held not only to account for the synchronic phonology of PIE better than the traditional model, but also for peculiarities of the diachronic development of the PIE daughters. For example, the presence of lengthened vowels in some words in Baltic and Slavic is supposed to reflect an earlier glottalic consonant:

Lithuanian $\breve{e}du$ 'I eat' < *$h_1 ed$-, with lengthening of *e before *d
Lithuanian $ved\grave{u}$ 'I lead' < *wed^h-, with no lengthening of *e before *d^h.

This process of lengthening, sometimes called '*Winter's Law*' (see Collinge 1985: 225–7), is explained through the reconstruction of *d as a *pre*-glottalised stop [ʔt]. When this sound merged with the outcome of PIE *d^h as a voiced stop [d], it is argued that the glottal stop [?] was reanalysed as a separate segment and was subsequently lost with compensatory lengthening of the preceding vowel. Although this suggestion is ingenious, it is not the only possible explanation. All the long vowels in the words under discussion can all be explained in other ways, not reliant on the glottalic theory. In comparison with Lithuanian *ĕdu*, for example, a long vowel is found in the present tense stem of the root *$*h_1ed-$* elsewhere, including Hittite (*edmi* 'I eat'), and a morphological explanation seems likely.

According to the glottalic model, Armenian and Germanic best preserve the PIE stop system: in Germanic, one need only assume the deglottalisation of the glottal series to arrive at a system not far removed from Proto-Germanic; and some Modern Eastern Armenian dialects could preserve the PIE system exactly. Under the traditional model, both language branches had undergone independent, but similar, sound shifts in which the voiced *$*d$* series were devoiced and the voiceless *$*t$* series became aspirates in Armenian and fricatives in Germanic. The glottalic model would therefore appear to give a better account of these languages. However, further investigation reveals that the picture is not so simple: comparison of all Modern Armenian dialects reveals that the three-way opposition between voiceless aspirated, glottalic and voiced aspirated stops in some varieties is likely to be secondary, and the original system most probably constituted an aspirated, a plain voiceless and a plain voiced series (Vaux 1998: 238f.). Moreover, very early loanwords into Germanic and Armenian appear to have undergone the devoicing of voiced stops postulated by the traditional model. The word for 'kingdom' in proto-Germanic is *$*r\bar{i}kja-$* (OE *rice*, Goth. *reiki*, Old Saxon *riki*), which is borrowed from Celtic *$*r\bar{i}g-yo-$* 'kingdom', and Iranian *$*pardaiza$* 'walled enclosure' is borrowed by Armenian, giving the word for 'garden' *partêz*.

The most controversial aspect of the glottalic model is the reconstruction of changes assumed for language branches other than Armenian and Germanic. If the *$*d$* series is reconstructed as glottalic consonants, then a shift from glottalic to voiced consonant must have been made independently in at least seven separate branches of IE: Latin and Sabellian, Celtic, Baltic, Slavic, Albanian, Greek and Indo-Iranian, and probably also Anatolian, although the writing systems of the early Anatolian language cause some uncertainty about the actual realisation of the stops transcribed as *d* etc. Not many languages with glottalic stops are known over a long time-span, but, among those that are, the change from glottalic stop to voiced stop is infrequent (Job 1989, 1995). It therefore seems less than likely that this change should take place independently in seven different proto-languages. The glottalic model therefore prioritises the *synchronic* typology of PIE over the *diachronic* typology of phonological change of the daughters.

Adherents of the glottalic theory like to present the rejection of the traditional model of PIE consonants as a 'paradigm shift' in the study of PIE (note the title of the volume of papers devoted to the glottalic theory: *The New Sound of Indo-European* (Vennemann 1989)). However, recent publications in PIE phonology show that the traditional paradigm remains resolutely in place, and the number of articles published in support of the glottalic model seems to be declining.

In retrospect, the glottalic model was never likely to provide the paradigm shift which it promised, since it actually affected our picture of PIE very little: there is no difference to the number of phonemes reconstructed for PIE; all that has really changed are the labels attached to the phonemes. We shall always be in a position of some ignorance about the phonetic realisation, and even the distinctive features, of reconstructed phonemes, and consequently the debate between adherents of the glottalic model and the traditional model is to a large extent a non-argument. The debate has, however, had the unfortunate effect of polarising views between 'glottalicists' and 'traditionalists', and the demise of the glottalic model has been seen in some quarters as vindication of the traditional model and as justification of the reconstruction of the $*d^h$ series as both voiced and aspirated. However, as we have seen, there is some evidence to suggest that PIE $*d$ was in fact more marked than $*d^h$, and consequently the impression given from the terminology that $*d^h = *d + aspiration$ is misleading.

In conclusion, it is time to seek a reconstruction of the stop series that combines the diachronic explanatory power of the traditional model, while seeking to explain the apparent markedness of the $*d$ series. There is a growing awareness among phoneticians of the complexity of different stop systems, and there are increasing numbers of languages which oppose stop series not easily described simply in terms of oppositions such as voiced / unvoiced, aspirated / unaspirated and glottalic / pulmonic. The process of voicing itself can be realised in many different ways, depending on the airflow through the glottis, the space between the vocal folds and the amount of vibration of the vocal folds. Ladefoged and Maddieson propose a continuum of five voicing types, from 'breathy voice', where the glottis is most open, to 'creaky voice', where the glottis is constricted (1996: 49):

breathy voice   slack voice   modal voice   stiff voice   creaky voice.

Several languages oppose two stop series with different types of voicing, but there is not always agreement among phoneticians about how exactly these differences should be classified. Hence, Javanese, for example, has two series labelled 'stiff voice' and 'slack voice' by Ladefoged and Maddieson, although these series have also been labelled 'light versus heavy, tense versus lax, voiceless unaspirated versus voiceless aspirated, and unaspirated versus aspirated' (Ladefoged and Maddieson 1996: 63). The idea of a continuum of voicing types has clear pay-offs for Indo-European. Some scholars have already noticed that the traditional label 'voiced aspirates' for PIE $*d^h$ could be replaced with the more accurate 'breathy-voiced stops' or 'murmured stops' (e.g. Garrett 1991), and this is how the Sanskrit and Hindi descendants of these stops, *dh* etc. are now usually described. We could correspondingly make a case for relabelling the $*d$ series as 'stiff-voiced' or 'creaky-voiced', and this might make clearer the status of $*d$ etc. as more 'marked' than the $*d^h$ series. Such a change in terminology would bring the traditional model closer to a system which has some typological support.

Exercise 2.5

The words in the following table are all cognate, yet the correspondences for the initial consonants do not fit into any of the correspondence sets. Use the correspondence tables 2.5, the results from exercises 2.1 and 2.3, and one of the laws given in table 2.3 to explain how these forms are all cognate.

Sanskrit	Latin	Greek	English	Meaning
	fidēs	*peíthomai*	*bide*	'trust'
budh-		*punthánō*	*bode*	'make aware'
bandh-	*-fend-*		*bind*	'bind'
dih-	*fingō*	*teîkhos*	*dough*	'daub'
bāhu-		*pêkhu*		'fore-arm'

Exercise 2.6

Assume that the glottalic reconstruction is true, and work out possible pathways of change for the derivation of a) the Latin stop system and b) the Greek stop system from PIE (material from exercises 2.1 and 2.2, and table 2.2, may be useful). Is it possible to derive either stop system without going through a 'typologically illegal' phase?

Exercise 2.7

Proponents of the glottalic theory argue that *Grassmann's Law* (see table 2.3) can operate as a phonological rule of PIE, rather than a separate process within Greek and Sanskrit, since aspiration is an allophonic feature of the $*t$ and $*d^h$ series. Assess the results of exercise 2.5 in the light of this claim. What changes must be assumed in order to arrive at the attested Greek and Sanskrit forms?

2.4   Mergers and splits: PIE velars

In the PIE phonemic inventory given in table 2.5 the dorsal consonants were grouped into three different places of articulation: 'palatal' ($*k'\ *g'\ *g'^h$); 'velar' ($*k\ *g\ *g^h$); and 'labio-velar' ($*k^w\ *g^w\ *g^{wh}$). The basis for this reconstruction can be seen by comparing the correspondence sets for the voiceless member of each set in table 2.9 (gaps in the table reflect gaps in the evidence).

The 'palatals' are widely attested and are characterised by their development to affricates and sibilants in Indo-Iranian, Baltic, Slavic, Albanian and Armenian. These languages are often called *satem* languages, after the Avestan word for 'hundred' (*satəm*), and contrasted with the *centum* languages (Latin *centum* 'hundred'). The velars surface as velars in all languages; and the third series, the labio-velars, have velar reflexes in the *satem* languages, but in *centum* languages are retained either as velars with simultaneous lip-rounding (Latin

Table 2.9 *The PIE dorsal series.*

	Hittite	Greek	Sanskrit	Latin	Gothic	Old Church Slavonic	Lithuanian	Armenian	Old Irish
*ḱ	k	k	ś	k	h	s	š	s	k
*ḱ´erd- 'heart'	kard-	kardía		cor	hairto	srĭdĭce	širdìs	sirt	cride
*ḱ´won- 'dog'		kuōn-	śván-	can-is	hund		šuõ	šun	cú
*k	k	k	k	k	h	k	k	k´	k
*krewh₂- 'flesh, blood'		kréas	kráviṣ-	cruor	hrá¹	krŭvĭ	kraũjas		crú
*kʷ	ku	k/p/t	k	qu-	hw	k/č	k	k´	k
*kʷi-/	kuis	tís		quis	hw	čĭto	kàs		
*kʷo- 'who, what'			kā-	quod	hwa	kŭto			

¹ meaning 'raw'; the form is Old Norse.

qu, Mycenaean Greek *q* and Hittite *kw*), or show various independent and some-times complex developments. For example, in most dialects of alphabetic Greek (i.e. Greek in the first millennium BC), $*k^w$ becomes *t* before front vowels, *p* before back vowels and consonants, and *k* in the vicinity of *u*. The designations '*satem* languages' and '*centum* languages' reflect a now discredited theory that the different behaviour of the velars reflected a dialectal division within the parent language, with the *satem* group positioned on the east of the IE language area and the *centum* group on the west. This theory was exploded by the discovery of two new *centum* languages, Tocharian and Hittite, at the beginning of the twentieth century, both of which were situated in the east. It is now clear that the *centum* languages share nothing other than a failure to participate in the palatalisation of the palatal series, and as such they cannot be held to be a subgroup of PIE. It is not clear, however, whether the palatalisation found in the *satem* languages is a common innovation or merely separate developments along the same lines. There are parallel palatalisations of velar consonants and loss of labio-velars even within the *centum* branches of IE: the Anatolian language Lycian and the Western Romance languages have independently undergone these developments.

The question of the reconstruction of velar series may therefore seem better suited to be discussed as a matter of IE dialectology or language contact rather than as an issue of PIE phonology. However, if the palatalisation of $*k'$, $*g'$ and $*g^{\prime h}$ is a shared innovation of the *satem* languages, it would have important ramifications for the picture of PIE phonology. This arises out of the fact that the only languages to make a distinction between the palatal and the plain velar series are the *satem* languages. If they have innovated in common, there is the possibility that the palatal and velar series were not originally separate in PIE, but represent a post-PIE split. Two alternative pictures of the PIE dorsals are therefore possible, as set out below:

A.   The two-dorsal series theory. PIE originally opposed velars ($*k$, $*g$ and $*g^h$), in words such as $*kerd$- 'heart', $*kwon$- 'dog' and $*krewh_2$- 'flesh', to labio-velars ($*k^w$, $*g^w$ and $*g^{wh}$), in words such as $*k^w i$-/ $*k^w o$- 'who, what'. These two series were retained in the ancestors of the *centum* languages, with specific developments in the later history of some languages. In the *satem* languages, most of the velar phonemes were palatalised (including $*kerd$- 'heart' and $*kwon$- 'dog'), but some were not (including $*krewh_2$-). The unpalatalised velars then merged with the old labio-velars, which lost labialised co-articulation.

B.   The three-dorsal series theory. PIE originally opposed three dorsal series, as set out in table 2.9. In the *centum* languages, the opposition between palatal and velars was lost, but in the *satem* languages the velar and labio-velar series merged, with independent development of the palatal series in different languages.

Proponents of the two-dorsal series theory offer in support the observation that the number of roots reconstructed with plain velars is relatively small, and many of them are of a phonetic shape that could have inhibited palatalisation:

*yug-óm 'yoke': Hittite *iukan*, Greek *zdugón*, Sanskrit *yugá-*, Latin *iugum*, Old Church Slavonic *igo*, Gothic *juk*

g^hosti- 'guest / stranger': Latin *hostis*, Gothic *gasts*, Old Church Slavonic *gostĭ*

The paradigm of the word for 'yoke' *yug-om* would have shown a palatalising environment only in the vocative *yug-e*, which is unlikely ever to have been in common usage, and the word for 'stranger' *g^hosti-* only ever appears with the vocalism *o*. It is possible, however, to find words with velars in the same environments as words with palatals: compare the word for 'flesh' given in table 2.9, *$krewh_2$-*, with a form with palatal *k'* such as *k'red* found in the collocation *k'red* *$d^h eh_1$-* 'trust, believe' reconstructed from Sanskrit *śrad dhā-* 'believe' and Latin *crēdō* 'I believe'.

A further argument given for the two-dorsal series reconstruction is that the supposed merger of palatal *k'* with velar *k* in the *centum* languages is unparalleled and *a priori* unlikely, since palatal stops generally develop forward in the mouth rather than to back consonants. However, this objection rests upon the phonetic identification of *k'* as a palatal and *k* as a velar, which is not required by the three-dorsal series theory. If we follow Huld (1997) and reconstruct *k'* as a true velar and *k* as a uvular stop (and there is nothing to prevent this), then the problem disappears. Finally, proponents of the two-dorsal theory point to the presence of words in Baltic which show unpalatalised velars alongside palatalised consonants in other *satem* languages, and doublet forms with both the palatalised and unpalatalised forms side by side:

pek'u- 'stock animal': Old Lithuanian *pēkus*, Sanskrit *páśu-*, Avestan *pasu-*

k'leus- 'hear': Sanskrit *śruṣṭí-* 'obedience', Old Church Slavonic *slušatĭ* 'listen', Lithuanian *kláusiu* 'ask' (with semantic shift)

$h_2$ek'mon- 'stone': Sanskrit *áśman-*, Avestan *asman-*, Greek *akmōn*, Lithuanian *akmuõ* 'stone', *ašmuõ* 'knife-edge' (see further section 7.1 for this word)

Such forms could be taken to reflect the fact that Baltic is geographically peripheral to the *satem* languages and consequently did not participate in the palatalisation to the same degree as other languages. Proponents of the three-dorsal theory would claim that such words result from an earlier mixture of palatalising and non-palatalising dialects, and as such they have little weight in the debate on the PIE forms.

In favour of the three-dorsal system, there is disputed evidence that some languages actually show an alternation between *k'* and *k*. Albanian and Armenian are sometimes brought forward as examples of the maintenance of three separate dorsal series. However, Albanian and Armenian are both *satem* languages, and, since the *k'* series has been palatalised in both, the existence of three separate series need not disprove the two-dorsal theory for PIE; they might merely show a failure to merge the unpalatalised velars with the original labio-velars. More convincing evidence comes from the *centum* Anatolian branch, where there is some evidence to suggest that the three-dorsal series have different outcomes:

> *k´   *k´erd-* 'heart' > Luwian *zart-* 'heart'
>   *k´ey-* 'lie down' > Luwian *zī-* 'lie down'
> *k   *ker-* 'cut' > Luwian *kars-* 'cut'
>   *kes-* 'comb' > Luwian *kisa-* 'comb'
> *kʷ   *kʷi-* / *kʷo-* 'who?, what?' > Luwian *kui-* 'who?'

This is strong independent evidence for three separate dorsal series, but the number of examples in support of the change is small, and we still have a far from perfect understanding of many aspects of Anatolian historical phonology. However, it is likely that this is one controversy in the reconstruction of PIE which may be laid to rest with an increased understanding of the Anatolian branch.

Exercise 2.8

The following table gives PIE reconstructions for the comparative material, except that the cover symbol K, G and G^h are used to indicate sounds that belong to one of the velar series (i.e. $*K$ could be $*k´$, $*k$ or $*k^w$). Where possible, identify which is the correct reconstruction to replace these cover symbols (n.b. you may need to refer back to the 'Law of the Palatals' in table 2.3 in order to understand the Sanskrit forms).

PIE	Sanskrit	Greek	Latin	English	Meaning
*Ke	ca	te	que		'and'
*derK-	dárś-	dérkomai			'see'
*Gmti-	gáti-	básis	-uenti-ō	gait	'going'
*Ge/onu	jắnu	gónu	genū	knee	'knee'
*dʰeGʰ-	dah-	tepʰ-	febris, fou-		'burn'
*leiK-	rik–	leípō	linquō		'leave'
*rGro-	rjrá-	argós			'quick'
*nGen		adḗn	inguen		'gland'
*deKm	dáśa	déka	decem	ten	'ten'
*leiGʰ-	réh-	leíkhō	lingō	lick	'lick'
*Gʰen-	hán-	theínō	-fendō		'kill'

2.5   Reconstructing lost phonemes: laryngeals

We have argued above that the glottalic model of the PIE stop system has not proved to be a paradigm shift in Indo-European studies. In contrast, the laryngeal theory really was a paradigm shift in the Kuhnian sense. A hundred years ago it would have been difficult to find an Indo-Europeanist teaching in a university post who would have accepted any need to reconstruct the laryngeal consonants *h_1, *h_2 and *h_3 (as we now designate these consonants); now it would be difficult to find one who does not accept it. In the first decade of the twentieth century the only scholars to write on the laryngeal theory were on the intellectual fringe of Indo-European and on the geographical fringes of German-speaking central Europe. The label 'laryngeal theory' itself dates from a period before its general acceptance, and most scholars would now hold that 'laryngeals' are no more nor any less theoretical constructs than any other phonological reconstruction.

The story of the genesis of the laryngeal theory has been told many times. In the simplest version, it features Ferdinand de Saussure, at the extraordinarily young age of 21, publishing in December 1878 the *Mémoire sur le système primatif des voyelles dans les langues indo-européennes* (Saussure 1879), which rethought the reconstruction of the vowel system in Indo-European and laid out a series of systematic vocalic alternations now commonly known as ablaut. Ablaut is as much a morphological as a phonological process, and we shall discuss it further in the next chapter. In its most basic form, it involves alternation between the vowel *e* and the vowel *o* in different formations from a verbal base. For example:

Latin *tegō* 'I cover': *toga* 'toga (a garment that covers)'
Greek *é-tek-o-n* 'I gave birth' (aorist): *té-tok-a* 'I have given birth' (perfect)

In other cases, where there was a member of the class of *resonants* (see section 2.2) in the vocalic base, there was a threefold alternation, between forms with an internal *e*, *o* and absence of either vowel:

Greek *leíp-o* 'I leave' (present): *lé-loip-a* 'I have left' (perfect): *é-lip-on* 'I left'
(aorist)
Greek *pénth-os* 'suffering': *pé-ponth-a* 'I have suffered' (perfect): *é-path-on* 'I suffered' (aorist) (with medial *a* in Greek stemming from a vocalic *$\underset{\circ}{n}$*)

These three different forms are termed the *e-grade* (as *leip-*), *o-grade* (as *loip-*) and *zero-grade* (as *lip-*). Saussure incorporated into these ablaut patterns reconstructed sounds such as vocalic nasals *$\underset{\circ}{n}$* and *$\underset{\circ}{m}$* which had only recently been posited for the parent language, and which were to remain controversial, since they did not survive as vocalic nasals in any single language, but always developed to a vowel or a combination of vowel and nasal.

Saussure isolated the morphological environments in which different ablaut grades were expected. Thus participles with a suffix *-to-* were formed in the zero-grade, present tenses of verbs could be formed by reduplication, and some aorist tenses were formed without any suffix and used the e-grade of the root in the singular active paradigm. Derived nouns often used the o-grade of the verbal root. Having set up these categories, Saussure attempted to reconcile the ablaut behaviour of roots which did not appear to show regular e-grades and o-grades, and it is here that we have the postulation of new reconstructed elements in the system. Three very widely attested roots which show anomalous ablaut patterns

Table 2.10 *'Irregular' ablaut series.*

'zero-grade'	'e-grade'	'o-grade'
	$*\bar{e}$	$*\bar{o}$
	$*d^h\bar{e}$ -	$*d^h\bar{o}$-
Greek *thetós* 'put'	Greek *títhēmi* 'I place'	Greek *thōmós* 'heap'
Skt *hitá*- 'placed'	Skt *dádhāmi* 'I place'	
Latin *factus* 'made'	Latin *fēcī* 'I made'	English *doom*
	$*\bar{a}$	$*\bar{o}$
	$*st\bar{a}$-	$*st\bar{o}$ -
Greek *statós* 'standing'	Greek *éstēn* 'I stood'	
Skt *sthitá*- 'stood'	(dialectal *estān*)	
Latin *status* 'stood'	Skt. *asthām* 'I stood'	
	$*\bar{o}$	$*\bar{o}$
	$*d\bar{o}$ -	$*d\bar{o}$
Greek *dotós* 'given'	Greek *dídōmi* 'I give'	
Skt -*ditá*- 'given'	Skt *dádāmi* 'I give'	
Latin *datus* 'given'		Latin *dōnum* 'gift'

are given in table 2.10. Exactly the same ablaut patterns are found in several other roots.

It will be seen from table 2.10 that some roots show long vowels in the e-grade and o-grade. In the e-grade the vowel appears as a long $*\bar{e}$, $*\bar{a}$ or $*\bar{o}$; in the o-grade it is always long $*\bar{o}$. But the vowels given in the zero-grade forms differ from language to language. In Sanskrit, and in other languages of the Indo-Iranian family, the result is *i*, in Latin *a*, but in Greek it appears to vary between *e*, *o* or *a*.

Faced with this anomaly, Saussure's next move is rightly famed. He suggested that by reconstructing two elements $*A$ and $*O$, which were not independently attested in any language, these 'irregular' ablaut types could be brought into line with the e / o / zero ablaut-type. Thus the root meaning 'give' could be reconstructed as $*deO$-, with a prehistoric change of $*-eO$- to $\bar{o}$, and the root meaning 'stand' could be reconstructed $*steA$- with a change of $*-eA$- to $\bar{a}$. The diverse developments seen in the zero-grade reflect language-specific treatments of $*dO$- and $*stA$-. Saussure reconstructed only $*A$ and $*O$, but realised that the ablaut series of the root $*dh\bar{e}$- was problematic. It was left to others to point out that a third element $*E$ could be reconstructed and to derive the root $*d^h\bar{e}$- from $*d^heE$- analogous to $*deO$ and $*steA$-.

Saussure also showed how these reconstructed elements could make sense of other areas of comparative grammar, most famously in the reconciliation of morphological alternations in Sanskrit verb classes. Compare the present tense forms of the verbs and their associated participles listed in table 2.11.

Table 2.11 *Sanskrit nasal infix verbs.*

Present	Past participle	Present class in Sanskrit grammatical works
riṇákti 'leaves'	*riktá-* 'left'	VII
*li-ne-kʷ-ti	**likʷ-to-*	
yunákti 'joins'	*yuktá-* 'joined'	
*yu-ne-k-ti	**yuk-to-*	
śṛṇóti 'hears'	*śrutá-* 'heard'	V
*kʹl-ne-u-ti	**kʹlu-to-*	
punā́ti 'purifies'	*pūtá-* 'purified'	IX
*pu-ne-A-ti	**puA-to-*	
(=*pu-neh₂-ti)	*(=*puh₂-to-)*	

Using the new reconstructed elements, Saussure was able to unify the three different verb classes under a single morphological type, with the present formed by infixation of an element **-ne-*. (It is necessary to remember that Sanskrit *-no-* is the regular development from **-neu-* in order to understand the Class V verb.) Verbs of Class IX had previously been thought to show the addition of a suffix **-nā-* to form the present stem, but by utilising the element **A*, Saussure could show that here again we had an infix. The length of the vowel in the uninfixed root in zero-grade, Sanskrit *pū-*, could easily be seen to be the result of the loss of **A*, in just the same way as **oA* became **ō*.

In the condensed form of the story of laryngeals, we skip forward fifty years after Saussure to 1927, when the Polish scholar Jerzy Kuryłowicz showed that in the recently deciphered Anatolian language, Hittite, the sound *h* corresponded to Saussure's predicted **A*, which he redesignated **H₂* (**E* became **H₁* and **O* became **H₃* at the same time; we here use the same notation, but with a lower-case **h* rather than upper-case **H*; in our notation **H* without a subscript numeral refers to any of **h₁*, **h₂* or **h₃*). In these intervening fifty years, however, the theory had developed far beyond Saussure's postulated **A* and **O*, which he clearly thought of as vocalic elements, rather than something which might surface as an *h* in a newly discovered language. The principal scholars involved in formulating the laryngeal theory, as Kuryłowicz used it, were the 'outsiders' Möller and Cuny, who developed the theory in the hope of finding a way to connect Indo-European to the Semitic language family, and who are forever in danger of being written out of history. It was Möller who first recognised that Saussure's system needed an **E*, and it was he who first identified **A* and **O* as consonants, and it is Möller's term, *laryngeals*, that has stuck. Cuny was the first to show clearly why the reconstructed **E*, **A* and **O* had to be consonants, arguing that if any of them followed a member of the class of resonants (**r, *l, *m, *n*) it was the resonant

Table 2.12 *Laryngeal developments in some early IE languages.*

After vowels

PIE	Latin	Sanskrit	Greek	Hittite
$*iH$	$\bar{\imath}$	$\bar{\imath}$	$\bar{\imath}$	$*ih_2 > ihh$
$*uH$	$\bar{u}$	$\bar{u}$	$\bar{u}$	$*uh_2 > uhh$
$*oH$	$\bar{o}$	$\bar{a}$	$\bar{o}$	
$*eh_1$	$\bar{e}$	$\bar{a}$	$\bar{e}$	e, i
$*eh_2$	$\bar{a}$	$\bar{a}$	$\bar{e}$ (dialectal $\bar{a}$)	ahh
$*eh_3$	$\bar{o}$	$\bar{a}$	$\bar{o}$	(?)

Before Vowels

PIE	Latin	Sanskrit	Greek	Hittite
$*Hi$	i	i	i	$*h_2i > hi$
$*Hu$	u	u	u	$*h_2u > hu$
$*Ho$	o	a	o	$*h_2o > ha$
$*h_1e$	e	a	e	e
$*h_2e$	a	a	a	ha
$*h_3e$	o	a	o	(?)

which became a vowel. Therefore $*E$ / $*A$ / $*O$ were more consonantal than the resonants. Cuny also stated clearly, and prophetically, that the lost consonants were 'a sort of *h*'.

The phonetic value of Hittite *h* (which is often written $\d{h}$ in handbooks) is uncertain. Hittite utilises the cuneiform writing system of Akkadian, where the same writing seems to represent a voiceless velar fricative, although this does not necessitate that it has the same value in Hittite. Our uncertainty about the value of this sound in Hittite means that there is still debate about the phonetic nature of the laryngeals in PIE, much of which is highly speculative. Current consensus tends to give $*h_1$ the value of a glottal stop, $*h_2$ is reckoned to be a back fricative of some sort, whether velar or pharyngal, and $*h_3$ a voiced back fricative, possibly also with lip-rounding.

In the period since Kuryłowicz's work on laryngeals a great deal of comparative work has been devoted to understanding their behaviour in different IE languages and their presence in particular reconstructed items. A real advance in our knowledge in recent years has been in the behaviour of laryngeals not just in Hittite, but in the Anatolian branch as a whole, and we are beginning to get a better picture of the phonetic environments in which laryngeals are lost in the Anatolian languages, their effects on neighbouring consonants and their outcomes in the different branches of the Anatolian group. It is clear that $*h_2$ is well attested in Anatolian, and there are now a sizable number of reliable etymologies with $*h_2$ exactly where Saussure would have predicted an $*A$. The following word-equations are just an illustration.

*peh₂-(s)- 'protect': Hittite *pahhs-*, Sanskrit *pā́ti*, Latin *pāscō*, *pāstor*

*dʰuh₂- 'breath / smoke': Hittite *tuhhuis*, Latin *fūmus*, Greek *thūmós*, Sanskrit *dhūmá-*

*h₂ent-: Hittite *hant-* 'front', Latin *ante*, Greek *antí*

*h₂erǵ´- 'white': Hittite *harki-* 'white', Sanskrit *árjuna-* 'silver', Greek *árguron* 'silver', Latin *argentum* 'silver', Tocharian A *ārki* 'white'

*h₂owi- 'sheep': Luwian *hawi-*, Lycian *xawa-*, Sanskrit *ávi-*, Greek *ó(w)is*, Latin *ouis*

It is clear from these and other comparisons that *h₂* is as securely reconstructed as any other PIE consonant. By contrast, *h₁* and *h₃* have proved more elusive, although there are recent claims that each of these might show clear and distinct reflexes in Anatolian languages other than Hittite. For the most part, however, our reasons for reconstructing these sounds come from aberrant ablaut patterns of the type noticed by Saussure and, more curiously, from Greek.

It is indeed not Anatolian, but Greek, which is now seen as the most reliable guide to when to reconstruct laryngeals in Indo-European, even though laryngeals nowhere survive as consonants in Greek. However, it has now become generally accepted that Greek shows a 'triple reflex' of laryngeals, preserving distinct outcomes of the laryngeals when they occur between consonants (that includes zero-grade forms such as *thetós* 'put' of table 2.10, which we now hypothesise comes from *dʰh₁to-). Greek also shows a distinct outcome for each of *h₁*, *h₂* and *h₃* when they follow a vocalic *r*, *l*, *m* or *n*, or stand initially before a consonant. The comparison of the Greek (Doric) outcomes of these sequences with the Latin and Sanskrit is shown in table 2.13.

In no other IE language is the 'triple reflex' of Greek paralleled. Indeed, Armenian is the only IE language outside the Anatolian branch to show a reflex of laryngeals in initial position before a consonant. However, there is some good corroborative evidence to their earlier presence in this position, in some cases from Anatolian, as shown in the examples below. More tantalising evidence comes from Indo-Iranian, where some compound words show lengthening of the vowel before a root presumed to have earlier had an initial laryngeal. Note the following:

*h₂ster- 'star': Hittite *hasterza*, Greek *astḗr*, Latin *stella*, Armenian *astł*, Sanskrit *tár-*

*h₂wes- 'live, spend time': Hittite *huis-* 'live', Greek *á(w)esa* 'I spent a night', Sanskrit *vásati* 'spend the night', English *was*

*h₂ner- 'man': No Anatolian cognate yet known, Greek *anḗr*, Armenian *ayr* (from *anir), Oscan *niir*, Sanskrit *nár-*, compound *sūnára-* 'vital' (*su-* 'well-')

*h₂uh₁-nt- / *h₂weh₁-nt- 'wind' (*h₂weh₁- 'blow'): Hittite *huwantes* 'winds', Latin *uentus*, Sanskrit *vā́ta-* 'wind', Greek *á(w)ent-* 'blowing'

The final example, the word for 'wind', provides further interesting evidence for the survival of laryngeals in an earlier stage of Indo-Iranian. When the Sanskrit word appears in the earliest, orally transmitted texts, the Vedic hymns, it regularly

Table 2.13 *The triple reflex of laryngeals in Greek.*

		*CHC	*HC-	*$r̥H$	*$l̥H$	*$m̥H$	*$n̥H$
*h_1	Greek	e	e	rē	lē	mē	nē
	Latin	a	lost	rā	lā	mā	nā
	Sanskrit	i	lost	īr/ ūr	īr/ ūr	ā	ā
*h_2	Greek	a	a	rā	lā	mā	nā
	Latin	a	lost	rā	lā	mā	nā
	Sanskrit	i	lost	īr/ ūr	īr/ ūr	ā	ā
*h_3	Greek	o	o	rō	lō	mō	nō
	Latin	a	lost	rā	lā	mā	nā
	Sanskrit	i	lost	īr/ ūr	īr/ ūr	ā	ā

has to be scanned as a trisyllable, *vaata-*. This scansion is not a usual metrical licence in these texts, and the trisyllabic form may reflect the reconstructed syllabification *h_2weh_1-n̥t-*, showing that during the time of the composition of the hymns there was still hiatus between two vowels which had once been separated by a laryngeal.

The example of Sanskrit *vā́ta-* 'wind', earlier *vaata-*, is not unique. Other forms in Vedic Sanskrit and the earliest Avestan hymns show similar examples of hiatus where laryngeals once stood between vowels. This phenomenon, and the examples of lengthening caused by laryngeals in compounds such as *sū-nára-* 'vital', show that laryngeals seem to have remained as consonants in some environments in Proto-Indo-Iranian, only to be lost just before the earliest texts. If we look at the other early language branches we find a similar picture. The 'triple reflex' of laryngeals in Greek precedes our earliest Greek texts, but since it is found in no other IE language it must have been a development unique to Greek. Greek must therefore have kept the three laryngeals as distinct elements in its prehistory. Recent work on Latin has also posited complex laryngeal developments which must be unique to its branch of IE.

The reconstruction of three laryngeals is now firmly accepted in IE linguistics, and there is much agreement on where laryngeals should be reconstructed and which laryngeal to reconstruct. The inclusion of laryngeals in the PIE phoneme inventory has proved an extremely powerful and effective tool in the comparative philologist's armoury, and is well supported by the historical data of the languages. Most Indo-Europeanists now see little need to tamper with the laryngeal theory as it is sketched out in this section.

However, some questions still remain. Particularly puzzling is the paradox that laryngeals are lost nearly everywhere, in ways that are strikingly similar, yet apparently unique to each language branch. We can of course assume some common developments already within PIE, such as the effect of the laryngeals

$*h_2$ and $*h_3$ to change a neighbouring $*e$ to $*a$ or $*o$, but the actual loss of laryngeals must be assumed to have taken place separately after the break-up of the parent language. We have already seen in section 1.4 that there is currently broad agreement on the family tree for the IE languages, and that the Anatolian branch is presumed to have split off from the other languages first. Given this model, it would have seemed a plausible assumption that the retention of $*h_2$, and possibly also $*h_1$ and $*h_3$, is an archaism of Anatolian, and the loss of the laryngeals was made in common by the other languages. But the current picture of laryngeal reconstruction necessitates repeated loss of laryngeals in each language branch. One could, of course, think up sociolinguistic reasons to explain this apparent 'time-lag'. If the IE languages outside the Anatolian branch were at one stage in close contact with languages without equivalent sounds to the laryngeals, it may have led to a widespread loss. It is certainly noticeable that the Semitic languages (such as Maltese and Modern Hebrew) which have been through stages of close contact with non-Semitic varieties have all tended to drop their inherited pharyngal and laryngal consonants, and these would provide a typological parallel for the loss of laryngeals.

If such a scenario is envisaged for the IE languages, it might lead to a reconsideration of the formulistic treatment of laryngeal developments in IE languages. To return to the example of Greek, current treatments search for rigid sound-laws in the development of laryngeals in Greek, which are supported by only a small set of definite correspondences. If we view the loss of guttural consonants in Maltese as a typological parallel to the diachronic development of laryngeals in Greek, the results may be instructive. The Maltese situation is well summarised by Comrie (1993: 94–5):

> These Maltese data shows that in cases where guttural consonants are lost, sometimes with changes in the quality of adjacent vowels, there are often idiosyncratic developments, and this is the case where we have access (via Classical Arabic and Modern Arabic vernaculars) to the original state before the loss of the gutturals and before the phonologisation of the changes in vowel quality. The idiosyncrasies discussed include loss of a guttural where it should have been retained, retention of a guttural where it should have been lost and irregular developments of vowel quality.

If the loss of laryngeals in Greek, and indeed in other IE languages, is viewed as comparable to the developments in Maltese, it would provide a challenge to the hypothesis that sound-change is regular and exceptionless. The loss of guttural consonants does not appear to have been a 'regular' change in Maltese, particularly as it affected neighbouring vowels. In both Maltese and PIE, vowel alternations are used as markers of morphological categories, and the interaction between morphology and phonology is therefore most apparent in the loss of consonants which may determine vowel quality. It would be wrong to imagine that there is no regularity at all in the sound-changes relating to laryngeals, but perhaps the researcher should not be surprised if laryngeal developments are not completely regular and exceptionless. As we saw in section 2.1, the comparative method does not rely on absolute regularity, and the PIE laryngeals may provide an example of where reconstruction is possible without the assumption of rigid sound-laws.

Exercise 2.9

An 'irregular' ablaut series not so far discussed involves roots which appear to have reflexes with two syllables in the e- and o-grades, and in the zero-grade a vowel which used to be reconstructed as a long syllabic resonant. Some examples are given in the table below (we have used the cover symbol *V* in the reconstructed e-grade forms, to show that a vowel occurs in the second syllable in the reflexes of the root).

zero-grade	e-grade
*$\acute{g}\acute{\bar{n}}$-	*$\acute{g}\acute{e}nV$-
*$\acute{g}\acute{\bar{n}}$-tó- 'born' Sanskrit *jātá*- Greek -*gnētos* Latin *(g)nātus*	*$\acute{g}\acute{e}nV$-tor- 'parent' Sanskrit. *janitar*- Greek *genétōr* Latin *genitor*
*$b^h\bar{u}$-	*$b^h ewV$-
*$b^h\bar{u}$-tó- 'created' Sanskrit *bhūtá*-	*$b^h\acute{e}wV$-tu- 'being' Sanskrit *bhávitum*
*$\acute{k}\acute{\bar{r}}$-	*$\acute{k}\acute{e}rV$-
*$\acute{k}\acute{\bar{r}}$-to- 'mixed' Sanskrit *śīrtá*- Greek -*krātos*	*e-$\acute{k}\acute{e}rV$-s- Greek *ekéras(s)a* 'I mixed'
*$g^w\acute{\bar{r}}$-	*$g^w erV$-
*$g^w i$-$g^w\acute{\bar{r}}$- 'swallow' Greek *bibrṓskō*	*$g^w erV$-tu- 'swallowing' Sanskrit *garitu*-

Use the laryngeal theory to rewrite this ablaut series, bringing it into line with the other ablaut series discussed in this section. (Hint: the sound-changes given in table 2.13 may be helpful.)

Exercise 2.10

One of the laws given in table 2.3, known as Brugmann's Law, states that in an open syllable, short *o* develops to $\bar{a}$ in Indo-Iranian languages. For example, compare Sanskrit *jā́nu* 'knee' with Greek *gónu* 'knee', Sanskrit *dā́ru* 'wood' with Greek *dóru* '(wooden) spear', Sanskrit *pā́dam* 'foot' (accusative) with Greek *póda* 'foot' (accusative). There are many exceptions to this law, including the following:

Sanskrit *jána-*, Greek *gónos* 'offspring'
Sanskrit *-gara-*, Greek *-boros* 'swallowing' (both second elements in compounds)
Can the results of exercise 2.9 help to explain these exceptions?

Further reading

Sound-change and reconstruction are both topics which have had an extensive scholarly coverage. Fox (1995), the articles in Joseph and Janda (2003) and handbooks of historical linguistics are good indications of some of the current issues and theories. A handy guide to the 'sound-laws' of PIE is given by Collinge (1985), with supplements at Collinge (1995) and Collinge (1999). The handbooks of Beekes (1995), Meier-Brügger (2003) and Fortson (2004) all offer extensive examples of correspondence sets to reconstruct PIE phonology. There is also a large number of publications devoted to specific developments in the IE branches: note especially Melchert (1994a) for Anatolian, Wackernagel (1896) and Hoffmann and Forssman (1996) for Indo-Iranian, Sihler (1995) and Rix (1976) for Greek, and Sihler (1995) and Meiser (1998) for Latin. Fortson (2004) also contains excellent overviews of the sound-developments from PIE to all the separate branches. Mayrhofer (1986) gives a detailed overview of the reconstructed phonology of PIE, with discussion of the realisation of allophones and combinatory effects; we have followed his analysis of PIE *b*, which in turn follows Schindler (1977a).

The glottalic model has attracted a great deal of discussion and debate. Vennemann (1989) includes many arguments in favour of glottalic consonants in PIE, and some against (for example, Job (1989)), and Salmons (1992) presents an attractive synthesis. Arguments against are marshalled most recently by Barrack (2002) and (2003). Job (1995) is an important investigation into the typology of change in language systems with glottalics.

Hiersche (1964) collected most of the evidence relating to voiceless aspirates in PIE; more recently their reconstruction has been defended by Elbourne (1998, 2000 and 2001). The history of the laryngeal theory from Saussure to the 1930s is well described by Szemerényi (1973); Mayrhofer (1981) gives a reassessment of the work in the light of contemporary research. Two volumes of collected papers have been very influential in the development of the laryngeal theory: Winter (1965) and Bammesberger (1988), and many of the articles in them are still very useful. Lindeman (1997) is useful but in disagreement with much current thinking. The most accessible account of the 'triple reflex' of laryngeals in Greek is given in Rix (1976: 68–76), but see Lindeman (1982) for criticism. Schrijver (1991) gives a detailed, and still in some respects controversial, review of the development of laryngeals in Latin. There is discussion of the possible phonetic realisation of laryngeals in Beekes (1994). For the developments referred to in Maltese and their use as a typological parallel to laryngeals in PIE, see Comrie (1993). Separate reflexes of *h_1 and *h_3 in Anatolian languages (Hieroglyphic Luwian and Lycian respectively) are argued for by Kloekhorst (2004) and Kimball (1987).

Discussion points

1.   How much is it possible to know about the phonetic realisation of PIE phonemes?
2.   In what respects is the phonology of a reconstructed language a) different from b) similar to the phonology of an attested language?
3.   How important are typological considerations of sound-systems and sound-changes for PIE reconstruction?
4.   Does the sociolinguistic study of sound-changes in progress have any bearing on the reconstruction of PIE phonology?

UNIVERSITY OF WINCHESTER
LIBRARY

3   Morphophonology

3.1   Introduction

This chapter deals broadly with issues that lie on the interface between phonology and morphology in reconstructed PIE. We first consider the phonological shape of reconstructed morphemes, before proceeding to discuss a process of vowel alternation known as *ablaut*. Ablaut is fundamental to much of PIE morphology, and this chapter consequently contains much that anticipates some of the reconstruction of morphological paradigms in following chapters. Current hypotheses to explain the origin and mechanics of ablaut in PIE relate it to the nature and location of the word-accent, and consequently we have also included in this chapter a section on the reconstruction of the PIE accent. We have titled this chapter *morphophonology* partly in the tradition of Trubetzkoy, who first proposed a separable sub-discipline covering the uses of a language's phonological resources in morphology, and partly as an indication of the historical uncertainty about how to describe ablaut, whether in phonological or morphological terms.

3.2   Morpheme structure constraints

The comparison of cognate forms in IE languages leads not only to the reconstruction of lexical items and phonemes, but also to lexical bases traditionally termed *roots*. The process of abstracting a root from the comparative reconstruction of PIE word-forms can be exemplified by the root **yug-* 'join'. Consider the following reconstructions:

1.   **yugóm* 'yoke' (nominative singular of a neuter noun): Hittite *iukan*, Greek *zdugón*, Sanskrit *yugá-*, Latin *iugum*, Old Church Slavonic *igo*, Gothic *juk*
2.   **yungénti* 'they yoke' (present tense): Sanskrit *yuñjánti*, Avestan *yuṇjiṇti*, Latin *iungunt*
3.   **n̥yugm̥* 'unyoked' (accusative singular): Sanskrit *áyujam*, Greek *ázduga*; the same second element is found in Latin *coniugem* 'spouse'

Reconstructions 1 and 3 can be directly related by reconstructing a root *yug-. The verbal stem of reconstruction 2 would at first sight appear to derive from an alternative form *yung-, but further investigation reveals that the *-n- is a tense-forming affix. In the early Indo-Iranian languages it only occurs in the present stem of the verb; compare the Sanskrit aorist (past) tense a-yuj-i 'I yoked'. In Latin the present stem iung- has been reanalysed as a lexical base, leading to its expansion throughout the verbal paradigm (Latin perfect iūnxī 'I yoked', past passive participle iunctus 'joined') and even to nominal forms, such as coniunx, a by-form of coniux 'spouse'.

The root *yug-, abstracted from the above forms, proves to be a powerful analytical tool when used to explain the formation of lexical items in many different IE languages. For example, the Greek verb meaning 'yoke, join', zdeúgnūmi, is formed differently from the verbs given above, and no other IE language has a verb meaning 'yoke' which is formed in the same way as the Greek word. Yet Greek zdeúgnūmi derives from another form of the root, *yeug-. Although the infixation of *e in *yeug- appears analogous to the infixation of *n in the form *yung-, the two processes are in fact quite different. Whereas the infixation of *n is associated primarily with the formation of a present-tense stem, the infixation of *e is not associated with any particular function, but plays a fundamental role in PIE morphology, which will be examined later in this chapter. It is normal to describe the form with *e, as *yeug-, as showing the e-grade of the root; the form without *e, as *yug-, is known as the zero-grade. The PIE root morpheme comprises a number of different morphs, including *yug- and *yeug-. The citation form for the root morpheme is standardly the e-grade, for example *yeug- 'join'.

The root is the base unit of lexical analysis in PIE, and the phonological constraints on the structure of PIE root and affix morphemes have been much discussed. The most influential theory of root-structure was put forward by Benveniste, in a chapter of a book concerning nominal formations in IE languages (Benveniste 1935). Benveniste used recent findings from work on the laryngeal theory (see section 2.5) to present a unified view of the PIE root, and his root-theory closely follows earlier work by Cuny and Kuryłowicz (see Szemerényi 1973). According to Benveniste, the basic structure of *all* PIE roots was *CeC- (C = any consonant), i.e. monosyllabic, with initial and final consonants. Examples of such a structure include some of the best-represented roots in the IE languages:

*sed- 'sit': Sanskrit sad-, Avestan had-, Greek hézdomai, Latin sedeo, Old Irish -said, Old Church Slavonic sĕd-, Lithuanian sĕd-, English sit

*bʰer- 'carry': Sanskrit bhár-, Avestan bar-, Greek phérō, Latin ferō, Old Irish -beir, Old Church Slavonic ber-, Armenian berem, Tocharian B paräm, Albanian bie, Gothic bairan, English bear

*ped- 'foot': Old Hittite pad-, Sanskrit pád-, Greek pod-, Latin ped-, Armenian ot-, Tocharian A pe, Old Norse fótr, English foot

Some well-attested roots have a more complex structure, such as *yeug- discussed above, or the root for 'snow', reconstructed as *sneig^{wh}- from comparison of Greek nípha (accusative), Latin nix, English snow et al. These were interpreted by Benveniste as extended forms of a root of *CeC- shape. The notion of extended forms of the root was adapted from the nineteenth-century idea of a root-determinative – that is, a consonant added to the end of a root. The idea was first formulated in order to account for the existence of parallel roots such as the following:

*g^heud- 'pour': Latin fundō, perfect fūdī, Gothic giutan
*g^hew- 'pour': Sanskrit juhóti 'libates, offers', Greek khéō, Tocharian B kewu

The longer form *g^heud- is easily taken to be composed of *g^hew- followed by a 'determinative' *d. According to Benveniste, every root with a structure more complex than *CeC- was an extended root (he used the term thème to denote what we call here 'extended root'). The root *yeug- can therefore be seen as an extended form of a more basic *yew-, a hypothesis which is supported by the fact that there is actually a root *yew- 'join' reconstructed from Sanskrit yuváti 'ties' and Lithuanian jáuju 'I mix'.

Benveniste further proposed that root-extensions were formed in two different ways, either by a suffix, or by an enlargement, with no root receiving more than one suffix and one enlargement. The difference between suffixes and enlargements is purely formal: a suffix was an extension which showed alternation between a form *eC and *C, whereas an enlargement could only take the form *C. When a root-suffix of the form *eC was added to a *CeC root, the *e of the root was dropped, giving an extended root of shape *CC-eC-. The idea of the root-suffix was formulated in order to take account of cases where the position of the *e in a root fluctuated, as in the root reconstructed from words denoting 'god' and 'sky' (or the 'sky-god'). This root appears to show two separate forms, both of which share the same zero-grade *diw-:

*dyew-: Sanskrit dyáu- 'sky(-god)', Greek Zdeús, Hittite Sius
*deiw-: Sanskrit devá- 'god', Latin deus 'god', dīuus 'divine', Lithuanian diēvas 'god'

Under Benveniste's analysis, behind all these forms there is a simple root *dey-, which, when extended with the suffix *-ew- / *-w-, takes two alternative forms:

I.   *dei-w-
II.   *dy-ew-

Benveniste also connected this extended root to another extended root *deih_2- meaning 'shine' (reconstructed from forms such as Sanskrit dīdáyati 'shines' and Greek déato 'shone'). The root *deih_2- shows the same *CeC- base, *dey-, but a different suffix, *-h_2-.

An extended root such as *dyew- shows only a root-suffix, but there are also roots which show both a suffix and an enlargement. For example, the lexical base meaning 'snow', *sneig^wh-, is explained in this way:

CeC root (*sen- / *sn-) + eC suffix (*-ei-) + C enlargement (*-g^wh-).

Benveniste proposed that when any further suffixes or enlargements were added to a root, these should be interpreted as nominal formations, rather than extensions of the root itself. One further feature of Benveniste's root-theory was that some roots could also occur with an optional initial *s-, thereby explaining pairs such as the following:

*teg- 'cover': Latin tegō, Old High German dah 'roof', Old Irish tech 'house'
*steg- 'cover': Greek stégō, Lithuanian stógas 'roof'

Benveniste's root-theory can be used to account for nearly all of the root-shapes actually attested for the reconstructed language, but few scholars now ascribe to the theory in its full form. The reconstruction of root-suffixes and root-enlargements meets with the objection that these could not be associated with any particular function. It is not clear, for example, what the function of the enlargement *g with the root *yew- is, nor of the enlargement *d with the root *g^h´ew-. Furthermore, in many cases, such as *sneig^wh- 'snow', analysis of the reconstructed form into root, suffix and enlargement proves ineffective in providing a semantic or morphological explanation for the reconstructed form. There is no reconstructed root *snei- or *sen- with a meaning anywhere close to 'snow'. These objections do not disprove the theory, of course; it is possible that roots were formed in this way at some point in prehistory but that by the time of reconstructed PIE the processes of formation were no longer productive, and we have only the remains of a once productive system.

Viewed as an attempt to find the origin of lexical bases, it is not clear exactly how Benveniste's theory of the PIE root *could* be falsified, and thus it has little worth as a scientific hypothesis. However, Benveniste's root-theory is falsifiable if it is considered not as an account of the prehistory of a root, but as an attempt to generate the attested shapes of reconstructed roots (and here we use the term 'root' to cover Benveniste's notion of an extended root as well as the base *CeC- roots). Viewed as a hypothesis of attested root-structure, the theory can be tested against actually occurring root-shapes. The shapes that are predicted by the root-theory are as follows:

CeC, sCeC, CeCC, sCeCC, CCeC, sCCeC, CCeCC, sCCeCC
where C = any consonant.

We can examine Benveniste's criteria by seeing how closely reconstructed PIE roots conform to these patterns. We shall rely on the most recent compendium of

PIE roots, the *Lexikon der Indogermanischen Verben* (Rix *et al.* 1998) as a reliable guide to current thinking on reconstructions. All of the root shapes predicted by Benveniste occur. But there are also three categories of exceptions to Benveniste's predictions:

1)   roots which contain the vowel *a rather than *e, such as *mad- 'be wet', *mag^h- 'be able'; note also the 'nominal' roots such as *nas- 'nose'.

2)   roots which contain more than two initial consonants (excluding initial *s) or more than two final consonants, including the following: *$h_3 sleyd^h$- 'slip', *$h_2 vyed^h$- 'injure', *$pster$- 'sneeze', *$ksweib^h$- 'swing', *$ksneu$- 'sharpen', *$menth_2$- 'whirl', *$meith_2$- 'change', *$h_2 eisd$- 'praise', *$welh_1 b^h$- 'confound'.

Some of these rely on questionable reconstructions, such as *$h_3 sleyd^h$- 'slip' and *$h_2 wyeid^h$- 'injure', and others, such as *$pster$- 'sneeze' and probably *$ksweib^h$- 'swing', are onomatopoeic. In other cases it is possible that the reconstructed 'root' is itself morphologically complex. Thus many of the roots with three consonants at the *end* have *h_2 as the final consonant, and this suggests that the laryngeal may earlier have been a separate verbal suffix.

3)   roots which contain no initial or final consonant. Only a small number of roots can be reconstructed without an initial or final consonant, including *k^w- the base of question words, *ne 'not', *en 'in', *ay- 'take / give'.

Most of the roots of this type are the bases of grammatical words, and the failure of these to conform to root-structure constraints is not a problem for Benveniste's theory. The root *ay- 'take / give' is reconstructed from the following comparison:

*ay- 'take / give': Hittite *pehhi* 'I give' (with pre-verb *pe-), Tocharian B *āyu* 'I give', Greek *aínumai* 'I take'

In Rix *et al.* (1998), this root is actually reconstructed with initial *h_1- in order to avoid infringing the hypothesis that no verbal root begins with a vowel. Unfortunately, there is no independent evidence to support or dismiss this reconstruction.

In conclusion, there seem to be very few root-types which cannot be explained within Benveniste's predicted root-structures. However, the problem with the root-theory is that it is too powerful: it predicts the existence of roots which do not in fact occur. We have noted several constraints on the possible combinations of consonants in the PIE root in section 2.3. There are no roots reconstructed with a consonant of the *d series in both the onset and the coda, (i.e. *$geid$-), and very few roots with both a consonant of the *t series and the *d^h series. There are also hardly any roots which have the same consonant repeated: *ses- 'sleep' is the best-attested example, with exactly matching verb-forms in Hittite (*seszi* 'sleeps') and

Sanskrit (*sásti* 'sleeps'), but it is possible that this verb is onomatopoeic (compare English 'take a ziz' for 'sleep'). Also rare are roots which use two stops with the same place of articulation, for instance $*ded^h$- or $*geuk$-. Moreover, the root-theory also predicts the existence of extended roots such as $**lpet$- or $**sedr$-, in which the root-form could potentially be vocalised with two syllabic peaks /ḹpet/ and /sedr̥/, but roots of this shape do not occur.

These considerations suggest that an alternative formulation of PIE root-constraints is possible. The PIE root was monosyllabic. The PIE root appears to have been based around a syllabic peak, with a progressive decline in sonority from this central peak to the edges of the root. The observed restriction in the number of consonants at the beginning and end of the root can be assumed to be in keeping with general constraints on the construction of PIE syllables, and the avoidance of roots of the shape $*lpet$- and $*sedr$- can be explained on the grounds that these sequences would have been vocalised as two syllables, not one, in the parent language. The monosyllabic rule also allows some of the roots which were difficult to fit into Benveniste's root-theory to be admitted as *bona fide* PIE roots, such as $*ay$- 'take / give', $*nas$- 'nose' and $*menth_2$- 'whirl'.

If the PIE root is reckoned to have been monosyllabic, it is possible to explain some of the constrictions on root-shapes. All PIE roots conform to a 'sonority rule': for roots of the general shape $C_1C_2eC_3C_4$, the outside consonants C_1 and C_4 cannot be more sonorous than the 'inside' consonants C_2 and C_3, allowing for the following scale of sonority:

$$\text{stops and } *s > *u, *i, *m, *n, *r, *l$$

However, two adjacent consonants can be of equivalent sonority, as demonstrated by the existence of roots such as $*d^hg^hem$- 'earth', $*mleuh_2$- 'speak' or $*tetk$- 'fashion'. Laryngeals would appear to pattern with the stops, since they can appear either further from the centre of the root than a stop or $*s$, such as $*h_1ger$- 'wake', or $*h_2seus$- 'dry'. We can further add the stipulation that all lexical roots are formed from syllables with a coda, which explains the restriction of roots of the shape $*Ce$-, such as $*ne$ 'not', to grammatical words. It should be stressed here that a monosyllable may not be realised as such in all daughter languages. A root such as $*ǵ'enh_1$- or $*dyew$- is presumed to have been monosyllabic in PIE even though its reflexes may not be monosyllabic in every daughter language, as the following reconstructions show:

$*ǵ'enh_1$-*ti*- 'birth': Greek *géne-sis*, Avestan *zaiṇ-ti*-, Old Norse *kind*
$*dyēm$ (from earlier $*dyew$-*m*, accusative singular): Latin *diem*, Greek *Zdēn*

The theory that all PIE roots are monosyllabic can be falsified by the reconstruction of a disyllabic root. In practice, however, disyllabic forms reconstructed for PIE tend to be analysed into conglomerates of root and suffix, or compounds of two roots, even when there is no good semantic reason to do so. For example, take the vocabulary of some basic kinship terms in PIE, reconstructed as follows:

*ph_2ter-	'father'
*meh_2ter-	'mother'
*b^hreh_2ter-	'brother'
*d^hugh_2ter-	'daughter'
*$yenh_2ter$-	'husband's brother's wife'

Since these words are not monosyllabic, it is normally assumed they must be analysable in smaller units. Thus, in some works they are analysed as *ph_2-ter-, *meh_2-ter-, etc., with a root followed by a suffix *-ter-, which is used elsewhere as an agent noun suffix (cf. Latin agent noun suffix -tor, Sanskrit -tar-). The root employed in the word for 'father' has been identified with the root of the Sanskrit verb *pāti* 'he protects', and the 'original' meaning of *ph_2-ter- was deduced as 'the protector'. An alternative division of these words is to analyse them as *p-h_2ter-, *me-h_2ter-, etc., with a common 'kinship suffix' *-h_2ter-. This reconstruction in turn meets with the objection that lexical roots of only one consonant are not found, and *p- 'father' and *me- 'mother' are consequently problematic.

The type of investigation of the kinship terms given above may seem futile. These terms are, after all, semantic primes, and in many of the world's languages the terms for 'mother' and 'father' do not lend themselves to analysis in terms of root and affix. Analysis of this kinship vocabulary in terms of root and suffix adds little to our understanding if neither the root nor the suffix can be connected with other lexical material reconstructed for PIE. Should terms such as *ph_2ter-, *meh_2ter-, etc. consequently be interpreted as 'roots' and our theory of monosyllabic roots be dropped? Certainly, this broad conception of the root would be the logical outcome of a formulation of the PIE root as 'the lexical base unit in the reconstructed language'.

However, there are other morphological reasons for viewing lexemes such as *ph_2ter-, *meh_2ter-, etc. as complexes of root and suffix, even though we cannot be sure how to make the cut between root and suffix. When further lexemes are derived from *ph_2ter- and *meh_2ter-, the suffixes used are always secondary suffixes, that is, suffixes which can attach onto other suffixes or compound word-forms, such as the adjectival suffix *-yo-. Primary suffixes, suffixes which elsewhere attach to unsuffixed roots, are not used in forming new derivatives from these kinship terms. It therefore seems most practical to define *ph_2ter-, *meh_2ter- and the other kinship terms as lexemes, or lexical bases, rather than roots, and accept that the details of their formation lie too far back in prehistory to be recovered.

Morpheme structure constraints for PIE suffixes and inflectional endings are easier to describe. Suffixes are not always monosyllabic, although longer suffixes, such as the comparative suffix *-tero- or the middle participial suffix *-mh_1no-, are sometimes further analysed into combinations of shorter suffixes. A suffix may be as short as a single phoneme, such as the PIE thematic vowel *-e/o-, used to derive secondary nouns from a lexical base, or *-t-, the marker of agent-nouns standing as the second member of compounds. More complex suffix-shapes include those that do not occur as roots, for example *-teh₂t-, the abstract noun-forming suffix, which has the same stop consonant repeated.

Inflectional endings also appear both as monosyllables, even single phonemes, and as polysyllables in PIE. For example, the third singular ending *-t or the accusative singular ending *-m, the imperative ending *-dʰi, and the first person plural middle marker *-medh₂; polysyllabic endings include the third person middle marker *-nto, the thematic genitive singular *-osyo and locative plural *-oisu, although all of these endings have been analysed as late creations within PIE.

3.3   PIE ablaut and word-structure

The term ablaut is here used to describe a process involving a change in the vocalism in any part of a word. Different types of ablaut are found in a large number of languages either as exclusive or subsidiary morphological markers. For example, compare the paradigm of English *man*, plural *men*, where a change of vowel functions as the exclusive marker, with the German paradigm *Mann* 'man', plural *Männer*, where a conditioned vowel change, called *umlaut*, acts as a subsidiary marker. For PIE it is usual to reconstruct different ablaut *grades*, that is, different forms of the root or affix distinguished by the presence or absence of specific vowels. Table 3.1 presents the paradigm of the word for 'foot' in several different IE languages and shows the possible variety of grades.

As is clear from the comparative data, there is a wealth of different ablaut grades in a single paradigm. The PIE forms given as reconstructions are not set in stone, and, as we shall see later, most scholars now reconstruct a very different paradigm for this word. There is a further grade not included in this table: the *zero-grade*, *pd-*, which can be reconstructed for this root from some compound forms such as Greek *épi-bd-a* 'day after a festival' (deriving from an earlier presumed meaning '[day] following the footsteps') and Avestan *fra-bd-a-* 'forefoot'. Table 3.2 shows the five different ablaut grades from the root *ped-* in summary.

The ablaut variation along the horizontal axis of table 3.2 is usually termed *quantitative ablaut*, and along the vertical axis *qualitative ablaut*. The *full-grades* *ped-* and *pod-* are far more frequent in PIE morphology than the *lengthened-grades* and are usually simply termed *e-grade* and *o-grade* for convenience.

It is possible to trace the fortunes of ablaut as a morphological process in the history of many of the IE languages: old ablaut patterns sometimes survive in non-productive paradigms, or sometimes they are revivified and reused. Alongside these survivals, new ablaut patterns are sometimes created after phonetic changes have eroded the conditioning factors which govern automatic vowel

Table 3.1 *'Foot' in various IE languages.*

	Nom. singular	Acc. singular	Genitive singular	Dative singular	Nominative plural	Locative plural
Sanskrit	*pā́t*	*pā́d-am*	*pad-ás*	*pad-é*	*pā́d-as*	*patsú*
Greek						
(Doric)	*pṓs*	*pód-a*	*pod-ós*		*pód-es*	
Armenian		*ot-n*			*ot-kʻ*	
Latin	*pēs*	*ped-em*	*ped-is*	*ped-ī́*	*ped-es*	
Old Norse	*fót-r*	*fót*	*fót-ar*	*føt-e*	*føtr*	
Albanian						*(për)-posh*
Old Irish						*ís*
PIE	**pṓd-s*	**pód-m*	**ped-ós*	**ped-éi*	**pód-es*	**péd-su*

Sanskrit *a* can derive from **e*, or **o*, *ā* from **ē*, **ō* or **o* in an open syllable.
Old Norse *ó* can derive from **ō* and *ø* is the result of *ó* before *i* or *j* in the next syllable.
Old Irish *í* and Albanian *o* can derive from **ē*.

Table 3.2 *Ablaut grades of* **ped-.*

	Zero-grade	Full-grade	Lengthened-grade
e	**pd-*	**ped-*	**pēd-*
o		**pod-*	**pōd-*

changes (as, for example, the English paradigm *man* plural *men*). In general, IE languages have shifted away from ablaut as a morphological device. In Ancient Greek and Sanskrit, derivational and inflectional suffixes were often associated with different ablaut forms, but in Modern Greek and Modern Indic languages this is no longer the case. It is possible to trace the decline of ablaut as an obligatory and productive marker even in the ancient languages. Extrapolation back in time, and comparison of paradigms such as in table 3.1, suggests that the parent language had a much more fully integrated system, where a greater number of morphological processes, inflectional and derivational, was necessarily encoded by ablaut as well as affixation.

This hypothesis is supported by the fact that in the ancient IE languages most of the workings of ablaut cannot be simply explained as the result of an earlier phonetic change, unlike umlaut plurals of the type *men* beside singular *man* in English. Ablaut must therefore have been at one stage a productive and widespread morphological process, and it is in these terms that it will be discussed. However, comparative philologists have repeatedly attempted to 'explain' ablaut in terms

Table 3.3 *The morphological structure of inflected words in PIE.*

Word	Lexical root	Derivational affix	Inflectional ending
	R	**S**	**D**
*pod-m **R + D**	**pod-*		**-m*
'foot' (accusative)			
*ped-o-m **R + S + D**	**ped-*	**-o-*	**-m*
'footstep' (nominative):			
Sanskrit *padám*, Armenian *het*,			
Old Norse *fet*			
*ped-yo-mh₁no-s **R + S + S + D**	**ped-*	**-yo- +*	** -s*
'going' (nominative):		**-mh₁no-*	
Sanskrit *padyamānas*			

of earlier phonetic change of some sort, no doubt influenced by the historical account of processes such as umlaut in English and German, and by a desire to trace allomorphic variation back to earlier unity. We need also to take account of such explanations, since the descriptions of ablaut that have been offered are frequently directly or indirectly tied in to a theory of how it arose.

A full understanding of ablaut also necessitates a theory of the make-up of complex words in PIE. Every inflected word (discounting compounds) must by definition contain a root and an inflectional ending, and it may also feature one or more derivational affixes between the root and ending. This can be represented schematically as in table 3.3.

Ablaut changes affect not only the lexical root of a word, but also the derivational affix (**S**) and the inflectional ending (**D**). For example, the agent-noun-forming suffix **-ter-* can appear in different ablaut forms, o-grade **-tor-* (as in Latin **actor** 'agent') and zero-grade **-tr-* (as Latin feminine **actrix** 'stewardess'); genitive singular inflection can be expressed by the allomorphs **-s, *-es* and **-os*. In any morphological element with more than two consonantal segments (here denoted as C) the ablaut vowel, if present, will fall somewhere after the first segment and before the last. Thus for bi-consonantal morphs the ablaut vowel will always fall between the two elements (CeC, CoC etc.), as in the root **ped-*, and the suffix **-ter-* given above. The only exceptions to this rule are affixes formed by a combination of nasal and dental which show ablaut **-nt- / *-e/ont-*. For a morph with only one consonant the picture is more complicated: suffixes, most inflections and the few mono-consonantal roots show an ablaut pattern of C: eC. However, sometimes the alternative, C: Ce, is found, as in the first person singular ending (**-h₂e: *-h₂*); the one PIE infix (**-ne-: *-n-*); and the negative particle (**ne: *n̥-*).

We have already seen in table 3.1 that some roots show alternative full-grade forms, as the root which is used to denote 'sky', 'heaven' and 'god' shows both a full-grade *deiw- and *dyew-. This apparent fluctuation of the full-grade vowel position is termed *schwebeablaut*, and does not affect all roots; some, such as the root *leik^w- 'leave', never show this alternation. It has sometimes been assumed that the alternation between *deiw- and *dyew- can be explained if an earlier form of the root *deyew- is reconstructed, with later syncope of one of the vowels. However, it seems more likely that schwebeablaut is in fact an illusion caused by the comparative method's inability to separate out different chronological stages of the parent language. For the root *dyew- / *deiw-, it is anachronistic to reconstruct both ablaut forms for the same synchronic stage of the parent language. Rather the original form of the root was *dyew- with zero-grade *diw-. At a later stage in PIE the zero-grade *diw- became the basis for a new full-grade *deiw- on the model of other roots which showed ablaut *CiC- / *CeiC-, such as *leik^w-. If this is the correct explanation, schwebeablaut then gives no support to reconstructing an earlier root *deyew-. Indeed, there is no reconstructed PIE formation which shows two full-grades in one root, and it is axiomatic that where there are two apparent full-grades in a reconstructed PIE word, there must be a morphological boundary between them.

This picture of IE word-structure is further clouded by the so-called thematic vowel (written *e/o). This is not a different IE vowel but rather a cover term to describe a formative which is realised either as *e or *o depending on context. The thematic vowel can stand directly before the inflectional endings of verbs and nouns, or it can be followed by further suffixes. It can function as a simple suffix on its own, or it can be part of a bigger suffix, for example the suffixes *-ye/o-, *-te/o-, *-tre/o-, *-sk´e/o- and *-re/o-. Note that these suffixes can further appear in e-grade or o-grade, for example *-eye/o-, *-ete/o-, *-tere/o- and *-ere/o-. The thematic vowel therefore seems to behave differently in affixation patterns from the ablaut vowels *e and *o. The rules given for placement of ablaut vowels apply only if the thematic vowel is not considered to count as an ablaut vowel.

Exercise 3.1

The Latin verb *gignō* 'I become' and Greek *gígnomai* 'I become' both derive from the root *g´enh_1-, Greek *píptō* 'I fall' derives from the root *pet-, and *mímnō* 'I stay' derives from the root *men-. Work out the derivation process of the verbal stem.

The following verbs share the same derivational process, although sometimes it has been obscured by phonetic changes. Explain the changes that have taken place.

Greek for 'I give birth' is *tíkt-ō* from a root *tek-.
Greek for 'I hold' is *ískh-ō* from a root *seg^h-.
Sanskrit for 's/he stands' is *tíṣṭh-ati* from a root *steh_2-.
Sanskrit for 's/he agitates' is *īj-āti* from a root *h_2eg´-.

Greek *hízd-ō-*, Sanskrit *síd-ati* and Latin *sīd-ō* – all mean 'sit'.
Identify the root which forms all three verbs and explain the phonetic changes.

Exercise 3.2

Sanskrit *nīḍá-*, Latin *nīdus*, Armenian *nist* and English *nest* all share the meaning 'nest'. Use the results of the last part of exercise 3.1 to reconstruct the IE word. Is it possible to analyse the PIE term morphologically and semantically as a compound?

3.4 PIE accent

It has long been recognised that PIE ablaut variation often correlates with a shift in the position of the reconstructed accent. This is exemplified by many nominal paradigms, note for example the reconstruction of inflected forms of the word for 'father' through comparison of Greek and Sanskrit in table 3.4.

Table 3.4 *Accent and ablaut in a PIE paradigm.*

	PIE	Greek	Sanskrit
nominative singular	*$ph_2tḗr$	*patḗr*	*pitā́*
nominative plural	*$ph_2tér$-es	*patéres*	*pitáras*
dative singular	*ph_2tr-éi	*patrí*	*pitré*
compounded nominative plural	* ´-ph_2tor-es	*a-pátores* 'fatherless'	*tvát-pitāras* 'having you as father'

It is immediately noticeable from table 3.4 that the e-grade (and lengthened ē-grade) coincide with the place of the accent. When the accent is shifted to the right, morphs which had e-grade under the accent switch to zero-grade, thus *$ph_2tḗr$*- becomes *ph_2tr*-, and when the accent is shifted to the left, e-grade morphs become o-grade. The leftward accent shifts generally involve compositional forms, as are the examples in table 3.4. Compounds such as these may have originated through the univerbation of two separate words, and hence it is possible to explain the leftward accent shifts not as shifts, but as the loss of the original word-accent on the second member of a compound in the univerbation process (note that, in the Greek example given in table 3.4, the expected accentuation is *á-patores*, but a rule of Greek limits the accent to the last three syllables of a word). If we accept this theory of leftward accent shift, we can reconstruct a stage of PIE where words had only one full vowel, which coincided with the position of the accent. This hypothesis of a coincidence of the full vowel with the accent has been fundamental in work on PIE ablaut patterns, and we shall explore it further below. But first we must ask what we mean by 'accent' for PIE, and how we can reconstruct it.

Only four of the IE branches present adequate information for the reconstruction of PIE accent. Little certain is known about the accent systems of Tocharian and Anatolian, and the fixed or predictable stress accents of Latin, Celtic,

Germanic and Armenian can be shown to be the result of (separate) innovations. In one of these branches, Germanic, there is, however, evidence of an earlier mobile accent traceable through its effect on neighbouring consonants. In Germanic, stops of the PIE *t series in medial position became either voiced or voiceless fricatives. Sometimes in the same paradigm there is variation between the voiced and voiceless outcome, as in the paradigm of the past tense of the Old High German word for 'pull', which is derived from the PIE root *deuk´-:

First person singular: *zoh* /tso:χ/ 'I pulled'
First person plural: *zugum* /tsugum/ 'we pulled'.

The best historical explanation for the voicing alternation is a proposed sound-change known as *Verner's Law* (see table 2.3). This states that fricatives are voiceless only if they were directly preceded by the PIE word-accent, otherwise they become voiced. In the paradigm above, the alternation is explained through assuming that the original accent fell on the root in the singular, and on the ending in the plural of the paradigm, a reconstruction which is supported by evidence from Sanskrit.

The Baltic and Slavic branches present a complicated array of different accent types, ranging from languages with a fixed-stress accent (e.g. Bulgarian) to others with mobile accent and tonal contrasts (e.g. Lithuanian). Unfortunately, most of these languages are only attested relatively late in the IE tradition, and we have no information on the accentuation of the earliest attested language: Old Church Slavonic. The divergences between the languages and the complexity of the internal developments they have undergone make the reconstruction of the ancestral accent patterns of these languages exceedingly difficult. We can be certain that it was a mobile system, but it is uncertain whether there is any need to reconstruct tonal contrasts, as in Lithuanian; recent work by Halle and others (see Halle and Vergnaud (1987), Halle (1997)) suggests that the Baltic and Serbo-Croatian tonal contrasts are an innovation.

Qualitatively our best evidence for PIE accent comes from two of the oldest and most conservative branches: Greek and Vedic Sanskrit. For both languages there is a large body of texts with word-accents marked and adequate metalinguistic descriptions of the nature of the accentual system. The accent of both Greek and Sanskrit was a mobile pitch-accent type, but there were differences between the two systems. Greek shows an accentual opposition on bimoraic nuclei between a rising tone *oíkoi* 'at home' (acute) and a compound rise and fall *oîkoi* 'houses' (circumflex). This opposition is paralleled in Baltic and Serbo-Croatian accentuation but is not found in Vedic Sanskrit. Restated in simple terms, however, this difference does not seem so great: in Vedic Sanskrit a *syllable* achieves prominence through rise in pitch with an associated fall in pitch on the following *syllable*; in Greek a *mora* achieves prominence through rise in pitch with an associated following fall in pitch (a short vowel counts as a single *mora*, a long vowel or diphthong counts as two *morae*). An innovation further restricts more than one *mora* between the rise and fall of the accent and the end of the Greek word; in effect this means that the accent can fall on the syllable three from the end if the final syllable has a short vowel. Since the two *morae* of some of the Greek circumflex nuclei have arisen from contraction of two syllables, it seems reasonable to assume that the syllable-based accent of Sanskrit is original (further discussion of the accentual innovations made in Greek and of moraic and syllabic approaches to Greek accent in a generativist framework is given by Noyer (1997)).

Comparison of Germanic, Baltic, Slavic, Greek and Sanskrit allows us to reconstruct the *place* of the PIE word accent with some confidence, and gives some indication of the main properties of the accentual system:

a)   The accent can fall on any element which functions as a syllabic nucleus.

b)   The accent can fall on any syllable of a word.

c)   No word has more than one accent.

It might be expected that every well-formed nominal or verb would have one and only one accent, but even this cannot be proved. Indeed, Sanskrit accentuation practice implies that a finite verb in a main clause was unaccented, and the rules for the accentuation of finite verbs in Greek can best be accounted for under the assumption that the same rule also applied in prehistoric Greek.

All in all this is a somewhat disappointing description of an accentual system. Comparative reconstruction of the *nature* of the PIE accent, beyond the fact that it was mobile, is difficult and controversial. This is because accentual change is not unidirectional, and there is no hierarchy for the likely direction of accentual change. It has sometimes been stated that there is a long-term diachronic development from tone accent to stress accent, via restricted tone and pitch accent, but in practice languages rarely behave this neatly, and stress languages may develop a pitch accent, as, for example, Swedish and Norwegian have done. It could be argued that, since Greek and Sanskrit were both of a pitch-accent type, the most economical reconstruction would also be a pitch accent, but it seems preferable to reserve judgement until we have better knowledge of likely pathways of accent change.

Since there is no agreed diachronic typology of accentual change, the reconstruction of PIE accent usually rests on a rather ad hoc synchronic typology, reliant on assumptions that certain phonological processes are only associated with one type of accent. Consequently, the different processes of quantitative and qualitative ablaut are often supposed to be linked to different accent systems: syncope of unaccented vowels is thought to take place only in stress systems, and variation in vowel quality between accented and unaccented syllables is supposed to be an effect of pitch-accent systems. These assumptions are set out in tabular form in table 3.5.

Since it is also normally assumed that stress and pitch accent are mutually exclusive, some scholars believe that PIE went through both a stress-accent and a pitch-accent period, a conclusion repeated in some handbooks. However, a simple chronological progression between two accent types is not enough. If the

Table 3.5 *Putative correlations of accent and ablaut.*

Ablaut type	Presumed cause	Presumed accent
quantitative ablaut: *ph₂tér-es / *ph₂tr-éi*	syncope	stress
qualitative ablaut *ph₂tér-es / *´-ph₂tor-es*	musical tones	pitch

stress period is assumed to have preceded the pitch period, then syncope cannot have affected all unaccented vowels, otherwise there would be no possibility of o-grades following the accent, as **´-ph₂tor-es*. If the pitch period preceded the stress period, then why were the unaccented vowels of **´-ph₂tor-es* retained? In order to meet these objections, it is usually assumed that the stress accent came first, and there was a subsequent loss of accent in some environments, such as the second members of compounds. However, the basic assumption that there must have been a separate stress- and pitch-accent phase of PIE need not be correct. Certainly it is true that syncope does occur in many stress-accented languages, but it also occurs in languages with other accent systems (such as Lithuanian). Likewise, change of vowel quality in unaccented syllables is by no means limited to pitch-accent languages, but occurs in languages, such as Russian, with different accent systems.

A further possibility is that PIE was in fact a tone language. This position has been advanced by Lubotsky (1988) based on his analysis of Sanskrit accentuation and on typological considerations. Lubotsky shows that the lexical accent of o-stem, i-stem and u-stem nouns in Sanskrit can be predicted with a large degree of success from the phonological shape of the word. For example, the accent of o-stem nouns with one obstruent in the root can be deduced from the following rules:

a)   if root obstruent [−voice] > barytone (i.e. accent on first syllable).
b)   if obstruent [+ voice] > oxytone (i.e. accent on final syllable).

Lubotsky concludes that this distribution of accent type is consistent with a tone system in which obstruent voicing is directly correlated with tone, as it is in other tone languages. At present, Lubotsky's findings are uncorroborated by other research. The nature of the PIE accent consequently remains unknown. It is possible to give reasons *for* reconstructing a stress, a pitch or even a tone accent, but there are no conclusive arguments *against* the reconstruction of any one of these. The reconstruction of accent is thus analogous to the reconstruction of the phonetic properties of PIE phonemes as discussed at section 2.2: we can reconstruct a position of accentual prominence in a PIE word, but we cannot securely know how that prominence was achieved.

3.5   Accent and ablaut paradigms

We have already seen that in some inflectional paradigms, such as the word for 'father' *ph_2ter-, there is a regular correlation between accent and ablaut. We have also seen, in our discussion of the laryngeal theory in section 2.5, that different ablaut forms of roots are associated with different derivational formations. In recent years, there has been much work in IE studies attempting to provide a unified theory of the morphological factors governing changes in accent and ablaut in both inflectional and derivational morphology. In this section, we shall examine some of these attempts.

We must first give a better account of the conditions for paradigmatic alternations of the type between *$ph_2téres$ and *$ph_2tréi$. Paradigmatic slots in which the accent and correlating e-grade are positioned further to the left of the word are traditionally termed *strong*, those with accent and e-grade further to the right, are called *weak*. In all nouns and verbs which show these alternations, the strong and the weak forms are predictable from the morphological category, as shown in table 3.6. (Note that in the reconstruction of the verb form *h_1i-mé we have followed the Sanskrit accent as evidence for the PIE accent position, since an innovation of Greek has led to the accent becoming fixed on the first permissible mora of the word in most verbal paradigms.)

Table 3.6 *Strong and weak forms of nouns and verbs.*

	Strong	Weak
Nouns	nominative singular / dual / plural accusative singular / dual / plural locative singular e.g. *$ph_2tér$-es	all other cases e.g. *ph_2tr-éi
Verbs	First person singular active Second person singular active Third person singular active e.g. *$h_1éi$-mi 'I go' Greek *eîmi*, Sanskrit *émi*	all other active forms all middle forms e.g. *h_1i-mé 'we go' Greek *ímen*, Sanskrit *imás*

The paradigm for 'father' also shows a different ablaut form, the lengthened ē-grade in the reconstructed nominative singular *$ph_2tḗr$. This appears to upset the parallelism between the nominal and verbal forms, since the noun paradigm has a further ablaut alternation not found in the verbs. However, comparison of this nominative singular with other paradigms shows that there is another way to explain the lengthened grade of *$ph_2tḗr$. Nouns in the same declension class which end in a final stop mark the nominative singular with the ending *-s, as, for example, the compound *$ņyuk$-s 'unyoked' cited in section 3.2. We can account for both the lengthened vowel of *$ph_2tḗr$, and the lack of a final *-s, if we suppose

Table 3.7 *Accent / ablaut paradigms.*

		Fixed accent
Acrostatic 1	Strong	$R(\acute{\bar{e}}) + S(z) + D(z)$
	Weak	$R(\acute{e}) + S(z) + D(z)$
Acrostatic 2	Strong	$R(\acute{o}) + S(z) + D(z)$
	Weak	$R(\acute{e}) + S(z) + D(z)$
		Mobile accent
Kinetic	Strong	$R(\acute{e}) + D(z)$
	Weak	$R(z) + D(\acute{e})$
Proterokinetic	Strong	$R(\acute{e}) + S(z) + D(z)$
	Weak	$R(z) + S(\acute{e}) + D(z)$
Hysterokinetic	Strong	$R(z) + S(\acute{e}) + D(z)$
	Weak	$R(z) + S(z) + D(\acute{e})$
Amphikinetic	Strong	$R(\acute{e}) + S(o) + D(z)$
	Weak	$R(z) + S(z) + D(\acute{e})$

that an earlier stage of PIE *$ph_2tér$s* existed, but underwent assimilation of *-rs* to *-rr*, with subsequent transfer of the length to the preceding vowel. The envisaged sound-changes in this account, assimilation, simplification of a consonant cluster and compensatory lengthening of a preceding vowel, are very common in the histories of many languages. If we allow this change, the nominal and verbal alternations are also brought into line.

Both paradigms cited in table 3.6 show accented e-grade in the syllable before the ending in the strong forms, and accented e-grade in the ending of the weak forms. However, the same alternation cannot explain all paradigms. If we return to the paradigm of the word for 'foot' reconstructed in table 3.1, it seems to show a strong stem *pód-*, but a weak stem *ped-*, with lengthening in the nominative singular and locative plural (in both cases when preceding *s*). The word for 'foot' is not the only example of a paradigm which does not fit the pattern: the widespread class of neuter nouns formed with a suffix *-e/os-* provides another example. This declension type can be reconstructed as follows from comparison of the Greek and Sanskrit words for 'spirit, courage'. Note that the nominative singular in this neuter declension class has a zero-morph as its ending.

Strong nom. sing.	Gk *ménos*	Skt *mánas*	PIE *mén-os-ø*
Weak gen. sing.	Gk *méneos*	Skt *mánasas*	PIE *mén-es-os*

In order to explain these different paradigms, a group of Austrian and German scholars (principally Schindler, Eichner, Klingenschmitt and Rix and their pupils) have developed the theory that there are in fact a number of different accent / ablaut paradigms, showing different alternations between strong and weak forms. There is general agreement on reconstructing the following types, as laid out in table 3.7, where the notation $R(\acute{e})$ means 'root in accented e-grade' and $S(z)$ means 'suffix in zero-grade', etc.

It will be seen that these paradigms mostly follow the principle that the e-grade coincides with the locus of the accent, and hence that there is no e-grade which is unaccented. The one exception is the 'acrostatic 2' paradigm, where an accented o-grade is found, which we shall examine in more detail below. Some PIE nominal paradigms that we have already discussed can be immediately explained in this framework. The hysterokinetic type is preserved in a number of nouns: the word for 'father' is a clear-cut example. Examples of what we have called the kinetic type, where there is no suffix between root and ending, can be most clearly seen in verbal formations such as the paradigm of the verb meaning 'go': *$h_1éi$-mi 'I go', *h_1i-mé 'we go'. This type is also well attested in the so-called *root-nouns*, nouns without a suffix between root and the inflexional endings.

However, there is much less direct evidence for the other paradigm types. An example of an amphikinetic paradigm may be found in the reconstructed word for 'path' in Indo-Iranian, already discussed in section 2.3:

	Vedic	Avestan	PIE
Strong nom. sing.	*pánthās*	*paṇtå̊*	*$pént-oh_2$-s*
Weak gen. sing.	*pathás*	*paθō̄*	*$p\underset{\circ}{n}t-h_2$-és*

Note that the analysis of *$péntoh_2s$* as root, suffix and ending, rather than simply root and ending, is based solely on the rule that no root can contain two full-grades, and synchronically this noun may have been viewed as a root-noun, since the nominal suffix *h_2* was not productive.

The explanation for the rarity of direct survivals of paradigm types other than the kinetic and hysterokinetic is straightforward. All the other types involve a change in the ablaut grade of the root morpheme within the paradigm. In the attested IE languages, only very rarely do suffixed nominal forms show any alternation in their root syllable. In most paradigms in the daughter language a rule operates that limits paradigmatic ablaut to operation in the syllable before the ending, and no further back in the word. Furthermore, in many nominal paradigms there is a tendency to use full-grade forms of the nominal endings in the weak cases, in order to mark them more clearly.

Despite this, the reconstructed paradigm types are a powerful tool to help explain the alternations which do occur in the daughter languages. Firstly, let us look again at the word for 'foot'. The reconstructed paradigm given in table 3.1 had nominative *$pṓd$-s* but genitive *$ped-ós$*, which fits in with none of the types given. This word is now reconstructed as acrostatic type 2, nominative *$pód$-s* and genitive *$péd$-s*. The lengthened grade of the nominative singular is explained as the outcome of the sequence *Vds*, with assimilation of the consonant cluster and compensatory lengthening. All languages have reformed the genitive, using the full-grade form *-os*, and in Greek and Sanskrit the accent has shifted from the root to the ending in the weak cases, through analogy with the kinetic root-nouns. Every language except Sanskrit has generalised a particular grade of the root throughout the paradigm.

The neuter nouns formed with a suffix *-e/os- have also undergone radical restructuring. As we saw, these alternate between a strong stem R(é) + S(o) + D(z) (*mén-os-ø) and a weak stem R(é) + S(e) + D(o) (*mén-es-os). This is explained as a development from an original proterokinetic paradigm, with strong stem R(é) + S(z) + D(z) and weak R(z) + S(é) + D(z). In Greek and Sanskrit, the e-grade and the location of the accent of the strong cases was generalised throughout the paradigm. The o-grade is introduced to re-mark the ending in the genitive. The o-grade of the suffix in the strong stem *mén-os could be explained as generalisation of the full-grade of the suffix from the weak cases, at a time when a rule was in operation that every *e which was not accented was realised as *o.

The number of prehistoric changes needed to get from the hypothetical paradigms to the attested forms may seem to be large in both the case of the word for 'foot' and the *-e/os- suffixed neuter nouns, and the accent and ablaut paradigms have seemed overly speculative to some. However, there is some support for these reconstructions from isolated case-forms which have survived in fossilised phrases. For example, the hypothetical original nominative-accusative singular *mens 'spirit' or 'mind' apparently survives in an archaic combination with the verbal root *dʰeh₁-, retained in the Avestan verb mazdā- meaning 'put in mind'.

Exercise 3.3

The following tables give some comparative material for PIE singular paradigms of the words *dyew- 'sky / god', *nébʰos 'cloud', *yekʷ- 'liver' and *gʷenh₂ 'woman'. Can you assign any of these nouns to the classes in table 3.7? (The paradigms of these words will be reconstructed in the next chapter.)

*dyew- 'sky / god'	Hittite	Sanskrit	Greek	Latin
nominative	sius	dyáus	Zdeús	diēs
genitive	siunas	divás	Diwós	Iouis
dative	siuni	divá	Diwéi	Iouī
locative	siuni	dyávi	Diwí	Ioue

*nébʰos 'cloud'	Hittite	Sanskrit	Avestan	Greek	Old Church Slavonic
nominative	nepis	nábhas	nabas-	néphos	nebo
genitive	nepisas	nábhasas	nabaṇhas-	népheos	nebese

*yek^w- 'liver'	Sanskrit	Greek	Latin
nominative	yák-ṛt	hêp-ar	iec-ur
genitive	yák-nas	hêp-atos	ioc-ineris

*g^wenh_2 'woman'	Vedic Sanskrit	Old Irish	Armenian
nominative	jáni	ben	kin
genitive	gnā́s	mná	knoǰ

The paradigms with fixed accent on the root have proved to be of particular importance for the reconstruction of PIE ablaut and accent. We have already seen a possible example of the acrostatic 2 paradigm in the reconstruction of the word for 'foot'. Acrostatic 1 is better attested in verbal formations, for example the root present tense from the root *stew- meaning 'praise' or 'declare':

	Sanskrit	Greek	PIE
Strong 3rd singular active	stáuti		*stéu-ti
Weak 3rd singular middle	stáve	steútai	*stéu-(t)oi

Verbal paradigms of this type, which show fixed accent on the root and an alternation between lengthened grade in strong forms and e-grade in the weak forms, were first recognised and described by Johanna Narten, and this type of ablaut is consequently known as *Narten ablaut*. Narten ablaut is also supposed for some nominal paradigms; an example is the neuter noun meaning 'old age' reconstructed as *g ´erh_2-s-/ *g ´erh_2-s-, which is supposed to lie behind both the Greek nouns gêras 'old age' and géras 'prize' (with semantic shift from 'old-age' to 'honour given in recognition of old age'). Formations with Narten ablaut occur in exactly the same morphological environments as other formations with mobile accent types: the fixed-accent present tense of *steu- is parallel to the kinetic present tense *$h_1éi$-; the Narten ablaut of the neuter noun *g ´erh_2-s- formed with a suffix *-s- is parallel to the hysterodynamic s-stem noun *mén-os-.

It is not clear why some words follow the acrostatic 1 paradigm (the Narten ablaut type) and others acrostatic 2. Schindler theorised that some PIE roots have a tendency to favour Narten ablaut formations (Schindler 1994). Consider the root meaning 'rule', *reg ´- (sometimes reconstructed with an initial laryngeal, *h_3reg ´-). In Vedic Sanskrit the strong stems of the unsuffixed verb formed from this root show a Narten ablaut, with strong stem from *rēg ´-, as in the third person singular active rā́ṣṭi 'he rules', and weak stem *reg ´-, which may be continued in the cognate verb in Latin regō. Nominal formations from the same root also show Narten ablaut; note in particular the derived noun in Avestan meaning 'order':

Strong nominative singular   *rāzarə* $< *rēg´-r$
Weak instrumental singular   *rašnā* $< *reg´-n-$

Schindler accordingly proposed that there was a distinction between 'Narten roots', which always carried the accent on the root and showed an ablaut pattern of lengthened ē-grade and e-grade, and other, 'non-Narten' roots, which allowed the accent to move away from them and showed an alternation between e-grade and zero-grade.

If Schindler's observation is correct, it opens the door to a different approach from the description of the workings of PIE accent, in line with work by Hock (1993) and Halle (1997). These scholars have attempted to derive the prosody of a well-formed PIE word from the action of rules upon underlying forms which are stored in the lexicon. All roots, suffixes and endings are held to be inherently accented or non-accented. What we have previously termed the accent of a full word is renamed *stress*, in order to avoid confusion between the inherent properties of morphemes and the prosody of the full word. The word-stress may fall on an inherently accented morpheme, but it need not do so. If a word contains one accented and one or more unaccented morphemes, the accented morpheme is stressed unless an intermediate rule has motivated a change of accent.

Combining Halle's and Hock's accounts, it is possible to sketch out one model showing how this might work for PIE paradigms. As we have seen, for the Narten ablaut the root is assumed to be inherently accented, and is stressed in both strong and weak cases. The amphikinetic type alternates between accentuation on the root in the strong cases, and accentuation of the ending in the weak cases. Let us assume that in this paradigm the root is inherently unaccented, and the ending is unaccented in strong cases but accented in the weak. It is possible to generate both the acrostatic accent paradigm and the amphikinetic by the assumption of three accentual rules:

1)   Words with only one accented morpheme stress that morpheme.
2)   In words with two accented morphemes, the leftmost is stressed.
3)   Words with no accented morpheme receive stress on the leftmost element.

The proterokinetic and hysterokinetic accents could be accounted for in the same way, if we assume that suffixes could also bear an inherent accent, and that more complex rules operate in cases where two accented morphemes are adjacent to each other, with the end-result that if either an accented root or an accented ending stands next to an accented suffix, the suffix accent loses out to either one, but if all three of the elements root, suffix and ending are accented, the suffix

Table 3.8 *Generating accent paradigms from inherent accents.*

		Inherent accent				Word prosody		
		R	S	D		R	S	D
Acrostatic	nom.	+	−	−	⇒	+	−	−
	gen.	+	−	+	⇒	+	−	−
Amphikinetic	nom.	−	−	−	⇒	+	−	−
	gen.	−	−	+	⇒	−	−	+
Proterokinetic	nom.	+	+	−	⇒	+	−	−
	gen.	+	+	+	⇒	−	+	−
Hysterokinetic	nom.	−	+	−	⇒	−	+	−
	gen.	−	+	+	⇒	−	−	+

receives the stress. These rules will generate the accentual paradigms set out in table 3.8.

Exercise 3.4

How would you formulate further accentual rules, in addition to the ones given, to arrive at the correct outcomes for the proterokinetic and hysterokinetic paradigms in table 3.8?

Despite Schindler's surmise that some PIE roots were inherently accented, a generative account of accent and ablaut paradigms of the type set out in table 3.8 is not generally followed in IE studies. Current thinking instead operates with morphological rules for deriving one accentual paradigm from another, i.e. derivation through accent shift and not through affixation (termed *internal derivation* in the literature). Thus, for example, a rule may operate on a proterokinetic paradigm to give a derived hysterokinetic paradigm. The proterokinetic neuter noun with suffix *-e/os–*, *mén-os-*, is consequently held to have a hysterokinetic counterpart *m(e)n-és-*, which is attested in compounded words in Greek and Indo-Iranian:

dus-m(e)n-és- 'ill-minded, hostile': Avestan *duž-manah-*, Greek *dus-menḗs*

The evidence for derivations through a shift in the accent paradigm outside compounded words is scarce: there is no uncompounded *m(e)n-és-* attested. Where there are derivatives of this sort in the early IE languages, they can often be shown to be later formations. For example, in Greek the adjective *pseudḗs* 'false' beside the noun *pseûdos* 'lie' appears to show exactly the same process of derivation as hypothetical *m(e)nḗs-* next to *ménos-*. However, closer examination of the textual occurrences of *pseudḗs* shows that it is actually a back-formation from a compound *apseudḗs* 'without falsehood'. The derivational chain is therefore:

$$pse\hat{u}dos \quad \rightarrow \quad apseud\acute{e}s \quad \rightarrow \quad pseud\acute{e}s$$

and the apparent derivation of this adjective through accent shift alone is a mirage. Despite the scarcity of examples of internal derivation as a productive process in early IE languages, most work on word-formation now relies heavily on the assumption that PIE formed new lexemes through shift from one accentual paradigm to another.

The reconstruction of accent and ablaut paradigms, and the best explanation for the genesis of these paradigms, is the locus of much current research in IE studies. As we have seen, there is disagreement over whether these accentual paradigms can be explained through accentual properties inherent in roots and stems, or whether they should be viewed as morphological operations.

3.6   The relation of accent and ablaut

The accent and ablaut paradigms discussed in section 3.5 were reconstructed following an assumption that PIE ablaut was dependent upon accent, and that e-grades systematically became zero-grades when they did not fall under the accent. Following this hypothesis, accentual paradigms were reconstructed on the evidence of ablaut variation. This can be seen in the reconstruction of the original paradigm of the word for 'foot' and the forms cited in table 3.1. Greek and Sanskrit both show a genitive singular of the word 'foot' with the accent falling on the second syllable, the ending. However, the alternation between original *pod-* and *ped-*, found in the daughter languages, led to the reconstruction of an acrostatic paradigm. The genitive singular was accordingly reconstructed *péd-s*, with accented root syllable. The original accent was therefore reconstructed principally on the basis of ablaut patterns, and not the attested accent of the daughter language.

It is possible that both Greek and Sanskrit made the same innovatory change in the accent pattern of the word for 'foot' when they replaced the inherited paradigm, following their separation from PIE. However, other comparative evidence makes it likely that, at the later stages of PIE, the hypothesis that each word has only one *e* vowel which was positioned in the locus of the accent cannot be true. We have already seen cases where the vowel *o* can also stand in accented syllables in opposition to *e*, as in the very same paradigm, nominative *pód-s* and genitive *péd-s*. There are also roots and suffixes which always show *o* and never *e* in any language, such as *póti-* 'master'; reconstructed words which show two e-grades, such as *pénkʷe* 'five'; and words where the comparative evidence suggests that the location of the accent was other than where the vowel *e* stood, as *septṁ* 'seven' and *wóid-e* 'he/she knows'.

*póti- 'master': Sanskrit páti-, Greek pósis, Latin potis, Lithuanian -pats
*pénkʷe 'five': Sanskrit pánca, Greek pénte, Latin quīnque, Gothic fimf
*septḿ 'seven': Greek heptá, Skt saptá, Gothic sibun
*wóid-e 'he/she knows': Greek (w)oîde, Sanskrit véda

   Furthermore, certain roots, and nominal and verbal suffixes and endings which theoretically should show ablaut forms in fact never do. Thus the root meaning 'become', which survives in all the IE branches except Anatolian and Tocharian, is reconstructed as a non-ablauting form *bʰuH-; apparent ablaut forms in Celtic, Italic and Indo-Iranian are all better explained differently (see Jasanoff 2003: 122). The (non-neuter) nominative plural ending is *-es, although it never carries the accent in any reconstructed paradigm. The 'weak' case-endings, locative and instrumental plural, never show a full grade, although they carry the accent in the majority of paradigms.
   One possible course of response to these difficulties would be to reject the hypothesis linking the e-grade and accent altogether, but without any rival theory to put in its place this is too drastic a reaction to the problem. The more profitable option is to modify our reconstruction to limit the scope of the hypothesis. This can be done in different ways. The usual solution, and one we have already mentioned in section 3.4, is to put back the time at which the vowel *e was uniquely associated with the accent to an earlier chronological stage of PIE, and explaining the exceptions to it as later chronological developments. Thus, it has often been assumed that *pénkʷe represents the juxtaposition of an original numeral *pen(k)- 'five' with the enclitic conjunctive particle *kʷe 'and' (although the existence of an enclitic with a full e-vowel is in itself a problem). The word for 'seven' *septḿ is assumed to have been influenced by the neighbouring number 'eight' which had accent on the final syllable, continued in Greek oktṓ and Sanskrit aṣṭá-.
   Another way of limiting the scope of the link between *e and the accent would be to reconstruct two (or more) separate vowel phonemes, which all merge as *e in the last stage of PIE, and one of which would be subject to loss when unaccented, and the other(s) not. We saw in section 3.3 that the so-called 'thematic vowel' *e/o does not behave as an ablaut vowel in the formation of suffixes, allowing for suffixes with two apparent e-grades, such as *-eye/o-, and this appears to be a good candidate for a separate vowel phoneme which is immune to the effects of the accent. This type of solution to the difficulties of the relationship between accent and ablaut has generally been avoided by scholars in the past century, although Rasmussen has moved towards it in recent work (Rasmussen 1989). Such a solution has, however, appeared too drastic, if not bizarre, to most IE specialists.
   Much of the divergence observable in the reconstruction of ablaut and accent schemata reflects different attitudes towards reconstruction. There is a constant tension between scholars who seek to reconstruct the 'last stage of IE' and those who wish to find the underlying, and chronologically earlier, basis for that reconstruction. Many have sought a phonological account for ablaut, reasoning

that all morphological variation can be traced back to earlier invariance armed with the right set of sound-changes. The attempts to explain accent and ablaut phenomena under either morphology or phonology in IE studies mirror the various treatments of morphophonemic alternations within general linguistics. The changing place of accent and ablaut reflects not only the chronological perspective of the researcher, but also the linguistic model which is used.

Further reading

The best recent survey of PIE root- and morpheme-structure constraints is Szemerényi (1996: 97–101 and 130–3), and we have followed him in positing a monosyllabic PIE root. A recent attempt to etymologise the kinship terms into conglomerates of root- and agent-noun suffixes is given in Tremblay (2003).

Accounts of the operation of ablaut, the reconstruction of different ablaut grades, IE word-accent and some of the morphological functions of ablaut can be found in the standard handbooks and grammars of individual languages: Wackernagel (1896), Meillet (1964), Beekes (1995) and Szemerényi (1996) all have accessible accounts. Kuryłowicz (1968) contains a mine of comparative data on accent and ablaut, but many of his arguments are marred by excessive use of analogy as an explanation. In the outline of current thinking on ablaut and accent given above, we have deliberately eschewed discussion of some of the books and monographs which have been devoted to giving a causal / genetic explanation of IE accent / ablaut (e.g. Borgström (1949), Schmitt-Brandt (1967), Fulk (1986)). Table 3.1 is largely based on the table presented by Koch 1996: 231.

Our account of schwebeablaut given here is largely based on Anttila (1969), Francis (1970) and Schindler (1970). Generativist work on IE accentology is associated with Halle and Kiparsky, who have published separately and jointly a number of important articles (Kiparsky (1973), Kiparsky and Halle (1977), Halle (1995), Halle (1997)).

There are many works which deal with the reconstructed accent and ablaut paradigms set out in section 3.4. The most recent comprehensive account is given in Widmer (2004), who also sets out the case for internal derivation. Narten ablaut stems from the work of Narten (1968), but the original article covers only Indo-Iranian verb forms and makes no mention of PIE. Strunk (1987) covers the example of the root *reg´ discussed here, and an overall coverage of Narten ablaut in verbs is given by Isebaert (1992).

Discussion points

1.   How much weight should be accorded to a) semantics and b) morphology in reconstructing PIE roots?

2.   Assess the role and function of morphological vowel or accent alternations in a branch of IE with which you are familiar.

3. What role does morphological analogy play in altering inherited paradigmatic alternations?

4. What justification is there for reconstructing accent / ablaut paradigms which are not attested in any IE language?

4 Nominal morphology

4.1 Introduction

Many handbooks on PIE give handy overviews of the nominal declensions of the parent language. The reader is presented with neat tables, with eight nominal cases running down the side, three numbers (singular, dual and plural) and an array of nominal declensions, partly corresponding to the three grammatical genders of masculine, feminine and neuter. There may be discussion about which of the competing morphs was the original exponent of a particular category, such as the genitive singular of the masculine and neuter o-stem, but there is in general little explanation of how these categories are the ones which must be reconstructed, and even less discussion of what these categories actually represent.

The primacy of Sanskrit in the early days of research into PIE has had lasting effects on the reconstruction of the nominal system. The reconstructed categories of the PIE noun are exactly the same as those of the Sanskrit noun. Sanskrit has eight cases: nominative, vocative, accusative, genitive, dative, ablative, locative and instrumental; three numbers: singular, dual and plural; and three genders: masculine, feminine and neuter. The only languages to have a wider array of nominal cases are some Baltic variants and Tocharian, but the additional case markers are easily discernible as postpositions or adverbial elements added to more basic case forms, and it is clear that these cases have arisen secondarily, probably through contact with languages with well-developed systems for expressing local cases. The other old IE languages known in the nineteenth century show a more reduced nominal system, with fewer cases: Gothic, Greek and Old Irish have only a nominative, vocative, accusative, genitive and dative; Latin has these cases and an ablative case, with some vestiges of a locative too; Old Church Slavonic has all the cases of Sanskrit except the ablative; Armenian has all the cases except the dative. Furthermore, within the languages with fewer cases than Sanskrit it is often clear that a single case can correspond to more than one Sanskrit case, both in form and in function. For example, the Greek dative singular marker of one noun class in the fifth century BC was -i, which corresponds to a Sanskrit locative singular marker -i. However, the Sanskrit dative singular ending -e (which derives from *-ei) is also attested in Mycenaean Greek as a dative singular marker -ei. The Greek 'dative' represents both the case of the indirect object, which corresponds to the Sanskrit dative, and the case denoting position in space or time (both independently and with the support of a preposition), exactly equivalent to the Sanskrit locative. It is thus straightforward to assume that in Classical Greek the original locative and dative cases in the singular have coalesced (in Mycenaean Greek the process of merger of the two cases may still be taking place). The standard grammatical term for the merger of two nominal categories into one is *syncretism*, and the causes and processes of case syncretism have been well studied and documented across the IE languages. Case syncretism and the concomitant decline in the number of cases is the norm in the diachronic history of most IE languages: in Modern Greek there is no longer a separate dative case, its grammatical functions having been subsumed by the genitive and its local functions largely by the accusative; in the Western Romance languages there is no longer any grammatical case at all.

The other nominal categories of number and gender have undergone similar reductions in the history of the IE languages. The dual is lost prehistorically in Germanic (in nouns), Latin, Albanian and Armenian, and although attested in Classical Greek, Old Irish and Old Church Slavonic, it only fully survives today in some Slavic languages. The three separate nominal genders found in Sanskrit, Greek and Latin have been merged in many different branches. Several languages have 'lost' one gender: in Romance, Modern Celtic and Modern Baltic, the neuter has been assimilated into the other two declensions; in Dutch and Scandinavian the distinction between masculine and feminine is lost, the surviving distinction being between common and neuter nouns. Some languages have lost the nominal category of gender completely: in Armenian, gender was lost from both nouns and pronouns before the language is attested in written form in the first millennium of the Christian era, and English retains gender only in pronouns (although vehicles such as boats, cars and motorbikes may still be referred to by feminine pronouns).

It is no surprise, then, that with so much erosion of the nominal system, Indo-Europeanists have in general wanted to restore the maximal system of case, number and gender differentiation for PIE. Of course, there are examples from among the IE languages of the creation of new nominal categories. For example, in Russian animate masculine and feminine nouns are distinguished from inanimate nouns in the formation of the accusative. In Modern Breton, a new number system has developed in which a singulative can be formed from a noun generally used in the plural (such as 'fish'), and a new plural can be formed from this singulative. But such developments are on the whole language-specific and stand as isolated phenomena in a general tendency towards loss of nominal categories.

However, as with so much else in IE linguistics, the decipherment of Hittite and the greater understanding of Anatolian languages have challenged scholars to rethink some of the assumptions that were encoded in the nineteenth-century model of the nominal system. Indeed, one does not need to have the Anatolian languages to see that there are some inherent problems with the traditional model. Firstly, if syncretism is widespread across the IE languages, why is it assumed that there has been no earlier syncretism, and that the Sanskrit noun has not collapsed different categories together from a richer system? Secondly, can one be so sure that the slots which are reconstructed for PIE are as impermeable as this model assumes, and that the categories did not run into each other? The comparison of the nominal paradigms of the Anatolian languages with the rest of the IE language family brings both of these issues to light and will be illustrated by two related studies, on the reconstructed categories of number and gender. In order to simplify the ensuing discussion, it will be useful to have here an overview of the principle reconstructed paradigms of PIE.

4.2   Overview of nominal declensions

In broad outline, there are three separate classes which can be reconstructed for PIE nouns showing different systems of case-marking:

a)   Nouns formed with the thematic vowel *e/o before the case-endings (see section 3.2 for the thematic vowel; the term *thematic* is a convenient way of labelling the vowel without specifying whether it is *e or *o). Since in most IE languages this declension uses *o almost to the complete exclusion of *e, this class is frequently referred to as the *o-stem declension*.

b)   Feminine nouns formed with a suffix *$-eh_2$ or *$-ih_2$. In most daughter languages these nouns have the stem-final vowels *$-ā$ and *$-ī$, and the nominal declensions are consequently sometimes termed the *ā-stems* and *ī-stems*.

c)   The third class has no characteristic theme vowel or suffix and is accordingly labelled the *athematic* class. It comprises a number of separate sub-classes, including nouns which show no suffix before the derivational endings (*root-nouns*), nouns formed with suffixes involving the semi-vowels *i and *u, and several sub-classes of neuter nouns.

In respect of the reconstructed case-endings, the class of feminine nouns in b) shows clear affinities with the athematic class c), and the o-stem declension diverges more radically from both. In the daughter languages, however, there is a general tendency for the o-stem class and the feminine ā-stems to become more closely associated, almost certainly through the combination of the two classes in a number of pronominal and adjectival declensions as masculine and feminine alternatives. For example, one widespread demonstrative pronoun is formed on a base *$t-$, with a masculine stem *$to-$ and feminine stem *teh_2- (*$tā-$).

For ease of explanation, the endings of the athematic nouns will be described first. In Greek and Sanskrit, many athematic noun paradigms still show accent shift and associated changes of ablaut which were discussed in section 3.4, and which will not be considered in detail here. Any overview of this nominal class

Table 4.1 *The singular paradigm for 'father' in PIE.*

	PIE	Sanskrit	Greek	Latin	Gothic	Old Church Slavonic	Armenian
nominative	*$ph_2tēr$ < *$ph_2tér$-s	pitā́	patḗr	pater	fadar	mati	hayr
vocative	*ph_2ter	pítar	páter	pater	fadar	mati	
accusative	*$ph_2tér$-**m**	pitáram	patéra	patrem		materĭ	hayr
genitive / ablative	*ph_2tr-**és**	pitúr	patrós	patris	fadrs	matere	hawr
dative	*ph_2tr-**éi**	pitré	patrí	patrī		materi	hawr
locative	*$ph_2tér$-**i**	pitári		patre		materi	hawr
instrumental	*ph_2tr-**eh₁**	pitrā́				materija	harb

is initially confusing, largely because of the effects of the different reconstructed ablaut patterns. Furthermore, the daughter languages have all regularised these patterns in different ways. This has the effect that two nouns reconstructed to this class may have very different outcomes and belong to completely different declension classes in Sanskrit, Greek or Latin. Two well-understood nominal paradigms are the words for 'father' and 'sky / god', which share the same shift of ablaut between the nominative, vocative, accusative and locative on the one hand (the so-called *strong* cases) and a different ablaut pattern in the rest of the paradigm (the *weak* cases). In table 4.1, the declension of words meaning 'father' in a number of different IE languages is given (in Old Church Slavonic, the inherited word for 'father' does not survive and so the word for 'mother' is given in the paradigm).

In table 4.2, only words from the oldest languages have been given. The paradigms given for Latin and Greek appear strange, since these forms are gathered from scattered relic forms which accord better with the earliest Sanskrit evidence. The Latin paradigm given includes words taken from different paradigms: *diēs* 'day' and *Iupiter* the name of the god Juppiter, who is indeed called *Dies-piter* 'Father Sky' in some early Latin texts. The word can mean both 'sky' and 'sky-god' in Latin and Sanskrit but has been restricted to refer to a single important god in Greek and Hittite. Note also that in Hittite the cases outside the nominative have been transferred into a different declension class.

Tables 4.1 and 4.2 taken together should make clear that the exponents of the cases are the same in the different paradigms, particularly after the plausible internal reconstruction of the nominative singular of the word for 'father' *$ph_2tēr$ < *ph_2ter-s is taken into account (see section 3.4). In table 4.2, two alternative reconstructions for the nominative are given, since it is not clear whether the length of the vowel *$ē$, which is guaranteed by the Sanskrit outcome, is in fact original or analogical to lengthened ē-grade in words such as *$ph_2tēr$. Masculine and feminine nouns in the athematic class share exactly the same endings, but neuter

Table 4.2 *The singular paradigm for 'sky / god' in PIE.*

	PIE	Hittite	Sanskrit	Greek	Latin
nominative	*$dyéw$-**s** or *$dyéw$-**s**	sius	dyáuṣ	Zdeús	diēs
vocative	*$dyéw$			Zdeû	Iū-
accusative	*$dyḗm$ < *$dyéw$-**m**	siunan	dyā́m	Zdḗn	diem
genitive / ablative	*diw-**és**	siunas/siunaz	divás	Di(w)ós	Iouis
dative	*diw-**éi**	siuni	divé	di-we	Iouī
locative	*$dyéw$-**i**	siuni	dyávi	Di(w)í	Ioue
instrumental	*diw-**éh₁**	siunit	divā́		

nouns do not mark any difference between the nominative and accusative. In the singular, most neuters show no overt ending for the nominative / accusative; in the plural, there is a special ending *-h_2- which will be discussed in more detail in section 4.3. Table 4.3 provides an example of a reconstructed neuter paradigm. The word given in the table means 'cloud' or 'heaven' in Hittite, Sanskrit, Avestan, Greek and Old Church Slavonic. Note also that the genitive singular in the reconstruction given is *-os, an ablaut variant of *-$és$ seen above (see section 3.4 for discussion of the origins of this alternation in the genitive endings).

Table 4.3 *The paradigm for 'cloud' in PIE.*

	PIE	Hittite	Sanskrit	Avestan	Greek	Old Church Slavonic
nominative / accusative singular	*$néb^hos$	nepis	nábhas	nabas-	néphos	nebo
genitive singular	*$neb^hés$-os	nepisas	nábhasas	nabaṇhas-	népheos	nebese
nominative / accusative plural	*$neb^hés$-h_2		nábhāṁsi	nabā̊s-	néphea	nebesa

An example of a sub-class of neuter nouns in the athematic class is given in table 4.4. It is included here since this class shows a curious allomorphy between a stem with final *-r in the nominative-accusative singular, sometimes extended to *-rt, and a stem formed with *-n- in all other cases. This declension type (usually termed the *r/n-stem* declension) has only limited productivity in the oldest branches of IE and is generally replaced by other, more regular, paradigms in most languages. The word given in table 4.4 means 'liver', and the PIE reconstruction given assumes that the word was originally declined in the acrostatic 1 paradigm (discussed in section 3.4) with an ablaut alternation between ē-grade of the root in the strong

Table 4.4 *The paradigm for 'liver' in PIE.*

	PIE	Sanskrit	Greek	Latin	Hittite
nominative / accusative	*yĕkʷ-r(t)	yákr̥t	hễpar	iecur	(sakkar)
genitive	*yékʷ-n-s	yáknas	hḗpatos	iocineris	(saknas)

cases and e-grade in the weak cases. The table also includes a Hittite example of an r/n-stem neuter, *sakkar*, meaning 'dung'.

Exercise 4.1

The Greek and Sanskrit words for 'dog' were introduced in section 2.2. Fuller paradigms are given below. Reconstruct the PIE paradigm, using the case-endings already given as a guide.

	Hittite	Sanskrit	Greek
nominative	kuwas	śvā́	kúōn
accusative	kuwanan	śvā́nam	kúna
genitive	kunas	śúnas	kunós
dative	kuni	śúne	kuní

Exercise 4.2

The following table gives the paradigm of the word for 'winter' (the Greek word means 'snow'). The paradigm can be reconstructed as a kinetic paradigm from a root *gʰyem-. Give the original paradigm, and work out what changes have taken place in each language. (Hint: in Avestan word-final *ēn and *ōn develop to å̄, and word-final *es and *os develop to -ō; in Greek word-final *-m becomes *-n.)

	Avestan	Greek	Latin
nominative	ziiå̄	khiṓn	hiēms
accusative	ziiạm	khióna	hiemem
genitive	zimō	khiónos	hiemis

Exercise 4.3

Paradigms of the word for 'cow' in IE languages (with some selection of archaic forms) are given in the table below. The original paradigm has been reconstructed by some scholars as a kinetic paradigm, by others as acrostatic 2 (see table 3.7 for these terms). Can you reconstruct the root? (Hint: the root begins with *gʷ-, and a special change has taken place in the accusative singular which also affects the word for 'sky / god'.) Which reconstruction of the paradigm do you think is more likely, and why?

	Sanskrit	Greek	Latin
nominative	gáuṣ	bous	bōs
accusative	gā́m	bôn	bouem
genitive	góṣ	bo(w)ós	bouis
locative	gávi		

Many of the same endings that we have met in the athematic nouns reoccur in the paradigm of the feminine noun class formed with $*-h_2$ as shown in table 4.5. The representative noun of this paradigm is the word for 'mare' which occurs in Sanskrit, Latin and Lithuanian. We cannot be sure that this word can be securely reconstructed for PIE (see further section 4.4), but it is given as a representative of the type. The Greek word given means 'goddess' and the Gothic 'gift'. Table 4.5 gives two alternative reconstructions for this paradigm type, one using the reconstructed laryngeal $*h_2$, the other giving the sound which resulted after the loss of the laryngeal. This declension type does not occur in Hittite.

There are two important differences between the feminine nouns in $*-eh_2$ and the athematic class. Firstly, the nominative singular is not marked by a final $*s$. As we have seen, in other declensions masculine and feminine nouns always mark the nominative singular, and where $*s$ is not preserved, as in the word for 'father' reconstructed in table 4.1, it is possible to reconstruct it at an earlier stage in the language. Secondly, the ablaut patterns of the $*-eh_2$ nouns appear to have been unique among athematic nouns, in that they show no alternation between the ablaut of the strong and weak case, but instead retain the full-grade of the suffix $*-eh_2-$ throughout the paradigm. The other exponent of this declension type, feminine nouns formed with the suffix $*-ih_2-$, lack any trace of $*s$ in the nominative singular in the best-attested paradigm type. But they do show better evidence for an original paradigm with ablaut alternations of the type we have seen for athematic words. The affix $*-ih_2-$ of the strong cases alternates with $*-yeh_2-$ in the weak cases.

For one word, given in table 4.6, some scholars have reconstructed a complete proterokinetic paradigm, with a change in ablaut in the root syllable and in the affix between the strong and weak cases. The Sanskrit word, which means 'female god', preserves the vocalism of the strong cases in the root; the Greek word, which is synchronically the feminine of an adjective meaning 'divine', preserves the ablaut grade of the weak cases. The reader will note that the root is the same as that which gives the athematic noun denoting the 'sky-god' in table 4.2 above; it should be noted that the word is semantically closer to the term for 'god',

Table 4.5 *PIE feminine stems in* *-eh₂*.

	PIE	Sanskrit	Greek	Latin	Gothic	Lithuanian
nominative	*ek´w-eh₂ (*ek´w-ā)	áśvā́	the-ā́	equa	giba	ašvà
vocative	?	áśve	the-ā́	equa		ašvà
accusative	*ek´w-eh₂-m (*ek´w-ām)	áśvām	the-ā́n	equam	giba	ašvą̃
genitive / ablative	*ek´w-eh₂-es (*ek´w-ās)	áśvāyās	the-âs	equae	gibos	ašvõs
dative	*ek´w-eh₂-ei (*ek´w-āi)	áśvāyai	the-âi	equae	gibai	ãšvai
locative	*ek´w-eh₂-i (*ek´w-āi)	áśvāyām				ãšvoje
instrumental	*ek´w-eh₂-eh₁ (*ek´w-ā)	áśvā				ašvà

Table 4.6 *PIE feminine stems in* *-ih₂*.

	PIE	Sanskrit	Greek	Gothic
nominative	*déiw-ih₂ / *déiw-ī	dev-ī́	dî̂-a <*diw-ya	(mawi)
genitive / ablative	*diw-yéh₂-s / *diw-yā́s	dev-yā́s	dî̂-ās <*diw-yās	(maujos)

déiw-os, reconstructed from the correspondence given below, and is usually seen as a derivative of that word:

déiw-os 'god': Sanskrit *devá-*, Latin *deus*, Old Norse *tívar* 'gods', Lithuanian *diẽvas*.

The Gothic word for 'girl' is included in table 4.6 as an example of the morphological type and does not derive from the same root.

The third major class of nouns, the o-stem or thematic class, stands apart from the other two classes, as can be seen in table 4.7. The example used in this table is the widespread word for 'wolf'. The Hittite paradigm is taken from another word, meaning 'father', and the example of a locative in Latin is taken from the place-name meaning 'Delos'.

Uniquely for the thematic class, there is a separate ablative singular case form, reconstructed with the ending *-ōd* in the table. In the other nominal classes the ablative singular is expressed by the same case markers as express the genitive case, and the ablative plural is syncretic with the dative plural. The form of the genitive singular case shows considerable variation across different languages. In Indo-Iranian, Greek, Armenian and one early Latin inscription the

Table 4.7 *The paradigm for 'wolf' in PIE.*

	PIE	Hittite	Sanskrit	Greek	Latin	Gothic	Lithuanian
nom.	*wlk^w-**os**	(attas)	vŕ̥kas	lúkos	lupus	wulfs	vil̃kas
voc.	*wlk^w-**e**	(atta)	vŕ̥ka	lúke	lupe	wulf	vilkè
acc.	*wlk^w-**om**	(attan)	vŕ̥kam	lúkon	lupum	wulf	vil̃ką
gen.	*wlk^w-**os**	(attas)	vŕ̥kasya	lúkoio	lupī	wulfis	vil̃ko
abl.	*wlk^w-**ōd**	(attaz)	vŕ̥kād		lupō(d)		vil̃ko
dat.	*wlk^w-**ōi**	(atti)	vŕ̥kāya	lúkōi	lupī	wulfa	vil̃kui
loc.	*wlk^w-**oi**	(atti)	vŕ̥ke		Deloi		vilkè
inst.	*wlk^w-**oh₁**	(-it)	vŕ̥kā				vilkù

ending *-*osyo* is found; in Latin and Celtic the productive morph is *-*ī*; and in Germanic, Baltic and Slavic other endings are used, including the ablative singular marker. However, in Hittite the genitive singular in this declension looks the same as the nominative singular. If Hittite has retained the original status, this may explain the other genitive singular endings as attempts to create a new case marker to disambiguate the genitive and nominative.

As the above table shows, in the thematic declension there is no clear evidence for an ablaut difference between the strong and the weak cases. Some nouns, it is true, show a variety of different vocalisms in different IE languages, but these normally do not need to be explained through generalisation of paradigm variants. Table 4.8 shows the possible original ablaut grades for the widespread word for 'sleep, dream' in various daughter languages. In some cases, a word appears in two different columns in the table, since it is not possible to tell what the original vowel in the root was, owing to later phonological mergers.

Table 4.8 *Possible ablaut grades for PIE 'sleep, dream'.*

e-grade *swep-no- (or *sep-no-)	o-grade *swop-no- (or *sop-no-)	zero-grade *sup-no-
Sanskrit svápna-	Sanskrit svápna-	Greek húpnos
Avestan xᵛafna-	Avestan xᵛafna-	Old Church Slavonic
Latin somnus	Latin somnus	sŭnŭ
Old Norse svefn	Lithuanian sãpnas	Albanian gjumë
Tocharian A ṣpäṁ	Armenian kʻun	
	Old Irish súan	

Although one way to explain this allomorphy would be to presume an original paradigm with *swep-no- or *swop-no- in some cases, *sup-no in others, there seems to be no ablaut alternation in the suffix. Furthermore, there are no archaic forms which favour this explanation, as was the case with the reconstruction of ablaut alternations in the athematic stems. Another explanation for the variation is therefore currently favoured: the words for 'sleep' which follow the thematic declension are all replacements of an older word, which followed the r/n-stem neuter declension. The old PIE neuter nouns of this type are gradually replaced by more 'regular' declension classes in the daughter languages, and the assumption of an early replacement of an athematic noun by a thematic noun is not controversial. Furthermore, there is good evidence for an original word meaning 'sleep' with nominative *swép-or and genitive *sup-nés. This is the explanation for the Latin noun *sopor* (which can derive from *swepor) 'sleep' and Greek *húpar* 'dream', and it explains the Hittite verb meaning 'sleep' *suppariya-*, which can represent a derivative of an unattested nominal stem *suppar*. It appears that the explanation for the variation in the ablaut of the thematic noun in this case is that each language generalised a different ablaut grade of the original paradigm in the new formation.

Table 4.9 *The paradigm for 'yoke' in PIE.*

	PIE	Hittite	Sanskrit	Greek	Latin	Old Church Slavonic
nominative / accusative singular	*yug-óm	iukan	yugám	zdugón	iugum	igo
genitive singular	*yug-ós	iukas	yugásya	zdugoîo	iugī	iga
nominative / accusative plural	*yug-éh₂	iuka	yugā́	zdugá	iuga	iga

The thematic declension, like the athematics, has a separate paradigm for neuter nouns. The nominative-accusative plural ending of the neuters shows the same ending as the athematics, but the nominative-accusative singular shows not just the bare stem, as in the athematic nouns, but a case-ending *-m, which immediately recalls the accusative singular of the masculine thematic paradigm. The example for the neuter paradigm given in table 4.9 is the widespread word for 'yoke'.

Exercise 4.4

In the athematic declension, the reconstructed plural endings of non-neuter nouns are as follows (see also table 1.2 and the discussion there of the dative, ablative and instrumental plural endings).

nominative / vocative	*-es
accusative	*-ns
genitive	*-om
dative / ablative	*-mos
locative	*-su
instrumental	*-bʰi

The table below gives comparative evidence for the plural of the IE thematic non-neuter nouns. Which of these endings are the same as the athematic endings and which are different? Which endings can you reconstruct?

	Sanskrit	Greek	Latin	Gothic	Lithuanian
nominative / vocative	vŕkās	lúkoi	lupī	wulfos	vilkaĩ
accusative	vŕkān	lúkous	lupōs	wulfans	vilkus
genitive	vŕkānām	lúkōn	lupōrum	wulfe	vilkų̃
dative / ablative	vŕkebhyas	lúkois	lupīs	wulfam	vilkáms
locative	vŕkeṣu				vilkuosè
instrumental	vŕkais				vilkaĩs

Exercise 4.5

The following table gives the reconstructed paradigm for the plural declension of the non-neuter (masculine) stem of the PIE demonstrative pronoun *to- (the dative-ablative plural cannot be reconstructed with certainty). Use this paradigm to help explain some of the thematic endings in exercise 4.4 which do not agree with the athematic endings. Why do you think this thematic declension has 'borrowed' endings from the declension of *to-?

nominative / vocative	*toy
accusative	*tons
genitive	*toisom
locative	*toisu
instrumental	*tōis

4.3   Reconstructing number: the collective

It is possible to reconstruct a singular, dual and plural number for the PIE noun. The dual and plural show the same categories of case as found in the singular, but with a greater degree of syncretism. In every plural declension the ablative is marked with the same ending as the dative, and the vocative is marked the same as the nominative; in every dual declension the nominative, vocative and accusative all share the same marker. The same dimensions of the category of number are found in the reconstructed PIE verbal conjugations, with separate singular, plural and dual endings. However, closer inspection of the older IE languages alone is enough to reveal that the category of number is not as straightforward as it might at first appear. Even the marginal category of the dual has unexpected distribution and uses. The dual does not just denote that there are two of something: it can also be used as an associative marker, in a construction standardly referred to as the *elliptical dual* in grammars and handbooks. Vedic Sanskrit provides the best examples of this use of the dual. When the name of the god *Mitrá* appears in the dual, *Mitrā́*, it refers to Mitra and his companion Varuna. Other languages show the same construction: the Greek dual *Aíante* in the text of Homer was once thought to refer to two separate heroes, Ajax the Greater and Ajax the Lesser, until Wackernagel showed by a combination of comparative linguistics and textual analysis that it was more likely to refer to Ajax and his brother and fighting companion Teucer. Languages which have lost the dual can use the plural as an associative to denote pairs: in Latin *Castorēs*, the plural of the name 'Castor', is used to denote the semi-god Castor and his twin Pollux. The dual is reconstructed for pronouns, animate nouns and inanimate nouns, but it is likely that its usage was optional at least with words denoting inanimates (that is, the lower end of the 'animacy hierarchy'). Note that in the two early IE languages with a paradigmatic dual, Greek and Sanskrit, pairs of body parts, such as hands, eyes, legs, knees etc., may be denoted either by the plural or by the dual, and the plural is in fact more common for body-part terms in Homeric Greek (for example, in the frequent Homeric formula to describe Achilles 'swift of foot', the plural 'feet', not the dual 'two feet', is used).

The agreement patterns of plural nouns are even more complex. All reconstructed neuter nouns have a special marker, $*h_2$, for the nominative and accusative plural. In Greek and the Anatolian languages (and in the ancient Iranian language Avestan, although the picture here is clouded by a partial collapse of number agreement in the verb), plurals of neuter nouns do not collocate with plural forms of the verb, but with the singular, as in examples (1) and (2).

(1)   Homer *Iliad* 5:428
          oú toi   téknon emòn   dédotai   poleméia   érga
          not you-DAT,   child my,   is-given-3 RD.SG   violent-NEUTER.PL   deeds-NEUTER.PL
          'My child, violent acts are not in your nature'

(2)   Anatolian example (from Palaic)
          tilila   hāri
          tilila-NEUTER.PL   is-warm-3RD.SG
          'The *tilila* foodstuffs are warm'

(Note that in Palaic, as in the other Anatolian languages, the laryngeal $*h_2$, although preserved word-initially and word-internally, seems to have been lost when it stood in final position.) This peculiar agreement pattern is found only for nouns which are grammatically neuter. The set of PIE neuter nouns is not the same as the set of nouns denoting inanimate or unsexed referents: the words for 'liver' and 'yoke' are neuter, but 'foot' and 'snow' are not neuter. Verbs in Greek and Anatolian which are collocated with plural forms of non-neuter inanimate

Table 4.10 *Nouns with two plurals.*

Nominative singular	Nominative plural	*h_2 plural
Greek		
kúklos 'wheel, circle'	*kúkloi* 'circles'	*kúkla* 'set of wheels' (of a chariot, a robot, etc.)
mērós 'thigh'	*mēroí* 'thigh-pieces'	*mêra* 'agglomeration of thigh-meat'
Hittite		
alpas 'cloud'	*alpes* 'clouds'	*alpa* 'cloud-mass'
	gulses 'the fates'	*gulassa* 'fate'
Latin		
locus 'place'	*locī* 'places'	*loca* 'places'
Latin / Umbrian		
Latin *uir* 'man'	Latin *uirī* 'men'	Umbrian *uiro* 'people'

nouns regularly show plural endings. The marking of verbs as plural is therefore not semantically conditioned, but relies solely on the grammatical gender of the noun. In order to account for this discrepancy in number-marking of the verb, it has been suggested that what is now known as the neuter plural was earlier a separate morphological category, a *collective* or *comprehensive*. This theory is supported by the fact that, in some early IE languages, 'plural' cases formed with the marker *h_2 can be used with non-neuter nouns alongside their regular plurals, giving these nouns an apparent distinction between two different plurals. Examples from Greek, Hittite, Latin and the Sabellian language Umbrian are shown in table 4.10 (the text containing the Umbrian word will be discussed in section 6.5).

The examples in table 4.10 are mostly restricted in occurrence, and interpretation of the significance of the original distribution is not always possible. But as far as our understanding allows, it appears that what we have called the *h_2 plural* has more of a collective meaning, and the regular plural has a more distributive meaning; the glosses given in the table are supposed to reflect the most appropriate meanings in context. However, it should be noted that the contrast between these two formations is lexically restricted. Furthermore, it is not difficult to fit a distributive or collective meaning to a certain form according to context, particularly in the case of languages where we only have a restricted corpus, and we should be careful to extrapolate a semantic distinction from only a few attestations. Unfortunately, in the one case where we do have the forms attested in significant numbers, Latin *locī* and *loca*, it is impossible to disentangle separate meanings in the Classical language, and in any author or text where it is possible to find an instance of, for example, *loca* with a collective sense, it is also possible to find the same form used as a distributive plural.

Table 4.11 *Number in PIE nouns.*

non-neuters	singular	dual	distributive	? collective?
neuters	singular	dual	? distributive?	collective

Taken together, the agreement-marking of verbs when collocated with neuter nouns with the $*h_2$ ending, and the existence of these formations alongside regular plural formations for non-neuter nouns, does offer support to the hypothesis that the $*h_2$ plural was in fact a collective, and this has profound implications for our reconstruction of the whole category of number in the PIE noun. Unfortunately, there are no clear answers to most of the outstanding questions. Should the collective be considered a subdivision of the plural, a separate category, or a subdivision of the singular? Verbs do not have a separate category of collective, and the agreement of neuter plurals with singular verb-forms suggests that at one time the collective may have been grammatically singular, a possible derived form of a noun just as exists in modern languages such as German (for example, *Gebirge* 'mountains' alongside *Berg* 'mountain'). However, the evidence of the case-marking argues the other way. In neuter 'plurals', the genitive, dative and other cases share the same markers as those found in the non-neuter plurals. In the same way, the collective formations given in table 4.10 are distinguished from the regular plurals only in the nominative and accusative: the Latin genitive plural *locōrum* 'of places' serves both the nominatives *loca* and *locī*; the Greek genitive plural *kúklōn* 'of wheels' serves both *kúkloi* and *kúkla*.

Table 4.11 sets out one possible categorisation of number for PIE. The shaded parts of the table indicate areas of uncertainty in the reconstruction. We have seen that for non-neuters there are some collectives which can be reconstructed, but these are limited in their occurrence. Most of the examples are nouns denoting inanimates, such as clouds, thighs, wheels and places. Umbrian *uiro*, supposedly the collective of the word for 'man', stands out as the only example of a collective of an animate noun. It is not clear whether this is a relic of a wider pattern or an extension of the collective: the word always occurs in a formula alongside other neuter plural nouns and it is possible that it has gained the ending by analogy to them. It certainly is strange that there are no other reflexes of collectives of animate nouns if they were more prevalent in the parent language; flock animals, such as sheep and cattle, form a semantic class which would lend itself well to a collective formation. Note also that there is no clear evidence for separate collective or distributive forms in the pronominal declensions. Table 4.11 also raises the possibility that a neuter noun could have a distributive plural. We know that some neuters had a separate category of the dual, from comparisons such as the word for 'eyes':

UNIVERSITY OF WINCHESTER
LIBRARY

$*h_3k^w\text{-}ih_1$ 'eyes': Greek *ósse*, Avestan *aši*, Armenian *ač'k'*, Old Church Slavonic *oči*, Lithuanian *akì*, Tocharian B *eśane*

If neuters did have duals, but not distributive plurals, we would be left with a curious situation in PIE. Neuters could be marked for a dual, but not a distributive plural; a PIE speaker would be able to count 'two yokes' but not 'three yokes'. This runs counter to the typological universal that the existence of a dual presupposes the existence of a plural.

4.4   Reconstructing gender: the feminine

Our increasing understanding of the Anatolian languages has led to substantial revisions in all areas of the reconstruction of PIE, and nominal morphology is no exception. The area of greatest current controversy is the status of the PIE feminine stems in $*\text{-}h_2$. Hittite, the first Anatolian language to be deciphered and still the best understood, has no gender distinction between masculine and feminine, but shows just two genders, termed *common* and *neuter*. As we have seen above, the neuter stems in Hittite correspond closely to those in other IE languages: reconstructed neuter nouns such as PIE $*néb^h\text{-}os$ 'cloud' and $*yug\text{-}óm$ 'yoke' are continued by neuter stems in Hittite with paradigms which can be easily derived from the reconstructed declensions. Masculine nouns in other IE languages appear as nouns of the common gender in Hittite, but Hittite has no nominal declension corresponding to the feminine stems in $*\text{-}eh_2$ or $*\text{-}ih_2$. The lack of a feminine gender in Hittite has led scholars to ask whether the feminine ever existed in the Anatolian branch. In general, scholars have explained the absence of the feminine in Hittite in two ways. The first possibility is that the Anatolian branch did inherit a separate feminine gender, but that it was lost as a separate category. Such a scenario is not *a priori* implausible: in other IE languages the distinction between three genders has progressively been eroded. Indeed, in the IE branch in closest geographical proximity to Hittite, Armenian, all gender distinctions, including a separate neuter category, have been lost without trace by the time of the first recorded texts in the middle of the first millennium of the Christian era.

An alternative model to explain the lack of a separate feminine gender in Hittite is that there had never been a separate feminine gender in Hittite or Proto-Anatolian, and that the language branch diverged from PIE at a stage before the feminine had developed in the parent language. By this theory, the creation of a separate feminine gender was an innovation of late PIE. Even before the decipherment of Hittite, there were good grounds for thinking that the distinction between three genders rather than two may have been relatively recent in the history of PIE. The distinction between neuter and non-neuter stems appears to have been more fundamental than the tripartite division between masculine, feminine and neuter. For some morphological forms there is no separate feminine exponent. For example, the PIE question word is $*k^wis$ 'who?' for both masculine and feminine, with a separate form $*k^wid$ 'what?' for the neuter (compare Greek *tís* 'who', neuter *tí* 'what'; in the Latin paradigm *quis* (masculine), *quae* (feminine), *quid* (neuter) a new feminine form has been introduced on the analogy of other declensions). Similar patterns are found in some adjective declensions in the daughter languages; in Greek, for example, compound adjectives, such as *rhododáktulos* 'rosy-fingered', have no form distinguishing the feminine from the masculine, although they do have a separate neuter form (in this case *rhododáktulon*). Furthermore, the neuter is distinguished from the other two genders by its case-marking, since it shows merger between the nominative and accusative cases in all numbers.

The correlation between gender and declension class is also skewed. Nouns of all genders can occur in the athematic declension. Non-neuter animate nouns are usually assigned gender through correspondence with the natural sex of the referent, non-neuter inanimate nouns are assigned gender by convention. Hence $*ph_2ter$- 'father' is masculine, and $*d^hugh_2ter$- 'daughter' is feminine, since fathers are male and daughters are female, but the inanimate noun $*pod$- 'foot' is assigned masculine gender and $*sneig^{wh}$- 'snow' is assigned feminine. In Sanskrit and other languages, there is a restriction of the thematic declension to masculine and neuter nouns, but in Greek and Latin the thematic declension can also include feminine nouns. It is usually reckoned that Greek and Latin have retained the original situation, since it is possible to reconstruct the word for 'daughter-in-law' as an o-stem noun $*snusó$-:

$*snusó$- 'daughter-in-law': Sanskrit *snuṣā́*-, Greek *nuós*, Latin *nurus*, Armenian *nu*

In Sanskrit, the word has transferred to the feminine declension in *-ā*, in line with the restriction of the thematic stems to non-feminine words. In Greek and Armenian the word is an o-stem; in Classical Latin *nurus* is a u-stem by analogy to the kinship term *socrus* 'mother-in-law', but the transfer in declension class is easiest to explain if the Latin word was earlier an o-stem. Therefore the only one of the three major declension classes to show a restriction to a single gender is the class of feminine nouns formed with the suffix $*-eh_2$ or $*-ih_2$. Where IE languages show masculine nouns in this declension class, such as Latin *agricola* 'farmer' or Greek *neānías* 'young man', they can be explained as post-PIE developments. The feminine is only therefore distinguished in one declension type, and it is this same declension that is absent in Hittite. It appears that the category of feminine gender is to be closely associated with the declension class in $*-h_2$.

As we saw in constructing tables 4.5 and 4.6, there is no good single example of a feminine $*-eh_2$ or $*-ih_2$ noun preserved across the IE languages. However, the languages outside the Anatolian branch show the same derivational processes by

Table 4.12 *Feminine abstract nouns derived from verbal stems.*

	Verbal stem $*Ce(R)C$-	Abstract noun $*Co(R)C$-eh_2-	Abstract noun $*C(R)C$-eh_2-
Sanskrit	*árcati* 'praises'	*arcā́* 'praise'	
	íṣṭe 'is master of'		*īśā́* 'mastery'
Greek	*phérō* 'I carry'	*phorā́* 'tribute'	
	pheúgō 'I flee'		*phugḗ* 'flight'
Latin	*tegō* 'I cover'	*toga* 'covering, toga'	
	fugiō 'I flee'		*fuga* 'flight'
Gothic	*wilwan* 'rob'		*wulwa* 'robbery'
Old Church Slavonic	*tek-* 'run, flow'	*pa-toka* 'flowing'	

which feminine nouns are formed. The suffix $*$-eh_2- is used in two main functions: to form feminine nouns and adjectives besides masculine nouns and adjectives; and to form abstract nouns derived from verbs. A good example of the first process of derivation is the word used in table 4.5, the word for the female counterpart to $*ek\acute{}wos$ 'horse', $*ek\acute{}weh_2$ 'mare'. The word is reconstructed on the basis of the correspondence between Sanskrit *áśvā*, Latin *equa* and (Old) Lithuanian *ašvà*. However, it is fairly certain that this word is not in fact inherited from PIE, but a separate individual creation of these three different language groups. We can be sure of this because in Greek the cognate word for 'horse', *híppos*, designates both male and female horses. There seems to have been no good reason for Greek to have lost the distinction between a word for stallion and mare if it once had had it, since the category of feminine is not lost in Greek. Indeed, we can see in the diachronic development of Greek a process whereby the distinction between masculine and feminine in adjectival declensions is extended to some nouns. For example, the word *theós* originally meant either 'god' or 'goddess', but in some Greek dialects a new word *theā́* 'goddess' was created alongside *theós*, which was accordingly restricted in meaning to just 'god'. We can account for the presence for a word for 'mare' in Sanskrit, Latin and Baltic by assuming that in these languages there were prehistoric independent creations of a new feminine alongside the inherited word $*ek\acute{}wos$, and we cannot reconstruct $*ek\acute{}weh_2$ 'mare' for PIE with confidence.

The second derivational process which leads to feminine nouns in IE languages is the formation of abstract nouns through addition of the suffix $*$-eh_2- to a verbal root, either in the o-grade, or in the zero-grade. This is a very productive means of word-formation in Greek and is also found in other languages, as shown in table 4.12 (note that in the Greek dialect from which these forms are taken the outcome of $*$-eh_2 is -*ā* when it follows *r* (and *i* and *e*), but otherwise -*ē*). But here again, although the process appears to be shared, there is no single word-equation which holds good across several languages.

The lack of good word-equations for the $*h_2$ declension class, and its absence in Hittite, offers support to the hypothesis that this declension class, and with it the creation of a separate feminine gender, is a late development within PIE, taking place after Hittite and the Anatolian languages have branched off from the parent. It leaves open the question of why and how a new declension class arose. To answer this, we should consider again the category of 'collective' considered in section 4.3. We saw there that it might be possible to reconstruct a category of a collective number, which was marked in the nominative by the morph $*-h_2$. The collective is a good candidate from a morphological point of view for the origin of the feminine declension in $*-h_2$. As the reconstruction given in table 4.5 shows, the feminine nouns in $*-eh_2$ do not mark the nominative singular with $*-s$, a marker found with all other non-neuter nouns. The absence of a nominative $*-s$ therefore links the feminine nouns with the collective. It is true that the other paradigmatic cases outside the nominative show no similarity to the neuter plural declension, but these could be explained as analogical creations based upon the model of the athematic declension. There is also an area of possible semantic overlap between collective formations and the abstract nouns formed with suffix $*-eh_2$. In many languages, the derivational means of expressing abstracts and collectives are linked. Indeed, the history of the Romance and Slavic languages provides neat parallels for a close relationship between collective nouns and feminine abstracts. In the Romance languages, some inherited neuter plurals develop to feminine singular nouns: for example, French *joie* (feminine) 'joy' derives from Latin *gaudia* 'joys', originally a plural of the neuter noun *gaudium* 'joy'. In Slavic, some plurals derive from earlier feminine collective forms, for example Russian *brat'ya*, the plural of *brat* 'brother', derives originally from a collective noun 'brotherhood'. A more striking example of the interaction is found in Classical Armenian, where the affix *-an-*, which is regularly used to derive abstract nouns from verbs, is a borrowing from Middle Iranian, where it functioned as a plural marker *-ān*.

Some scholars have accordingly reconstructed an earlier stage of PIE when there was no separate feminine gender, but rather just two genders, 'common' and neuter. Hittite and the rest of the Anatolian branch is explained as reflecting this stage of PIE. Then, in a period after the Anatolian languages had split from the rest of PIE, the feminine gender arose through reanalysis of neuter plural 'collective' formations and is accordingly found in the other IE language branches. A major problem with this theory is finding an explanation for why the formations in $*-h_2$, which originally had a 'collective' or 'abstract' meaning, became associated in particular with the nouns denoting people and animals of female sex. One view is that the crucial pivot was the noun which denoted 'woman' $*g^wenh_2$. It is proposed that since this noun ends in the laryngeal $*h_2$, it became associated with the new class of abstracts and collectives, which also ended in $*h_2$. Speakers then began to think of the whole class of nouns in $*h_2$ as 'feminine', since $*g^wenh_2$ denoted the human female. However, as can be seen from table 4.13, the noun $*g^wenh_2$

Table 4.13 *The paradigm for 'woman' in PIE.*

	PIE	Vedic Sanskrit	Old Irish	Armenian
nominative	$*g^wenh_2$	*jáni*	*ben*	*kin*
genitive	$*g^wneh_2s$	*gnā́s*	*mná*	*knoǰ*

does not decline like the other feminine nouns in $*-eh_2$, but instead it shows an ablaut variation between nominative and genitive. Note, however, that it does lack a final $*-s$ in the nominative singular.

Even if we accept that the association of the noun meaning 'woman' with collective and abstract formations with final $*h_2$ led to the rise of the feminine gender, there are still problems with the theory that a new declension class arose after the separation of the speakers of Anatolian languages from the rest of the PIE speech community. Firstly, it is not clear how the collective ending $*-h_2$ could at once become the marker of a new declension class, but retain its old function as the marker of neuter plurals. In the parallel case in Romance, some neuter plurals were reinterpreted as feminine singular nouns, but this reinterpretation could only happen because the neuter was lost as a category altogether. Under the scenario sketched out above, forms in $*-h_2$ appear both to retain their collective function and take on a new life as markers of the new feminine gender. It may also be significant that while we have seen that there is some evidence for the retention of old collectives in forms such as Greek *kúkla* 'set of wheels' and Latin *loca* 'places', these survivals function synchronically as neuter plurals, not as feminine singulars. Indeed, there is no good example of a well-attested IE feminine noun which can be derived from a neuter in the way French *joie* is related to Latin *gaudium*.

Recent work on Anatolian languages other than Hittite has also brought back into vogue the hypothesis that there was once a gender distinction between masculine, feminine and neuter even in the Anatolian branch. Although we have the most extensive textual remains of Hittite, the last thirty years have seen increasing advances in our knowledge of other Anatolian languages, in particular Luwian and Lycian. We are still hampered in both these languages by a relative paucity of textual remains, but it is becoming clear that we are now no longer able to state with such certainty that there is no equivalent to the $*-eh_2$ and $*-ih_2$ declensions in Anatolian. The new findings may be dealt with under two separate heads: apparent survivals of the $*-eh_2$ and $*-ih_2$ declensions, and a morphological process know as *i-motion*. Before discussing these phenomena in detail, it is worth reminding the reader that in all Anatolian languages word-final $*h_2$ is lost.

There are several scraps of evidence from different Anatolian languages to suggest that the $*-eh_2$ and $*-ih_2$ declensions did continue into this language branch. The best evidence comes from Lycian, a language attested over a thousand years later than our earliest Hittite texts. We have enough Lycian surviving to be able to isolate several different nominal declensions which, broadly speaking, can be grouped into *a*-stems, *i*-stems, *e*-stems and consonant stems. Some lexical correspondences imply that the Lycian *e*-stems continue the IE thematic or o-stem declension, including the following:

*pedom 'place, ground': Lycian *pddẽ*, Hittite *pedan*, Greek *pédon*, Umbrian *perso*
*ek´wos 'horse': Lycian *esbe*, Skt *áśva-*, Greek *híppos*, Latin *equus*, Old Irish
   ech, Old English *eoh*, Tocharian A *yuk*

Note that in the word for 'place', the Hittite word *pedan* has an ending *-an* from **-om*, showing the regular Hittite development of *a* from **o*. In Hittite, and the other Anatolian languages except Luwian, PIE **a* and **o* have merged as *a*, but in Lycian this merger does not seem to have taken place. Consequently, the Lycian *a*-declension cannot derive from the PIE thematic declension, but could continue the **-eh₂* stems. The word for 'altar' gives a possible equation of a Lycian *a*-stem with a Latin *a*-stem in support of this, although unfortunately the Lycian word shows a further suffix *-di-*:

*h₂eh₁s-eh₂ 'altar, hearth': Lycian *xaha-di-* 'altar', Hittite *hassas* 'hearth', Latin
   āra 'altar', Oscan *aasa-* 'altar'

In this equation, the Hittite word *hassas* has fallen into the class of the thematic stems (originally with ending **-os*) after the merger of **a* and **o*. If this equation is correct, then we may have been too hasty in assuming that the **-eh₂* declension is a development of Post-Anatolian PIE. The Lycian *a*-declension is not, it is true, specifically feminine: nouns denoting males, such as *kumaza* 'priest', belong to the class. However, this could be seen as a later development in the language, just as we saw that in Greek and Latin masculine nouns are incorporated into the *ā*-declension. Unfortunately, this explanation of the Lycian *a*-stems is still contentious, since the behaviour of vowels in Lycian is far from straightforward; there is good evidence for widespread umlaut in the prehistory of the language, and we are not yet certain of the rules by which it operated.

   The second important recent discovery is a morphological phenomenon called *i-motion*, which can be exemplified by the declension of adjectives in Luwian. In this language, some adjective paradigms show a different stem in agreement with common nouns from the stem used with neuter nouns. Table 4.14 gives an example, the partial paradigm of the suffix *-mma-*, which is used to form participles from verbs (such as *piiamma-* 'given' from the verbal stem *piia-* 'to give').

   In this paradigm, the suffix *-mma-* (which derives from Proto-Anatolian **-mo-*) is replaced by a suffix *-mmi-* (derived from Proto-Anatolian **-mi-*) in the nominative and accusative singular and plural of the common gender. In the other cases, the same suffix *-mma-* is used for both genders. The evidence for i-motion is clearest in Luwian, but in all the other Anatolian languages, including Hittite, similar phenomena can now be identified. For example, in Lydian the adjective meaning 'of Sardis' alternates between a stem *sfardeti-*, used in the

Table 4.14 *i-motion in Luwian participles.*

	Common	Neuter
nominative singular	*-mmis*	*-mman*
accusative singular	*-mmin*	*-mman*
nominative plural	*-mminzi*	*-mma*
accusative plural	*-mminz*	*-mma*
dative plural	*-mmanz*	*-mmanz*

non-neuter nominative-accusative, and *sfardeta-* in the oblique cases. In Hittite, i-motion is not used within adjectival paradigms, but there is evidence to suggest that Hittite did inherit two distinct adjectival stems. For example, the Hittite adjective meaning 'pure' has the stem *parkui-*, although a stem without *-i-*, *parku-*, appears in the factative verb-form *parku-numi* 'I make pure'. The comparative evidence therefore suggests that i-motion is an inherited morphological process within Anatolian.

One theory to account for Anatolian i-motion relates the process to the formation of PIE feminine stems with a suffix *-ih_2. We have already seen that the feminine *$deiw$-ih_2, 'goddess', discussed in section 4.2, is derived from *$deiw$-os 'god'. This seems analogous to i-motion, since the thematic vowel *o of *$deiw$-os is replaced by *i in *$deiw$-ih_2, just as *-mmi-* (earlier *-mi-*) replaces *-mma-* (earlier *-mo-*) in the paradigm given in table 4.14. Indeed, the suffix *-ih_2 is regularly used to form the feminine stem to athematic adjectives in other IE languages. For example, the adjective *$sweh_2du$-* 'sweet' forms a feminine with a suffix *-ih_2:

$sweh_2du$- 'sweet': Sanskrit *svādú-*, feminine *svādvī́*; Greek *hēdús*, feminine *hēdeîa*

Note, however, that the suffix *-eh_2, not *-ih_2, is usually deployed to form the feminine of adjectives which follow the thematic declension, as, for example, the adjective meaning 'new':

$newo$- 'new': Sanskrit *náva-*, feminine *návā-*; Latin *nouus*, feminine *noua*, etc.

We could therefore explain i-motion in Anatolian if we envisage that at an earlier stage of this language branch there was a separate feminine form marked in adjectives by a suffix *-ih_2. By this theory, when the distinction between masculine and feminine was lost in the prehistory of the Anatolian branch, the suffix *-ih_2 was redeployed as a more distinctive marker of the common stem to oppose the neuter stem in adjectives. Note that, in thematic adjectives, the accusative singular masculine ending *-om is not differentiated against the accusative singular neuter ending *-om. An original feminine accusative singular *-ih_2m, which would have developed to *-im in Anatolian, was therefore chosen to distinguish the common stem from the neuter.

The *a*-stems of Lycian and the existence of i-motion in Anatolian could therefore be taken as two pieces of evidence in support of the theory that Anatolian did originally have a distinction between the masculine and feminine gender. The evidence is not yet conclusive, however. As we saw, the development of the Lycian vowels is still not yet fully explained, and until it is, some scholars remain sceptical that Lycian does preserve a distinction between **a* and **o* lost in all other Anatolian languages. The link between i-motion and the formation of feminine adjectives in PIE is rendered uncertain by the fact that o-stem adjectives elsewhere in IE do not form feminine stems with the suffix **ih₂* (although some o-stem nouns do). Moreover, the arguments put forward to suggest that the feminine stems were a recent creation in PIE are still valid, even if we believe that their genesis did occur before the Anatolian languages split off from the parent.

The Anatolian evidence suggests another way to look at the rise of the feminine gender in PIE. It is possible that processes such as i-motion do directly continue PIE morphological processes, but that these had not yet been specifically associated with the feminine gender, or that the feminine gender was not yet fully differentiated throughout the nominal system. It may be indicative that one of the few words for which an Anatolian cognate to a feminine in other IE languages is proposed is the word for 'altar' PIE **h₂eh₁s-eh₂* discussed above. This is a completely uncharacteristic feminine *eh₂*-stem noun. It is neither derived as an abstract from a verbal root, nor as a feminine counterpart to a masculine noun or adjective. Indeed, it is one of a very few such *eh₂*-stem nouns attested across the IE languages. If it is correctly reconstructed, it may indicate that at an earlier stage of PIE the *eh₂*-stem nouns were not specifically feminine at all. However, this still leaves the question of how we are to account for all the diverse formations using a marker **h₂*: nouns denoting females formed with suffixes **-eh₂* and **-ih₂*; collective or neuter plural formations in **-h₂*; and verbal abstracts formed in **-eh₂*. Most Indo-Europeanists believe, at some level, that there is a connection between the collective or neuter plurals and the feminine. But reconstructing a plausible pathway and a chronology of change for the attested situation in the IE languages still remains to be done.

Exercise 4.6

The Sanskrit and Greek paradigms of the adjective meaning 'sweet', PIE **sweh₂du-*, are as follows (the neuter form declines like the masculine in both languages, but has nominative-accusative *svādú* in Sanskrit and *hēdú* in Greek).

	Masculine		Feminine	
	Sanskrit	Greek	Sanskrit	Greek
nominative	*svādús*	*hēdús*	*svādvī́*	*hēdeîa*
genitive	*svādós*	*hēdé(w)os*	*svādvyā́s*	*hēdeíās*

The masculine / neuter stem is generally thought to have been a proterokinetic paradigm (see table 3.7). What changes have taken place in the Sanskrit and Greek masculine paradigm? How should the feminine paradigm be reconstructed? (Hint: compare table 4.6.)

Exercise 4.7

The Latin adjective meaning 'sweet' is *suāuis* and is from the same root as Greek and Sanskrit. The masculine and the feminine have the same form throughout the paradigm. How can you explain the form of the adjective in Latin, using the data from exercise 4.6?

Further reading

On the process of syncretism and some case studies in IE languages, see Meiser (1992). Tremblay (2003) gives comprehensive evidence for the paradigm of the word for 'father' in PIE and the daughter languages. Table 4.6 follows Meier-Brügger (2003: 286), and table 4.8 and the discussion of the word for 'sleep' are based on Schindler (1966).

There is much written on the category of the 'collective'. Eichner (1985) and Harðarson (1987b) are the starting-points for much recent research. For some of the many attempts to explain the link between the collective and the feminine in a viable relative chronology, see Nussbaum (1986: 118–36), Euler, (1991), Tichy (1993) and Matasovic (2004). Matasovic (2004) also gives a recent overview of theories on the origin of the distinction between masculine and feminine stems, and he examines in some detail the principles on which gender is assigned to nouns in attested IE languages. However, he does not include a discussion of the Lycian a-stems or Anatolian i-motion, for which the most accessible discussions are Starke (1990), Melchert (1994b) and Rieken (1999). The category of the dual has also received attention in recent years, with three articles devoted to it in the same volume of papers: Fritz (2000), Lühr (2000) and Malzahn (2000), and a recent unpublished habilitation by Fritz (Fritz (2003), cited in Meier-Brügger (2003: 190–1)). For discussions of the word for 'altar', see Harðarson (1994: 35–9) and Rieken (1999: 247–8). See also Harðarson (1987b) for more information and on the word for 'woman' (table 4.13), and Jasanoff (1989) for its idiosyncratic development in Old Irish, where it is of neuter gender.

Discussion points

1.   Discuss the case syncretisms which have taken place in any branch of IE with which you are familiar. What have been the motivating factors for these case syncretisms?

2.   Some scholars have attempted to reconstruct the origins of the PIE inflectional endings, noting, for example, that the dative singular ending *-ei* is an ablaut variant of the locative singular ending *-i*. Do you think this is a valid exercise?

3.   Assess the arguments for considering formations such as the collective as a derivational, rather than inflectional, category.

5 Verbal morphology

5.1 Introduction

In the documented history of many IE languages, the verbal system has undergone complex restructuring, while the nominal system remains largely unaltered. In Russian, for example, the nominal cases largely continue the forms and functions of the cases of Common Slavic, with the most significant change the loss of the dual number, but the Russian verb is radically different from the Common Slavic verb. The category of aspect has come to dominate the verbal paradigm, with a concomitant loss of tenses such as the imperfect, and the creation of new tenses such the imperfective future. In Modern German the case system of Old High German is more or less maintained, but new periphrastic verbal formations, such as the *werden* future, have developed over the same time. In other languages, such as the Romance group or English or Swedish, the noun has lost case differences, but the categories of the verb have been maintained and even expanded (note, for example, the 'conditional' tense of French, or the *-ing* present of English). It appears, in Indo-European languages at least, that verbal systems undergo greater changes than nouns. If this is the case, it is not difficult to see why. Verbs typically refer to processes, actions and events, whereas nouns typically refer to entities. Representations of events are likely to have more salience in discourse, and speakers seek new ways of emphasising different viewpoints of events in discourse.

It is certainly true that, as we shall see later in this chapter, the verbal systems of the earliest IE languages are less congruent to each other than the nominal paradigms. The reconstruction of the PIE verb is correspondingly less straightforward, and there is greater room for disagreement. Indeed, there is no general agreement even about what verbal categories should be reconstructed for PIE, let alone the ways in which these categories were expressed in the verbal morphology. The continuing debate over the PIE verb makes it one of the most exciting and fast-moving topics in comparative philology. In this chapter we shall not argue for one particular reconstruction, but present and assess some of the different reconstructions that have been put forward.

Before proceeding to consider the verbal categories of PIE, we shall first emphasise an important difference between the methodology of verbal and nominal reconstruction. In section 4.2, if two different markers are used to mark the same category of the noun, we generally attempted to explain the difference between them through phonetic changes. For instance, final *-s is used to mark the nominative singular in most non-neuter declension classes in PIE, but the r-stem *ph₂ter- has a nominative singular ending *-ēr, without *-s. In our reconstruction, we assumed that the category of nominative was originally the same in the r-stem declension as in the other athematic declensions, and that the allomorphy could be explained by hypothesising a change from *-ers to *-ēr in prehistory. Our reconstruction of a single marker for the nominative singular was built on the assumption that the nominal categories of case which we find in the earliest IE languages are unchanged in PIE.

For the reconstruction of the verb, however, scholars have tended to view reconstructed categories with less confidence and pay more attention to reconstructed markers. For instance, the verbal marker *-r is used 1) in some languages to mark middle-voice forms, and 2) to mark the third person plural in the perfect paradigm (the third person plural is marked by *-nt in other paradigms). In general, scholars have agreed that the *-r marker of the third plural is unconnected to its allomorph *-nt, but there have been attempts to link it to the third plural *-r with the middle-voice marking *-r. One theory proposes that the *-r marker was originally used as a third plural and from there was associated with an impersonal meaning, which was later extended to middle forms (see Jasanoff (1977)). This is, perhaps, an extreme example of the tendency to accord more importance to markers than categories, but it does reflect the fact that verbal categories such as 'tense', 'aspect' or 'middle' are extremely 'fluid': they run into one another, and markers may be transferred easily from one category to another. The actual reconstructed morphs are consequently seen as providing the most secure foundations on which to build the reconstruction.

5.2   The Greco-Aryan model of the PIE verb

We have already seen in sections 2.4 and 2.5 the effect that the recognition of the Anatolian branch as IE has had on the reconstruction of PIE. Earlier models of PIE phonology and nominal morphology have been substantially revised in order to incorporate the evidence from Anatolian. In the case of the verb, the impact of Anatolian has been even more dramatic. Indeed, in order to follow the current debates on the PIE verb, it is necessary to have a full understanding of the model reconstructed before the discovery of Hittite and its sisters. This model, which we call the *Greco-Aryan model*, since it is based largely on Greek and Sanskrit, has provided a very good explanation for the origin of the verbal systems of Latin, Baltic, Slavic, Germanic, Armenian and Celtic. However, the Greco-Aryan model does not work well as an explanation for the Anatolian verb. In this section, we shall reconstruct the PIE verb as if the Anatolian languages did not exist and then examine more closely some of the ways in which the model might be modified in later sections.

Table 5.1 *Greek verbal stems.*

	Present	Aorist	Perfect	Future
Indicative	past & non-past active & medio-passive	past active & medio-passive	past & non-past active & medio-passive	non-past active & medio-passive
Subjunctive	active & medio-passive	active & medio-passive	active & medio-passive	
Optative	active & medio-passive	active & medio-passive	active & medio-passive	
Imperative	active & medio-passive	active & medio-passive	active & medio-passive	
Infinitive	active & medio-passive	active & medio-passive	active & medio-passive	active & medio-passive
Participle	active & medio-passive	active & medio-passive	active & medio-passive	active & medio-passive

We start by presenting the verbal system as it stands in Greek, Vedic, Latin and Gothic. All of these languages use fused morphs to encode a number of different categories, leading to highly intricate inflectional systems. As an example of the morphological complexity, we shall analyse a single verbal form taken from Homeric Greek, which will also serve as an introduction to the comparison of verbal systems.

tetást^{h}ēn 'the two of them were stretched'
3rd person dual pluperfect medio-passive indicative

The form *tetást^{h}ēn* can be broken down into a personal ending *-st^{h}ēn* attached to a stem *teta-*. The ending *-st^{h}ēn* is the marker of the third person dual of the medio-passive voice in a past tense and cannot easily be further divided into morphs for third person, dual, medio-passive or past. The stem *teta-* is an allomorph of the *perfect* stem, used in Homeric Greek to form a set of tenses and moods all referring to the resultant state following the verbal action of stretching. The perfect stem contrasts with a *present* stem *tein-* which refers to the action of stretching in the imperfective aspect, an *aorist* stem *tein(a)-* used as a perfective, and a *future* stem (not attested in Homer) referring to the action in the future. The stem *teta-* is formed with reduplication of the first consonant of the verbal root, which is normally a concomitant marker of the perfect stem, although there are perfect stems formed without reduplication and non-perfect stems which are formed with reduplication. The language user must know the place of the stem within the system to be able to decode the fact that in this verb *teta-* functions as a perfect stem.

The analysis of *tetást^{h}ēn* as the combination of a tense-aspect stem with a personal ending is fundamental. As mentioned above, in Greek different tenses and moods can be formed from the same stem, as shown in table 5.1. From the

Table 5.2 *Vedic Sanskrit verbal stems.*

	Present	Aorist	Perfect	Future
Indicative	past & non-past	past	past & non-past	non-past
	active & middle	active & middle	active & middle	active & middle
Subjunctive	active & middle	active & middle	active & middle	
Optative	active & middle	active & middle	active & middle	
Imperative	active & middle	active & middle	active & middle	
Injunctive	active & middle	active & middle	active & middle	
Participle	active & middle	active & middle	active & middle	active & middle

perfect stem, the following can be formed: a past-referring and non-past indicative tense (named the *perfect* and *pluperfect*); two separate modal formations, inflected for all persons and numbers (called the *subjunctive* and *optative*); second and third person imperatives inflected for all numbers; and two nominal formations, the infinitive and participle. For each one of these categories, there is a separate paradigm for the two voices of Homeric Greek, active and medio-passive. Exactly the same array of forms can be derived from the Greek present stem and from the aorist (perfective) stem, with the exception that the aorist forms only one indicative tense (the past-referring tense), not two. The future stem is exceptional in that it only exhibits nominal forms, the infinitive and the participle, besides the indicative. The future stem and aorist stem in later Greek show a three-way opposition of voice between active, middle and passive, but this is not systematic in Homeric Greek, which only marks a paradigmatic difference between active and forms which we have labelled medio-passive, which correspond in function to either the later Greek middle, or the passive.

We can set out in summary the verbal stems of Vedic Sanskrit in table 5.2. As in Greek, there are four different tense-aspect stems, with indicative tenses and modal and nominal forms associated with each stem. Vedic Sanskrit does not show the regular correlation of an infinitive with a stem, as Greek does, so this is missing from the table. But it does have a further modal formation besides the subjunctive and optative, termed the injunctive.

Table 5.3 shows the verbal stems formed to the Latin verb. Here we see a different system from either Greek or Vedic. There is a reduction in the number of stems for each verb, and a split between the perfect active stem and the perfect passive stem. Furthermore, perfect passive indicative tenses are not given in the table, but such forms do exist in periphrastic constructions: for example, the perfect passive indicative can be expressed through a periphrasis of the participle and the present indicative of the auxiliary verb 'to be'. In Latin, there is a reduction in the number of separate moods and participles in comparison with Greek and Sanskrit, although there is a new modal feature, the distinction between two subjunctive moods marked as past or non-past. The table does not include periphrastic infinitive forms.

Table 5.3 *Latin verbal stems.*

	Infectum	Perfect Active	Perfect Passive
Indicative	present imperfect future active & passive	perfect pluperfect future perfect	
Subjunctive	past & non-past active & passive	past & non-past	
Imperative	present active present passive future active		
Infinitive	present active present passive	active	
Participle	present active		passive

Table 5.4 *Gothic verbal stems.*

	Present	Preterite Active	Preterite Passive
Indicative	active & passive	active	
Subjunctive	active & passive	active	
Imperative	active		
Infinitive	active	active	
Participle	present active		passive

Table 5.4 shows the situation in Gothic. Here the system is even further reduced than in Latin. There are only two indicative tenses distinguished (not counting periphrastic constructions): the present and the preterite (a past-referring tense).

Most other IE languages also show some kind of distinction between a present and a preterite or past-referring stem. Some, including the Celtic languages, also show a separate stem for the future. However, no language, other than Greek and Indo-Iranian, shows a distinction between aorist and perfect stems. Where some IE languages show a verbal category and others do not, it is possible to explain the disparity in two ways. Either the category should be reconstructed for PIE, and was lost in some IE branches, or the category is an innovation made in the individual histories of the languages. One way to decide between these different accounts is to compare specific lexical forms which mark each category. If there is agreement across languages that a particular lexical form is associated with a particular verbal stem, this increases the likelihood that the category is a PIE inheritance. As table 5.5 shows, if we compare lexical forms in Greek (including early dialectal forms) and Vedic Sanskrit, there is a good correlation between specific formation types and different stems.

In Latin, Gothic and other IE languages, formations which build presents in Greek and Vedic form present stems. For example, Latin *agō* 'I drive' and *sīdō* 'I sit down' are formed in exactly the same way as the Greek and Sanskrit cognates

Table 5.5 *Comparison of stem formations in Greek and Vedic Sanskrit.*

	Greek	Vedic Sanskrit
Present stems		
verbal root $*h_2eg'$-	ag-	aj-
suffixed form $*g^wm$-sk´-	bask-	gacch-
reduplicated form $*si$-sd-	hizd-	sị̄d-
Aorist stems		
verbal root $*steh_2$-	stē-	sthā-
suffixed form $*weg^h$-s-	wex-	vakṣ-
reduplicated form $*we$-wk^w-	eip-	voc-
Perfect stem		
reduplicated form $*de$-$dork'$-	de-dork-	da-darś-

given in table 5.5. But Latin 'perfect' formations match both the Greek and Sanskrit aorist stems and the perfect stem. For example, Latin *uēx*- is the perfect stem of *uehō* 'I drive', derived from $*weg^h$-s-, which is an aorist formation in Greek and Sanskrit; Latin *cecin*-, the perfect stem of *canō* 'I sing', is an original perfect, formed in the same way as $*de$-$dork'$- 'see'. In Old Irish, the preterite *-dairc* 'saw' is derived from the perfect stem $*de$-$dork'$-, and other preterites match Greek and Sanskrit aorists, such as *luid* 'went', formed in the same way as Greek *éluthon* 'I went'. Hence, the Greek and Sanskrit three-way split between a present, aorist and perfect stem seems to be an original distinction which has been lost in other languages.

On the other hand, if we compare future stem formations in Greek and Sanskrit, it is more difficult to find similarities of formation. Both languages use affixes involving $*$-s- to form future tenses, for example Greek *dérksomai* 'I shall see' and Sanskrit *drakṣyáti* 'he shall see', from the root $*derk'$- 'see'. However, the match between the forms is not exact. When we compare future formations in other languages, we find: a) completely different formations (as in Latin and Armenian); b) formations with similarities to the Greek and Sanskrit futures (as in the Sabellian languages, Baltic and some futures in Celtic); and c) some languages where the non-past indicative or modal formations are used to describe events in the future (as in Germanic and Slavic). Since the affix $*$-s- is also used to form present stems with desiderative meaning, it is possible to explain all the future formations which use this marker as secondary in origin, and there is consequently no need to reconstruct a future for PIE. In what follows we shall leave the future out of our discussion.

Comparison of the different modal formations also shows substantial agreement between Greek and Indo-Iranian. In Sanskrit and the early Iranian languages there are two modal formations alongside the indicative and imperative which show the same means of formation as the Greek subjunctive and optative. (Table 5.2 also gives a further modal form, the injunctive, which will be discussed more

Table 5.6 *The Greco-Aryan model of the PIE verb.*

	Present stem	Aorist stem	Perfect stem
Indicative	Present/imperfect	Aorist	Perfect/?Pluperfect
Subjunctive	Present	Aorist	?
Optative	Present	Aorist	?
Imperative	Present	Aorist	?
Participle	Present	Aorist	Perfect

fully below.) The subjunctive and optative can also be thought to lie behind the verbal systems in other languages. In Latin, for example, inherited subjunctive forms are continued as futures, and inherited optative forms are continued as subjunctives.

Accordingly, a model of the PIE verb based upon the different stems found in Greek and Indo-Iranian appears to lie behind the verbal systems of the other IE branches. Table 5.6 shows a schematic arrangement of the reconstructed verb under the Greco-Aryan model. The principal opposition is between three different stems. From each stem a number of paradigms are derived, including indicative tenses and modal formations. Where the table shows ? in a slot, this indicates that there is uncertainty about the reconstruction of a category.

The present and aorist are marked off from the perfect. The perfect stem stands apart from the other two reconstructed stems for a number of reasons. Firstly, it is morphologically distinct: as we shall see below, a basic set of endings can be reconstructed behind all the paradigms which derive from the present and aorist stems, but the perfect originally had its own special set of personal endings, and a distinct participle suffix *-wos-*. Secondly, the voice distinction between active and middle is securely reconstructed for all the present and aorist formations, but not so for the perfect. Although a distinction between a perfect active and middle / passive is found in the earliest Greek and Indo-Iranian texts, there are reasons to believe that this is a recent development. In both early Greek and Indo-Iranian, verbs which only show middle endings in the present and aorist will use the 'active' endings of the perfect. For example, in early Greek the verb *gígnomai* 'I become' has middle endings in all paradigms except for the perfect stem, where forms which are synchronically active occur, such as *gégona*. In Vedic Sanskrit, the verb *rócate* 'shine' inflects in the middle in the present and aorist, but in the perfect active forms occur such as *ruroca* 'shines'. Pefect forms inflected as middle in Greek and Indo-Iranian appear to have originated by analogical extension of the active and middle distinction in the present and aorist. Indeed, the spread of the middle endings to the perfect can be seen in the history of Sanskrit and Greek. In post-Homeric Greek a new perfect form to the verb *gígnomai* appears, with middle endings: *gegénēmai*. In Vedic Sanskrit the active perfect *ruroca* means 'shine', but in the later language *ruroca* is restricted to a causative sense 'make bright', and the middle form *rurucé* is used to signify 'shine', in line with the middle inflection of the present and aorist stems. Thirdly, as indicated on table 5.6, the reconstruction of the pluperfect and the modal formations of the perfect is uncertain. In both Greek and Indo-Iranian it is possible to form a past tense and moods from the perfect stem; these do not have special perfect endings, but instead show the endings of the equivalent present and aorist paradigms. It is not clear whether these paradigms are another example of the encroachment of the present and aorist system into the perfect.

Alongside its peculiar morphological status, the perfect appears to have been semantically distinct. In Greek the difference between the present and aorist stem is aspectual: broadly speaking, the present stem is imperfective, and the aorist stem perfective. The perfect principally denotes a state: for example, the perfect *téthnēke* means 'he is dead', distinct from present *thnḗiskei* 'he is dying', imperfect *éthnēiske* 'he was dying' and aorist *éthane* 'he died'. As can be seen in this example, the state described in the perfect follows as a result of the action described in the other tenses. In early Greek the perfect is restricted to describing the state of the subject, not the resultant state of the object. A striking example of the use of the perfect is provided by the verb *tíktō* 'beget' (of a man) or 'give birth to' (of a woman). The perfect of this verb in early Greek, *tétoka*, is collocated only with women or female animals as subjects, since in these cases the subject has undergone a physical change of state; since male parents undergo no change of state, the perfect is not used. The Greek semantics of the perfect are matched by perfect forms in other languages and can be reconstructed for PIE. For example, the perfect **woid-* 'know' is reconstructed from the following correspondence:

*woid- 'know': Sanskrit *véda*, Greek *oîda*, Gothic *wait*, Old Church Slavonic *vědě*

In all the languages in which it appears, **woid-* functions semantically and syntactically as a *present* tense, although showing the characteristic PIE perfect endings and formation (including o-grade of the root). In order to connect it with the normal use of the perfect in early Greek, the semantics of **woid-* could be glossed as 'he has found out and consequently is now in a state of knowing' (the same root **weid-* is found in verbs meaning 'see' or 'find' in IE languages:

*weid- 'see, find': Sanskrit *vindáti*, Greek *eîdon*, Latin *uideō*, Armenian *gtanem*).

Similar correspondences could be found for other roots: Latin *meminī* 'I remember' and Gothic *man* 'I think' can be derived from an original perfect meaning 'I have had an idea'; Vedic Sanskrit *dadhárṣa* 'he dares' and Gothic *ga-dars* 'he dares' both continue an original perfect meaning 'he has summoned up courage'.

However, in most languages such survivals of inherited perfects with present meaning are not numerous (although they did spawn a whole class of 'perfecto-presents' in Germanic), and the perfect has mainly been reinterpreted as a tense with past reference. We should note that this shift to past reference offers support for the notion that the perfect originally referred to the state *following an action in the past*, and was not just a stative. In this new past-reference function the perfect

Table 5.7 *Mergers of the inherited preterite formations.*

	Inherited verbal stem		
	Perfect	Aorist	Imperfect
Latin and Sabellian	Merged to create new preterite formations		Lost
Celtic	Merged to create new preterite formations		Lost
Germanic	Continued as preterite	Lost except for relic formations	Lost
Baltic and Slavic	Lost except for relic formations	Merged to form new preterite	
Armenian	Lost except for relic formations	Merged to form new preterite	
Albanian	Lost	Merged to form new preterite	

consequently overlapped with old aorist and imperfect formations, leading to the collapse of the three-stem system in languages outside Greek and Indo-Iranian. This merger of the perfect, aorist and imperfect seems to have taken place independently in the languages concerned, and in some cases it is possible to see two forms surviving alongside each other without difference in function. For example, in early Latin there are several examples of old aorist forms surviving alongside old perfect forms from the same root, without any functional difference between the two stems but reflecting the relatively late fusion of the aorist and perfect in the new preterite. Furthermore, across the IE languages different patterns of merger are found, as summarised in table 5.7. Many languages also created new imperfective preterite forms (usually called 'imperfect' tenses), including Latin, Slavic and Armenian.

We have seen at the beginning of this section that in the Greek verb *tetásth̄ēn* the ending *-sth̄ēn* is a fusional marker of the third person dual medio-passive past indicative. This one morph encodes the five different categories of person, number, voice, tense and mood, and in this respect is typical of verbal endings in IE languages. We shall now examine briefly the reconstruction of these categories, before moving to the reconstruction of the endings themselves. The marking of the categories of person and number is found in every branch of IE. All languages distinguish three persons: first (the speaker), second (the addressee) and third (neither speaker nor addressee). Some languages, such as Celtic and perhaps Umbrian, show evidence for a distinct fourth person, i.e. an impersonal form. These impersonal forms can be connected to ways of marking passives and middles, and are almost certainly late and independent developments. Indeed, IE languages typically use third person forms for verbs which prototypically lack a subject, such as the verbal expressions of weather, 'it rains' and 'it snows'. All IE languages show a distinction between singular and plural number, and a dual is also found in Baltic, Slavic, Gothic, Greek and Indo-Iranian. Although the dual was clearly a category of the PIE verb, its endings are more difficult to reconstruct, and we shall leave them out of the discussion in the remainder of

Table 5.8 *Active personal endings in Sanskrit.*

	Primary	Secondary	Perfect	Imperative
1.	-mi	-m	-a	
2.	-si	-s	-tha	-hi / ø
3.	-ti	-t	-a	-tu
4.	-mas	-ma	-ma	
5.	-tha	-ta	-a	-ta
6.	-nti / -anti	-n /-an	-ur	-ntu

this chapter. The distinction between 'inclusive' and 'exclusive' uses of the first person plural and dual (i.e. 'I and others including you' opposed to 'I and others excluding you') is not marked on the verb in any early IE language. The category of 'voice' will be discussed in detail at section 5.5.

The interplay between tense and mood and the personal endings is complex, and can best be explained by considering the personal endings used in Sanskrit. The sets of active personal endings in table 5.8 have been abstracted from a number of different verbal paradigms. In this table, and subsequently in this chapter, we shall denote the personal endings by numbers 1–6, with 4 representing the first person plural, 5 the second person plural and 6 the third person plural.

The distribution of the endings in table 5.8 cuts across the categories of tense, aspect and mood. The set of *primary* endings are restricted to two tenses: the present indicative and the future indicative. The *secondary* endings are used for the imperfect indicative (the past tense formed from the present stem), the aorist indicative, the optative and the injunctive mood. The subjunctive mood can use either primary or secondary endings. The set of perfect endings is used only in the perfect indicative. The imperative has distinct endings, and is the only mood to do so. Sanskrit employed a further morphological marker for all persons of past-referring indicative tenses (i.e. the aorist, imperfect, and the pluperfect, the past tense of the perfect) which is also preserved in other Indo-Iranian languages, Greek, Armenian and Phrygian. This is a prefix, reconstructed as **e* and called the *augment*, following Greco-Roman grammatical terminology. In Classical Greek and Sanskrit the augment is an obligatory marker of past tenses, but it appears to have been optional at earlier stages of these languages. In Classical Armenian it is only used if the verb-form would otherwise be monosyllabic (similarly in Greek and Indo-Iranian there is a tendency to use the augment to avoid forms that would otherwise be monosyllabic with a short vocalic nucleus).

There is a further important feature in the primary and secondary endings in Sanskrit which has correspondences in other IE languages and must be reconstructed for PIE. This is the opposition between *thematic* and *athematic* endings, which appears in Sanskrit and Greek to be purely morphological, and not to have any significance for the meaning of the forms (compare the thematic and athematic nominal paradigms reconstructed in section 4.2). Some stem formations are associated with thematic endings and others with athematic. For example,

Table 5.9 *Athematic active primary endings: PIE 'to be'.*

	PIE	Sanskrit	Greek	Latin	Gothic	Lith.	O.C.S.
1.	*$h_1$és-**mi**	ásmi	eimí	sum	im	esmì	jesmǐ
2.	*$h_1$és-**si** (or *$h_1$ési)	ási	eî	ess, es	is	esì	jesǐ
3.	*$h_1$és-**ti**	asti	estí	est	ist	ĕsti	jestŭ
4.	*h_1s-**mé**	smás	esmén	sumus	sijum	esme	jesmŭ
5.	*h_1s-**té**	sthá	éste	estis	sijuþ	este	jeste
6.	*h_1s-**énti**	sánti	eisí	sunt	sind		sǫtŭ

the root aorist, of the type *$steh_2$- given in table 5.5, and the aorist formed with the suffix *-s- (as *weg^h-s- in table 5.5), both take athematic endings, whereas the reduplicated aorist of the type *$wewk^w$- takes the thematic set of endings. Thematic endings generally show a vowel, which surfaces as *e or *o (termed the *thematic vowel*) between the stem and the personal markers. In Sanskrit the endings following the thematic vowel are generally the same as the athematic endings, but as we shall see later, the similarity between thematic and athematic may have been a recent development.

All other IE languages show sets of active personal endings which can be connected to the four sets given in table 5.8, primary (thematic and athematic), secondary (thematic and athematic), perfect and imperative. Moreover, there is no set of endings which cannot be linked to these types. Through comparison of paradigms with these endings we can consequently reconstruct paradigms in the Greco-Aryan model of PIE. In table 5.9 we set out the basis for comparison of one athematic active paradigm, which uses primary endings, the present tense of 'to be'.

The paradigm reconstructed in table 5.9 shows a shift in accent and ablaut between the singular and plural, comparable with the accent and ablaut shift reconstructed for the strong and weak cases in kinetic paradigms discussed in section 3.4. Other verbal paradigms are reconstructed with a static accent fixed on the root. The fluctuation in the third person plural ending between *-enti in some languages and *-onti or *-nti in others stems from the generalisation of alternants associated with different original paradigms. The first and second person plural forms show considerable variation from one language to the other. For example, the first person plural ending in Latin derives from *-mos, not *-me; in Attic-Ionic and other East Greek dialects the ending *-men is found. Most of these developments seem to be particular to separate branches of IE, and their significance is unknown.

In table 5.10 we give the basis for reconstruction of the secondary athematic endings, starting from a comparison of the imperfect of the verb 'to be' in Greek and Sanskrit. In the other IE languages, the original imperfect is lost as a separate category, as we saw above, and forms labelled 'imperfect' in the grammars, such as Latin *eram* 'I was' or Old Church Slavonic *běxŭ* 'I was', are new creations

Table 5.10 *Athematic active secondary endings:*
PIE 'to be'.

	PIE	Vedic Sanskrit	Greek
1.	$*e\text{-}h_1\acute{e}s\text{-}\boldsymbol{m}$	*ásam*	*êa*
2.	$*e\text{-}h_1\acute{e}s\text{-}\boldsymbol{s}$	*ás*	*êstha*
	(or $*e\text{-}h_1\acute{e}s$)		
3.	$*e\text{-}h_1\acute{e}s\text{-}\boldsymbol{t}$	*ás*	*ês*
4.	$*e\text{-}h_1s\text{-}\boldsymbol{m\acute{e}}$	*āsmá*	*êmen*
5.	$*e\text{-}h_1s\text{-}\boldsymbol{t\acute{e}}$	*āstá*	*êste*
6.	$*e\text{-}h_1s\text{-}\boldsymbol{\acute{e}nt}$	*āsán*	*êen*

of the languages. Even in Sanskrit and Greek the imperfect paradigm of 'to be' has been remodelled, and table 5.10 includes forms from the older stages of the languages and, in the case of Greek, a dialectal form of the third person singular.

Note the presence of the prefix $*e$- (the augment) in the reconstructed forms. In persons 1, 2, 3 and 6 the secondary endings are equivalent to the primary endings minus their final $*\text{-}i$. The PIE endings for 4 and 5 appear to be the same for both primary and secondary, but these are reconstructed with less confidence.

Exercise 5.1

The verb meaning 'strike' or 'kill' in Hittite and Sanskrit comes from a root $*g^{wh}en\text{-}$, and some attested forms of the present tense are given in the table below. Reconstruct the PIE paradigm. (Note that $*ti$ develops to *zi* in Hittite.)

	Hittite	Sanskrit
1.	*kuenmi*	*hánmi*
3.	*kuenzi*	*hánti*
6.	*kunanzi*	*ghnánti*

Exercise 5.2

The table below gives the present paradigm of the verb meaning 'go' in Sanskrit, Greek and Latin. Reconstruct the PIE paradigm. (Note that $*ti$ develops to *si* in Greek.)

	Sanskrit	Greek	Latin
1.	*émi*	*eîmi*	*eo*
2.	*éṣi*	*eî*	*is*
3.	*éti*	*eîsi*	*it*
4.	*imás*	*ímen*	*imus*
5.	*ithá*	*íte*	*itis*
6.	*yánti*	*íāsi*	*eunt*

Which forms in the individual languages are replacements of the original forms?

Exercise 5.3

The table below gives some forms of the paradigm of the verb *duh-* 'milk' in Sanskrit. Work out what sound-changes have taken place to give these forms from the inherited paradigm. (Hint: you may wish to refresh your memory of some of the sound-changes given in table 2.3.)

	Present active	Imperfect active
2.	*dhókṣi*	
3.	*dógdhi*	*ádhok*
6.	*duhánti*	*áduhan*

The thematic conjugation is in many respects analogous to the thematic nominal declension reconstructed at section 4.2. Both paradigms show a vocalic affix which surfaces as either **e* or **o*, and neither paradigm appears to show any evidence for the accent and ablaut alternations reconstructed for the corresponding athematic classes. We have already seen how the thematic nouns share some endings with the athematic noun classes, but show some endings which are unique to them (such as the ablative singular **-ōd*). In the same way, the thematic verbal endings cannot be reconstructed simply as an agglomeration of thematic vowel and athematic endings. In the primary first person singular active, the thematic ending is not, as might be expected, **-e/o-mi* but **-ō* (probably from original **-oh₂*). This ending is widespread across IE languages: compare the reconstruction of the first person singular of the verb meaning 'carry':

*bʰer-ō 'I carry': Greek *phérō*, Latin *ferō*, Gothic *baira*, Old Irish *-biur*.

In Sanskrit, the primary first person ending of the thematic class is *-āmi*, except in the subjunctive paradigm, where the ending *-ā* is found in early texts. The thematic ending consequently appears to have been 'extended' in Sanskrit with the athematic marker **-mi* added to the original ending **-ō*. Avestan, the ancient representative of the Iranian branch, still shows *-ā* as a first person indicative marker. The other reconstructed thematic endings in the Greco-Aryan model are usually reconstructed as in table 5.11.

There are some problems with this reconstructed paradigm. It has been argued that the thematic endings of the second and third person singular in Latin and Sanskrit have been assimilated to the athematic paradigm, and that the original endings were substantially different. This hypothesis rests on the Greek endings *-eis* and *-ei*, which cannot directly continue **-esi* and **-eti* without the assumption of ad hoc sound-laws (see Cowgill 1985). However, while some languages (such as Baltic and Slavic) also show different endings in the thematic singular, their endings cannot be easily reconciled to the ones found in Greek, and it is not possible to reconstruct an alternative set of thematic endings with any confidence.

Table 5.11 *Reconstructed thematic primary and secondary endings.*

	Primary				Secondary		
	PIE	Sanskrit	Greek	Latin	PIE	Sanskrit	Greek
1.	*-ō	-āmi	-ō	-ō	*-om	-am	-on
2.	*-esi	-asi	-eis	-is	*-es	-as	-es
3.	*-eti	-ati	-ei	-it	*-et	-at	-e
4.	*-ome	-āmas	-omen	-imus	*-ome	-ama	-omen
5.	*-ete	-atha	-ete	-itis	*-ete	-ata	-ete
6.	*-onti	-anti	-ousi	-unt	*-ont	-an	-on

Exercise 5.4

The following tables give the present of the thematic verbal stem built from the root
*h_2eg´-, meaning 'lead' or 'drive' in Sanskrit, Greek and Latin, and the imperfect in
Sanskrit and Greek. Reconstruct the PIE paradigms. (Hint: remember that in Greek
long *ē* can derive from an earlier long *ā*, which may in turn derive from a contraction
of vowel or vowels with the laryngeal *h_2.)

Present tense

	Sanskrit	Greek	Latin
1.	ájāmi	ágō	agō
2.	ájasi	ágeis	agis
3.	ájati	ágei	agit
4.	ájāmas	ágomen	agimus
5.	ájatha	ágete	agitis
6.	ájanti	ágousi	agunt

Imperfect

	Sanskrit	Greek
1.	ā́jam	êgon
2.	ā́jas	êges
3.	ā́jat	êge
4.	ā́jāma	êgomen
5.	ā́jata	êgete
6.	ā́jan	êgon

The perfect endings are reconstructed through comparison of the terms for
'know' attested in different IE languages, which, as we saw above, continued an
old perfect form. The perfect paradigm also showed an alternation of ablaut and

Table 5.12 *The reconstructed perfect: PIE 'know'.*

	PIE	Greek	Sanskrit	Latin	Gothic
1.	*$w\acute{o}id$-h_2e	oîda	véda	uīdī	wait
2.	*$w\acute{o}id$-th_2e	oîstha	véttha	uīdistī	waist
3.	*$w\acute{o}id$-e	oîde	véda	uīdit	wait
4.	*wid-m-	ídmen	vidmá	uīdimus	witum
5.	?*wid-$\acute{e}$	íste	vidá	uīdistis	wituþ
6.	*wid-r-	ísāsi	vidúr	uīdēre	witun

accent, again with a difference between the singular and the plural. However, the ablaut pattern of this paradigm is dissimilar to that of any nominal paradigm in that there is an alternation between accented *o* and zero-grade in the root, rather than the more usual accented *e*. Table 5.12 sets out the basis for the reconstruction of the perfect endings.

The endings of persons 4 and 5 are again reconstructed without much certainty, but it is clear that for the second person plural the forms in all languages other than Sanskrit have been influenced by the active ending of the present and aorist systems. Influence from the active paradigm also explains the third person plural forms of Greek and Gothic, where the original ending has been replaced. In one sense the paradigm for 'know' appears to be atypical of perfect formations: it is not formed with reduplication of the initial consonant of a root. In Greek and Indo-Iranian, reduplication is a characteristic mark of the perfect, and reduplicated perfect stems are also found in Latin and Germanic, although reduplication there is not obligatory. It is uncertain whether the lack of reduplication in the paradigm for 'know' is a preservation of an archaic feature or not; it has been argued that the loss of reduplication in this paradigm is an innovation originating in the participle, where the expected **we-wid-wos- was simplified to *$weid$-wos- (Greek *eídōs*).

The final set of endings to be considered are the markers of the imperative. The Sanskrit forms given in table 5.8 can be compared to material in other IE languages. In the second person singular active, most languages exhibit either the bare stem as an imperative or a marker *-d^hi. The bare stem is found as an imperative in both athematic stems (e.g. Latin *ī* 'go!' $< $ *h_1ei) and thematic stems (e.g. Greek *phére* 'carry!' $< $ *b^her-e), but the overt marker *-d^hi is only found attached to athematic stems (Greek *íthi* 'go!' $< $ *h_1i-d^hi). Given this distribution, and the fact that there are examples of both types of formation for the same verbal stem, it seems likely that the marker *-d^hi was originally an optional particle, which became partially grammaticalised to mark out the athematic imperatives and add phonological weight to monosyllabic forms.

The second person singular imperative is, in a sense, the only 'true' imperative form reconstructable for PIE. The original form of the second person plural imperative is the same as the indicative *-*te*, and the difference between an imperative and indicative use of this form must have been derived from context. What grammars traditionally call 'third person imperatives' are not in fact imperatives at all. They are modal forms signifying the speaker's desire that a third party should act in some way. There are many different ways of expressing these third person imperatives in different languages, of which two can certainly be reconstructed for PIE: 1) a suffix *-u* added to the secondary third person endings *-t*, *-nt*, and 2) a suffix *-ō*, also added to the secondary endings:

-u: Sanskrit *ástu* 'let it be', derived from *$h_1$es-t-u*
-ō: Latin *estō*, Greek *éstō* 'let it be', derived from *$h_1$es-t-ō*

The identification of secondary endings at the base of these forms corresponds to the employment of injunctive forms, that is, verb-forms with secondary endings but no augment, in negated imperatives in Indo-Iranian (see further discussion in section 5.3), and the most likely ultimate origin of these third person imperatives is through a combination of the precursor of the injunctive with additional particles.

5.3   Reconciling Anatolian to the Greco-Aryan model

The Anatolian verbal system is radically different from that of Greek and Vedic and from that reconstructed for PIE. Each verb has a present and preterite indicative, marked only by different endings, and a separate set of imperative endings. There are no verbal moods other than indicative and imperative, there is no separate 'perfect' system, there is no distinction between aspect-marked stems, and there are no separate thematic and athematic conjugations. In Hittite, the Anatolian language for which we have by far the greatest amount of information, verbs either follow the *-mi* conjugation (with a third person singular ending *-zi* derived from *-ti*), or the so-called *-hi* conjugation, which has a first person singular *-hi* and third person singular *-i*. In this very different verbal landscape there are, however, exact formal matches to stems, suffixes and whole paradigms in other IE languages, as shown in table 5.13.

However, the number of exact matches is small, and sometimes the conjugation of a root in Hittite is at odds with the evidence of other IE languages. For example, the verb which means 'guide' in Hittite continues a root *ney(H)-* which is also found in Indo-Iranian (the bracketed *(H)* at the end of the reconstructed root means that there is doubt whether the root originally ended in a laryngeal, and, if it did, which laryngeal was involved). The Hittite third person singular of the present *nai* 's/he leads' looks unlike the Vedic third person singular present *náyati* 's/he leads'. The third person singular of the preterite of this verb in Hittite is *nais* 's/he led', which can be directly compared with the Vedic Sanskrit aorist *anait* 's/he led', and both forms can be derived from an original verb-form *(e)-nēy(H)-s-t*. However, in Hittite the final *-s* is a personal ending, whereas the *s* of the Vedic aorist (although lost through particular sound-changes affecting the third person) is a suffix present throughout the aorist paradigm, for example, the subjunctive *neṣat* 'may s/he lead'.

In general, scholars have adopted three different approaches to reconstruction of the verb following the decipherment of Hittite. The first, in its crudest form,

Table 5.13 *Exact matches between Anatolian and Sanskrit verbal forms.*

Anatolian form	Sanskrit form	PIE	Category
Hittite *estu* 'let it be'	*ástu* 'let it be'	*h_1es-tu*	Imperative
Hittite *kuenmi* *kuenzi* *kunanzi* 'I, s/he, they kill'	*hánmi* *hánti* *ghnánti* 'I, s/he, they kill'	*$g^{wh}en$-mi* *$g^{wh}en$-ti* *$g^{wh}n$-enti*	Present Tense Active
Luwian *ziyar* 's/he lies'	*śáye* 's/he lies'	*$k\acute{e}y$-o-*	Present Tense Middle
Hittite *tepnuzzi* 's/he makes small'	*dabhnóti* 's/he cheats'	*d^heb^h-ne-u-ti*	Causative Present Tense Active

accepts the Greco-Aryan model, or something not radically dissimilar from it, as essentially correct, and seeks to explain the Anatolian divergences from this model through specific developments in the prehistory of this branch, principally the loss or merger of categories. An alternative is to redraw the picture of the PIE verb altogether and to construct a new model for the verbal system, which may entail a more complicated prehistory for Greek and Indo-Iranian. In this model, the PIE verbal system has fewer categories than previously thought, and some languages, in particular Greek and Indo-Iranian, have expanded the number of verbal moods and tenses. The third approach, championed most notably by Cowgill, combines the two alternatives. Something like the Greco-Aryan model is reconstructed for the stage of PIE after the Anatolian languages (and probably also Tocharian) broke off from the other languages, and a different model is constructed for an earlier stage of the PIE verb (see further section 1.4 on the question of the original PIE 'family tree'). The last two approaches assume a rather different type of change in the verbal system from that observed in the prehistory of most IE languages, where categories are lost and merged. In these accounts there would actually have been an expansion of verbal categories, and a creation of new tenses and new formations, in post-Anatolian PIE.

In the rest of this chapter, we shall examine some of the features reconstructed in the Greco-Aryan model in more detail, in light of the Anatolian material. In this section we examine areas where the categories reconstructed in the Greco-Aryan model can be 'slimmed down' in order to bring them closer to the picture of the Anatolian verb. In the next section, we examine the problems posed by the Hittite *hi*-conjugation, and possible analogues in the rest of PIE.

Even without the Anatolian perspective on the PIE verb, some of the verbal categories reconstructed on the base of shared stems and endings in Greek and Indo-Iranian could be assumed to be recent developments. The clearest example is provided by consideration of the injunctive. As we saw, this modal formation is only extant as a separate category in Indo-Iranian. Its distinctive morphological

Table 5.14 *The injunctive compared with indicative tenses.*

	Sanskrit	PIE
Present indicative	*bhárati* 's/he carries'	**bheret-i*
Imperfect indicative	*ábharat* 's/he was carrying'	**e-bheret*
Present injunctive	*bhárat* 'carry'	**bheret*

feature is the absence of special markers, rather than any particular affix. This is illustrated by comparing the Sanskrit third person singular of the present injunctive, alongside the same person in the present and imperfect indicative, as in table 5.14, which also gives the reconstructed forms.

In morphological terms, the injunctive is unmarked with respect to both the present tense, which can now be analysed as containing an extra affix **-i*, and the past imperfect tense, which has an extra prefix **e-* (the augment). In the earliest Sanskrit texts (the Vedic hymns) and the Iranian language Avestan, the injunctive has two principal functions. It occurs 1) in prohibitions with a negative particle *mā́*; and 2) as a replacement for another tense or mood in a string of verb-forms. The second function can be explained through what Kiparsky termed *conjunction reduction*: the overt markers of tense or mood are not repeated in strings of verbs with the same tense or mood reference. The following textual examples can serve as an illustration. Note that in (1) there is a change of subject between the two verbs, which marks conjunction reduction off from serial verb constructions in other languages.

(1)   *RV 5.29.7 . . . ápacat . . .   pibat*
                cook-IMPERFECT   drink-INJUNCTIVE
        '(Agni) cooked . . . (and) (Indra) drank . . .'

(2)   *RV 9.95.1 . . . kr̥ṇute . . .   . . . janayata*
                make-PRESENT   cause-to-be-born-INJUNCTIVE
        'he makes . . . (and he) causes to be born'

(3)   *RV 2.2.5   pári bhūtu . . .   citayat*
                encompass-IMPERATIVE   quicken-INJUNCTIVE
        'let him encompass . . . (and) let him quicken'

This function of conjunction reduction can lead to further nuances of the injunctive. For example, in a classic study by Hoffmann (1967), it is shown that in the Vedic hymns the injunctive refers to events which were already known to the hearer, for example in reference to the action of gods and heroes in mythical context. In this case, the context is enough to guarantee to the hearer that the action took place in the past, and so there is no need to indicate this by a past verb-form. Indeed, it may be possible to see the use of the injunctive in prohibitions as a further example of conjunction reduction. In this case, the particle *mā́* gives sufficient indication of the illocutionary force, so that it need not be encoded in the verb.

Table 5.15 *PIE eventive endings.*

	Athematic	Thematic
1.	*-m	*-om
2.	*-s	*-es
3.	*-t	*-et
4.	*-mé	*-ome
5.	*-té	*-ete
6.	*-ént / *-nt	*-ont

There is little available comparative evidence for the injunctive in languages outside Indo-Iranian. The only languages other than the Indo-Iranian group which preserve the augment are Greek, Armenian and Phrygian, so it is only here that we might find oppositions between augmented and non-augmented verb-forms with secondary endings. In early Greek there are a few examples of non-augmented past tenses following present-tense forms, all referring to habitual actions of divine beings: in Hesiod *Theogony* 4–10 a description of the Muses' activities begins with a verb in the present *orkheûntai* 'they dance', which is later followed by *steîkhon* 'they process', an imperfect without augment. It is possible that examples such as this show a relic of the same conjunction reduction which is found in Indo-Iranian.

The injunctive in Indo-Iranian therefore appears to be in origin a verb-form unmarked for tense or mood. To arrive at the most economical picture of the PIE verb, we need not reconstruct a present, imperfect and injunctive, but merely a single category unmarked for tense. The extra *-i* found in the present-tense endings and the augment of the imperfect can be explained as having arisen later through grammaticalisations of originally independent, adverbial elements. Some accounts of the PIE verb refer to this unmarked verb form as the injunctive, since it does underlie the Indo-Iranian injunctive verb-forms, but we shall use the term *eventive* in order to avoid confusion.

The reconstruction of an eventive verb-form therefore slims down our reconstruction for verbal categories. The primary and secondary endings of the present and aorist system, reconstructed in tables 5.9, 5.10 and 5.11, can be derived from a single set of endings, given in table 5.15. Nearly all the primary endings can be derived from the eventive endings by the addition of final *-i*. The exceptions are the first and second person plural endings and the first person singular ending of the thematic conjugation, reconstructed as *-ō or *-oH. The reduction in the marking of the first and second person plural forms is not particularly troublesome for the theory, since it is paralleled in other paradigms cross-linguistically; a comparable case is the loss of person distinction in the plural of the passive paradigms in Gothic. More problematic is the thematic ending of the first person singular, which cannot be derived from an eventive ending *-om followed by

-i without resorting to unparalleled phonetic changes. The explanation for this ending is obscure; see further section 5.4.

The PIE present and aorist paradigms share the same set of endings, and it is possible to explain both of these as the outgrowth of a single paradigm, thereby further reducing the reconstructed categories of the verb. It is important, however, to keep in mind that the two paradigms must both be reconstructed to explain the non-Anatolian languages. Although the distinction between present and aorist is preserved only in Greek and Indo-Iranian, the opposition between them cannot be explained as a separate creation of these languages, since aorist formations underlie preterite formations in several of the other IE languages. The aspectual distinction between the two stems, reconstructed on the basis of Greek, also seems to underlie other IE verbal systems (despite the doubts of e.g. Szemerényi (1996)). Support for the reconstruction of aspect comes from the expression of prohibitions in IE languages. In Vedic Sanskrit, where prohibitions were expressed by the particle *mā́* and the injunctive, there is an observable difference between present-stem injunctives, which are used to stop an ongoing action (inhibitives) and aorist-stem injunctives which are employed in circumstances where a future action is forbidden (preventatives). Latin and Tocharian may show a similar distribution of stems in inhibitives and preventatives, and it is possible that this is an inherited PIE syntactic rule (see further 6.1). The opposition between inhibitive and preventative functions can be seen to correspond to one of aspect: inhibitives refer to ongoing activities, as do imperfective verbs, whereas a preventative envisages the verbal action as a whole in the same way as the perfective aspect.

Despite these signs of the antiquity of the aorist and present opposition, many scholars have argued that they both ultimately derive from a single paradigm. The reasoning behind this view is clear: both present and aorist paradigms use the same personal endings, and both can be formed by attaching the endings directly onto the verbal root. Indeed, in Greek and Indo-Iranian it is not possible to tell whether an isolated root formation with secondary endings is an imperfect or an aorist. The identification of a stem as present can only be guaranteed by the use of primary endings (which are not used in the perfective aorist forms); the identification as aorist is made by the opposition with a present stem in the same paradigm. As illustration, compare the following two reconstructions:

$*d^heh_1$-*t* 's/he put': Greek (dialectal) *éthē*, Sanskrit *ádhāt*, Armenian *ed*
$*h_2weh_1$-*t* 's/he blows': Greek *áwēsi*, Sanskrit *vā́ti*.

The verbal formation $*h_2weh_1$-*t* 's/he blows' must be reconstructed as a present stem, since it can occur with primary endings in Greek and Sanskrit, but the stem $*d^heh_1$-*t* 's/he put' does not occur with primary endings, and it is opposed in Greek, Sanskrit and Armenian by different present-tense stems (Greek *títhēsi*, Sanskrit *dádhāti* and Armenian *dnê*). If there is no difference between the endings or the stem-formation of the present and aorist stems, what governs the assignment of one verb to the aorist and the other to the present? The usual answer given is that the distinction between the two stems relies upon the inherent lexical aspect of the root. Some verbal roots refer to states of affairs which are most naturally understood to be 'perfective', such as 'put', 'give', 'die'. All of these describe events which are envisaged as having an end-point, and are consequently termed *telic* (Greek *télos* 'end'). Root-formations from telic verbs are normally classed as aorists (as *d^heh_1-t* 'put' cited above). Other verbal roots, termed *atelic*, refer to processes or events without reference to an end-point, and root-formations from these are usually presents (as *h_2weh_1-t* 'blow' cited above). Other examples of telic roots include *deh_3-* 'give', *g^werh_3-* 'swallow', *mer-* 'die', *$pleh_1$-* 'become full', for all of which there is good evidence for an original root-aorist. The roots *b^heh_2-* 'speak', *h_1es-* 'be', *h_1ey-* 'go', *ses-* 'sleep' and *$sneh_1$-* 'spin' all have presents formed directly from the root and are all clearly atelic. In some cases, however, the meaning of the verb and that of the root-formation appear to be at odds. Take the case of the root *g^weh_2-*, which forms a root-aorist (Greek *ébē* 's/he went', Vedic *ágāt* 's/he went'), but appears to have atelic meaning 'go'. This would be a problem for the theory, were it not possible to show through more careful consideration of the original attestations and the meaning of derived forms (such as Greek *bêma* 'a step' and Avestan *jāman-* 'a step') that the original meaning was actually telic 'step', from which 'go' was a secondary development. Similar discrepancies are found with other roots, which cannot always be explained so easily: *g^when-*, cited in table 5.13, forms a root-present, but its meaning is 'kill' or 'hit' in all the early IE languages. Other examples include *g^wem-* 'come', which forms a root-aorist 'come'; *$k'lew$-* 'hear', which forms a root-aorist; and *$wemh_1$-* 'vomit', which forms a root-present in Sanskrit.

Given the formal equivalence in the personal endings, it is therefore possible to reconstruct a stage of PIE at which time there was no difference between the present and aorist; and this becomes especially attractive if one is attempting to account for the absence of the category 'aorist' in Anatolian languages. By this hypothesis (sketched out most fully by Strunk (1994)), at an early stage of PIE there would have been no difference of aspect, just eventive forms of the type *d^heh_1-t* and *h_2weh_1-t*. Alongside these forms, there would have been characterised forms, with additional affixes signifying some extra nuance of meaning – for instance, reduplicated *de-d^hoh_1-t* might mean something like 's/he keeps putting'. Root-formations with telic meaning would not normally have been used in reference to events or processes ongoing at the same time as the utterance; for these a speaker would use a characterised form. But both telic and atelic root-formations could be used with reference to past time. If one hypothesises that at this same stage of the language tense is beginning to become grammaticalised, we can imagine a scenario as presented in table 5.16.

At the stage represented in table 5.16, there was a contrast between two past-referring formations meaning '(s)he put, placed', one of which had a perfective meaning (*$(e-)d^heh_1$-t*), and the other an imperfective meaning (*$(e-)de$-d^hoh_1-t*). Telic verbs could thus at this stage exhibit aspectual differences between a perfective root and a characterised imperfective form, but aspect was not yet fully

Table 5.16 *Eventive formations in early PIE.*

	Atelic root	Telic root	Characterised telic root
present-referring:	$*h_2weh_1-t(-i)$		$*de-d^hoh_1-t(-i)$
past-referring:	$*(e-)h_2weh_1-t$	$*(e-)d^heh_1-t$	$*(e-)de-d^hoh_1-t$

systematic. The crucial step in the grammaticalisation of aspect appears to have taken place when atelic verbs were also able to form characterised perfective stems. The means of forming a perfective stem to an atelic root appears to have been the affix $*s$, which survives as an aorist marker in Greek and Indo-Iranian and lies behind past-tense stems in many IE languages (compare the aorist stem $*weg^{'h}-s-$ 'drove' referred to in table 5.5).

This is a plausible hypothesis for the creation of an aspect distinction in PIE, but when did the process of the grammaticalisation of aspect occur? It has been argued that the spread of $*s$ as a marker of the aorist took place late in PIE, and in some languages it even post-dates the end of the common period (for details see Strunk (1994)). Significantly, there is no evidence for an $*s$ as a perfective stem formant in Anatolian, and one theory suggests that the suffix originated in the generalisation of a marker once restricted to the third person singular (as in Hittite *nais* 's/he guided' discussed above). This would fit with the theory that the creation of aspect was a recent event in PIE. However, we must be careful not to confuse structures with markers. It is perfectly possible for an old category to be formally renewed, and the apparent spread of $*s$ as a marker of the aorist does not necessarily mean that the category of aorist is itself late. Similarly, the co-existence of root-aorists and root-presents need not entail that the creation of separate grammatical categories of perfective and imperfective is a recent phenomenon, and there are some grounds for believing that such an opposition does underlie all IE languages, including Anatolian.

We saw above that semantic change has in some cases obscured the relationship between the original lexical aspect of the root and the formation of a root-present or a root-aorist. For instance, the root $*g^weh_2-$ changed its meaning from telic 'step' to atelic 'go' within the recent history of IE languages. Some problematic cases were left unresolved, including the telic root $*g^{wh}en-$, meaning 'strike' or 'kill', which forms a root-present. Several scholars (see especially García Ramón (1998)) have proposed that the root originally had an atelic meaning, something like 'beat' rather than 'strike'. The change of meaning must have occurred after the separation of different aspect stems, or otherwise the root-formation would have been assigned to the aorist rather than to the present. If the grammaticalisation of aspect, and the creation of separate present and aorist stems, arose after the isolation of the Anatolian languages, we would expect to find $*g^{wh}en-$ meaning 'beat' in Anatolian, but 'strike' elsewhere. However, as we saw at table 5.13, Hittite *kuenzi* is an exact formal and semantic match with Sanskrit *hánti*, which suggests that the change of meaning of the root had taken

Table 5.17 *The athematic optative of PIE 'to be'.*

	PIE	Sanskrit	Greek	Early Latin
1.	*h_1s-yéh$_1$-m*	syā́m	eíēn	siēm
2.	*h_1s-yéh$_1$-s*	syā́s	eíēs	siēs
3.	*h_1s-yéh$_1$-t*	syā́t	eíē	siēd
4.	*h_1s-ih$_1$-mé*	syā́ma	eîmen	sīmus
5.	*h_1s-ih$_1$-té*	syā́ta	eîte	sītis
6.	*h_1s-ih$_1$-ent*	syúr	eîen	sient

place before the separation of the Anatolian languages. Further research into the prehistory of the Anatolian verbal system may help to decide the question of when the split between present and aorist stems took place.

The categories of optative and subjunctive can also be seen as late developments in PIE. The endings of these moods are not marked against the indicative, and they can be derived from the same set of eventive endings reconstructed in table 5.15. In some IE languages the optative and subjunctive are formed to the verbal root, rather than associated with a particular tense-aspect stem. This is the case for Tocharian (Pinault 1989: 124f.), and in the Sanskrit of the Vedic hymns optatives and subjunctives formed to verbal roots significantly outweigh those formed to derived stems. This suggests that the formations which later became optatives and subjunctives originally existed alongside other derived stems and were not formed from derived stems. In other words, they were themselves separate derived stems, and only later became grammaticalised as markers of mood and incorporated into the verbal paradigm.

Some evidence to support this theory comes from the details of the formation of the moods in the IE languages. The optative is constructed differently with athematic and thematic stems in the daughter languages. For athematic stems, an ablauting suffix *-yeh$_1$- / *-ih$_1$-* can be reconstructed, as seen in table 5.17. The Latin forms included in the table are known as the subjunctive in the grammars, but they in fact represent the continuation of the original optative.

For thematic stems, an optative suffix *oi* can be reconstructed from the correspondence of Gothic (again the forms are usually called subjunctive in grammars), Indo-Iranian and Greek. This suffix does not ablaut, as the following correspondence sets reveal:

bher-oi-t 's/he might carry' (optative): Greek *phéroi*, Sanskrit *bháret*, Gothic *bairai*

bher-oi-me 'we might carry' (optative): Greek *phéroimen*, Sanskrit *bhárema*, Gothic *bairaima*.

The thematic optative endings are clearly connected in some way to the athematic endings, but it is difficult to account for the shape of the thematic affix *-oi-*, apparently without a laryngeal, beside the athematic affix *-yeh$_1$- / *-ih$_1$-*.

In Tocharian, the thematic optative is formed differently: the affix $*-ih_1-$ is added directly to the verbal stem, with loss of the thematic vowel:

Tocharian B thematic present *klyauṣäṃ* 'I hear', derived from a stem $*k\textit{'lew-s-e/o-}$
Tocharian B optative *klyauṣim* 'I might hear', derived from a stem $*k\textit{'lew-s-ih}_1\textit{-m}$

This unusual formation may well be original, as it is closer to the athematic optative formation. It is possible to see that the thematic optative suffix *-oi-* is in fact a creation of late PIE, after the Tocharian branch has split from the parent. The form of the suffix can be explained by analogy to the athematic suffix, and its form might be explained if at the time of its creation the combination $*-ih_1-$ had developed to $*-\bar{\iota}-$:

	$*h_1s\textit{-mé}$	$: *h_1sih_1\textit{-mé}$	::	$*b^h\acute{e}ro\textit{-me}$	: X
or	$*s\textit{-mé}$	$: *s\bar{\iota}\textit{-mé}$	::	$*b^h\acute{e}ro\textit{-me}$	: X
	'we are'	'we might be'		'we carry'	'we might carry'
	athematic indicative	: athematic optative	::	thematic indicative	: thematic optative

X $=*b^h eroih_1me$ or $*b^h ero\bar{\imath}me$, then simplified to $*b^h eroime$.

If this is correct, it offers some support for the hypothesis that the optative was only grammaticalised late in the prehistory of PIE, since we can see the process whereby it develops separate forms for the thematic and athematic paradigms. The details of the formation of the PIE subjunctive may also reveal something about the immediate prehistory of the IE verb (see further section 5.6). Subjunctives of athematic stems are formed by the simple addition of the thematic vowel. Subjunctives of athematic verbs consequently look exactly like thematic indicative forms. For example, Sanskrit *gámat* 's/he may come' is the third person singular subjunctive of the root-aorist, which has an athematic indicative *ágan* 's/he came'. The PIE equivalents of these Sanskrit forms are subjunctive $*g^w em\textit{-}e\textit{-}t$ and aorist $*e\textit{-}g^w em\textit{-}t$. The subjunctive is therefore formed in exactly the same way as the thematic stem, such as Sanskrit *bhárati* 'he carries' from $*b^h er\textit{-}e\textit{-}t\textit{-}i$. The thematic subjunctive is formed with lengthened thematic vowel, as can be seen from the reconstructed third person singular subjunctive of the thematic present of the root $*b^h er\textit{-}$ (in Latin, the subjunctive is used as a future):

$*b^h er\textit{-}\bar{e}\textit{-}t(i)$'s/he may carry': Sanskrit *bhárāti*, Greek *phérēsi*, Latin *feret*

It is easy to see how the thematic subjunctive may have arisen by analogy to the athematic form through generalisation of a rule that the subjunctive is formed by the insertion of a thematic vowel between the stem and endings. We shall return to examine the origin of the curious similarity between the thematic stems and the subjunctive in section 5.6.

In conclusion, we have seen how many of the categories reconstructed for the verbal system in the Greco-Aryan model may be seen as recent developments. In comparison with the reconstructed system sketched out in table 5.6, an 'improved'

Table 5.18 *An 'improved' Greco-Aryan model of the PIE verb.*

	Eventive	Perfect
Indicative	Eventive indicative	Perfect indicative
Imperative	Eventive imperative	?Perfect imperative
Participle	*-nt-* participle	*-wos-* participle

model of the PIE verbal categories would take the form of the system given in table 5.18.

The categories of the Anatolian verb can be accounted for by the improved model reconstructed in table 5.18. The PIE eventive paradigm must lie behind the present and the preterite paradigms of the Anatolian -*mi* conjugation; we have already seen the close fit between the Hittite verb *kuenmi* 'I kill' and the Sanskrit cognate in table 5.13. In the prehistory of Anatolian, as in all other IE languages, the optional marker *-i* of non-past endings has become obligatory to give the endings of the -*mi* conjugation. In the next section we shall consider how the reconstructed category of the perfect corresponds to forms in Hittite.

Our improved model of table 5.18 works on the assumption that the distinction between a 'present' and 'aorist' stem arose recently in the history of PIE. This is far from certain, and it would be equally possible to explain the Anatolian from a model such as that given in table 5.19, where there is a nascent distinction between present and aorist stems in PIE. Indeed, this model might explain some of the supposed relics of specifically aorist forms in Anatolian.

Table 5.19 *An alternative 'improved' Greco-Aryan model of the PIE verb.*

	Eventive		Perfect
	Present	Aorist	Perfect indicative
Indicative	Present	Aorist	Perfect indicative
Imperative	Present imperative	Aorist imperative	?Perfect imperative
Participle	*-nt-* participle	*-nt-* participle	*-wos-* participle

5.4   The Hittite -*hi* conjugation

One of the most puzzling aspects of the Hittite verb for Indo-Europeanists has been the existence of a parallel verbal conjugation to the -*mi* conjugation. This is called the -*hi conjugation*, after the first person singular ending, and is given in table 5.20.

Many verbs in the -*hi* conjugation show ablaut differences between the singular and plural. It is generally agreed that the ablaut pattern seen in Old Hittite verbs

Table 5.20 *The Hittite* -hi *and* -mi *active conjugations.*

	-*hi* Conjugation		-*mi* Conjugation	
	Primary	Secondary	Primary	Secondary
1.	-*hi*	-*hun*	-*mi*	-*un*
2.	-*ti*	-*ta*	-*si*	-*ta*
3.	-*i*	-*s*	-*t*	-*ta*
4.	-*weni*	-*wen*	-*weni*	-*wen*
5.	-*teni*	-*ten*	-*teni*	-*ten*
6.	-*anzi*	-*ir*	-*anzi*	-*ir*

such as *sākki* 'he knows', *saktēni* 'you (pl.) know', or *āri* 'he arrives', *aranzi* 'they arrive' is original, the root-vowel *ā* reflecting an accented *o in the singular of the paradigm and the vowel *a* in the plural deriving from an earlier zero-grade. This ablaut pattern, with accented o-grade in the strong forms and zero-grade in the weak, is not matched by any paradigm in the Hittite *mi*-conjugation. There is no functional difference between verbs conjugated in -*hi* and verbs in -*mi*. The -*hi* conjugation appears to have been common to the whole Anatolian branch. Note the correspondence between third person singular forms such as Hittite *pai* 'he gives' and Hieroglyphic Luwian *pi-ai-i* 'he gives'.

Hittite -*hi* conjugation verbs often have respectable etymological links with verbal roots in other languages, but there is no clear correspondence between them and a particular paradigm of the other IE languages, as can be seen by the following comparisons of Hittite -*hi* conjugation verbs and their cognates:

Hittite *dai* s/he takes' derived from PIE *$*deh_3$-* 'give'
    reduplicated present *$*de-doh_3-ti$* in Sanskrit *dádāti*, Greek *dídōsi*
    root aorist *$*(e-)deh_3-t$* in Sanskrit *ádāt*, Armenian *et*
Hittite *nai* 's/he guides' derived from PIE *$*ney(H)$-* 'lead'
    thematic present *$*ney(H)-e-ti$* in Sanskrit *náyati*
    s-aorist *$*(e-)nēy(H)-s-t$* in Sanskrit *ánaiṭ*
Hittite *pasi* 's/he swallows' derived from PIE *$*peh_3-s$-* 'drink'
    reduplicated present *$*pi-ph_3-e/o$-* in Sanskrit *píbati*, Latin *bibit*
    root aorist *$*e-peh_3-t$* in Sanskrit *ápāt*

Two of the above verbs are cognate with verbs which form root-aorists elsewhere, but it does not make sense to connect the Hittite -*hi* conjugation with the root-aorist, since other reconstructed root-aorists have Hittite cognates which are -*mi* verbs – for example, the root-aorist with third singular *$*(e-)d^heh_1-t$* meaning 's/he placed, put' (Greek (dialectal) *éthē*, Sanskrit *ádhāt*, Armenian *ed*) is cognate with Hittite *temi* 'I say'.

Hittite is the earliest attested IE language, and the -*hi* conjugation appears to be an archaism even in Anatolian (the difference between the -*hi* and -*mi* conjugations is levelled in the youngest Anatolian language, Lycian). The fact that the -*hi* conjugation does not slot conveniently into a single reconstructed category of PIE calls for an explanation if we are to have any confidence in the reconstructed models of PIE given in tables 5.18 and 5.19. There are many explanations for the origin of the -*hi* conjugation. We shall first examine in turn the grounds for seeing a connection between the -*hi* conjugation with the thematic conjugation and the PIE perfect.

The endings of the -*hi* conjugation were first compared to the endings of the thematic verbs by Kuryłowicz as long ago as 1927, and there are some similarities which encourage the connection. Firstly, the morphological distinction between thematic and athematic personal endings corresponds to no functional opposition in the attested IE languages, just as there is no functional difference between -*hi* and -*mi* conjugations in Hittite. Secondly, there is a similarity between the first person singular in -*hi* and the reconstructed first person singular of the thematic conjugation *-*oH*. The -*hi* conjugation ending of the third person singular, -*i*, can be directly compared to the Greek thematic third singular ending -*ei*. Moreover, if the -*hi* conjugation does continues the PIE thematic conjugation, then we can keep our reconstructed model of the verbal system largely intact. Unfortunately, the connection cannot be upheld, for the following reasons:

i)   There are very few good etymological correspondences of -*hi* class verbs to thematics (the connection between Hittite *nai* 'he guides' and Vedic *náyati* 'he leads' given above is one of them). Hittite -*hi* conjugation verbs are often cognate with athematic verbs in other IE languages, for example *dai* 'he takes' < *deh_3- 'give'.

ii)   Verbal suffixes which take thematic endings in other IE languages are continued by Hittite -*mi* class verbs – for instance, a reconstructed PIE suffix *-*ske/o*- is inherited into Hittite with -*mi* endings, third person singular -*skizzi* < *-*sketi*.

iii)   The root-ablaut of the -*hi* conjugation (with o-grade of the root in the singular and zero-grade in the plural) has no counterpart in the PIE thematic conjugation. Thematic verbs in IE languages show no ablaut or accent differences between the singular and plural.

Most scholars now see the perfect as the most likely ancestor of the -*hi* conjugation. Hittite does not have a perfect, and, if the -*hi* conjugation does continue the original perfect, then Hittite would fit well with the 'improved' Greco-Aryan model. Formally, the link between the perfect and the -*hi* conjugation is much better than the link with the thematic conjugation. Almost all the endings of the -*hi* conjugation can be derived from the perfect endings reconstructed in table 5.12 or else explained as contaminations from the -*mi* conjugation. The primary endings also show the addition of a final *-*i*, which is paralleled in the eventive endings. Furthermore, the distinctive o-grade of the verbal root in the strong forms of the perfect is matched by the ablaut of the -*hi* conjugation. There are, however, two formal differences between the PIE perfect and the -*hi* conjugation.

Firstly, reduplication is closely associated with the perfect in other branches of IE (although it is lacking with the verb *woid- 'know' reconstructed in table 5.12), but is not found in the -hi conjugation. Secondly, in Hittite it is possible to form derived stems in the -hi conjugation – for example, verbs formed with the suffixes -ess- and denominative verbs in -ahh- use the set of -hi endings. But in the other IE languages, the perfect was originally attached only to roots, and there is only one perfect formed from each root.

The formal match between the perfect and the -hi conjugation is therefore close, if not exact. The semantic and functional equation is much more difficult. As we have seen, the PIE perfect was used to denote the state resultant from an action. Although some Hittite verbs, such as sākki 's/he knows' are stative, many are not, for example aki 's/he dies', waki 's/he bites', dai 's/he takes', pai 's/he gives' and nai 's/he guides'. How do we get from a stative meaning to these forms? According to the proponents of the theory linking the -hi conjugation with the perfect, the process must have taken place in separate stages. One must first assume that the small class of stative verbs, such as sākki, are relics of true perfect forms, but for most other verbs the perfect must have developed to a simple preterite, as it has in Latin and Germanic. The new preterite perfect formation did not merge with the preterites to -mi verbs (which continue PIE imperfects and aorists). Next, by analogy to verbs of the sākki type, a new present was developed alongside these preterite forms. Existing verbal paradigms were then assigned to the -mi and -hi conjugations, with some interchange on the basis of root-vocalism and root-shape.

This explanation of the -hi conjugation is now widely accepted by scholars in the German-speaking world, but it has found less favour in the USA, and has particularly been criticized by Cowgill and Jasanoff. Cowgill's objections are three-fold. Firstly, Hittite is our earliest attested language, and it is not feasible that such an extensive restructuring of the verbal system had taken place (without leaving any relics of the earlier system) so much sooner than it happened in other IE languages. Secondly, he knew of no parallel to the back-formation of a new present tense from a preterite. And thirdly, there are very few good word-equations between Hittite -hi verbs and PIE perfects. Indeed, we can go further and say that some -hi verbs derive from roots which are unlikely ever to have had a perfect of the type reconstructed for PIE, where the perfect is surmised to have denoted the state of the subject following a verbal action. This is an unlikely formation for a root such as *deh₃- 'give' (Hittite dai 'takes') or *neyH- 'lead' (Hittite nai 'guides'). Admittedly, a perfect with preterite function does develop in other IE languages for the root *deh₃-, cf. Latin dedit 's/he gave, s/he has given', but this appears to be a separate, and fairly late, development. The active perfect in Greek, dédōka 'I have given', is first attested in the language after the earliest Mycenaean and Homeric texts. In order to explain the Hittite verbal system according to this model, one must assume that the language has already progressed far beyond the stage reached in Greek only in the sixth century BC, a thousand years later than the Old Hittite texts.

Cowgill's arguments against the 'perfect' model are not conclusive; it is *possible* that the Anatolian branch radically recast its verbal system at a much faster rate than any of the other IE languages, and the absence of evidence for a good parallel to the creation of a marked present paradigm from a past tense does not necessarily mean that the change has not happened. However, it follows from the arguments put forward in section 5.3 that we can get a closer fit between Hittite and the Greco-Aryan model if we assume that considerable changes to the PIE verbal system took place after the separation of Anatolian from the rest of PIE. It accordingly makes sense to revise our model of the perfect as well, and to derive both the Greco-Aryan perfect and the Anatolian *-hi* conjugation from an earlier formation, not one from the other. We shall move on to consider two alternative ways of doing this in the next section. Before we can look at the proposed models of the early PIE verb, we must first look in detail at the reconstruction of the PIE middle, which we have delayed considering until now.

5.5   The PIE middle

We have already mentioned the opposition of voice or diathesis, which could be reconstructed for the present system and the aorist system but not for the perfect. The two voices traditionally reconstructed for PIE are known by the rather unhelpful labels *active* and *middle*, taken over from Ancient Greek grammatical terminology; and the opposition between them is not altogether clear-cut. Whether a particular verb is conjugated as active or middle is partly determined lexically, as shown in table 5.21. In this table, roots which form verbs with active or middle diathesis are grouped together, and two roots are included which show variation within the same paradigm between active and middle forms.

We shall return to the semantics of these verbal roots below. But first we should consider how the middle functions in opposition to the active. Active and middle paradigms are preserved in Anatolian, Greek, Indo-Iranian, Celtic, Tocharian, Latin and Gothic. In Latin and Gothic the middle functions as a passive, except for a few *deponent* verbs in Latin which are conjugated as middles but without passive sense; *fātur* in table 5.21 provides an example. In Celtic, and for the most part in Tocharian, the choice between the active and middle conjugation is wholly lexically determined. The three branches to retain a productive opposition between active and middle are therefore Greek, Indo-Iranian and Anatolian. In these languages, the following functions are associated with middle forms when in opposition to the active of the same verb (note that the active can be reckoned as the unmarked voice):

1.   Personal involvement: Greek *lúō* (active) 'I set free', *lúomai* (middle) 'I ransom'; Vedic *yájati* (active) 's/he performs a sacrifice' (said of

Table 5.21 *Lexical assignments of roots to active or middle paradigms.*

Active		Middle
*h_1es- 'be'		*$k'ey$- 'lie'
*$wemh_1$- 'vomit'		*men- 'think'
*$sneh_2$- 'swim'		*wes- 'wear'
*men- 'wait'		
	*b^heh_2 -'speak'	
Greek present *phḗmi*		Greek aorist *éphato*, Latin *fātur*
	*h_1eh_1s- 'sit'	
Old Hittite present *eszi*		Sanskrit *ā́ste*, Greek *hêstai*, Hittite preterite *esa*

the priest), *yájate* 's/he performs a sacrifice' (said of person for whose benefit the sacrifice is made).

2.   Reflexivity: Greek *loúō* (active) 'I wash', *loúomai* (middle) 'I wash myself.'

3.   Reciprocity: Hittite *appanzi* (active) 'they take', Hittite SU-*za appan-tat* (hand take-MIDDLE) 'they took each other by the hand'.

4.   Passivity: the default meaning in Latin and Gothic, also found in Greek and Anatolian.

It is worth stressing that the active and middle diathesis does not seem to be connected with an opposition between transitivity and intransitivity, or with a reduction in the valency of the verb. Some verbs which are conjugated as active may be used transitively or intransitively without any change in voice, and in function 1) above verbs may be conjugated as middle with no effect on their syntactic arguments. The distinction between active and middle is therefore not a syntactic one, but semantic. Combining the functions of the middle in opposition to the active and the semantics of the lexical stems which are associated with the middle, we can say something of the prototypical use of the middle, which appears to be dependent on how speakers view the semantic role of the subject. The middle is the voice used to denote that the subject is in some way affected by the verbal action. Thus, for transitive verbs the active typically represents the subject as the actor, and the middle represents the subject as the undergoer. For intransitive verbs the middle is preferred when there is some notion of control over the verbal action (hence the middle inflection of 'think' and 'speak'), but if the verb denotes an event or action where the participant cannot have control, the active is used (thus 'be', 'vomit' and 'wait').

The endings of the middle have proved difficult to reconstruct. The attested personal endings are set out in table 5.22. For Latin, Old Irish and Gothic there is no distinction between primary and secondary endings preserved, and the same endings have been repeated twice in the table.

Table 5.22 *Middle endings in IE languages.*

	Hittite	Tochar. A	Sanskrit	Greek	Latin	Old Irish	Gothic
	Primary endings						
1.	*-ha(ri)*	*-mār*	*-e*	*-mai*	*-r*	*-ur*	*-da*
2.	*-ta(ri)*	*-tār*	*-se*	*-oi*	*-ris*	*-ther*	*-za*
3.	*-(t)a(ri)*	*-tär*	*-te*	*-toi*	*-tur*	*-thir*	*-da*
4.	*-wasta*	*-mtär*	*-mahe*	*-metha*	*-mur*	*-mir*	*-nda*
5.	*-tuma*	*-cär*	*-dhve*	*-sthe*	*-mini*	*-the*	*-nda*
6.	*-anta(ri)*	*-ntär*	*-nte*	*-ntoi*	*-ntur*	*-tir*	*-nda*
	Secondary endings						
1.	*-hat*	*-e*	*-i*	*-mān*	*-r*	*-ur*	*-da*
2.	*-tat*	*-te*	*-thās*	*-o*	*-ris*	*-ther*	*-za*
3.	*-at*	*-t*	*-ta*	*-to*	*-tur*	*-thir*	*-da*
4.	*-wastat*	*-mät*	*-mahi*	*-metha*	*-mur*	*-mir*	*-nda*
5.	*-tuma*	*-c*	*-dhvam*	*-sthe*	*-mini*	*-the*	*-nda*
6.	*-antat*	*-nt*	*-nta*	*-onto*	*-ntur*	*-tir*	*-nda*

Exercise 5.5

The following table gives the present paradigms of the middle (or, in the case of Latin, the passive) indicative of the thematic stem *$*h_2eg´-$*, which we have already met in exercise 5.3. Compare these endings with the ones given in exercise 5.3 and identify possible motivating factors for the choice of *$*e$* or *$*o$* as the realisation of the thematic vowel. (There is no need to attempt to reconstruct the endings. Hint: in Latin both *$*e$* and *$*o$* develop to *i* in open medial syllables; in closed medial syllables *$*o$* regularly develops to *u*.) Now compare the thematic nominal endings from table 4.7 and exercise 4.4. Do the same factors govern the choice of thematic vowel in the nominal endings?

	Sanskrit	Greek	Latin
1.	*áje*	*ágomai*	*agor*
2.	*ájase*	*ágeai*	*ageris*
3.	*ájate*	*ágetai*	*agitur*
4.	*ájāmahe*	*agómetha*	*agimur*
5.	*ájadhve*	*ágesthe*	*agiminī*
6.	*ájante*	*ágontai*	*aguntur*

Hittite, Tocharian, Latin and Old Irish have a final element *-r* or *-ri* attached to the middle forms. Two of these languages, Hittite and Tocharian, show forms with *-r* that appear in the primary endings only. The morph *$*-r$* appears therefore to have acted as the analogue to *$*-i$* in the active endings and originally marks the

Table 5.23 *Reconstruction from archaic middle endings.*

	PIE	Hittite	Sanskrit	Tocharian A	Old Irish
1.	*-h₂-*	-ha(ri) / -hat	-e / -i	-e	
2.	*-th₂-*	-ta(ri) / -tat	-thās	-tār / -te	-ther
3.	*-o*	-a(ri) / -at			

'here and now' of middles. This explanation, proposed by Cowgill (1968: 25–7), also accounts for the absence of *-r* in Greek and Vedic middle endings: at one stage these languages must have replaced the primary marker *-r* with *-i* on the analogy of the active endings.

The personal endings given in table 5.22 are not susceptible to normal processes of comparative reconstruction. There is no phonetic similarity between, for example, the Latin first person singular ending *-or* and Greek *-mai*. The reason for this divergence in the personal endings appears to be interference from the active forms. We have already mentioned that the middle was the marked member of the pair of active and middle, and in the history of many languages the personal endings of the middle appear to have been refashioned following a general analogical principle that the middle endings were equivalent to active endings with an additional middle marker.

This process can be seen in the history of Latin, where the original third person singular and plural endings *-tor* and *-ntor* have been reinterpreted as active endings *-t* and *-nt* followed by a marker involving *-r*, leading to the replacement of the inherited first person singular with a new ending *-or*, formed by combining the active ending *-ō* with *-r*, and a first person plural ending *-mur* by analogy to active *-mus*. Similar analogical patterns have affected the middle endings of many other languages. In Greek and Tocharian, for example, the first person singular ending incorporates the characteristic *-m* of the first person singular active. Indeed, in all but a few paradigms, the middle endings in the singular can be connected to the active singular markers *-m* (or *-ō*), *-s* and *-t*. The middle endings of table 5.22 which do *not* show any connection to the active morphs may therefore be taken to be archaic forms. Table 5.23 uses the archaic forms found in the singular of the middle paradigms as a basis for the reconstruction of PIE middle endings. It should be noted that in the Tocharian active the second person singular ending is also marked with a *-t*. The Gothic first person singular ending is excluded from the above table, since it appears to show a different sort of analogy, the spread of the ending from the third person to the first person.

The reconstructed markers of table 5.23 appear to be based on little comparative evidence, but they can help to explain the detailed development of the middle endings in other languages. As an example, let us consider the case of the first person markers *-mai* and *-mān* in Greek. As we have seen, these can be explained through incorporation of the active first singular marker *-m-* into the middle

Table 5.24 *Vedic Sanskrit third singular middle forms without* t.

	'lie'	'give milk'
3. (primary) without *t*	*śáye* < *$k^{'}éy$-oi*	*duhé* < *d^hug^h-oi*
3. (primary) with *t*	*śéte* < *$k^{'}éy$-toi*	
3. (secondary) with *t*	*á-śayat* < *e-$k^{'}ey$-o-t*	*á-duh-at* < *e-d^hug^h-o-t*

ending. The reconstructed middle endings given can be used to explain exactly how this change took place:

primary   *-h_2ei → *-mh_2ei > -mai
secondary   *-h_2 → *-mh_2 > *-mā.

The actual secondary ending of Greek, -*mān*, can be explained as a further re-marking of *-*mā* through the adoption of the *-*m* of the secondary active ending (which regularly developed to Greek -*n*).

The reconstructed ending for which there is the least comparative support in table 5.23 is the third person singular ending *-*o*. The evidence, how-ever, is not completely limited to Anatolian; a few verbs inflected in the mid-dle in Vedic Sanskrit also have third person singular forms without *-*t*-. The relevant forms from the verbs *śe*- 'lie' and *duh*- 'give milk' are given in table 5.24.

The forms without *t* are completely replaced by the forms with *t* in the later language, showing the influence of the active third person singular ending -*t*. The secondary forms synchronically look like active forms, but it would be unusual to have an active secondary ending alongside a primary middle ending, and these forms are better explained diachronically if they derive from middle forms which are secondarily re-marked with the active ending -*t*. It is possible to observe the same process of replacement of an older middle form without *t* in Hittite, where an archaic middle ending -*a* loses out to -*ta* – for example, Old Hittite *hi-in-ga* /hinka/ 's/he bows', and Old and Middle Hittite *hi-in-kat-ta* /hinkta/ 's/he bows' (see Yoshida (1990: 70 n.18)). There are also scattered examples of a puta-tive original ending *-*o* outside Anatolian and Indo-Iranian. For example, some verbs in Old Irish have a passive or impersonal form derivable from *-*or(i)*, as *berid* 's/he carries', which forms a passive *berair / ·berar* 's/he is carried'. It is likely, therefore, that the process of replacement of the original ending *-*o* by *-*to*, which can still be observed in Sanskrit and Hittite, took place prehistori-cally in all other branches of IE, and perhaps had even begun during the PIE period.

Once the third singular ending *-*to* has been generalised, it can serve as an analogical pivot for the replacement of other parts of the paradigm. The original second person ending was reconstructed as *-*th_2- in table 5.23. In many languages this is replaced by *-*so*, which lies behind the endings -*se* in Sanskrit, -*ris* in Latin,

Table 5.25 *Vedic Sanskrit third plural middle forms with* r.

	'lie'	'give milk'
6. (primary)	*śére* < **kéy-ro+i*	*duhré* < **dʰugʰ-ro+i*
6. (secondary)	*áśeran* < **e-k´ey-ro+nt*	*aduhrán* < **e-dʰugʰ-ro+nt*

-oi in dialectal Greek and *–za* in Gothic. This ending can be derived by a four-part analogy:

-t (3 active) : *-to* (3 middle) :: *-s* (2 active) : X (2 middle)
X= *-so*.

If **-so* and **-to* are to be explained as replacements of earlier middle endings, then it seems likely that the widespread third plural middle ending **-nto* is also an analogical formation, constructed by combining the active ending **-nt* and the middle **-o*. The earlier form of the third plural middle may be preserved in the plurals of the Vedic Sanskrit verbs with a third singular without *t*, *śáye* and *duhé* given in table 5.24. Table 5.25 gives the endings which occur for these verbs, which both show evidence of an archaic third plural ending.

The endings in table 5.25 can be explained if we posit an original third plural ending **-ro(i)*. In the imperfect the form *aduhrán* shows re-marking of an anomalous verb-form **aduhrá* with the active ending **-nt* (with loss of *t* in word-final position after a consonant) in exactly the same way that the third singular **áduha* was re-marked with active *-t* to give *áduhat*. There is not as much comparative support for an original ending **-ro* as there is for an original third singular ending **-o*. However, Latin and the Sabellian languages and Celtic share a middle third plural ending **-ntro*, which is directly continued in the Sabellian (Marrucinian) form *ferenter* 'they are carried' < **bʰer-ntro*, and can be argued to lie behind various other forms (such as Old Irish third person singular deponent endings *-thir / -tar* < **-tro* formed by analogy to **-ntro*). Combining all the evidence for the archaic middle endings, it is possible to reconstruct the singular and the third plural as in table 5.26.

Table 5.26 *Reconstruction of PIE middle endings.*

	PIE	Hittite	Sanskrit	Tocharian A	Sabellian	Old Irish
1.	**-h₂-*	*-ha(ri) / -hat*	*-e / -i*	*-e*		
2.	**-th₂-*	*-ta(ri) / -tat*	*-thās*	*-tār / -te*		*-ther*
3.	**-o*	*-a(ri) / -at*	*śáy-e*			
6.	**-ro*		*śé-re*		*-nter*	

Note that only one set of endings is reconstructed; the difference between primary and secondary endings may be a secondary grammaticalisation of originally separate particles, as we saw with the eventive endings reconstructed in table 5.15.

Table 5.27 *Comparison of PIE middle endings, perfect endings and the* -hi *conjugation.*

			Hittite -*hi* conjugation	
	PIE Middle	PIE Perfect	Primary	Secondary
1.	*-h_2-	*-h_2e	-hi < *-h_2ei	
2.	*-th_2-	*-th_2e	-ti < *-th_2ei	
3.	*-o	*-e	-i < *-ei	
6.	*-ro	*-r-		-ir

The comparative evidence does not allow us to be certain about the final vowel of the first and second person endings.

Exercise 5.6

Look again at table 5.22 and see which of the middle endings of the different IE languages you can explain using the reconstructed endings of table 5.26 and the analogical processes of changed described in this section.

The endings reconstructed in table 5.26 share a number of similarities both with the endings in the Hittite -*hi* conjugation and the endings of the reconstructed PIE perfect, as is shown in table 5.27. Since these endings have been reconstructed for three different categories, we shall refer to them as the h_2-*series* of endings to avoid confusion (and from now on we shall call the set of endings 1. *-*m*, 2. *-*s*, 3. *-*t*, 6.*-*nt* the *m-series*). The coincidence of form between original perfect and middle endings is not necessarily a problem for the comparativist. Both the perfect and the middle are 'subject-orientated': the perfect is reconstructed as the paradigm which denotes the state of its logical subject following the verbal action, and the middle typically has as its subject the undergoer of the action, or the affected participant. Although verbs conjugated as middles and verbs conjugated as perfects may take complements, they are both subject-focussed. More difficult is the association of the same series of endings in both the middle and the Hittite -*hi* conjugation. Since Hittite has a fully functioning paradigmatic middle, the -*hi* conjugation cannot be a direct continuation of the middle, and such an explanation helps little to explain why verbs such as 'take' and 'guide' are in this conjugation.

Not everyone agrees that the middle endings have undergone such widespread restructuring, and one current theory holds that it is incorrect to reconstruct 'original' middle endings 2. *-*th_2$-, 3.*-*o* and 6. *-*ro*, and a set of later replacements 2. *-*so*, 3. *-*to* and 6. *-*nto*, but instead that there were two separate sets of endings, associated with two different categories. Indeed, a few verbs in Indo-Iranian appear to show both sets of endings in the third person, with a difference of meaning between the two formations. For example, besides the plural form *duhré* 'they give milk', cited in table 5.25, there is also a middle form *duhaté* which means 'they milk', with an ending which continues PIE *-nto-i*. In other verbs the semantic opposition between the two formations is clearer: verbs with third person endings derived from *-o* or *-ro* function as passives or as statives (for example, *mahe* 'is capable', *ávasran* 'they wear'). Consequently, scholars who reconstruct an original opposition between two sets of endings propose that the paradigm with *-o* and *-ro* is an original *stative*, opposed both to the active and the middle (Kümmel 1996). The similarity between the stative and the perfect endings reflects the fact that the perfect denotes a state. The paradigm with endings 2. *-so*, 3. *-to* and 6. *-nto* is seen as an independent medio-passive, ultimately derived, according to Rix (1986), from an original reflexive, formed by the combination of the active endings with a pronoun *o*.

The two theories for the explanation of the middle endings lead to two very different prehistories of the IE verb, which we shall sketch out briefly. The first theory has been most fully put forward by Jasanoff (2003), and we shall call it the 'middle theory'. This proposes that at an early stage in PIE there were two separate paradigms which lie behind the PIE active and middle, marked by the *m*-series of endings and h_2-series respectively. It is no longer possible to recover the original functional opposition between these paradigms. Within the history of PIE, the original h_2-series endings were used both for the formation that became the PIE perfect and the Hittite *-hi* conjugation. Whether the Hittite *-hi* conjugation was once the same formation as the perfect, or whether it represents a separate paradigm which took middle endings but lost distinctly middle semantics, is uncertain. This system underwent further alterations, as the middle endings were progressively assimilated to the active endings, and the connection between the perfect, *-hi* conjugation and the middle was lost, leading to the creation of a new perfect middle paradigm and a new middle to the *-hi* conjugation. Since relics of the old middle endings still survive in Vedic and Hittite and perhaps elsewhere, these changes must have taken place after the period of shared IE unity.

The alternative theory, which we call the 'stative theory', sees the fundamental opposition between an active and a stative paradigm at the earliest reconstructable period of PIE, with the stative marked by the h_2-series. The stative endings were used in one particular paradigm to denote the state resultant from a verbal action, and this formation was grammaticalised as the PIE perfect (and through a secondary series of changes, the Hittite *-hi* conjugation). The grammaticalisation of active forms followed by a reflexive pronoun led to a new category, the middle. At the last stage of PIE we therefore have to reconstruct four separate paradigms: active, stative, middle and 'proto-perfect'. In the subsequent prehistory of the IE languages, the perfect paradigm became detached from other stative formations, which were merged, to a lesser or greater extent, with the new middle. The merger of the old stative and middle reflects an overlap of function: the middle originally denoted reflexivity, from which arose secondary meanings of personal involvement and passivity; the stative is naturally the voice used to denote passive states. As we have seen, the stative still survives opposed to the middle in some relic formations in Indo-Iranian.

These two competing theories operate at stages of reconstructed PIE a long way removed from the attested IE languages. But they do have consequences for the interpretation of historical data, as we shall demonstrate through the analysis of one particular root, *wes-, according to the rival theories. The root relates to wearing clothes, and can be reconstructed from the following correspondence set:

*wes- 'wear': Hittite wes-, Sanskrit vas-, Greek heîmai, English wear, Armenian zgenum, Tocharian B wäs-, Albanian vesh

The following verbal root-formations of *wes- are found in Greek, Hittite and Indo-Iranian:

*wés-o nowhere attested
*wés-ro Vedic third plural ávasran interpreted as 'they have clothed themselves' or 'they were wearing'
*wés-to Vedic váste 's/he wears' / 's/he puts on'; Hittite westa 's/he was wearing'; Greek hésto 's/he was wearing'
*wés-nto Vedic vásate 'they wear', 'they put on'; Hittite wessanta 'they were wearing'; Greek heíato 'they were wearing'

The forms *wés-to and *wés-nto everywhere have the meaning 'wear'. According to the middle theory, *wés-to and *wés-nto must be replacements of earlier *wés-o and *wés-ro, made separately but in exactly the same way in Greek, Vedic and Hittite. The root meaning must have been something like 'dress', and the verb could refer either to getting dressed or wearing clothes. Vedic preserves that original double sense of the middle in váste, but only the secondary meaning 'wear' in the relic formation *wés-ro. In Hittite and Greek, derived formations have taken the sense of 'put on'.

For proponents of the stative theory, the meaning 'wear' was originally restricted to the stative paradigm, and the meaning 'put on' of Vedic váste must reflect the original meaning of the middle *wés-to. However, *wés-to 'put on' was replaced separately in Hittite and Greek by new formations, and then Greek, Vedic and Hittite have separately replaced *wés-o 'wears' by *wés-to 'wears'. Thus the stative theory still has to operate for a replacement of the endings *-o by *-to and *-ro by *-nto. For this root, the stative theory consequently requires the reconstruction of an additional category, but without any pay-off in reducing the number of changes which must be reconstructed.

The process of working out the best model for the prehistory of the PIE verb is still taking place. The correspondence between the personal endings of three very different categories – the -hi conjugation, the PIE perfect and archaic middle formations – provides a tantalising avenue into the earlier verbal system of PIE. Fitting all the pieces together in terms of their original function, within a viable chronology, is still contentious, and research into the PIE verb is likely to continue for many years to come.

5.6   Roots and stems

Pour se faire une idée du système verbal indo-européen, il faut oublier la
≪conjugaison≫, telle qu'elle apparaît en latin, en germanique, en baltique,
en slave, en arménien, en grec moderne, etc.   (Meillet 1964: 195)

In order to get an idea of the verbal system of IE, it is necessary to forget
'conjugations' as they appear in Latin, Germanic, Baltic, Slavic, Armenian,
Modern Greek, etc.

Meillet's injunction stands at the beginning of his chapter on the verb in his classic handbook of IE reconstruction (Meillet 1964). Meillet saw the organisation of verbal stems in PIE as fundamentally different from the system found in modern IE languages, where each verb will belong to a *conjugation* with a discrete number of stems and forms. Comparative study of the verb shows a wide range of differing formations attested as present or aorist tense stems from the same root. Table 5.28

Table 5.28 *Present and aorist formations from three roots.*

Root	Present	Aorist
$*leik^w$- 'leave'	1. $*li\text{-}ne\text{-}k^w$- Sanskrit *riṇákti*, Latin *linquit* 2. $*leik^w\text{-}e$- Greek *leípō*, Gothic *leihwan*	1. $*leik^w$- Sanskrit *rikthā́s* 2. $*leik^w\text{-}s$- Sanskrit *áraik* 3. $*lik^w\text{-}e$- Greek *élipon*, Armenian *elik'*
$*deik\acute{}$- 'show'	1. $*deik\acute{}\text{-}nu$- Greek *deíknūmi* 2. $*di\text{-}deik\acute{}$- Sanskrit *dídeṣ*- 3. $*deik\acute{}\text{-}e$- Latin *dīcō* 'I say', Gothic *ga-teihan*	1. $*deik\acute{}$- Sanskrit *ádiṣṭa* 2. $*deik\acute{}\text{-}s$- Greek *édeiksa*, Latin *dīxī* 'I said'
$*d^heh_1(y)$- 'suckle'	1. $*d^hi\text{-}d^heh_1$- Luwian *titaimi*- 'nurtured' 2. $*d^hi\text{-}ne\text{-}h_1$- Sanskrit *dhinóti* 3. $*d^heh_1\text{-}ye$- Armenian *diem*, Old High German *taen* 4. $*d^hh_1\text{-}eye$- Sanskrit *dháyati*	1. $*d^heh_1\text{-}s$- Greek *thḗsato*

UNIVERSITY OF WINCHESTER
LIBRARY

gives some of the different present and aorist formations found in IE languages from three different roots.

In order to explain the number of different stem formations with the same function, Meillet supposed that in the parent language not just one present stem was opposed to one aorist stem, but rather it was possible to form several present and aorist stems from the same root. These stems were held to show different 'nuances' of aspectual meaning (or, to use the German term, *Aktionsart*), such as punctual, repeated or incipient action. Each root could show a wide variety of different formations, none of which presupposed the other. The two modes of forming a present of the root *leik*^{w}- in table 5.28 were consequently reconstructed with different meanings: the nasal infix present (1) was 'perfective' and the thematic formation (2) 'imperfective' (Pokorny 1959: 669).

Exercise 5.7

The table below gives the present paradigm of the verb *riṇákti* 'leave' in Sanskrit. Work out what the reconstructed PIE paradigm is likely to have been, using the athematic endings given in table 5.9 and deciding on the most likely pattern of ablaut variation in the verb.

	Present active
1.	*riṇájmi*
2.	*riṇákṣi*
3.	*riṇákti*
4.	*riñjmás*
5.	*riṅkthá*
6.	*riñjánti*

However, better knowledge of the earliest attested IE languages has led to a revision of this view, and researchers have increasingly become aware that if two stems can be reconstructed for PIE, one may represent an archaism and the other an innovatory replacement. Thus athematic verbs are in general a relic class, replaced over the history of individual languages by thematic formations. Motivation for the replacement of athematic verbs is not difficult to find: the juxtaposition of root-final consonants and the athematic endings (mostly consonant-initial) led to clusters which were often simplified or otherwise altered, so that the boundary between root and desinence, or suffix and desinence, became opaque to speakers. In some languages, paradigms still survive which exemplify the extent to which regular phonological developments can conceal the form of the root and the suffix. For example, the active conjugation of the athematic present formed to the root *duh-* 'milk' in Vedic Sanskrit gives second person singular *dhókṣi* 'you milk', third person *dógdhi* 's/he milks'. This paradigm is later replaced by a present formed with a suffix *-ya-*, *duhyati* 's/he milks' in Classical Sanskrit.

It is possible, therefore, that the thematic presents *$leik^w$-e-* and *$deik'$-e-*, and the thematic aorist *lik^w-e-*, reconstructed in table 5.28, are in fact replacements of earlier athematic formations. Support for this hypothesis comes from the observation that thematic presents formed on the pattern of *$leik^w$-e-* and *$deik'$-e-*, with the root in e-grade and thematic vowel added directly to it, are extremely rare, if not completely absent, in the Anatolian languages (and there are only very few verbs of this type in Tocharian). This suggests that the process of replacement of athematic verbs by thematics may not have been underway at the time when the ancestor of Hittite separated from the other IE languages. The class of thematic aorists of the type *lik^w-e-* is found in several languages, but there is little cross-linguistic agreement on which verbs formed an aorist of this type, and it was argued by Cardona (1960) that hardly any thematic aorists could be securely reconstructed for PIE. Similarly, many examples of the aorist formed with a suffix *s can be explained as post-PIE extensions of the suffix.

Consequently, the most recent dictionary of PIE verbs, edited by Rix *et al.* (1998), reconstructs only one present formation for the root *$leik^w$-*, the nasal infix present *li-ne-k^w-*, and one aorist formation, the athematic root aorist *$leik^w$-*. Since the semantics of 'to leave' are basically telic, this is in accord with the theory sketched out at section 5.2, that there is a relationship between the root-formation and the inherent lexical aspect of a verb, with telic verbs assigned to the aorist. We are therefore back to something like a 'conjugation' for the verb *$leik^w$-* in PIE, rather than the reconstruction of a verbal root with many possible formations.

Meillet's rejection of the reconstruction of paradigms was based on his contention that the existence of one verbal stem did not presuppose or rely upon the existence of any other: each stem was separately derived from the root. Some roots do still show a bewildering array of different formations. The root *$d^heh_1(y)$-* in table 5.28 is one such example. It is not possible to reduce the four present stems given there down any further (the reconstruction follows Rix *et al.* (1998)). But Meillet's claim is looking less likely for a number of other roots, where patterns of associations between certain present stems and aorist stems have started to emerge. Nasal infix presents, of the type of *li-ne-k^w-t*, are overwhelmingly found beside root aorist formations, as can be seen by the count of aorist formations beside reconstructed nasal infix presents in table 5.29 taken from the material in Rix *et al.* (1998). Since root aorists are hypothesised to reflect originally telic roots, the nasal infix present can be seen as a productive way of forming imperfective forms to verbal roots with an inherently perfective aspect. The nasal infix need not have any particular *Aktionsart* in late PIE: it is just one marker of the present stem.

Although affixes such as the nasal infix may have been grammaticalised as markers of tense and aspect stems in late PIE, there is much current research attempting to elucidate their earlier function. In some cases we may be fortunate enough to have sufficient clues to unearth earlier functions of suffixes. For example, the nasal infix retains a causative function in the verb *d^heb^h-ne-u-* 'makes small' which is derived from the adjective *d^heb^h-u-* 'small', and was, as we saw

Table 5.29 *Aorist formations from nasal infix presents.*

Root aorist	Sigmatic aorist	Reduplicated aorist	No aorist attested
129	17	1	90
(32 uncertain)	(7 uncertain)	(1 uncertain)	(37 uncertain)

in table 5.13, one of the examples of an exact correspondence between Hittite and Sanskrit.

d^heb^h-ne-u-ti 'makes small': Hittite *tepnuzzi* 'makes small', Sanskrit *dabhnóti* 'cheats'
d^heb^h-u- 'small': Hittite *tepu-*, Sanskrit *dabhrá-* < *d^heb^h-ro-*

The nasal infix can also be seen to have a causative function in other derivatives, such as Latin *pangō* 'I fix' (from a root *peh_2g- 'firm, fast'). However, for many other verbs, including the root *$leik^w$-, a causative meaning is not appropriate. In order to address this problem, Meiser (1993) has argued that the nasal infix originally functioned, not as a causative, but as a marker of transitivity. In order to explain the use with the root *$leik^w$- 'to leave', Meiser further proposes that the root originally had an intransitive meaning 'to get away (from)', a use that survives in Avestan, and the form *li-ne-k^w- originally denoted the transitive sense 'leave'. Meiser's reconstruction of the original function of the nasal infix clearly operates at an earlier level of the language than the paradigmatic opposition of present and aorist, where, as we saw, the nasal infix is just one way of forming a present stem. The reconstruction of the nasal infix as a marker of transitivity is one possible way of explaining a number of various facts. However, fitting the pieces of the jig-saw together is still problematic. The nasal infix is used in late PIE to form imperfective present stems from telic verbs. Cross-linguistically, transitivity aligns with the perfective, rather than the imperfective, aspect. For example, a punctual act, such as 'kill', is typically more readily encoded as a transitive than a non-punctual one such as 'fight'. We might therefore expect to see a marker of transitivity used to mark the perfective aspect (i.e. the PIE aorist) rather than the imperfective, but in fact the opposite happens.

For other stem-forming affixes, the reconstruction of the PIE background may be even more complex. We have already seen that the thematic vowel is used as a suffix to form present stems for some roots, often replacing earlier athematic stems. In section 5.2 we noted that the thematic vowel also forms subjunctives to athematic indicatives, and that the subjunctive mood has the hallmarks of a derived formation which had been grammaticalised as a mood. The thematic vowel is consequently used in two different ways in the verbal system. With some roots, it has become a lexicalised marker of the present, or the aorist, stem. With all roots, it has become grammaticalised as a marker of mood. However, there is no subjunctive mood in the Anatolian languages, and scarcely a good example of a present stem formed in the same way as *$leik^w$-e-, with the root followed by the thematic vowel and personal endings. This suggests that both extensions of the thematic vowel took place only recently in the prehistory of PIE. In Tocharian, a language branch which probably also derives from an early stage of PIE, only a handful of inherited presents were formed through the addition of the thematic vowel directly to the root, but there is better evidence for original subjunctive formations with the thematic vowel (see the data collected by Ringe (2000)). This suggests that the thematic vowel was originally a functional suffix which was later reanalysed, but the details of the development are difficult to work out (Jasanoff (2003) is the latest to attempt to answer this question). Why were some occurrences of root and the thematic vowel reinterpreted as present indicatives, while others were not? And if thematics and subjunctives were not around at the time of the stage of PIE ancestral to Anatolian, how did they subsequently develop? These questions will continue to occupy linguists in the future.

Further reading

Introductory surveys in English of the verb in IE languages are provided by Kerns and Schwarz (1972), which contains verbal paradigms for all IE languages, but is very unreliable with many errors, and Hewson and Bubeník (1997), which provides an overview of different tense / aspect systems within the individual branches. Sihler (1995) gives a comprehensive overview of the Greek and Latin verbal systems, and one of the more readable introductions to the reconstructed system. Sihler's work builds largely on the teaching of Warren Cowgill, who drew attention to the inadequacy of the Greco-Aryan model as a way of explaining Hittite (see in particular Cowgill (1979)). Cowgill (1985) argues against a special 'thematic' set of verb-endings (this paper was published posthumously and is consequently rather condensed).

Calvert Watkins published two important books on the PIE verbal system early in his career (Watkins 1962 and 1969); his 1969 book has been heavily criticised for its over-ambitious attempts to reconstruct on the basis of personal endings alone, and Watkins himself has since rejected some of the claims he made. Watkins' former student Jasanoff has advanced and modified Watkins' approach (see particularly Jasanoff (1978 and 2003)), and he has constructed elegant models of the PIE verb which do not rely on the primacy of the Greco-Aryan model (it should be noted that the 'Stative' referred to in Jasanoff's 1978 book 'Stative and Middle' is a different category from the 'stative' discussed in section 5.5). The first chapter of Jasanoff (2003) sets out the problems concerning the connection of the Hittite -*hi* conjugation with the reconstructed PIE verb brilliantly, and we have used it in the above discussion, and one scenario for the internal history of the PIE verb according to the 'middle theory', given in section 5.5, follows Jasanoff's explanation of the Hittite -*hi* conjugation.

While the focus of much American research into the verb has been the elucidation of the history of personal endings, the best of the European research has been directed at elucidating the categories of the verb and the relationship between different stem-building processes. This tradition of research is crowned by the *Lexikon der Indogermanischen Verben* (Rix *et al.* 1998, second edition 2001), which includes a concise introduction to the PIE verb as reconstructed by Rix and his students. Rix is himself partly responsible for the 'stative theory' sketched out in section 5.5 (see Rix (1988), who develops the idea of Oettinger (1976)), although the fullest expression of the stative theory is in the work of Kümmel (1996 and 2000). Rix's explanation of the secondary character (Rix 1986) of the IE moods is a classic piece of internal reconstruction.

There are numerous treatments of individual aspects of the reconstructed PIE verb and the development of the verb in individual languages. For the PIE verb, the perfect has recently been handled by di Giovine (1990–6, see also Kümmel 2000). Bendahman (1993) discusses the reduplicated aorist; Drinka (1995) the sigmatic aorist; Cardona (1960) the thematic aorist; Giannakis (1997) and Niepokuj (1997) reduplication; Strunk (1967) and Meiser (1993) the nasal present; Forssman (1985) the imperative; Rix (1986) and Euler (1992) moods; and Stempel (1996) (supported by Klaiman (1991) and Kemmer (1993)) voice. Further references, particularly to discussion of individual paradigms and stem formations, are given in Szemerényi (1996: 230–338) and Meier-Brügger (2003: 163–87).

Discussion points

1. The paradigm of the verbs 'to be' and 'to know' are 'irregular' in most of the IE languages, yet they are reconstructed as regular paradigms for PIE. Should this worry the comparativist?

2. Many IE languages have a category of 'infinitive', yet this is not reconstructable for PIE. How might infinitives have arisen? What other categories of the verb are new creations in any branch of IE with which you are familiar, and what is their origin?

3. 'The middle is the voice used to denote that the subject is in some way affected by the verbal action.' How can this prototypical meaning of the middle be related to a) the meanings which develop in the daughter languages, and b) the middle verbs in any branch of IE with which you are familiar?

4. 'Indo-Europeanists are very good at finding ways of linking morphological forms in different languages. They are less good at finding convincing semantic pathways to explain the morphology.' Is this fair criticism?

6 Syntax

6.1 Syntactic reconstruction

> Diachronic syntax is where it's at.
>
> (Campbell and Mithun 1980)

To judge from the number of conferences, books and theses, diachronic syntax is still where it's at in the first decade of the twenty-first century, in IE studies as in the rest of historical linguistics. Despite this, recent introductions to IE linguistics either omit syntax altogether (Beekes (1995) and Szemerényi (1996)), or accord it much less discussion than morphological and phonological reconstruction (Meier-Brügger (2003) and Fortson (2004)). There is still much pessimism about how much of IE syntax can be reconstructed, exemplified by the words of Penney (2000: 35):

> [I]t is not clear that any substantial reconstruction of syntactic patterns, with the exception perhaps of elements of word order, can be achieved without recourse to morphology, so that the study of the syntax of IE can appear to be essentially the study of the function of forms, and whether a theoretical linguist of today would accept this as an adequate approach to syntax must be open to doubt.

In this chapter we shall begin by asking why syntactic reconstruction is so difficult, and assess what syntactic reconstruction is possible and what is not. We shall then proceed in the remainder of the chapter to examine areas of current debate in IE syntactic studies.

Although the early comparativists were not uninterested in syntax, most accounts of the history of IE syntax begin with Berthold Delbrück (1842–1922), particularly with his three-volume work on comparative syntax (Delbrück 1893–1900), which is still frequently described as 'unsurpassed'. Delbrück's conception of syntax is different from the modern one: some parts of his work would nowadays be treated under the heading of word-formation rather than syntax. For example, topics such as the assignment of gender to nouns according to word meaning or morphological formation, or the original function of the active and middle opposition in verbs, are now commonly discussed in conjunction with the reconstruction of the morphology that encodes these forms. But Delbrück's work on case usage, word-order and hypotaxis provided a model for later research, and for much of the twentieth century general works on IE were not embarrassed to include a section on syntax. Indeed, the 1970s saw two publications entitled *Proto-Indo-European Syntax* (Lehmann (1974) and Friedrich (1975)). These works concentrated principally on word order, and their shortcomings result from an over-eagerness to fit PIE into a rigid Subject-Verb-Object (SVO) or Subject-Object-Verb (SOV) typology.

Criticism of Lehmann and Friedrich's works was coupled with a more general set of concerns about the feasibility of syntactic reconstruction, articulated by scholars such as Jeffers (1976) and Lightfoot (1980). They saw syntactic reconstruction as impossible, since syntactic change was unlike phonological change. They argued that correspondence sets for syntactic phenomena are not equivalent to correspondence sets for phonemes, since, while lexemes could be 'cognate', sentences could not (although we shall see later in section 6.5 that there are examples of possible 'cognate phrases' among IE languages). Furthermore, if correspondences are set up, there is no way of knowing which, if either, of two competing constructions is original. We do not even have any clear idea about whether syntactic change is more likely to proceed in one direction or another. Jeffers (1976: 22) compares the reconstruction of a phonological feature with the reconstruction of a syntactic feature in two related languages, L1 and L2. If the sound s in L1 corresponds to r in L2, knowing that the change of $s > r$ is common, but the reverse change is exceedingly rare, enables the linguist to reconstruct $*s$. However, faced with an equation between SVO in L1 and SOV in L2, we have no reason *a priori* for supposing that either SVO or SOV, or indeed any other word-order pattern, was the original.

It is easy to find fault with this reasoning (see the discussion of Harris and Campbell (1995: 344–76)). Here we would like to stress that syntactic reconstruction is a different type of enterprise from phonological reconstruction, and it is not possible to compare the two directly. Phonological reconstruction is a 'first-order' reconstruction: it is not reliant on any other reconstructed data, and the establishment of correspondence sets in phonology is normally sufficient evidence to justify the supposition of a genetic relationship between languages. Syntactic reconstruction is a 'second-order' operation, as is morphological reconstruction and the reconstruction of lexical fields; all rely upon both the reconstructed phonology and the knowledge that the comparanda come from genetically related languages. Syntactic reconstruction, like morphological reconstruction, has to go beyond simple comparison and pay special attention to the most archaic forms to establish what is the most likely scenario to explain the data in the daughter languages. Syntactic reconstruction consequently often involves weighing up two or more rival hypotheses, and judging which changes fit better with the picture of the reconstructed language and with what we know of syntactic change. Sometimes (and we shall see examples of this discussed in detail below) there may be no means of deciding between two alternative reconstructions, or indeed there may be no means of identifying any satisfactory reconstruction.

A further crucial difference between syntactic reconstruction and phonological (and morphological) reconstruction is the very diverse nature of what is covered by the term syntax. We have already mentioned how Delbrück's discussion of syntax includes many topics which are not nowadays normally considered part of syntax. Even if we sub-divide syntax into, say, nominal syntax (case syntax), verbal syntax, sentence syntax and text syntax, each of these areas covers very diverse aspects of language, so we cannot say that 'syntactic reconstruction is possible or impossible' or even that the reconstruction of 'sentence syntax is possible or impossible'.

What then can we reconstruct? What are the necessary data we need in order to attempt a reconstruction? In our view there are certain prerequisites for the reconstruction of any syntactic phenomenon:

a) There must be sufficient evidence of the construction in early IE languages, the facts of the attested languages must be carefully and fully detailed, and comparative work on the individual branches of IE must be used to isolate language-specific developments as far as possible.

b) The attested forms of the construction must share one or more of the following comparable elements: morphology, lexical particles, word-order agreement. Where there is very little actual material for the construction, then we are unable to proceed further.

c) The patterns in daughter languages must be explicable in terms of a recognised process of syntactic change. By 'recognised' we mean a syntactic change that can be paralleled in another language of the world, or one that is in keeping with observed and established mechanisms of syntactic change. If we are unable to give an adequate explanation for the developments from our reconstructed IE syntax to the constructions of a daughter language, the chances are that the reconstruction is wrong.

We shall illustrate here some of the principles and some of the possible pit-falls of syntactic reconstruction by looking at three different reconstructions. Firstly, we shall examine how 'yes-no' questions were formed in PIE. In all languages of the world there are a limited number of patterns for forming 'yes-no' questions: i) interrogative particle; ii) special word-order; iii) special intonations; iv) the A-not-A structure; v) tag questions; or a combination of these (Harris and Campbell 1995: 294). In IE languages there is evidence for all of these types of construction, although some formations, such as tag questions, are not well attested for early IE languages. We give first a necessarily brief survey of the question-forming devices in IE, focussing on languages attested before the Christian era:

1. Anatolian: in Hittite and Luwian 'yes-no' questions appear no different from statements. There are no special particles or changes in word-order, except that negatives may stand at the beginning of the sentence, rather than in their regular position before the verb.

2.   Indo-Iranian: in the early Vedic Sanskrit and Gathic Avestan texts there are few 'yes-no' questions attested. In the Rg-Veda, where 'yes-no' questions are attested only a few times in the late Book Ten (see Etter (1985) for a full survey), they either take the same form as the direct statement or, on two occasions, they show lengthening of the final vowel in the question sentence (represented in written texts with a special sign, the *pluti*, here transcribed *3*). Disjunctive questions can be formed by juxtaposition of a verb with a negated verb, as in the following example from a Vedic Sanskrit prose text:

(1) *TS* 1, 7, 2, 1 (Sanskrit): *chinátti sā́ ná chinattī3*

cut-3.SG she not cut-3.SG *pluti*

'Does she divide or not?'

The particle *nu* is found both in 'yes-no' questions and wh-questions in early Sanskrit. A particle *na* occurs in wh-questions in Avestan.

3.   Greek: in early Greek texts most 'yes-no' questions are introduced by a particle *ê*, although there are examples of questions with no introductory particle. Disjunctive questions are generally formed with a particle *ē(w)é* before the second alternative. The particle *nu* is found in 'yes-no' and wh-questions.

4.   Latin: in early Latin there are abundant examples of 'yes-no' questions in the comedies of Plautus. 'Yes-no' questions can be formed by using a particle *ne* which is enclitic on the emphasised word (normally the first word of the sentence), or they can be formed in exactly the same way as a statement, examples (2)–(3).

(2) Plautus *Bacchides* 247 (Latin): *uēnit=ne?* B. *uēnit.*

A. 'Has he come?' B. He has come.

(3) Plautus *Captiui* 882 (Latin): 882. A. *uēnit?*

A. 'Has he come?'

Questions expecting an answer 'no' are introduced by a particle *num*. Disjunctive questions have *an* before the second alternative.

5.   Germanic: in Gothic and the other early Germanic languages it is also possible to form a question without a particle and with unchanged word order, but various particles are also used (details in Lühr (1997b)). Other IE languages variously require an interrogative particle (Old Irish, Old Church Slavonic, Lithuanian, Tocharian A) or do not (Armenian, Tocharian B, some modern Slavic languages).

For PIE there are (at least) four possible reconstructions of the form of the interrogative sentence:

A)   'Yes-no' questions were marked only by sentence intonation. This is the reconstruction favoured by most of those who have addressed the issue (Delbrück 1893–1900: III, 267, Meier-Brügger 2003: 244), and it has the advantage that it requires no change to have taken place in the two earliest attested languages, Hittite and Vedic Sanskrit. However, since we have information (and far from full information) about the actual phonological processes of question intonation in only *one* early language, Vedic Sanskrit, we do not know if the Hittite or early Greek intonation patterns were in fact comparable, and it is not possible to reconstruct the intonation for PIE.

B)   'Yes-no' questions were marked by an interrogative particle. Since there are etymological connections between the interrogative particles in various different languages (and note in particular the support for a reconstructed particle **nu* from Greek and Vedic Sanskrit), it is difficult to exclude the possibility that speakers of PIE had at least the option of using an interrogative particle. However, the particle **nu* is extremely widely used in non-interrogative sentences in Hittite, becoming the default particle to introduce new clauses in Middle and Late Hittite, and is also found in non-interrogative sentences in Sanskrit and Greek. It is not clear which use is original.

C)   Lehmann (1974: 102), following Delbrück (1893–1900: II, 540) and Eichner (1971: 32), argued that the Latin interrogative particle *-ne* was the original interrogative particle, since its post-placement accorded with the typology of OV languages, in which interrogative particles are placed sentence-finally. He further observed that the interrogative particle would then be of the same form as the reconstructed negative particle **ne*, and noted that the use of the negative in 'yes-no' questions to encode is also found in non-IE languages with OV word-order.

D)   It can also be argued that the Sanskrit pattern of disjunctive questions of the type of (1) (i.e. A-not-A) continues an original PIE usage. If PIE questions took the form *verb* *ne *verb*, one could explain Latin questions such as that given in example (2) through ellipsis of the verb.

These different reconstructed hypotheses are not mutually exclusive: it is possible that different types of 'yes-no' question formation existed alongside each other in PIE. Indeed, systems of marking through intonation exist alongside other systems in many languages of the world. In French, for example, there are three different ways of forming 'yes-no' questions: *Il vient?*, *Est-ce qu'il vient?* and *Vient-il?* all mean 'Is he coming?' Research on syntactic change gives us no help on which of the PIE reconstructions to prioritise: interrogative patterns change in all sorts of different ways among documented languages. It may, however, be possible to accord different probabilities to different reconstructions, so that we can say that we have more confidence in the reconstruction of sentence intonation (A) than the reconstruction of an A-not-A structure (D), on the grounds that the former is more widely attested than the latter. Reconstruction (C), which is based largely on data from one language, looks far from likely, especially since the typological considerations which Lehmann relies upon do not hold good for all OV languages. But we do not have sufficient information to be certain of any single reconstruction for PIE. We could, of course, decide that reconstructions (A), (B) and (D) are all possible PIE means of forming questions: this has maximal diachronic explanatory power, but minimal adequacy as a synchronic description. All the constructions found in the early IE languages would be explained, but we cannot distinguish between the uses of these three constructions in PIE. Furthermore, there are many other questions for which we do not have sufficient evidence to begin to answer. For example, PIE indefinite pronouns are normally reconstructed with the same form as PIE interrogative pronouns, *$k^w i$- or *$k^w o$-. How were indefinites handled in 'yes-no' questions? Was it possible to make a difference between 'Did you see the dog kill something?' and 'What did you see the dog kill?', and, if so, how was this encoded?

As a second example of the process of syntactic reconstruction, we shall examine the construction of prohibitive sentences in the IE languages. Some languages show a difference between *inhibitives*, commands to stop doing something that the hearer is engaged in, and *preventatives*, commands or warnings not to do something in the future; we shall signal this only where relevant.

1. Anatolian: a special negative marker *$n\bar{e}$ (Hittite *lē*, Cuneiform Luwian *nis*, Hieroglyphic Luwian *ni*, Lycian *ni / nipe*) is used in prohibitives, and followed by the indicative, or in some cases the imperative.

2. Indo-Iranian: the negative *$m\bar{a}$ (Sanskrit *mā́*, Avestan *mā*) introduces prohibitions which are formed with the injunctive mood (see section 5.2). The injunctive formed from the present stem forms inhibitives, from the aorist stem preventatives.

3. Greek: prohibitions are formed by the negative particle *mḗ* followed either by the present imperative or the aorist subjunctive. In Homeric Greek the usage *mḗ* followed by the present imperative predominates and generally is used as an inhibitive (Ammann 1927).

4. Latin and Sabellian: here there are several different constructions, all of which use an introductory negative particle *$n\bar{e}$. Rix (1998) argued that the earliest construction employed a non-indicative mood formed with a suffix -$\bar{a}$-, but this has been disputed by de Melo (2004). In early Latin, the imperative and other modal formations are used, including the perfect subjunctive. Latin also forms prohibitives through a combination of the grammaticalised imperatives meaning 'beware' and 'don't want to', *cauē* and *nōlī*, followed by the infinitive.

5. Tocharian: the introductory particle has the form *mā* in Tocharian B, *mar* in Tocharian A. Both languages distinguish between inhibitives, which show the present indicative, and preventatives, which are formed with the subjunctive mood.

6. Celtic: Old Irish may also show a difference between the inhibitive, for which a particle *na* is followed by an imperative verb, and the preventative, with particle *ni* and verb in the subjunctive mood.

Table 6.1 *Comparison of negative particles in prohibitions and statements.*

	PIE	Anatolian	Indo-Iranian	Greek	Latin	Tocharian A	Armenian
Prohibition negative	*mē	*nē	mā́	mḗ	nē	mar	mi
Statement negative	*ne	*na	ná	oú	nōn	mā	oč'

7.   Armenian: a special particle *mi* is used which is followed by a 'pro-
        hibitive' form of the verb, formed from the present stem with sec-
        ondary verb-endings.
8.   Germanic: in Gothic prohibitions are formed by *ni*, the normal nega-
        tive particle, followed by an optative verb-form.
9.   Slavic: Old Church Slavonic uses the negative particle *ne* with the
        present imperative (which is historically derived from the PIE opta-
        tive).

This comparison allows us to reconstruct two features for the PIE prohibitive
sentence. Firstly, prohibitions seem to have employed a distinct negative particle.
Note that in a number of languages the negative used in prohibitions is different
from the normal negative particle, as shown in table 6.1.

    Secondly, comparison of the verb-forms allows us to reconstruct the indicative
stem, unmarked for tense, as the form used in prohibitions. The unmarked indicative, which we called the eventive in section 5.3, is retained as the Indo-Iranian
injunctive and has been replaced by the tense-marked indicative in Tocharian and
Hittite. In languages such as Greek and Latin, which have replaced, or partially
replaced, these old forms with an imperative, the original syntax has changed
according to a recognised process of syntactic change: extension. Imperative
forms have become seen as the markers of all commands, and the particle *mē*
has been reanalysed as a 'modal negative' rather than in itself having any force of
command. This extension can be described in the same way that 'four-part analogy' operates in morphology, as can be shown by the following putative examples
of positive and negative statements and positive and negative commands in PIE:

(4)   *e-$g^w em$-t
         'he came' (aorist)
(5)   *ne *e-$g^w em$-t
         'he did not come' (aorist)
(6)   *$g^w ṃsk´e$
         'come' (imperative)
(7)   *$mē$ *$g^w ṃsk´es$
         'stop coming' (indicative form unmarked for tense)

    The negative of a statement is formed by the use of a negative particle before
the same form of the indicative as was used in the positive form (cf. (4) and (5)).

A prohibition has both a negative particle and a different inflectional form. In languages where the indicative form is replaced by the imperative in prohibitions, speakers have presumably interpreted (4) and (5) as a rule that 'negative utterances are formed by adding a negative particle to the positive utterance', to give a structure which in PIE terms would be:

(8) $*m\bar{e} *g^w \eta sk\acute{}e$

Note also that several languages have opted to use modal forms (subjunctive and optative) in prohibitions. The most likely explanation for this is that speakers have extended the secondary functions of these modal forms, which include marking requests, wishes and other directive expressions, to embrace negative commands as well.

It is much less easy to construct a model of semantic change which would explain the forms in the daughter languages if we reconstruct an original pattern for the prohibitives with an imperative or modal form. There is no motivation for replacement of these forms by the indicative or the tenseless 'injunctive' forms; moreover, as we saw in section 5.3, the injunctive is a relic category, only clearly attested in the Indo-Iranian branch (although there may be traces in Greek), and in retreat even there. The reconstruction of a tenseless indicative in PIE prohibitions is therefore likely to be correct. We can even reconstruct something of the word order of prohibitions in PIE: in all daughter languages the prohibitive particle precedes the verb, and this was most probably the word order in the parent language.

The construction of conditional clauses offers a third example of syntactic reconstruction. Across the IE languages there are numerous different conditional constructions and markers; indeed, there are so many that Meillet (1964: 377) used conditional clauses as an example where syntactic reconstruction could never be achieved. We shall not attempt to list the variety of conditional clause types here, but rather shall give a brief discussion of a particular marker which appears to be used to introduce conditional clauses in at least three different early branches of IE. The marker is $*k^we$, which is widespread in IE languages as a connective enclitic (although it also has other functions), both at the word level and, less generally, clause level. The Sanskrit derivative of $*k^we$, *ca*, is used in thirty-one passages in the Rg-Veda, the corpus of early Sanskrit hymns, to introduce subordinate conditional or temporal clauses. We can be sure that the clauses are subordinate, since the verb at the head of the clause is marked as accented, and in Vedic Sanskrit main clauses verbs are unaccented; in all cases the clause with the clitic *ca* stands before the main clause. Wackernagel (1942) had noticed similar, marginal, uses of the cognates of Sanskrit *ca* to introduce subordinate, and in particular conditional, clauses in Gothic, Latin and Greek. This support for a PIE use of $*k^we$ to introduce conditional clauses then appeared to be confirmed by Hittite, since the element *-ku* of the conditional particle *takku*, 'if', can be derived from $*k^we$. However, the issue is not settled. Some of the Latin and Greek uses of the particle can be explained differently, and it is not impossible that different language branches have separately extended *k^we from a co-ordinating to a subordinating context. We can compare examples from Early Modern English, where 'and' is used in conditional clauses, and non-IE Mingrelian, where *da* has developed in meaning from 'and' to 'if'. What we are seeing here is merely a syntactic example of the problem familiar in reconstruction: possible 'over-reconstruction' on the basis of similar developments in the daughter languages.

We have seen therefore that we have not had much success in the reconstruction of one PIE sentence type, 'yes-no' questions, but considerably more success in another sentence type, prohibitives, whereas for the reconstruction of conditionals we are not certain whether we can attribute a shared syntactic construction to PIE. The differences between these three examples are instructive. For the reconstruction of prohibitives we have access to material which admits comparison, with particles which can be directly compared in six different branches and morphological forms which can be related to paradigmatic forms, and which can allow us to judge between older and more recent creations. Our reconstruction is not dependent on any typological arguments or preconceptions about the nature of PIE. Where we have no identifiable or special morphology, as in 'yes-no' questions, it is much more difficult to judge between relic and innovatory forms. In the case of conditionals, we have limited material grounds for the reconstruction, and similarities may arise out of changes which are cross-linguistically not uncommon.

6.2   Word order

The reconstruction of PIE word order has received a lot of attention in recent years. Word order achieved greater prominence in syntactic studies of the 1960s and 1970s following the attempts to construct 'transformational grammars' for English and other languages, and books and articles written on PIE syntax in the 1970s followed this trend. However, many aspects of the reconstruction of word order are still controversial, not least because the analysis of some of the early IE languages is still unclear. Hale (1987a: 2) noted the difficulties which face the scholar attempting to reconstruct word order when encountering languages such as Greek and Vedic Sanskrit:

> Discontinuous NPs, no fixed Adj/N-N/Adj or Gen/N-N/Gen order, no fixed verb position, and unusual relative clause structures (to name but a few characteristics) are constantly encountered in the texts in these languages. Indeed the same complications clearly continue to mystify typologists, who have claimed PIE to have been SVO, SOV and VSO in their efforts to fit that language into their neatly designed 'ideal' types.

As Hale states, one of the central problems with reconstructing PIE word order is that word order in some of the daughter languages shows a considerable amount of freedom. Linguists who attempt to explain IE word order in terms of rigidly fixed word order systems are often unable to explain how this freedom arose. The investigation of PIE word order in terms of rigid SVO and SOV patterns was rightly criticised as a 'pseudo-problem' by Watkins in a much-cited article of 1976. It would be wrong, however, to think that because word order cannot be expressed in terms of strict SOV or SVO patterns it is somehow unimportant, or that it was free. If PIE were a 'non-configurational' language, with completely free word order, we would still have to explain why the unmarked place of the verb is sentence-final in Hittite, Sanskrit and Latin, and why word comparisons which reflect original juxtapositions of noun and dependent genitive agree in showing the order genitive – head noun, as in the reconstructed collocation meaning 'master of the house' (9).

(9)   *dems potis house-GEN master 'master of the house': Sanskrit dám pati-,
         Avestan də̄ng patih-, Greek déspotis (Lithuanian viẽšpats with different first
         element)

Agreements such as these could lead to the conclusion that the unmarked order was SOV for the PIE sentence, and head-final for the PIE noun phrase. But variation from these patterns is widely attested, particularly in poetic or highly stylised texts, which make up a large part of our corpus of many early IE languages. Scholars have made some progress in the investigation of what possible deviations from the unmarked orders were permissible, and what motivated variation. One of the first aberrant word-order patterns to be explained was originally termed 'sentence amplification' or 'sentence expansion', but would now be recognised by linguists as a process of *right-detachment*. Right-detachment, which is frequent in many early IE languages, describes the process whereby appositional phrases and other adjuncts are tacked on to the end of a grammatical sentence. The first verse of the Sanskrit Ṛg-Veda provides a textbook example (10):

(10)   RV 1.1 (Sanskrit): agním īḷe puróhitaṃ yajñásya devám ṛtvíjam hótāraṃ
         ratnadhā́tamam
         Agni-ACC I-praise domestic-priest-ACC sacrifice-GEN god-ACC
         sacrificer-ACC invoker-ACC best-bestower of treasure-ACC
         'I praise Agni the domestic priest, god of the sacrifice, sacrificer, invoker,
         best-bestower of treasure'

All of the necessary grammatical information is contained in the first two words, which could stand on their own as a complete sentence, but the sentence is then expanded by the addition of five noun phrases which are in apposition to the accusative *agním*. Right-detachment can be observed in other early IE languages, and there is no objection to its reconstruction for PIE.

Just as material can be added to expand the end of the sentence without affecting the syntactic nucleus, in the same way early IE languages show evidence for *left-detachment*, or the addition of material before the beginning of the sentence. It is important to distinguish left-detachment from the process of *fronting* (also called *focus*): left-detachment moves an element outside its clause, whereas fronting typically involves movement of a focal element within the clause. The difference can be illustrated from English and Icelandic. In English, a noun phrase in a sentence can be fronted for focus: as '**that** I do not like'; '**What** did you give him?'; '**Where** are you going?' The fronted elements are still a necessary part of the sentence and cannot be omitted. But if a noun phrase is left-detached, it stands outside the grammar of the sentence, reference to it within the sentence must be made anaphorically, and it is often followed by a pause or intonation break: '**As for Paul**, I don't like him.' Left-detached elements may occur before a focussed noun phrase or question word: '**Next year**, where are we going on holiday?' In Icelandic, there is a clear syntactic difference between fronted focal and left-detached elements: verbs come second in Icelandic, but left-detached elements do not count in the calculation of where 'second position' in the sentence is.

Some early IE languages show a clear distinction between the left-detached and fronted position in the sentence. Consider first Hittite. Hittite word order is more rigid than Greek or Sanskrit, and sentences generally follow an SOV pattern. However, any constituent, even the verb, can be fronted, and the first full word of the sentence is followed by the particle chain, as in (11):

(11)   *StBoT* 8, 2, 22 (Hittite): *harkanzi=ma=an* ^{d}*Hantasepes anduhsas harsa[r]=a* $^{GIS}SUKUR^{<HI>A}=ya*
         they-hold=CONN=PART H-NOM.PL man-GEN head-ACC=and spear-PL=and
         'The Hantasepa-divinities hold both human heads and lances'

If the sentence includes one of the introductory particles *nu*, *su* or *ta* (sometimes termed S-adverbs), then these normally precede the fronted element. Left-detachment, although rare, is attested for Hittite, and other early IE languages, as examples (12)–(14) show. In these sentences, left-detached nominal phrases are picked up by anaphoric pronouns in the body of the sentence. Enclitics and sentence adverbs are positioned as if the left-detached element was absent:

(12)   *THeth* 11 II 13 (Hittite): *V SES^{MES}=SU nu=smas É^{MES} taggasta*
         5 brothers=his CONN=them-OBL houses he-assigned
         'As for his five brothers, he assigned them houses'

(13)   *Thes.* II 309.5 (Old Irish): *maisse doíne ní=s toimled*
         glory of-men, not=of-it he-partook
         'The glory of men, he did not partake of it'

(14)   CIL I^2 675 (Latin): *N. Pumidius Q.f.* [11 other names omitted] *heisce magistreis Venerus Iouiae muru aedificandum coirauerunt*
         Pumidius-NOM . . . these-NOM magistrates-NOM Venus-GEN
         of-Juppiter-GEN wall-ACC to-be-built-ACC supervised
         'Numerius Pumidius son of Quintus [and 11 others], these magistrates supervised the building of a wall to belong to Venus daughter of Juppiter'

These examples suggest that the pattern of left-detached elements at the beginning of the sentence should probably be allowed as a possible permutation in

the parent language, but it is more difficult to find clear-cut examples from other
IE languages; in Avestan, for instance, the left-detached position is only found
occupied by a vocative (Hale 1987a: 48f.), and in Greek, sentence connectives
attach to the left-detached slot, rather than the sentence proper as in Hittite:

(15)   *Odyssey* 2.28 (Greek): *nûn dè tís hôd' égeire*
            now CONN who thus gathered-AOR
            'Now who has collected them thus?'

In this sentence the left-detached slot is filled with the adverb *nûn*, and the
question word *tís* occupies the focus slot. We shall return to the question of the
beginning of the sentence in PIE below.

The difference between the left-detached and the focus slot becomes important
when we consider '[o]ne of the few generally accepted syntactic statements about
Indo-European' (Watkins 1964: 1036): *Wackernagel's Law* (henceforth abbrevi-
ated to WL). The law can be simply stated: 'enclitics stand in the second position
of the sentence'. This word-order rule had already been noticed at the end of
the nineteenth century and was strikingly confirmed after the decipherment of
Hittite, where, as we have seen, particle chains always follow the first word in
the sentence. The following sentences exemplify the law well; they are all taken
from early IE texts which mark word-division (and two of which were not known
to Wackernagel), and they all show enclitics attached to the first word of the
sentence.

(16)   *KUB* 35 102 + 103 III 4 (Luwian): *zam=pa=kuwa* DUMU-*nin wallindu*
            this-ACC=PART=PART child-ACC they-shall lift
            'They shall lift this child'
(17)   PY Ep 704 6 (Mycenaean Greek): *da-mo=de=mi pa-si ko-to-na-o*
            ke-ke-me-na-o o-na-to e-ke-e
            people-NOM=CONN=she-ACC say plot-GEN communal-GEN use-ACC
            have-INFIN
            'But the people say that she has the use of the communal plot'
(18)   XPh 32 (Old Persian): *pasāva=maiy Auramazdā upastām abara*
            then=me-DAT Ahura-Mazda-NOM aid-ACC he-brought
            'Then Ahura-Mazda brought me aid'

In each language the enclitics are written without any word-break after the first
word of the sentence; the lack of any word-break shows that the scribes did not
consider the unaccented forms as comprising a full word, and we are consequently
justified in seeing this as evidence for their phonological status as clitics.

In recent years, WL has come under closer scrutiny from a number of different
angles. This attention has clarified what we understand by the notions enclitic
and second position, and as we shall see, WL now looks more problematic than
it did forty years ago. We have already seen how, in Hittite, 'second' position
counts as second position excluding the left-detached elements in a sentence, but
in the Greek example (15) above, second position means immediately after the

left-detached phrase. The situation is even more complicated in Vedic Sanskrit, as has been shown by Hale (1987a and 1987b). In this language, question words are typically fronted and followed by enclitics, as seen in example (19). Note that in this example the pronoun *te* is enclitic and does not carry an accent; the verb is unaccented, as is standard in main clauses.

(19)   *RV* 4.18.12a (Vedic Sanskrit): *kás te mātáram vidhávām acakrat*
         who you-GEN mother-ACC widow-ACC he-made
         'Who made your mother a widow?'

Where an element precedes the question word, it makes sense to interpret this as a left-detached element, and it appears that in Vedic Sanskrit, as in Hittite, left-detachment does not count in the calculation of second position.

(20)   *RV* 6.27 1b (Vedic Sanskrit): *índrah kím asya sakhyé cakāra*
         Indra-NOM what-ACC he-GEN friendship-LOC he-did
         'What did Indra do in his friendship?' (or perhaps better:
         'As for Indra, what did he do in his friendship?')

Other Sanskrit examples show yet more complex patterns. In example (21) there are two enclitics, the disjunctive particle *vā*, which follows the left-detached slot, and the personal pronoun *nas* following the relative pronoun, which occupies the 'front' slot (the pronoun *nas* appears as *no* by a process of sandhi).

(21)   *RV* 2.23.7a (Vedic Sanskrit): *utá vā yó no marcáyād ánāgasah*
         and PART rel-NOM us-ACC harm-OPT innocent-ACC.PL
         'Or also who would harm innocent us . . .'

It should be noted that the position of the particle *vā*, which has scope over the whole sentence following the left-detached element, is exactly paralleled by the behaviour of connectives and adverbs with scope over the sentence in Greek, which, as we saw with example (15), stand immediately after the left-detached element. Hale (1987a and 1987b) collected evidence for second-position enclitics in Indo-Iranian and showed that, in general, enclitics with scope over the sentence and connectives occurred after left-detached elements, which he refers to as the TOPIC position, whereas enclitic pronouns were placed after the fronted element. Hale claims that the behaviour of these two different sets of enclitics reflects an inherited difference between the two sentence positions, and others have used Hale's results to explain word-order patterns in Lycian (Garrett 1992 and 1994), Germanic (Kiparsky 1995) and more generally in IE (Krisch 1990).

However, if we look at some of Hale's examples more closely, it appears that there is some fluctuation between his definition of TOPIC and what would be judged as left-detached. In examples (22) and (23) Hale takes the material highlighted in **bold** as in TOPIC position.

(22)   *RV* 4.23.2b (Vedic Sanskrit): **sám āmamśa sumatíbhih** *kó asya*
         PREVERB he-attained good-will-LOC who-NOM he-GEN
         'Who has attained his good-will?'

(23)   *RV* 4.12.2a (Vedic Sanskrit): **idhmám** *yás te jabharác chasramānáḥ*
           kindling-ACC rel-NOM you-DAT he- bears exulting
           'Who, exulting, bears the kindling to you . . .'

However, in neither case can the TOPIC phrase be detached from the rest of
the sentence, and both contain essential features of the sentence which are not
reprised. These constituents in fact appear to be fronted, rather than detached. But
if this is the case, how are we to explain the position of those pronominal enclitics
that do not occur in second position either after the left-detached element or the
fronted element? One approach, which has proved illuminating for the placement
of pronominal enclitics in Latin, is to consider the nature of the element that
precedes the enclitic, rather than simply its position. This is the approach taken
by Adams, in research into Latin word order, and his conclusion is worth citing
in full.

> Unemphatic pronouns in Classical Latin prose, far from always being placed
> mechanically in the second position of their colon, are often attracted to
> particular types of hosts, namely antithetical terms, demonstratives / deictics,
> adjectives of quantity and size, intensifiers, negatives, temporal adverbs and
> imperatives. I have suggested that what these hosts have in common is their
> focused character, and have accordingly argued that enclitic pronouns had a
> tendency to gravitate towards focused constituents. The prominent constituent
> serving as a host may be at the head of its colon, in which case the clitic will
> indeed be second, in apparent conformity with Wackernagel's law. But often
> the host is in the second or a later position, thereby entailing a place later
> than second for the pronoun.   (Adams 1994a: 130–1)

We should also include relative and interrogative pronouns in this list of preferential hosts for enclitics. Adams' findings for Latin also appear to apply well to
cases of enclitic pronouns which do not follow WL (or even Hale's modifications
of it) in Vedic Sanskrit. Note the placement of enclitic pronoun *vām* in example
(24), which is unexplainable in terms of 'second position', but can be explained
if we consider the temporal adverb *adyá* 'today' as a preferential host.

(24)   *RV* 1.93.2 (Vedic Sanskrit): *ágnīṣomā yó adyá* **vām** */ idáṃ vácaḥ*
           saparyáti
           Agni-and-Soma-VOC, rel-NOM today you-two- DAT this- ACC speech- ACC
           he-praises
               'Agni and Soma! The one who today hymns you this praise . . .'

In other languages too there is evidence for breaches of WL, and for the placement of pronominal enclitics after items identified by Adams as preferential hosts.
Consider the Greek sentence cited as example (25), which is taken from Krisch
(1990: 71) and used by him to support Hale's arguments:

(25)   *Odyssey* 20. 47–8 (Greek): *autàr egṑ theós eimi, diamperès hḗ se phulássō*
           CONN I-NOM god-NOM am, thoroughly who-NOM you-ACC I-protect
               'But I am a goddess, the one who protects you steadfastly'

Table 6.2 *Position of enclitics in early IE languages.*

	Hittite	Sanskrit / Greek / Latin
Enclitics after left-detached elements?	No enclitics allowed.	Sentence enclitics can stand after left-detached element.
Enclitics delayed after fronted element?	No enclitics allowed later than second position.	Pronominal enclitics may be delayed.

Here the enclitic *se* follows the relative pronoun *hé*, which comes second in the clause after the emphatically placed adverb *diamperés*. The relative here can easily be seen as a preferential host, the focussed element in its clause.

We have shown here that there may be other factors at work in the placement of pronominal enclitics than just working out where second position in the sentence lies. We have also seen that the behaviour of enclitics in Hittite is quite different from that in Sanskrit, Greek and Latin. For the purpose of comparison we have set out the differences in table 6.2.

It is difficult to know whether the model of Hittite or the other early IE languages should be reconstructed for enclitics in PIE. It would be easy to see the more rigid word order of Hittite as a later reanalysis of the placement of enclitics after a 'preferential host', which was also fronted, but it is also possible to explain the situation in Sanskrit, Greek and Latin as the result of reanalysis of left-detached elements belonging to the sentence proper, and thereby leading to patterns where fronted elements are not first in their clause.

6.3   Clause-linking and subordination

The reconstruction of subordination procedures for PIE is a controversial topic, and before considering the particular case of relative clauses, we shall examine some of the assumptions which lie behind much of the research into historical change and the reconstruction of the formation of complex sentences. The first assumption that has dominated research into IE complex constructions since the early nineteenth century is that *hypotaxis*, i.e. subordination procedures, developed from *parataxis*, i.e. juxtaposed, independent clauses. Undoubtedly this assumption is grounded in observations from the history of languages, and the history of English provides a couple of apparently clear-cut examples. Firstly, sentences with relative clauses using a marker 'who' or 'which' can be derived from two juxtaposed clauses, i.e. 'I met the man who married her' has its origin in: 'Who married her? I met the man.' Secondly, complement structures of the type 'I know that he is king' can be derived from separate clauses: 'I know that; he is king.' Since some subordination processes admit explanations of this type, Indo-Europeanists have always been tempted to explain most, if not all, subordination procedures through the amalgamation of loosely connected clauses or sentences into more rigid structures. This approach has been justified by the etymological research into the elements used to mark subordination, which frequently show connections with demonstratives and anaphorics, question words and sentence connectors. Typology has also been used to confirm the reconstruction of a paratactic PIE sentence structure. Lehmann (1980: 124), working on the assumption that PIE was a language of strict OV type, assumes that there was no formal distinction between main clauses and subordinate clauses, and that subordination was marked only through word order, since this is how SOV languages express subordination. A different type of typology is used by Devine and Stephens, who argue that '"flat" i.e. non-configurational languages have a tendency for parataxis' (1999: 148), and that consequently we should not expect to find hypotaxis in early Greek or PIE, which are taken by Devine and Stephens to be non-configurational.

A challenge to the widespread assumption that there was minimal subordination in PIE has come from Harris and Campbell, who argue in their work on historical syntax that it is important to separate out the history of subordination *structures* from the etymology of the *markers* used as subordinators.

> Since subordinators in many languages originate as markers of questions – either yes/no or content questions – it is sometimes assumed that the subordinate clauses they mark must have originated in actual questions. Many languages have subordinators that originated as demonstrative pronouns, and some investigators see this as evidence that those pronouns were 'pointing to' a loosely adjoined clause. Notice that it is by no means necessary to assume that the structure in which a particular innovative grammatical element is found developed out of the structure in which that grammatical element originated. It is logically possible that one *word* simply developed from another, with little reference to context. It is also possible that structural marking that developed in one context was later *extended* to another.   (Harris and Campbell 1995: 284)

They give as an example the development of relative pronouns from old question words in English (of the type 'I met the man who married her' cited above): rather than replacing old paratactic structures, relative pronouns from question words replaced earlier structures where relatives were formed with the marker *ðe*. An example from early IE languages may be the extension of *k^we* from co-ordinating structures to subordinating structures discussed in section 6.1. While the changes involving *k^we* (Sanskrit *ca*) in its move from 'and' to 'if' may at first appear to show that co-ordination was re-evaluated as subordination, in fact this is not the case. As Klein notes (1985: 248), in Vedic Sanskrit the accentuation of the verb 'from the very beginning marked the clause as subordinate'. Hence, we should see the change in *ca* clauses in Sanskrit (and probably in the other IE languages which use a derivative of *k^we* to mark conditional clauses) as examples of the extension of the marker, rather than a change of structure. This fits with the findings of Harris and Campbell, who claim that 'while most languages have parataxis, we have no direct evidence of it developing into hypotaxis'. As we shall see, Harris and Campbell's argumentation provides a particular challenge for Indo-Europeanists.

Relative clauses have been much more widely discussed in the reconstruction of PIE than any other subordination process. The attention they have received corresponds to their widespread attestation in IE languages; even languages which are attested in only very small corpora, such as Phrygian or Gaulish, show clear examples of relative-clause structures. The reconstruction of IE relative pronouns also presents a paradigmatic example of the difficulties of reconstruction. Two separate relative markers can be reconstructed for PIE. Greek, Indo-Iranian, Phrygian, Slavic and Celtic have inherited a stem $*yo$-, but Anatolian, Latin, Sabellian and Tocharian derive their relative pronouns from a stem $*k^wo$-/$*k^wi$-. This distribution cuts across other isoglosses separating the IE languages and does not seem to reflect a 'dialectal' difference of the parent language. In order to explain the divergence, scholars have consequently resorted to one of four different explanations:

a) $*yo$- is the original IE relative pronoun, and $*k^wo$-/$*k^wi$- is an innovation made separately by some languages;

b) $*k^wo$-/$*k^wi$- is the original IE relative pronoun, and $*yo$- is an innovatory form;

c)   PIE did not have relative clauses, and the competing relative clause markers (and others, such as the use of *that* and cognates in Germanic) reflect post-PIE innovations;

d)   PIE had both $*k^wo$-/$*k^wi$- and $*yo$-, but the two pronouns had different functions, corresponding to different relative clause types.

It is difficult to make a choice between these hypotheses *a priori*, although we have already given reasons to question whether hypotactic structures such as relative clauses necessarily arise out of paratactic structures, as option c) suggests, and, as we shall see, some of the syntactic similarities between relative clauses in the daughter languages are extremely close. The pronominal stem $*k^wo$-/$*k^wi$- also functioned in PIE as an indefinite pronoun, whereas $*yo$- had no other reconstructable function. This may suggest that the extension of $*k^wo$-/$*k^wi$- at the expense of $*yo$- is more likely, but the languages which share $*k^wo$-/$*k^wi$- are geographically isolated and share other archaic material (the *r*-endings of the primary endings of the middle – see section 5.4), which has led some to suppose that $*yo$- is the innovation. Option d) is criticised by Klein (1990: 90) on the grounds that it is 'virtually unfalsifiable': 'given the possibility of the generalization of one form or the other in any given dialect, the argument remains forever impervious to the objection that a given dialect (say, Indo-Iranian, Italic or Anatolian) shows only one relative pronoun and gives no evidence of having ever had the other'. This does not mean, however, that it cannot be reconstructed; if all the other options have been dismissed, it must remain a possibility.

The discussion over the differing *markers* of relative clauses has the drawback that it focusses attention away from similarities of *structure* in relative clauses across the IE languages; however, recent work has advanced our knowledge of relative clauses in the early IE languages considerably. A crucial element of the recent work has been the difference between *restrictive* or *defining* relatives and *non-restrictive* (also called *descriptive* or *appositional*) relatives. Restrictive relatives delimit the head of the relative clause, but non-restrictive relatives merely add extra information about their head. Compare the following sentences:

(26)   The tea that I drank was cold.
(27)   The tea, which I eventually drank, was cold.

In (26) the relative defines and restricts the referent, whereas in (27) the relative gives incidental information, and is in effect a separate assertion from that of the main clause. In English, if the relative pronoun is omitted, only a restrictive interpretation is possible. Some English speakers prefer, or are taught, to use *that* as a relative pronoun in restrictive clauses.

In Hittite, restrictive relatives generally precede the matrix clause, and this pattern is also widely found in early Latin and the Indo-Iranian languages, although there the relative clause may also follow the matrix clause. In Vedic Sanskrit, the most common pattern is the order 'relative clause before matrix clause', with the antecedent of the relative, if it is mentioned, within the relative clause, and an anaphoric pronoun ('correlative') picking up the relative in the main clause. The similarities of structure of relatives in some IE languages is shown by examples (28)–(31). All these examples show the relative clause preceding the main clause, with a correlative pronoun at the beginning of the main clause.

(28)   *IBoT* I 13 (Hittite): *nu tarhzi kuis dan pedass=a kuis nu=smas II TUG^{HIA}
         ERÍN^{MES} [p]ianzi*
         CONN wins who-NOM second place=and who-NOM CONN=them-OBL 2
         uniforms they-give
         'Whoever wins and whoever gets second place, to them they give two
         uniforms'
(29)   *AB* 4,7,4 (Sanskrit): *sa yo na ujjeṣyati tasya idam bhaviṣyati*
         CONN who-NOM us-GEN will-win, his this-NOM will-be
         'Whoever of us will win, this will be his'
(30)   IG I Suppl. 492a (Greek): *hos nun orkhēstōn pantōn atalōtata paizdei tō
         tode k[. . .*
         who-NOM now dancers-GEN all-GEN most-sportively plays, his this-NOM
         k[
         'Whoever dances most sportively of all the dancers, this k[. . .] (will be) his'
(31)   Eznik I 45 (Armenian): *or ok' i noc'anê val aṙ is hasc'ê, zna t'agawor
         araric'*
         who-NOM INDEF from them-ABL first to me-ACC will-come, him-ACC
         king-ACC I-will-make
         'Whichever of them comes to me first, I shall make king'

Hittite also has examples of non-restrictive relatives, although these are quite rare and not found in the Old Hittite text corpus at all (Lehmann 1984: 278).

Table 6.3 *Summary of relative clause types in early IE languages.*

Language	Hittite, Latin	Sanskrit, Homeric Greek
Origin of relative pronoun	*k^wo-/*k^wi-	*yo-
Most common type of relative clause in early texts	restrictive	non-restrictive
Most common order respective to matrix clause	relative–matrix	matrix–relative

Where they do appear in later Hittite, they function in a similar way to the appositional material added as an afterthought to the main sentence, as in example (32), taken from the Ullikummi epic, which shows a greater number of postposed relatives.

(32)   *KUB* 33, 98 (Middle Hittite): *nu=za* ^{d}*Kumarbis GALGA-tar ZI-ni kattan*
        daskizzi UD^{KAM}-an kuis LÚ HUL-an sallanuskizzi
        CONN=PTC Kumarbi-NOM wisdom-ACC mind-LOC into he-takes
        day-ACC who-NOM being-ACC evil-ACC he-causes-to-grow
        'Kumarbi takes wisdom into his mind, Kumarbi who brings up the day as
        an evil being'

The Hittite distribution is paralleled in Latin, where in the earliest texts most relative clauses are also restrictive and precede the matrix clause. However, this is not the case in the two other IE branches which are well attested before the Christian era. In Vedic Sanskrit, non-restrictive relatives are more common than in Hittite (they outnumber restrictive relative clauses in the Rg-Veda by a ratio of approximately 4:3), and for non-restrictive relative clauses the order of matrix clause followed by relative clause is over twice as common as the order with relative clause preceding the main clause. In Homeric Greek, appositive relative clauses are also more common, outnumbering restrictive relatives by around 9:5, and they generally follow or are contained within the matrix clause. The details of relative clauses in Latin, Hittite, Sanskrit and Greek are presented in summary form in table 6.3.

The differences between the languages which use the relative marker *yo- and those which use *k^wo-/*k^wi- are striking, although it is important to remember that the early texts in Greek and Sanskrit are poetic, whereas in Old Hittite and early Latin most of our texts belong to a different register: laws, annals, ritual prescriptions, etc., which have a less digressive style than epic poetry or hymns. Since there may be a universal tendency to postpose appositive relatives (see Lehmann 1980 and 1984), the different word-order tendencies observed in the *k^wo-/*k^wi- languages and the *yo- languages may not signify more than the different nature of the evidence. Even so, it is remarkable that the relative constructions in the two sets of languages correspond with earlier attempts to etymologise the relative markers from paratactic structures: $*k^w o$-$/*k^w i$- is the stem for the interrogative pronoun, and has consequently been taken to have originally *restrictive* meaning; $*yo$- is usually linked to the pronominal basis $*ei$-, and has been thought to have originated from an original anaphoric pronoun, suitable for its use as a non-restrictive relative. Should we then conclude that PIE had two separate relative pronouns, and different clause structures for restrictive and non-restrictive relatives? It is often a fault of Indo-Europeanists to over-reconstruct, and to explain every development of the daughter languages through reconstruction of a richer system in the parent language. We should also be wary of equating the origin of the markers of relative clauses with the origin of the structures; markers may be extended to existing structures, and there are documented examples of the extension of, for example, the $*k^w o$-$/*k^w i$- pronoun to structures formerly marked by the $*yo$- pronoun in Middle Iranian languages. However, the reconstruction of two relative pronouns for PIE does fit the attested facts better than any of the other theories on offer.

It has been noted that relative clauses in early Latin, Vedic Sanskrit and Hittite, and, by implication, PIE were adjoined and not embedded (Kiparsky 1995: 155). Relative clauses were positioned on the peripheries of the sentence, in the left-detached or right-detached positions (to use the terminology of section 6.2 above), and items in the relative clauses could be picked up by anaphorics in the main clause: they were consequently not included in the sentence proper. In all the IE languages, relative clauses eventually developed into embedded structures. It would, however, be wrong to see the process of embedding relative clauses as an example of the creation of a new structure. The older IE languages had other devices of clause-combining and clause-embedding using non-finite verb forms. Verbal nouns and adjectives, often associated with particular tense stems and functioning as infinitives and participles, doubtless played a part in subordination in the parent language, as they do for the attested IE languages. We can also reconstruct compounds, some of which have a first member which corresponds to a verbal stem which may have taken on some of the roles of relative clauses, as already noticed by Jacobi (1897: 91).

6.4   Alignment change

Alignment is the term used to describe the ways in which languages group notions of subject and object within case categories. The idea that PIE may not have had the nominative-accusative structure, which is observable at an early stage of the history of every branch of IE, was first put forward by Uhlenbeck in 1901 and is consequently one of the few important topics in IE syntax which was not discussed by Delbrück.

Before presenting the arguments which have been put forward about reconstructed PIE, it will be helpful to give a brief sketch of different patterns of

Table 6.4 *Nominative and ergative alignment systems.*

	A	S	O
Nominative system	nominative	nominative	accusative
Ergative system	ergative	absolutive	absolutive

alignment found cross-linguistically. One of the basic distinctions is between *nominative* systems and *ergative* systems, which make different categorisations between the following three grammatical roles: the subject of a transitive verb (**A**); the subject of an intransitive verb (**S**); and the object of a transitive verb (**O**) (see table 6.4). Nominative systems group subjects together and assign them to the nominative case, ergative systems group undergoers together and assign them to the absolutive case, reserving a special case, the ergative, for the grammatical role of agent.

Uhlenbeck first posited that PIE was an ergative language on the basis of reconstructed case-marking. As we have seen in section 4.2, PIE distinguished between neuter nouns, which have undifferentiated nominative and accusative cases, and non-neuter nouns, which have separately marked nominative and accusative cases, and in most declension classes mark the nominative singular with $*s$, a marker not found in the neuters. The morphological data can be best explained, it is reasoned, if PIE had gone through an ergative stage, in which the ergative case was marked with $*s$. Neuter nouns reflected the class of inanimates, which never functioned as subjects of transitive verbs, only as undergoers. Hence, an IE noun like $*wlk^{w}os$ 'wolf' has different forms for nominative and accusative ($*wlk^{w}om$) because it could function as both a transitive subject in a sentence such as 'the wolf eats the man', and as an intransitive subject or object. A neuter noun such as $*néb^{h}os$ 'cloud' could only have functioned as the subject of an intransitive verb: 'the cloud lifts', or as an object: 'we see the cloud'. At some point in the evolution of IE languages, the ergative system was replaced by a nominative system; for non-neuter nouns the case-marking of the ergative was continued as the case-marking of the nominative, but for neuter nouns, which had never had ergative case-marking, the nominative and the accusative continued the absolutive form (which was equivalent to the bare stem in most declensions).

Uhlenbeck's argument is wonderfully simple, and many scholars have accepted an 'ergative stage' for 'pre-PIE'. However, the argument from the reconstructed nominal case-marking is not on its own convincing. The principal drawback is the misassumption that inanimate nouns never receive ergative case-marking in an ergative system; although inanimate nouns may not be typical agents of transitive verbs, that does not mean that they are never so used, and cross-linguistic studies have shown that if languages use any ergative marking, they are more likely to mark inanimate nouns than animates or pronouns (Dixon 1994: 83f.). Some languages use nominative-accusative marking for pronouns and animate

Table 6.5 *Case-marking in active systems.*

	A	S		O
		Active	Neutral	
Active system	A-case			O-case

nouns, but ergative marking for inanimate nouns alone. Indeed, Hittite is an example of just such a language: inanimate neuter nouns receive a special case-marker (with the suffix *-anza*) when they stand as the subject of a transitive verb. Although this case-marking in Hittite has been seen as a survival of PIE ergativity, it is better explained as an innovation (Garrett 1990), possibly reflecting contact between speakers of Hittite and speakers of non-IE Hurrrian, which is ergative. Typological comparisons also show that the reconstructed PIE nominal system is better in accord with nominative-accusative systems than an ergative system. Just as inanimate nouns are the most likely to receive ergative marking cross-linguistically, in the same way they are least likely to receive accusative marking, since they most typically function as objects. The merger of nominative and accusative in the reconstructed PIE neuter can be viewed as an indication that neuter nouns lacked *accusative* marking. Indeed, in most declension classes this accords well with the morphology, since neuter nouns such as **nébʰos* have no marking in the nominative and accusative. The only problem for this theory is the fact that in one declension class (the thematic) the neuter nominative and accusative *are* marked with **-m*, as in the word for 'yoke' **yugóm*, and this is the same morph which forms the accusative in all other declensions.

More recent attempts to reassess PIE alignment patterns have moved away from the reconstruction of ergative structures and have looked at another type of alignment, named the active system. Languages with active systems split the category of the intransitive subject **S** depending on the nature of the intransitive verb. Verbs which express some notion of control of the action by the subject, termed *active* verbs, are separated from those which do not, termed *neutral*, *stative* or *inactive* verbs, reflecting the fact that they typically describe states rather than events. Agents of active verbs are grouped with agents of transitive verbs, and themes of neutral verbs are grouped with objects of transitive verbs, leading to a pattern as represented in table 6.5 (rather than label the nominal cases found in these languages with 'nominative', 'accusative' or 'ergative' or related terms, we simply refer to them as the *A-case* and *O-case*).

A wide variety of languages show active systems of some sort, and there are important differences between different types. In one type, labelled *split-S* by Dixon (1994), there is a fixed association between a class of nouns which are, or are considered to be, animate and a class of verbs which are transitive or intransitive but active. There is a corresponding association between neutral verbs and a set of inactive nouns. Animate nouns cannot act as the subject of neutral verbs, and inactive ones cannot be the subject of active verbs. Consequently,

Table 6.6 *Active and inactive verbs in PIE.*

Active verb	Neutral verb
$*h_1es$- 'be'	$*b^huh_2$- 'be'
$*ses$- 'lie, sleep'	$*\acute{k}ey$- 'lie'
$*steh_2$- 'stand'	$*h_3er$- 'stand, stand up'

there are some verb doublets, one of which is used for animates, the other for inanimates. Another type of active system, termed *fluid-S*, allows nouns to be marked as active or inactive depending on whether they are viewed as in some way controlling the action of the verb. Most proponents of an active structure for PIE assume a split-S system, but in recent years some scholars have put forward the case for fluid-S alignment (Horrocks 1996, Drinka 1999).

Both typological and morphological arguments have been brought forward in favour of reconstructing an active system for PIE. The typological arguments include claims that some features of reconstructed PIE, such as the lack of a verb for 'to have', are typical of active systems. However, this is hardly a compelling argument, since there are a number of languages without a word for 'have' which do not have an active system, for example Russian. The morphological arguments for an active structure are reached from consideration of the reconstructed verbal paradigms of PIE rather than the nominal paradigms, which provide little support for the theory. As we saw in section 5.4, the personal endings of the PIE verb can be explained from two separate sets, the m-series, which develop into the present and aorist active endings of Greek and Indo-Iranian, and the -*mi* conjugation of Hittite, and the h_2-series, which may lie behind the perfect endings of Greek and Indo-Iranian, the Hittite -*hi* conjugation and the middle endings. These two paradigms are held to reflect the original difference between active and neutral verbs, and we can actually reconstruct active and neutral verb doublets for PIE, which would originally have collocated with active and inactive nouns, as in table 6.6.

Unfortunately, the verb-pairs in table 6.6 do not stand up to scrutiny, since in each case there is a semantic discrepancy between the meanings accorded to the verbs and the meaning obtained through reconstruction. Thus the root $*b^huh_2$- means 'become' in daughter languages, not 'be', $*ses$- probably means 'sleep', not 'lie', and $*h_3er$- means 'rise'. The absence of reliably reconstructed pairs of verbs with active and inactive meaning respectively remains a problem for the reconstruction of a split-S system.

Proponents of a reconstructed fluid-S system base their arguments on the behaviour of the active and middle voice in early PIE languages. As we saw in section 5.4, the opposition between the active and middle distinction does not have any syntactic basis in reconstructed PIE. Some verb-stems can only be reconstructed inflected in the middle voice, such as $*\acute{k}ey$- 'lie', others only in the active voice, such as $*h_1es$- 'be', and a third group can appear in both voices, such as $*b^heh_2$- 'speak'. This fluid marking of voice is reminiscent of fluid-S systems, and Horrocks and Drinka have mused on the possibility that fluid-S marking was a feature of the verb at an early stage of PIE (or even 'pre-PIE'). However, even if the variable marking of the middle is reminiscent of fluid-S systems, that does not mean that the two were once equivalent, and at present there is no theory which describes how an original fluid-S system would have given rise to the PIE verbal system, and what the advantage of such a reconstruction would be.

6.5   PIE phraseology

The reconstruction of syntax sometimes meets with the objection that we do not possess cognate sentences in the same way that we possess cognate lexemes. However, many Indo-Europeanists have argued that it is possible to reconstruct PIE phrases, sentences and even texts, and in this final section of the chapter we shall examine these claims. Before considering what impact the reconstruction of PIE phraseology has had on the reconstruction of syntax, we shall devote some space to the methodology of phrasal reconstruction, reflecting the considerable recent interest in this area.

It has long been recognised that some early IE languages share collocations of which all the constituents are cognate. The most famous and most widely discussed example, and that which was identified first (by Adalbert Kuhn in 1853), is the correspondence between the Greek phrase *kléos áphthiton* (attested at *Iliad* 9.413, and in later poetry, see Floyd (1980)) with Vedic Sanskrit *ákṣiti śrávas* (*RV* 1.40.4b, 8.103.5b, 9.66.7c) and *śrávas . . . ákṣitam* (*RV* I.9.7bc). In both traditions, the phrase means 'imperishable fame', and since the words for 'fame' (Greek *kléos*, Sanskrit *śrávas*) and 'imperishable' (Greek *áphthiton*, Sanskrit *ákṣitam*) are exactly cognate, it appears possible to reconstruct a PIE phrase $*kléwos$ $*n-d^hg^{wh}itom$. Before we can be sure of this reconstruction, however, we must answer two questions: 1) Why should we think this phrase an actual fragment of PIE, rather than the result of a chance similarity in Greek and Vedic Sanskrit? and 2) How could an adjective-noun phrase of this type be transmitted diachronically?

The first question is more difficult to answer, and we shall return to it in detail below. To begin with we shall consider the second question, the answer to which has been provided by work on formulaic composition and oral poetry initiated by Milman Parry (and partly inspired by the Indo-Europeanist Antoine Meillet, see de Lamberterie (1997)). Parry identified Greek epic poetry as oral poetry, reliant on an oral tradition with stock phrase combinations. Parry used the term 'poetic formula' to define expressions 'which are regularly employed under the same metrical considerations to express a given essential idea' (Parry 1971: 270). Much research has been done on the system of formulaic composition in the

Greek epics, and it is clear that some formulae preserve linguistic features that are more archaic than the language of the Mycenaean Greek documents, which were written hundreds of years earlier than the establishment of the written text of the Homeric poems. If formulae can survive in an oral tradition for that long, it is clearly possible that some might survive for longer and perhaps even stretch back to PIE.

Scholars working on the reconstruction of PIE phraseology have been keen to embrace the notion of the formula, but they have made important modifications to the concept as put forward by Parry. The connection of formulae with metre has been largely dropped. There are two reasons for this: firstly, it is clear that there may be considerable modification of metres and metrical structure within the history of a single oral tradition, and we are uncertain what sort of metrical system (if any) can be reconstructed for PIE. Secondly, shared phraseology need not necessarily reflect a shared *poetic* tradition; formulaic utterances might also have been a feature of prayers, charms, rituals, myth and legal or quasi-legal pronouncements. We are therefore left with the formula defined as the fixed expression of an essential idea. This may seem uncontroversial, but different scholars have weighted the parts of this definition differently. For Matasovic, the 'fixed expression' is paramount; any syntagm which can be reconstructed for PIE on the basis of correspondent expressions which appear in 'at least partially correspondent contexts' is by definition a formula (1996: 54). For Watkins, the 'essential idea' is the key element of the equation, and he has repeatedly stressed that formulae should be viewed as surface expressions of an underlying *theme*, i.e. the semantic, cultural or mythical network of ideas that are expressed by a formula (Watkins 1995: 17).

The relationship between the fixed lexical expression and the essential idea is not always straightforward. To illustrate, let us consider the attestations of 'imperishable fame', *kléos áphthiton*, in Greek in a little more detail. In the *Iliad*, the phrase is used at a crucial moment in the poem, when the hero Achilles sets out the choice he has to make:

> For my mother Thetis the goddess of the silver feet tells me
> I carry two sorts of destiny toward the day of my death. Either,
> If I stay here and fight beside the city of the Trojans,
> My return home is gone, but my glory shall be everlasting [*kléos áphthiton*];
> But if I return home to the beloved land of my fathers,
> The excellence of my glory is gone, but there will be a long life
> Left for me, and my end in death will not come to me quickly.
> (*Iliad* 9. 410–16, translation by Richard Lattimore)

If Achilles chooses to have *kléos áphthiton*, the glory will be given to him after his death, and his fame will come from the tales and songs of poets. Elsewhere in early Greek the phrase is used slightly differently. In an early dedicatory inscription from Delphi, the phrase is used by the donor in an address to the gods, in the hope that his gifts might bring him imperishable fame. In a fragment of Pseudo-Hesiod, Zeus 'called her [reference uncertain] Leukothea, so that she might have unfading fame'. In both these passages it appears that the gods are able to grant fame, and that fame is compatible with a long life or prosperity. The Vedic formula is used similarly: mortals request imperishable fame from the gods, together with material benefits. Achilles' use of the formula is innovative, in that it specifically rejects the associations of life and prosperity and a divine origin; it is also syntactically innovative, since the adjective must be read predicatively rather than attributively. It thus appears that the *theme* of a formula may change, even if the words remain the same.

Conversely, the essential idea may remain unchanged, but a lexical element in the formula may be replaced. Thus in Greek one stock epithet of Achilles is *podárkēs*, 'defending with the foot' and hence 'swift-footed' in the formula *podarkḗs dîos Akhilleús* 'swift-footed, divine Achilles'. But if the word *dîos* is not present, the more easily understood (and metrically equivalent) *podṓkēs* 'swift-footed' stands in the same position in the line as *podarkḗs* (Hainsworth 1993: 29). Both of these epithets are still in use in the Homeric poems, but sometimes we can only see the later effects of lexical replacement. For instance, Schmitt (1967: 73f.) argues that the Vedic Sanskrit formula *śrávas pṛthú*, meaning 'broad fame', has replaced earlier **śrávas urú* 'broad fame'. The reconstruction of **śrávas urú* is supported by the existence of a Sanskrit proper name *Uruśravās* and by the fact that there is a cognate Greek phrase *kléos eurú* 'broad fame'.

It is even possible to go one step further and reconstruct a formula from a nexus of correlations, where no single language preserves the complete formula. Watkins reconstructs a PIE formula **peh₂- *wīro- *pek´u-* 'PROTECT MEN (and) LIVESTOCK' from the correspondence of phrases (33)–(36) (1995: 210f.):

(33)   *AV* 8 7.11 (Sanskrit): *trā́yantām asmín grā́me / gā́m áśvam púruṣam paśúm*
        protect-IMPTVE this-LOC village-LOC cow-ACC horse-ACC man-ACC flock-animal-ACC
        'Protect in this village cow, horse, man, and flock-animal'

(34)   *Yt* 13.10 (Avestan): *θrāθrāi pasuuā̊ vīraiiā̊*
        protection-DAT cattle-GEN.DUAL men-GEN.DUAL
        'For the protection of cattle and men'

(35)   Cato *Agr.* 141 (Latin): *pāstōrēs pecuaque salua seruāssīs*
        herdsmen-ACC farm-animals-ACC safe-ACC you-preserve-OPT
        'May you keep safe shepherds and livestock'

(36)   *Tab. Ig.* VIa 42 (Umbrian): *nerf arsmo uiro pequo castruo frif salua seritu*
        magistrates-ACC ordinances-ACC men-ACC cattle-ACC fields-ACC fruit-ACC safe-ACC let-him-preserve
        'May he keep safe the magistrates, ordinances, men, livestock, fields and fruit'

The Umbrian and Avestan phrases agree on the shared inherited vocabulary **wīro- *pek´u-* 'men' and 'livestock', although listed in different orders (Avestan *pasuuå vīraiiå*, Umbrian *uiro pequo*, see further below for discussion of the morphology). In Latin and Sanskrit, the term for 'man' has been replaced by different lexemes, *pāstōrēs* 'shepherds' in Latin and *púruṣa-* 'man' in Sanskrit. More strikingly, the original lexeme for 'protect' *peh_2-* has been replaced in all four languages, in the two languages from Italy by a complex expression 'keep safe', and in Indo-Iranian by the root *trā-*. The underlying theme remains the same, although there may be no surface equivalence in the expression of that theme.

The move from cognate expressions to themes has allowed Watkins and other scholars to find what they see as IE inherited material in a far wider array of languages and texts than was possible in an approach which only accepted etymologically cognate expressions, as exemplified by Schmitt in his 1967 book. When dealing with reconstruction through cognate themes, the question left unanswered at the beginning of this section becomes even more important: why should we think that the similar phrases are survivals of PIE, rather than later, independent developments in the daughter traditions? There are other ways to explain similar themes in different cultures, including borrowings from each other or a third source, or similar metaphors arising from a similar cultural background. Thus a description of a king as 'shepherd of the people', which Watkins classes as 'probably of IE antiquity' (1995: 45), on the basis of attestations in Greek, Sanskrit, Old English and Old Irish, is also widespread across the Ancient Near East (see Haubold (2000)) and could represent a borrowing or result from the fact that all these cultures were familiar with the practice of tending flocks.

One can, of course, construct criteria in order to assess the likelihood of a given phrasal reconstruction (following Matasovic (1996: 89)): it should contain cognate lexical material, not just shared themes, and it should be found as a formula in as wide an array of daughter languages as possible (and ideally would not be found in other traditions). A longer phrase which contains a more unexpected or unusual combination of elements is clearly also less likely to be an independent creation. Some of these criteria may be difficult to assess objectively, especially when dealing with languages with a limited surviving corpus of traditional oral material. Even in Greek, we have barely enough evidence to establish whether *kléos áphthiton* was really a formula. The criterion of unusualness or unexpectedness is particularly difficulty to judge, especially if we follow Matasovic in believing that '[r]econstructed formal elements of texts are more probable if they are typologically plausible'. The reconstructed prayer formula 'protect men and livestock' is certainly plausible, but does that not make it less unexpected, and more liable to be created independently? It is difficult to avoid a degree of subjectivity in textual reconstruction, and the acceptance or rejection of each particular case will probably remain a matter of personal taste.

We shall now consider what light reconstructed phraseology throws upon reconstructed syntax. Phrasal reconstruction is little help when it comes to word-order, as comparison of two reconstructed formulae shows: *$kléwos$ *$n-d^h g^{wh} itom$*

has the order noun – adjective, whereas *még 'h₂ *kléwos 'great fame' (Vedic Sanskrit máhi śrávas, Greek méga kléos, Schmitt (1967: 77f.)), has the reverse order. The comparison of the formulae for 'protect men and livestock' above showed different orders of the verb and its complements in the four languages. The tendency for unusual word-orders in early poetic texts has already been noted (section 6.2), and it seems likely that PIE poetry would have shared this freedom; from formulae alone we would have no idea which orders were marked and which unmarked in PIE.

Formulae may give more information on other matters, however. If we return to the comparison of Avestan *pasuuå̇ vīraiiå̇* (the formula is also attested in cases other than the genitive) with Umbrian *uiro pequo*, we see that in both languages the nouns are juxtaposed without any connecting particle. The omission of a word for 'and' is found in another phrasal parallel between Umbrian and Vedic Sanskrit: Umbrian *dupursus peturpursus* (*Tab. Ig*. VIb 10, 11) 'for two-footed (and) four-footed (creatures)', Vedic Sanskrit *dvípādas cátuṣpādas* 'two-footed (and) four-footed (creatures)'. The conjunction of noun phrases without a word for 'and' is attested in many early PIE languages, and the reconstruction of an original juxtaposition 'men (and) live-stock' is a pleasing confirmation of a suspected PIE syntactic rule. However, the comparison of the Avestan and Umbrian forms may reveal much more: both nouns in Avestan *pasuuå̇ vīraiiå̇* are in the dual, and this is an example of a peculiar construction whereby a pair of closely associated nouns joined asyndetically may both be marked as dual, in a construction similar to the elliptical dual which we met at section 4.3. This process is found also in Sanskrit juxtapositions of the type *Mitrā́-Várunau* Mitra-DUAL-Varuna-DUAL 'Mitra and Varuna'. It is not certain whether this usage is also attested outside Indo-Iranian, and thus whether it is to be reconstructed for PIE, but Wackernagel (1910: 295f. = 1953: 280f.) saw a parallel in the Umbrian formula *uiro pequo*, proposing that both nouns were also in the dual. Unfortunately, the uncertainties of the phonology of Umbrian written in the Latin alphabet leave the question undecided, and we have already noted that the ending of these Umbrian words could be explained as an original neuter plural or collective marker (section 4.3), and this explains the phonological outcome better. As often happens in the study of phrasal reconstruction, we are left without quite enough evidence to convince everyone of the exact correspondence between the Umbrian and Avestan phrases, and we remain uncertain whether to reconstruct asyndetic phrases in the dual in PIE.

In summary, it is fair to say that systematic phrasal comparison of the PIE daughter languages is still very much in its infancy. As our understanding of early IE languages beyond the Classical languages and Sanskrit improves, it is certain that our stock of phrasal reconstructions will increase, and close reading of texts may reveal better contextual correspondences. It is further possible that this will lead to an improvement in our understanding of PIE syntax.

Further reading

The only book-length treatment of IE syntax in English is Lehmann's (1974) work, *Proto-Indo-European Syntax*, which was written in the heyday of the period when word-order typology was seen as the key to understanding syntax. Lehmann has continued the typological approach in subsequent work (see, for example, Lehmann (1993)), principally investigating the syntactic consequences of classing PIE as a language of the 'active type'. A recent book by Brigitte Bauer (2000), somewhat confusingly entitled *Archaic Syntax in Indo-European: The Spread of Transitivity in Latin and French*, is one of the few works to flesh out in detail the consequences of reconstructing PIE as an active-type language, although, as Bauer emphasises, this must have been at a very early stage of PIE (and at an earlier stage than we have felt able to talk about in this chapter). A much better idea of what most Indo-Europeanists think about when reconstructing PIE syntax can be gathered from the papers of the colloquium commemorating the centenary of Delbrück's work on comparative syntax (Crespo and García Ramón 1997).

One of the principal difficulties in reconstructing PIE syntax is the inadequacy, or absence, of existing accounts of the syntax of the older IE languages. Two of the topics we have considered in this chapter, word-order and clause-linking, have benefited from new studies of the phenomena, particularly in Anatolian by Garrett (see Garrett (1992 and 1994)) and Hale (in particular the still-unpublished dissertation (1987a)), and work on the Anatolian languages in particular will doubtless continue to throw up fresh data for new research.

For textual examples and arguments on the status of $*k^we$ as a subordinator, see Eichner (1971) for Hittite, Klein (1985: 238) for Vedic Sanskrit and Hettrich (1988: 250). The comparison with English 'and' and 'an' comes from Klein (1985: 249), and the example of Mingrelian from Harris and Campbell (1995: 280).

For examples of 'right-detachment' in Vedic Sanskrit, Greek and Old Persian, see Gonda (1959). See McCone (1997: 371) for further examples from Hittite. The Icelandic and English examples of left-detachment are taken from van Valin and LaPolla (1997: 35f.). The terminology used to describe fronting and left-detachment varies: Garrett (1994) talks of TOPIC and FRONT, Kiparsky (1995) of TOPIC and FOCUS, and Krisch (1998) of TOPIC$_1$ and TOPIC$_2$. Much has been written about WL in different IE languages: see Krisch (1990), Hale (1987a and 1987b) on Sanskrit, Luraghi (1990b) on Hittite, Adams (1994a and 1994b) on Latin, and Ruijgh (1990) on Greek.

Lehmann (1984) and Hettrich (1988) are fundamental recent works on relatives in PIE; Hettrich (1988: 467–518) gives a very full *Forschungsgeschichte* of the topic. Examples (28), (29) and (30) are taken from Watkins (1976). Garrett (1994) and Probert (2006) both deal with relative sentences in Anatolian: Garrett describes the process whereby relatives move from adjoined to embedded clauses overtime in the Anatolian languages, while Probert argues for the presence of embedded relative clauses in Old Hittite and their later reanalysis as adjoined.

Villar (1984) and Rumsey (1987a and 1987b) discuss the ergative theory for PIE in detail, and Drinka (1999) provides the fullest arguments for an active system, building on earlier work including Gamkrelidze and Ivanov (1984) and Lehmann (1993). Table 6.6 is adapted from Gamkrelidze and Ivanov (1984: 295 and 1995: 256). The arguments against the theory presented here follow Schmidt (1999).

There is also an ever-growing amount of material on PIE phraseology and 'poetic language'; note in particular the publications of Schmitt (1967), Watkins (1995), Matasovic (1996), Costa (1998 and 2000) and Katz (2005). Costa (1998) in reality presents little more than an annotated bibliography of the subject; this can, however, serve as a useful appendage to the careful theoretical argumentation of Matasovic and the excitement and range of Watkins (1995). For details of Greek poetic formulae, and the very archaic nature of some formulae, see Hainsworth (1993: 1–31), West (1988) and Janko (1992: 8–19). The Greek phrase *kléos áphthiton* is discussed by Floyd (1980), Finkelberg (1986) and Nagy (1990: 122f.).

Discussion points

1.   What elements of PIE syntax are likely to be irrecoverable?
2.   How far is reconstructed syntax dependent on the reconstruction of morphology?
3.   How important are typological considerations of syntactic features and syntactic change for PIE reconstruction?
4.   Many of the reconstructed formulaic phrases of PIE, such as *$kléwos$ *$n\text{-}d^h g^{wh} itom$, are concerned with 'fame'. Why should this be so?

7 Lexicon and lexical semantics

7.1 The PIE lexicon

Comparative reconstruction begins with the comparison of lexical items across different languages, but most works on IE operate largely on the basis of *roots* and *affixes* rather than *lexemes*. The standard etymological dictionaries of IE (see Pokorny (1959), Rix *et al.* (1998) and Watkins (2000)) present the IE lexicon as a collection of roots, each of which has limited semantic scope and from which a number of derived stems can be formed. For example, the correspondence between Latin *agō* 'I drive, lead' and Greek *ágō* 'I lead' and Sanskrit *ájāmi* 'I drive' is listed under a root *$h_2eg´$- (or *$ag´$-) rather than as a separate lexical entry, and a unified meaning is given for the root as a whole. Listed in the same dictionary entry one may find nominal derivations such as *$h_2eg´$-mn, which is the hypothetical ancestor of Latin *agmen* 'procession, military column' and Sanskrit *ájman-* 'course, procession', or the adjectival form *$h_2(e)g´$-to-, continued as the Latin participle *āctus* 'driven' and found in the Celtic compound *ambactos* 'servant'. Furthermore, the word-equation of Latin *ager* 'field', Greek *agrós* 'field', Gothic *akrs* 'field' and Sanskrit *ájras* 'plain' is given by Pokorny and Watkins as a derivative of the same root, on the supposition that the original root was connected with animal herding, and *$h_2eg´$-ro- designated the space into which animals were driven.

The etymological dictionaries consequently structure the reconstructed PIE lexicon in a different way from how the attested IE vocabularies are normally viewed. In English, Russian, Latin, Greek and other languages, the lexicon comprises a large number of lexical bases, with some productive procedures of derivation, some semi-productive and some fossilised forms that can scarcely be related synchronically to etymologically related forms. Thus few speakers of English are aware of any connection between *loud* and *listen*, both of which derive from the PIE root *$k´lew(s)$- 'hear', and few speakers of Russian are aware of the derivational relationship between *slovo* 'word' and *slyšat'* 'hear' (both from *$k´lew(s)$- again). The PIE lexicon is thus represented as an 'ideal' system, where all the derivational procedures are capable of combining with all the lexical bases. In such a system every lexeme is a *potential* formation, but it is difficult to ascertain which reconstructed lexemes were *established* formations. Some scholars

have accordingly argued that for IE we are able to reconstruct few lexemes, and
that the reconstructed root should be seen as the basic unit of the lexicon. This
doctrine is expressed in an extreme form by Schlerath, in discussing the reconstruction of the word for 'fame' from the correspondence of terms in Greek and
Sanskrit (Schlerath 1987: 44). He argues that the comparison of Greek *kléos*
'fame' and Sanskrit *śrávas-* 'fame' allows the Indo-Europeanist to reconstruct
only a root *kʹlew-*, a nominal suffix *-e/os-*, and a rule that enables the formation
of a nominal stem *kʹlewes-*. He sees independent confirmation in the existence
of a PIE form *kʹlewes-* 'fame' from the correspondence of formulae meaning
'imperishable fame' in the Greek and Indo-Iranian poetic traditions (see section 6.5), but normally we do not have that extra evidence, and we do not know
whether the reconstruction of the actual lexeme is justified. Without any support
from other information, Schlerath argues, we cannot be sure that a potential form
actually occurred at any time before it surfaces in one or more of the daughter
languages.

Schlerath sees the reconstruction of individual words as subordinate to systematic correspondences of word-formation and the lexical root. We note further that
the reconstructed meaning of the word *kʹlewes-* cannot simply be 'fame', as the
same form is continued in Russian *slovo* 'word' and Avestan *sravah-* 'word'. If
we reconstruct 'fame' as the PIE meaning, we then have to explain two apparently
independent semantic shifts from 'fame' to 'word', and consequently 'that which
is heard' is preferable as the hypothetical original meaning. Other *s*-stem nouns
reconstructed in PIE also form verbal abstracts with similar semantics. Compare
gʹenh₁-es- 'that which is born', formed from the root *gʹenh₁-* 'give birth to',
and reconstructed from the following correspondence:

gʹenh₁-es- 'that which is born': Sanskrit *janas-* 'race', Greek *génos* 'race, kin',
    Latin *genus* 'family, offspring'

The case of *kʹlewes-* can be compared to the reconstruction of *$h₂eg$ʹ-mn-*
mentioned above. In the case of *$h₂eg$ʹ-mn-*, we have no evidence for a formation
in PIE, beyond the parallel of Latin *agmen* 'procession, military column' and
Sanskrit *ájman-* 'course, procession'. This lexeme is clearly a *potential* reconstruction for IE, in the same way that a form such as *Schlerathian* is a potential
lexeme of English. Since the suffix *-men-* continued to be productive both in
Sanskrit and in the early history of Latin, we cannot be certain that the two words
were not created separately in the two languages, despite the apparent overlap in
their meanings.

Not all reconstructed lexemes can be split so easily into root and suffix. At
section 3.1 we discussed the case of the kinship terms *ph₂ter-* 'father', *meh₂ter-*
'mother', *bʰreh₂ter-* 'brother', *dʰugh₂ter-* 'daughter' and *yenh₂ter-* 'husband's
brother's wife', and there we argued that these lexemes could not easily be seg-
mented into root and suffix, although their morphological behaviour was in line
with other lexical items which were formed from the combination of a root and

suffix. It is possible to add further reconstructed nominal lexemes to this list, for example *$g^{'h}esor$- 'hand', or *$g^{h}osti$- 'guest':

*$g^{'h}esor$- 'hand': Hittite *kessar*, Greek *kheír*, Tocharian A *tsar*, Armenian *jer̄n*
*$g^{h}osti$- 'guest': Latin *hostis*, Gothic *gasts*, Old Church Slavonic *gostĭ*

There is always room for speculation: the word for 'hand' may derive from a root meaning 'grasp' (see the etymological attempt by Rix (1991)), although in this case the derivational process involved is obscure. The word for 'guest' may derive from the root meaning 'eat' found in Indo-Iranian (Sanskrit *ághas* 'he ate'), with some particular semantic change.

For other reconstructed items, such as *$h_2eg\,'ro$- 'field' or 'plain' discussed above, it may be impossible to say with certainty what the original meaning of a word was. A striking example is the reconstructed term *$h_2ek\,'-mn$-:

*$h_2ek\,'-mon$-: Sanskrit *áśman*- 'stone, thunderbolt', Avestan *asman*- 'stone, heaven', Old Persian *asman*- 'heaven', Greek *ákmōn* 'anvil, thunderbolt', Lithuanian *akmuõ* 'stone', *ašmuõ* 'knife-edge'

The meanings in all the daughter languages can be related: the sense 'heaven' arises from a belief that the vault of heaven was made of stone, and a thunderbolt is a stone fragment which falls from heaven; the sense of 'knife-edge' may relate to the original use of stone tools and ties in with the normal derivation of the word from an adjectival root *$h_2ek\,'$- 'sharp'. However, we cannot be certain which of these meanings is to be reconstructed for PIE, nor do we know how 'heaven' was conceptualised by PIE speakers. The semantics of *$h_2eg\,'ro$- and *$h_2ek\,'mon$- are so unusual that they cannot be taken as potential PIE forms which are only realised after the PIE period. They must have existed as separate lexemes, even if we cannot ascribe a coherent single meaning to them.

We have therefore arrived at a picture of the PIE lexicon which contains both *established* and *potential* lexemes in the same way that attested languages do. Established lexemes are those of the type of *$k\,'lew-es$- 'that which is heard', *ph_2ter- 'father', *$g\,'hesor$- 'hand' and *$h_2ek\,'mon$- 'stone (?)', and *potential* those of the type of *$h_2eg\,'men$-. The difference between a reconstructed lexicon and the lexicon of a language such as English is one of degree: the number of established lexemes is small for PIE, but huge for English. The discrepancy between PIE and English is particularly large, since English is still spoken and has a very well-documented lexicon. If we were to compare PIE with a less well-documented corpus language, such as Avestan or Gothic, the difference would not be so great, since in these languages the corpus is relatively restricted and the number of established lexemes much smaller. The large number of potential PIE lexemes leads to a number of difficulties when discussing the reconstructed lexicon, and we shall look at a few of these, firstly concentrating on the problems for the linguist, and then the problems for the cultural historian.

7.2   Derivation

Etymological dictionaries of PIE usually operate with lexical roots from which derivations are formed through affixation, so that *$kʹlewes$- 'that which is heard' is derived from a root *$kʹlew$- 'hear', and an affix *-e/os-, and *$h_2ekʹ$-mon- 'stone' is derived from a root *$h_2ekʹ$- 'sharp' and an affix *-mon-. However, we cannot be sure that derivation operated in this way in PIE. It is possible that derivation operated from lexeme to lexeme, rather than from root and affix, and our rules for deriving affixed forms from roots may be a construct of the comparative process. We rely on roots as the base of derivation since we can reconstruct roots with more confidence than we can reconstruct individual lexemes. Roots may be shared across many languages, while a particular lexical formation is only found in a small number of languages. Table 7.1 illustrates this fact for the roots *$kʹlew$- 'hear' and *$h_2ekʹ$- 'sharp'. We can find cognate material for these roots in nearly all the branches of IE, but no derived form is found in all the languages which preserve the root.

However, there is evidence to suggest that in PIE derivation did not operate through affixation direct to a root. In section 4.2, we saw how the different IE words for 'sleep' – Sanksrit *svápna*-, Greek *húpnos*, Latin *somnus*, etc. – could be explained as secondary derivatives from an r/n-stem noun, rather than as direct formations from a PIE root. In section 5.5, we saw that the causative *$dʰebʰ$-ne-u- 'makes small' can be derived from the adjective *$dʰebʰ$-u- 'small'. Given that all of the IE languages also show derivation of lexemes from lexemes, it seems likely that this process of derivation was also operative in PIE. Of course, in some cases, the root may also have been a lexeme, and thus give the impression that derivatives are formed from the root, whereas in fact they are formed from a verbal or nominal form which consisted of the root and desinences with no suffixation. For example, the suffixed forms *$kʹlnew$- 'hear', *$kʹlewes$- 'that which is heard' and *$kʹluto$- 'heard' listed in table 7.1 are all best explained as formations from the root aorist *$kʹlew$- meaning 'hear'.

Some scholars also see processes of morphological derivation of new lexemes from inflected word-forms in PIE. One of the best examples of this supposed derivation pattern is a reconstructed word for 'human', *$dʰgʰ(e)m$-on- reconstructed from the following comparison (for the reconstruction of the initial cluster *$dʰgʰ$-, see section 2.2):

*$dʰgʰ(e)m$-on- 'human': Latin *homō*, Gothic *guma*, Lithuanian *žmuõ*

This reconstructed item is generally seen as derivative of the word for 'earth', *$dʰgʰom$-, discussed at section 2.2, and the comparative evidence for which we repeat below:

*$dʰgʰom$- 'earth': Hittite *tekan*, Sanskrit *kṣám*-, Greek *khthṓn*, Lithuanian *žḗmė*, Old Irish *dú*, Tocharian A *tkaṃ*

It would, of course, be possible to reconstruct a suffix *-on- to explain the derivation of this word, but, as Nussbaum points out (1986: 187), there is little comparative evidence for such a suffix with the required meaning. Nussbaum proposes instead that *$d^hg^h(e)m$-on- is derived from an original PIE locative of the noun for 'earth', *d^hg^hm-én, which is directly attested in Sanskrit *jmán* 'on the earth'. The noun *$d^hg^h(e)m$-on- would originally have meant '[a thing] on the earth', hence 'human'. Note that in order to get from the locative *d^hg^hm-én to the noun *$d^hg^h(e)m$-on-, one must assume a change in vocalism and accent. We have already met word-formation processes of this type in section 3.4, called *internal derivation*, involving a change in accent and ablaut but no overt suffixation.

Attempting to reconstruct the derivational chains which operated within PIE is a hazardous business, since we have lost so much of the material which may have been pivotal in new formations. For the word for 'sleep' and the causative 'make small' cited above, we are lucky to have the intermediary steps surviving. The original r/n-stem word for 'sleep' only just survives in Latin and Greek, and lies behind a derived verb in Hittite. The adjective *d^heb^h-u- 'small' only survives in Hittite; in Sanskrit the cognate adjective, *dabhrá-*, has a different suffix, *-ro-. Without these forms, our reconstruction of the derivational process would remain speculative and would rely on hypothesising what derivations were possible in PIE and which were not. The formations from the root *h_2ek´- given in table 7.1 provide an example of an extreme variety of different formations, many of which share similar meanings, where the derivational patterns are largely unclear. It may be possible to see the nominal stem *h_2e/ok´-ri- as a derivative of the adjective *h_2ek´-ro-, but beyond that it is difficult to find any order among the different attested formations, or even assign distinctive semantics to individual suffixed forms. Despite these difficulties, derivational morphology is one of the largest current sub-fields in IE studies.

7.3   PIE lexical semantics

The nature of the PIE lexicon has meant that semantic reconstruction has traditionally been centred around the meaning of PIE roots, rather than individual lexemes. Etymological dictionaries of PIE tend to assign meanings at the level of the root, and, in works such as Pokorny (1959), these meanings are arrived at either through abstraction or accumulation of the semantic features which apply to the derivations. This procedure for semantic reconstruction was criticised by Benveniste in a number of publications (see especially Benveniste (1954, 1969a and 1969b)). Benveniste proposed a different methodology for reconstructing the meaning of roots, emphasising the need for detailed examination of their derivatives in their textual and social context.

Table 7.1a *Derivatives of the root* *ḱlew-* *'hear'*.

PIE	Anatolian	Indo-Iranian (Sanskrit)	Greek	Latin	Germanic (Old English)	Slavic (Russian)	Celtic (Old Irish)	Armenian	Baltic (Lithuanian)	Tocharian (Tocharian B)	Albanian
*ḱlew- 'hear'											
*ḱlnew- present stem		śṛṇóti					ro-cluinethar	kalnem			
*ḱlu-sḱ'e- present stem											quhet
*ḱlews- present stem		śroṣ-				slyšat'			kláusiu	kljausām	
*ḱlewes- 'that which is heard' stem		śrávas-	kléos			slovo	clu			kälywe	
*ḱluto- 'heard'		śrutá-	klutós	inclutus	hlūd		cloth	lu			

Table 7.1b *Derivatives of the root* $*h_2e\acute{k}$- '*sharp*'.

PIE	Anatolian	Indo-Iranian (Sanskrit)	Greek	Latin	Germanic	Slavic	Celtic (Old Irish)	Armenian	Baltic	Tocharian	Albanian
$*h_2e\acute{k}$- 'sharp'											
$*h_2e\acute{k}$-ro-		áśri-	ákros	acer			ér				
$*h_2e/o\acute{k}$-ri-			ákris ócris	ocris							
$*h_2e\acute{k}$-on-		áśani-	ákōn		Gothic ahana						
$*h_2e\acute{k}$-u-				acus					Latvian ass		
$*h_2e\acute{k}$-u-r/n-	hekur										
$*h_2e\acute{k}$-i-			akís	aciēs	Old Saxon eggja						
$*h_2e\acute{k}$-i-l-						osla		asełn			
$*h_2e\acute{k}$-mon-		áśman-	ákmōn						Lithuanian akmuõ		

Table 7.2 *Selected derivatives of the root* *med-.

	Avestan	Greek	Latin	Umbrian	Gothic	Old Irish
Verbs derived from *med-		*médomai* 'provide for, plan' *mẽdomai* 'resolve'	*meditor* 'think' *medeor* 'cure'		*mitan* 'measure'	*midiur* 'judge'
Nouns derived from *med-	*vi-mad-* 'doctor'	*mẽdea* 'plans'	*modus* 'measure' *medicus* 'doctor'	*mers* 'law'		*mess* 'judgement'

For example, table 7.2 gives some of the derivatives in different IE languages of the root *med-. In Pokorny's dictionary, the meaning of this root is glossed as 'messen, ermessen', 'measure, assess' (Pokorny 1959: 705). By contrast, Benveniste proposed that the individual lexical items could all be explained by the covering idea of 'considered judgement of a figure in authority' (Benveniste 1969b: 123–32). The use of the root in the field of medicine, shown by the nominal derivatives meaning 'doctor' in Iranian and Latin, and the meaning 'law' in Umbrian (with related meanings in other Sabellian languages), were taken by Benveniste not to be parallel semantic extensions made in individual languages. Instead, they showed the continued presence of an underlying prototypical meaning of the root during the creation of language-specific derivatives.

Benveniste's approach to semantic reconstruction may seem far-fetched, almost mystical, but gains some credibility if we think in terms of a root-verb being at the base of most of the derivatives. There is other evidence which shows that there was a close semantic link between verbs and derived nouns in early IE languages. Firstly, there was widespread use of a trope known as *figura etymologica*, whereby two derived forms of the same root occur in the same phrase, as in example (1):

(1) Cato *Agr.* 139 (Latin): *bonās precēs precārī*
   good-ACC.PL prayers-ACC.PL to-pray
   'To pray good prayers'

In this example, the noun *precēs* and the verb *precārī* share the same root. In oral formulae of early Sanskrit there is a similar interplay between verb and derivatives. Watkins summarises this procedure: 'It is characteristic that the same root may appear in different semantic slots, with the appropriate derivational and inflexional morphology, as subject, verb, object, instrument' (Watkins 1995: 302). He illustrates the point with examples (2) and (3):

(2) *RV* 1.32.5b (Sanskrit): *áhan . . . vadhéna* 'he slew . . . with a weapon'
(3) *RV* 1.33.4a (Sanskrit): *vádhīs . . . ghanéna* 'you slew . . . with a weapon'.

The meaning of the two phrases is the same. In (2), a derivative of the root meaning 'slay', $*g^{wh}en$-, acts as the verb, and a derivative of the root $*wed^hh_1$-'strike' functions as the instrument; in (3), the verb derives from $*wed^hh_1$-, and the word for 'weapon' is formed from $*g^{wh}en$-.

The Benvenistean approach allows for considerable scope in lexical reconstruction. If we understand derived forms to relate back to the prototypical sense of a verb formed from a PIE root, we can link together diverse forms which share only the root and which can be derived from the same original meaning. Etymology of this sort, sometimes termed 'root etymology', still forms a large part of the study of IE, and offers researchers a chance to display ingenuity as well as learning. Attested examples of semantic change give parallels for all sorts of widening, narrowing or transfer of meaning. In the absence of specific contexts there is room for considerable hypothetical shifts and connection of words of very diverse meaning. To take just one example, Katz has recently argued that the Latin and Greek words for 'evening' should be related to a Hittite word for 'clothes (of the dead)' and a Greek word meaning 'pulse' or 'chickpea' (Katz 2000):

$*wesp$-: Hittite *waspa*- 'clothes (of the dead)', Latin *uespillō* 'undertaker'
$*wesper$-: Greek *hésperos* 'evening', Latin *uesper* 'evening'
$*wosp$-ro-: Greek *óspros* 'pulse'

All the words share a root $*wesp$- and can be linked together by derivational processes paralleled elsewhere. Katz explains the semantics through assuming an original meaning 'clothe' or 'shroud' and seeing the derived forms as semantic extensions: a pulse is a bean with a coating, the evening could have been referred to using a metaphor of 'the shroud of night'. Etymology of this sort leads to the reconstruction of a number of roots whose status is uncertain: it is possible that the etymological connection is right, and that a PIE formation does lie behind the various forms; but it is also possible, given the wide divergence in meaning of the terms in daughter languages, that the phonetic match between terms is entirely fortuitous, and that the reconstructed root is in fact a mirage.

The existence of so many potential, and so few established, reconstructed lexemes causes difficulties for research into the semantic structure of the PIE lexicon. It is largely impossible to discern where the boundaries between the meaning of one reconstructed root or lexeme and another lie, since we are so unsure about how much can be securely reconstructed. Despite these severe limitations, studies such as those of Benveniste have increased our knowledge of some parts of the PIE lexicon and shown how close examination of the contexts and uses of well-attested lexical fields in a range of languages can give some insight into the PIE vocabulary. In the following section we shall examine some specific lexical fields within PIE, in order to see whether it is possible to delimit hierarchies of meaning or structured semantics in any more detail.

7.4   Reconstructed lexical fields

Lexical change and replacement mean that we have large gaps in our knowledge about some areas of PIE vocabulary. For example, we know very little about PIE terms for different articles of clothing or footwear, although we can securely reconstruct verbs with the meanings 'wear (clothes)' and 'put on (shoes)'. Mallory and Adams (1997) list seven different reconstructed items under the lemma 'clothing' in their dictionary of PIE culture, but most of these are far from certain and show themselves to be post-PIE loanwords by their restricted geographical range. Our ignorance of PIE clothing terms reflects little more than the fact that the vocabulary of dress is frequently subject to changes, and that speakers of IE languages adopted clothes suitable to the diverse regions that they inhabited. In other lexical fields there may be individual gaps. Thus, as noticed by Benveniste (1969a: 239), although there are terms denoting relations by marriage, there is no reconstructable term for 'marriage', or even for 'husband' or 'wife'. In these cases, we are fortunate in recognising conceptual 'slots' in the vocabulary for which we have no separate reconstructed terms, and we can debate how these slots were filled: was there, for example, a lexeme with the sense 'husband' which is now lost, or was a word for 'man' also used in the sense of 'husband', as is the case in the majority of IE languages?

More often we do not know whether the absence of a reconstructed term means that the concept itself did not exist. We cannot reconstruct PIE terms for 'read' or 'write', but since the speakers of PIE constituted a pre-literate society, we can be sure that our lexical gap coincides with a conceptual gap. But we also cannot reconstruct a term for 'promise' or 'vow'. Does this mean that there was no concept of promising or vowing in PIE? Wachter (1998) has argued that we should reconstruct a conceptual framework for PIE alongside our reconstruction of lexical items, and that where a concept, such as promising, exists in all the daughter languages, it can be reconstructed for the parent language. This positivist approach is also followed in Mallory and Adams (1997), but must be viewed with caution, since it is clear that cultural practices can be diffused across wide areas in history and prehistory. For instance, even though the practice of writing and reading is a post-PIE development, words for denoting these activities have entered all the IE languages.

Our reconstruction of the PIE lexicon will consequently work best in areas where we can minimise the problem of gaps and explore fully the oppositions of meaning between reconstructed terms. With this in mind, we shall look at vocabulary in relatively discrete, bounded semantic fields. No semantic field is completely bounded, of course, and the overlap between different areas of the lexicon can cause considerable problems. Take, for example, the vocabulary of colour terms, long used as a paradigmatic case of a lexical field in works on semantics. For PIE it is difficult to reconstruct this as a bounded set: we can reconstruct three roots which have meanings 'red', 'white' and 'green/yellow', but only for the first does the meaning seem to be limited to colour:

*h_1reud^h- 'red': Sanskrit *rudhirá-*, Greek *eruthrós*, Latin *ruber*, Old Irish *rúad*, Old English *reod*, Lithuanian *raũdas*, Old Church Slavonic *rudŭ*, Tocharian B *rätre*

*h_2erg'- 'white': Hittite *harki-* 'white', Sanskrit *árjuna-* 'silver', Greek *árguron* 'silver', Latin *argentum* 'silver', Tocharian A *ārki* 'white'

*g'^helh_3- 'green/yellow': Sanskrit *hari-* 'green/yellow', Greek *khlōrós* 'green/yellow', Latin *heluus* 'yellow', Welsh *gell* 'yellow', Old High German *gelo* 'yellow', Old Church Slavonic *zelenŭ* 'green', Lithuanian *žel˜vas* 'green'

The root *h_2erg'- also refers to flashing brightness as well as colour: note the derivatives Sanskrit *arjrá-* 'bright, quick' and Greek *argós* 'quick'. The root *g'^helh_3- may originally have been restricted to denoting organic material, as indicated by the existence of the verb *žélti* 'to grow' in Lithuanian, which continues the same root. In a lexical field such as colour, there is no way of knowing for certain the direction of semantic change in these two roots, whether from 'white' to 'bright', and 'green' to 'grow', or vice versa, and we cannot be sure that they all originally belonged in the same lexical field. We shall look in more detail at the lexicon in three other fields which stand a better chance of being bounded: numerals, kinship terms and the taxonomy of animals.

Numerals

Numerals lie on the boundary between closed-class and open-class items in the lexicon. Lower numerals usually have fixed expressions, but there may be more variation in the formation of higher numbers. In table 7.3, we give the numerals 'one' to 'ten', 'twenty', 'fifty' and 'hundred' in five IE languages and the putative PIE reconstructions (in cases where the numerals decline we give the masculine forms only).

As can be seen from table 7.3, the Anatolian terms for cardinal numbers are only scantily attested, since texts generally use ideograms to represent numbers, and there is uncertainty over the meaning of the Lycian terms given – *aitãta* may mean 'eight' or 'eighty'. One of the few Anatolian terms we do have, the word for 'four', does not match the terms in the other languages or that reconstructed for PIE. The reasons behind this rather worrying divergence are not known.

There is a gap in the table for the reconstruction of the word for 'one', since there is no common agreement across the IE languages. Besides a root-formation *sem-* / *sm-* in Greek, Tocharian and Armenian, we also find suffixed forms of a different root: *oi-no-* in Latin, Germanic, Celtic, Baltic and Slavic, *oi-wo-* in Iranian and *oi-ko-* in Indic. In some languages both terms are found, for example,

Table 7.3 *IE numerals.*

	PIE	Anatolian (Hittite unmarked)	Sanskrit	Greek	Latin	Lithuanian
1			*ékas*	*heís*	*ūnus*	*víenas*
2	*duó-*	Luwian *tuwa/iza*	*dváu*	*dúo*	*duo*	*dù*
3	*tréy-*	*teri-*	*tráyas*	*treîs*	*trēs*	*trŷs*
4	*kʷétwor-*	*meiu-*	*catvā́ras*	*téssares*	*quattuor*	*keturì*
5	*pénkʷe*		*páñca*	*pénte*	*quīnque*	*penkì*
6	*swéks*		*ṣáṭ*	*héx*	*sex*	*šešì*
7	*septḿ̥*		*saptá*	*heptá*	*septem*	*septynì*
8	*okʹtṓ* (*h₃ekʹtéh₃*)	Lycian *aitãta*	*aṣṭáu*	*oktṓ*	*octō*	*aštuonì*
9	*néwn*	Lycian *nuñtãta*	*náva*	*ennéa*	*nouem*	*devynì*
10	*dékʹm̥*		*dáśa*	*déka*	*decem*	*dẽšimt*
20	*wīkʹmtī*		*viṁśatí-*	*eíkosi* (*wīkati*)	*uīgintī*	*dvì-dešimt*
50	*penkʷḗ-kʹomth₂*		*pancāśát*	*penté-konta*	*quīnquā-gintā*	*peñkiasdešimt-*
100	*kʹm̥tóm*		*śatám*	*hekatón*	*centum*	*šiṁtas*

in Greek *oino-* is continued as a rare word for an ace on a die *oínē*. The best explanation for this situation is that there was no word corresponding to English 'one' in PIE. Indeed, the numerical systems of some IE languages do without a word for 'one': for example, in Old Irish, *oen* 'one' (< *oino-*) is not required in numerical expressions. Old Irish *bó* can mean 'a cow' or 'one cow', and 'twenty-one cows' would be expressed as *bó ar fichit* 'cow plus twenty'. Where the numeral *oen ar fichit* 'one plus twenty' occurs, *oen* is in fact functioning as a replacing pronoun, rather than an actual number. As Gamkrelidze and Ivanov (1995: 742) remark, '[c]ounting or enumeration of objects begins with two or more'.

Table 7.3 does not include numbers between eleven and nineteen, or between twenty-one and twenty-nine, since these are formed from combinations of other numbers in the daughter languages. Numbers can be combined in different ways, most usually addition (Greek *hekkaídeka* 'six and ten' for 'sixteen'), subtraction (Latin *undeuīgintī* 'twenty less one' for 'nineteen'), or multiplication (Welsh *deunaw* 'two nines' for 'eighteen'), and in several languages there my be more than one possible way to arrive at a particular number. Given this variety in the construction of higher numbers, it is possible that there was no single method of formation, and reconstruction is in vain.

Table 7.4 *PIE formation of decads.*

Paradigm of PIE 'decad'	Formation of higher numbers
$*d(e)k'omt$- 'decad'*	
nominative dual *$*dk'mt$ -ih$_1$*	*$*dwi$-dk'mt -ih$_1$* 'pair of decads' > *$*wīk'mtī$*
nominative plural *$*dk'omt$-h$_2$*	*$*penk^we$ *dk'omth$_2$* 'five decads' > *$*penk^w ē$-k'omth$_2$*
genitive plural *$*dk'mt$-om*	*$*dk'mt$-om* '(group) of decads' > *$*k'mt$-om*

The forms given in table 7.3 for the reconstructed decads are arrived at by comparative reconstruction of the attested forms. However, if we compare the words for 'ten', 'twenty', 'fifty' and 'hundred', it is possible to refine our reconstructions to make the system more consistent. All of the forms can be related to a skeleton *$*dk'mt$-*, which may have been a derived form of *$*dek'm$* 'ten' with the meaning 'decad' (the original meaning survives in the Sanskrit word *daśát-* 'decad'). As shown in table 7.4, it is possible to build the numbers 'twenty' and 'fifty' through the reconstruction of original collocations, such as 'a pair of decads', with subsequent assimilation of consonant clusters and compensatory lengthening. The most questionable aspect of this reconstruction is the supposition of a genitive plural *$*dk'mtóm$* meaning 'a group of decads', and by extension 'ten decads, a hundred'. However, in some Germanic languages the outcome of PIE *$*k'mt$-om* does not mean 'hundred' but 'hundred and twenty', as Old Norse *hundrað*. This suggests that the fixing of the meaning of *$*k'mt$-om* may in fact have been late. Table 7.4 offers a neat and systematic picture of the formation of decads, but this should be viewed with some caution: there are still problems with explaining the formation of other decads, particularly those between sixty and a hundred.

The presence of a sub-system of decads within the PIE numerals has led scholars to look for other sub-systems. In the past two hundred years there have been many attempts to link the names of the numbers with other areas of the lexicon, seeing connections between 'five' and 'fist', for example, or 'nine' and 'new'. These etymologies seem less outlandish when one compares other counting systems in natural languages, where systems are based upon body-parts or a combination of smaller units. For example, many languages in Papua New Guinea use a body-part to express a numeral, and some Californian languages use a base of three to express 'six' and 'nine', while others express 'eight' as 'two fours' (Comrie (1999) gives examples). The problem with the attempts to find etymologies for the PIE numerals is that scholars have usually concentrated on individual numbers rather than looking at the system as a whole, and once one collects together the etymologies, 'in most cases we have to accept that the Indo-Europeans amused themselves by inventing a numeral system with no consistency at all' (Luján Martínez 1999: 203). The lack of consistency is problematic for most etymological accounts of the PIE numerals. If we think that 'five' originally meant 'fist', for example, we must explain why other numbers cannot also be obviously connected to a system of finger-counting. Whatever the ultimate origins of the names of the numbers, in the absence of any additional information we can only conclude that at the stage of PIE which we can reconstruct with the comparative method, the names of the numerals had no further significance.

Kinship terms

Kinship terms are a less tightly bounded group than numerals, but they offer a rich array of comparative terms preserved in several separate traditions. Since the reconstruction of kinship terms promises some insight into prehistoric social structure, it has attracted a number of independent studies, and we shall review the arguments over the reconstruction of individual items and the whole system. Table 7.5a gives an array of different kinship terms (and possible reconstructions) in most of the major IE branches. We shall not discuss here attempts to find etymological connections for the PIE kinship terms (see the discussion at section 3.1). Where there are gaps in the table, this is either because the evidence for the specific term is lacking (this is the case for most of the kinship terms in Anatolian), or the term is attested, but is formed by combining other elements, so that 'nephew', for example, is expressed as 'sister's son' or 'brother's son'. In order to make the table more comprehensible we have given terms in **bold** where they can be related to the reconstructed IE form. In general, kinship terms are well preserved, except in Anatolian, where the terms found elsewhere for 'father', 'mother', 'brother' and 'sister' do not occur. Loss of some members of the set is not unusual: Greek has replaced inherited terms for 'brother' and 'sister', and Latin for 'daughter' and 'son', but the extent of the apparent restructuring of the system in Anatolian is striking.

Table 7.5a gives the initial impression that all the comparative linguist has to do is construct a grid of this type and try to fill in the slots for PIE. That certainly gives results for the first items in the table, but begins to break down past the words for grandparents. The terms for 'uncle' and 'aunt' are split in most traditions between words denoting mother's and father's siblings, with many examples of independent derivations from the words for 'father' and 'mother'. Striking are the cases where languages show deviation from this pattern and instead use derivations from the word for 'grandfather': Latin *auunculus* 'mother's brother', Lithuanian *avýnas* and the family of words in Germanic, Celtic and Slavic. In a parallel fashion, words for 'nephew' and 'niece' are frequently new formations from 'brother' or 'sister', but in Germanic, Celtic and Slavic they appear to continue the words used elsewhere for grandchildren. In these cases there seems to be conflation between different areas of the kinship grid. This led some scholars in the 1960s and 1970s to propose that in PIE there was some conceptual 'skewing' of lines of descent; in particular, relations through the sister were equated to relations through the daughter. This skewing is known to anthropologists as a kinship system of the Omaha type. However, closer research into the occurrence of the terms in the relevant branches reveals that the skewing of kinship terms in at least two language branches took place within the historical period. Latin *nepōs* means 'grandson' until the second century AD, when it starts being used to mean 'nephew' as well, a sense which is continued into the Romance languages (Italian *nipote* 'nephew, grandson', etc.). Old High German *nevo* and *nift* mean 'grandson' and 'granddaughter', but in the later language they can also refer to 'nephew' and 'niece'. Hettrich (1985) has consequently explained the shift in meaning as a series of parallel changes in different IE languages, which, in his view, ultimately relate to the switch from a nomadic to a sedentary life.

In the case of the word for 'cousin' there is no possible reconstruction for PIE. Given the stability of most of the other reconstructed terms, it is unlikely that there once was a separate term for 'cousin' which has disappeared across the board. Instead, the term must either have been expressed through a combination of other terms, such as 'father's sister's son', or else another reconstructed term must have had a wider application. For instance, the term *$b^h reh_2 ter$-* 'brother' may also have denoted members of the same family of the same age. The latter explanation is supported by the use of derivatives of *$b^h reh_2 ter$-* to refer to wider social groups than the immediate family, as in Greek *phrā́tēr* 'clansman' and Latin *frāter* 'brother, cousin, member of a religious collegium'.

The set of reconstructed terms for relations by marriage are worth discussing in some detail, particularly since several scholars have used them to draw conclusions about prehistoric marriage practice. (See table 7.5b.) The array of reconstructed terms is impressive, and the survival of such a marginal term as 'husband's brother's wife' is remarkable. The column of reconstructed terms immediately reveals a dichotomy between the terms for the wife's relations and the husband's. In Indo-Iranian, Latin, Germanic, Celtic and Albanian, the same terms are used for both sets, while in Baltic, Slavic, Greek and Armenian, the inherited terms designate only the blood-relations of the husband. In these languages, the terms for the wife's parents and siblings are generally not related from one language to another. This gives the comparative linguist two options: the first is that a system can be reconstructed where the same terms covered the wife's and the husband's relations. In this case, Greek, Armenian, Baltic and Slavic must all have independently replaced the set with a new set of terms for the wife's relations. The second option is that there were only terms for husband's father, husband's mother, husband's brother and husband's sister in PIE, and no special terms by which the husband designated the close family of the wife. Following the lead of Delbrück (1889), most scholars have favoured the second option and explained the absence of specific terms for the wife's family through the supposition of patrilocal marriage – in other words, the wife went to live with her husband's family. Delbrück noted that some languages use more general terms for the wife's family: thus Greek *gambrós* can be used of the wife's brother or the wife's father, as well as

Table 7.5a IE Kinship terms: relations by blood.

PIE	Anatolian (Hittite)	Indo-Iranian (Sanskrit)	Greek	Latin	Germanic (English)	Celtic (Old Irish)	Baltic (Lithuanian)	Slavic (Russian)	Armenian	Meaning
*ph₂ter-	atta-	pitár-	patḗr	pater	father	athir	tévas	otec	hayr	'father'
*meh₂ter-	anna-	mātár-	mḗtēr	māter	mother	máthir	mótyna	mat'	mayr	'mother'
*bʰreh₂ter-	negna-	bhrátar-	adelphós	frāter	brother	bráthir	brólis	brat'	ełbayr	'brother'
*swesor-	nega-	svásar-	adelphḗ	soror	sister	siur	sesuõ	sestrá	kʻoyr	'sister'
*su-nu- / *su-yu-	Lycian tideimeśi	sūnú-	huiós	fīlius	son	macc	sūnùs	syn	ordi	'son'
*dʰugh₂ter-	Luwian tuwat(a)ri-	duhitár-	thugátēr	fīlia	daughter	ingen	duktė̃	dočʹ	dustr	'daughter'
*h₂ewh₂o-	huhha-	pitāmahá-	páppos	auus	Old Norse afi Old High German ana	senathir	sēnis	deduška	haw	'grandfather'
*h₂en-	hanna-	pitāmahī-	tḗthē	auia	Old High German ana	senmáthir	sénė	babuška	han	'grandmother'
		pitṛvya-	pátrōs	patruus	Old High German fetiro		dédė	Old Church Slavonic stryj		'father's brother'

PIE / Lycian	Sanskrit	Greek	Latin	Germanic	Celtic	Baltic	Slavic	Armenian	gloss
	mātula-	*mḗtrōs*	*auunculus*	Old High German *oheim*		*avýnas*	Serbian *ujak*	*k'eři*	'mother's brother'
	pitṛ̥ṣvasr-	*tēthís*	*amita*	Old High German *base*		*tetà*	*tekta*		'father's sister'
	mātṛ̥ṣvasr-	*tēthís*	*mātertera*	Old English *modrie*		*tetà*	*tekta*		'mother's sister'
Lycian *tuhe(s)-*	*bhrātrīya-*	*adelphidéos*		Old High German *nevo*	Welsh *nei*	*sunénas*	*plemmjannik*		'nephew'
Lycian *tuhe(s)-*	*svasrīya-*	*adelphidéē*		Old High German *nift*	Welsh *nith*	*dukterécia*	*plemmjanica*		'niece'
anninniyami-	*bhrātṛ̥ṇya-*	*anepsiós*							'cousin'
*nepōt- Lycian *hassa-, xahba-*	**nápāt**		**nepōs**		*aue*	**nepuotìs**	*vnuk*	*t'ořn*	'grand-son'
*neptih₂- Lycian *xahba-*	**naptī-**		**neptis**		*aue*	**neptē**	*vnučka*	*t'ořn*	'grand-daughter'

Table 7.5b IE kinship terms: relations by marriage.

PIE	Indo-Iranian (Sanskrit)	Greek	Latin	Germanic (Gothic)	Celtic (Welsh)	Slavic (Russian)	Baltic (Lithuanian)	Albanian	Armenian	Meaning
*deh₂iwer-	devár-	daér	leuir	Old English tacor		dever'	dieverìs	kunat	taygr	'husband's brother'
*glṓ-	giri- / giri-	gálōs	glōs			zolva	móša	kunatë	tal	'husband's sister'
						svojačenica	sváinė	k'eni		'wife's sister'
*swek'uro-	śváśura-	hekurós	socer	svaihr	chwegrwn	svekor	šēšuras	vjehër	skesrayr	'husband's father'
		pentherós	socer	svaihr	chwegrwn	test'	úošvis	vjehër	aner	'wife's father'
*swek'ruh₂-	śvaśrū́-	hekurā́	socrus	svaihro	chwegr	svekrov	anýta	vjehërë	skesur	'husband's mother'
	śvaśrū́-	pentherā́	socrus	svaihro	chwegr	tešča	úošvienė	vjehërë	zok'anč'	'wife's mother'
*snuso-	snuṣā́-	nuós	nurus	Old High German snora	gwaudd	snoxa	martì	nuse	nu	'son's wife'
*g'emh₂-ro-	jāmātar-	gambrós	gener	megs	daw	zjat'	žéntas	dhëndër	p'esay	'daughter's husband'
?*yenh₂ter-	yātar-	enátēr	ianitricēs			jatry	jéntė		nër	'husband's brother's wife'

the son-in-law, and he thought that some more general terms would have been used for the wife's family owing to the fact that day-to-day contact with them would have been less.

However, if we only reconstruct terms denoting the husband's relations, we do not necessarily have to follow Delbrück's explanation for the situation. Goody (1959) pointed out that the Laguna of the Western Pueblos in the USA had a typologically similar system of kinship terms to PIE, in that they have a set of terms for husband's relatives but no words for the wife's father etc. However, the Laguna are *matrilocal*: the husband goes to live with the wife's family and refers to her father as 'father'. The same linguistic evidence can thus be used to support an opposite conclusion about social structure. Despite this, no Indo-Europeanist has ever used the kinship terms to support an argument that PIE society was matrilocal. The existence of patrilineal naming systems in the early IE languages, and the survival of patrilocal social systems in many different IE speech-communities (and maintained until recent times among the South Slavs and Armenians), have led to a widespread assumption that the PIE linguistic community was also patrilocal. However, the only purely *linguistic* evidence against matrilocality is the use of the words for 'lead' to mean 'marry, take a wife'. For example, Latin *uxōrem dūcere* 'take a wife' literally means 'lead a wife', and Lithuanian *vèsti* means both 'lead' and 'marry'. However, it is not clear that the semantic range of these verbs really supports patrilocal marriage patterns and does not just refer to some aspect of the marriage ceremony.

We have not yet considered the other possibility for the reconstruction of the in-law terms, that the same set of terms was used to cover both the husband's and the wife's relations. Some support for this reconstruction comes from the geographical location of the speakers of languages with one set of in-law terms. Indo-Iranian, Celtic, Latin and Germanic are situated on the eastern and western edges of the IE linguistic area. The languages which have two sets of in-law terms are all spoken in the middle: Greek, Baltic, Slavic and Armenian. However, it cannot be the case that these languages jointly innovated a change of meaning for the in-law terms, restricting *swek´ruh₂-*, for example, from 'mother-in-law' to 'husband's mother', since they have not created a common set of new terms for 'husband's mother'. If this restriction in meaning is an innovation, it must have taken place independently. Why then are the inherited terms always restricted to the husband's relatives? A possible answer to this problem could be that the 'central' language communities shared a common social change, such as a common shift to a patrilocal system from an earlier system where the married couple settled with neither family. Such a change could lead to a common use of the inherited terms for the in-laws which were closest at hand, but a new set of names for the wife's family. In this way one could construct an argument based on the premise that the original custom was neither patrilocal nor matrilocal.

We have thus seen how it is possible to use the reconstructed set of kinship terms to reach three different conclusions about the social structure of the speakers of PIE. We do not endorse any of these three different reconstructions, but use

Table 7.6 *Some PIE animal names.*

PIE form	Meaning	Comparative evidence
*$pek\acute{}u$-	stock animal	Sanskrit *páśu*, Latin *pecū*, Umbrian *pequo*, Old Lithuanian *pēkus*, Old English *feoh*, Gothic *faihu*, Old Norse *fé* et al.
*h_2owi-	sheep	Luwian *hawi-*, Lycian *xawa-*, Sanskrit *ávi-*, Greek *ó(w)is*, Latin *ouis*, Irish *oi*, English *ewe*
*g^wow-	cow	Sanskrit *gáv-*, Greek *boûs*, Latin *bos*, Irish *bó*, Old English *cu*
*$g\acute{}^hwer$-	wild animal	Greek *thḗr*, Latvian *zvḕrs*, Old Church Slavonic *zvěrĭ*, Latin *ferus* 'wild'
*wlk^wo-	wolf	Sanskrit *vŕka-*, Greek *lúkos*, Latin *lupus*, Gothic *wulfs*, Lithuanian *vil̃kas*, Albanian *ujk*
*$h_2rtk\acute{}o$-	bear	Hittite *hartagga-*, Sanskrit *ŕkṣa-*, Greek *árktos*, Latin *ursus*, Middle Irish *art*, Armenian *arǰ*

them as an example of the way in which the reconstructed terms can be used to bolster any existing argument or set of assumptions. As we have seen, kinship terms can be very tenacious, but they can also shift their sense quite radically in the course of language history. These shifts of meanings can affect the most basic of terms, as in the case of the Albanian cognate to words for 'mother', *motrë*, which means 'sister'. It is perhaps through examination of these semantic shifts that we can gain a better insight into social systems, since we are forced to find a context in which the change of meaning is feasible. In the absence of extra-linguistic information for the PIE speech community it is hard to gain any insight into social systems from terminology alone.

Animal taxonomies

We shall finally look at the vocabulary relating to various animals and examine how far we are able to reconstruct a taxonomy for IE. Table 7.6 gives some reconstructions of lexical items for common animals and some superordinate terms.

This obviously does not represent the full range of reconstructable animal names; it would be possible to add to this table words for pigs, dogs, horses, hares, beavers, mice, flies, bees and others. But what interests us here is the ability to reconstruct higher-order terms such as *$pek\acute{}u$-* 'stock animal' and *$g\acute{}^hwer$-* 'wild animal'. The meaning of *pek´u-* as 'stock animal' is well attested and always refers to domesticated animals. There is disagreement over which domesticated animals were known to speakers of PIE, but it is clear that they had domesticated some animals. Only Latin and Baltic share both terms *$pek\acute{}u$-* and *$g\acute{}^hwer$-* (and Latin only preserves the derived adjective *$g\acute{}^hwero$-* 'wild'), but the cross-linguistic

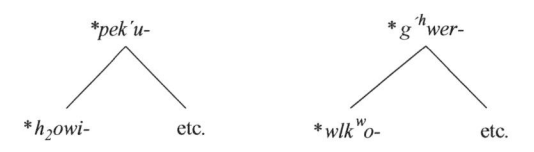

Figure 7.1   *A basic taxonomy for animals in PIE*

attestations of these terms support the reconstruction of both for PIE, giving us a clearer idea of the IE semantic structure. We can thus construct a very basic taxonomy for the semantic field of animal terms in PIE, shown in figure 7.1.

Before we examine whether this taxonomy can be further extended, it is worth considering the meanings of, and derivations from, **pek´u-* in IE languages more closely. In Germanic, **pek´u-* does not only mean 'cattle' but also 'property', in particular moveable property, thus Old English *feoh* refers both to 'cattle' and 'property', and in Gothic *faihu* is only attested with the sense 'money, property'. In Old Norse, the phrase *gangandi fé*, literally 'walking *fé*', is used to refer specifically to cattle and suggests that the meaning 'livestock' is a sub-set of the general sense of 'property'. The relationship between **pek´u-* and property is also found in Latin, where the derivative *pecūnia* means 'property' or 'money', and the derivative *pecūlium* refers to 'the property of a slave'. In Indo-Iranian there is also some evidence for a wider signification of **pek´u-* than just domesticated animals: Vedic Sanskrit texts denote *páśu* as either *cátuṣ-pad-* 'four-footed' or *dvi-pád-* 'two-footed' (Watkins 1979: 275); the two-footed variety refers to human slaves. Benveniste (1969a) used this evidence to argue that **pek´u-* originally denoted 'moveable property' and that the restriction to livestock was a later development undertaken separately in IE languages. The semantic restriction from 'property' to 'domestic animals' can be paralleled in many languages, including English *cattle* from late Latin *capitāle* 'wealth, possessions', or English *stock* used to refer to farm-animals, a specialised sense from the meaning 'fund, property'. A taxonomy under Benveniste's reconstruction would accordingly be along the lines of figure 7.2.

The term **pek´u-* is put in three separate levels in figure 7.2, since it acts as the unmarked term in the oppositions between inanimate and animate possessions, and between human and non-human property.

Benveniste's arguments have been accepted by some scholars, but difficulties with his position remain. Benveniste's conception of **pek´u-* has also been subtly revised by Watkins (1979), who takes it to cover *mobile* rather than *moveable* property, i.e. to cover the superordinate to humans and livestock (and, as the unmarked term, also 'livestock'), but not the top line in figure 7.2. Watkins proposes to keep the basic structure of the above taxonomy in place, however, but reconstructs different lexical items to fill the slots. For the concept of 'wealth' (which covers *mobile* and *immobile* property), Watkins tentatively reconstructs **h₁wesu-*, from the correspondence given below, even though there is no clear indication that this term was seen as superordinate to other terms in ancient texts:

UNIVERSITY OF WINCHESTER
LIBRARY

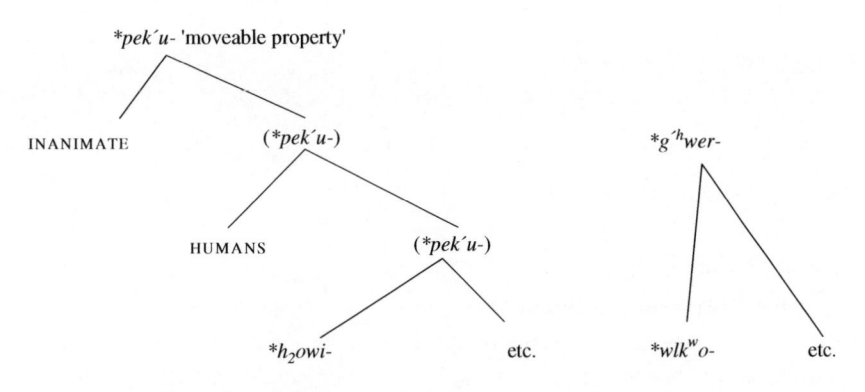

Figure 7.2   *Taxonomy of PIE terms following Benveniste*

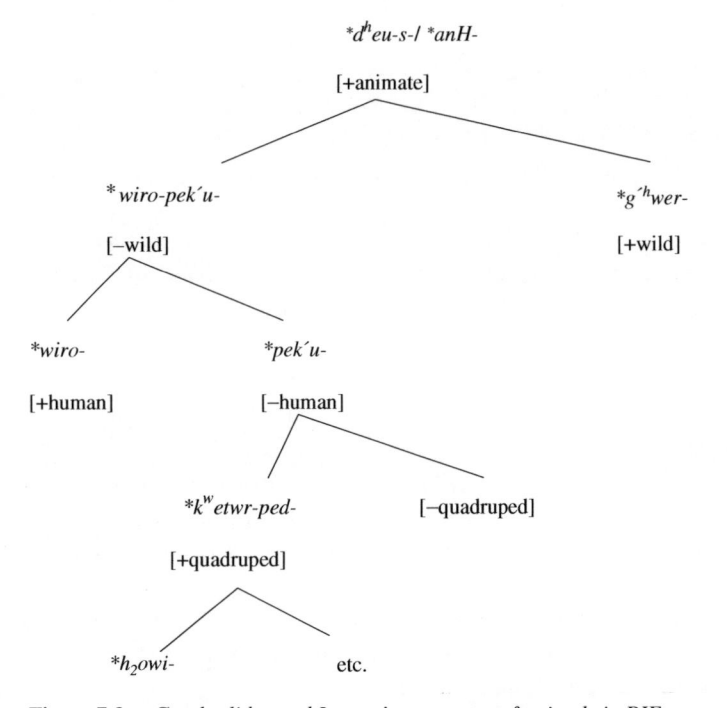

Figure 7.3   *Gamkrelidze and Ivanov's taxonomy of animals in PIE*

$h_1$wesu- 'wealth': Luwian *vasu*- 'property', Sanskrit *vásu*- 'property', Greek *dōtễres eáōn* 'givers of goods' (see Nussbaum (1998))

Another revision of Benveniste's reconstruction is given by Gamkrelidze and Ivanov (1984), who see the unity of humans and livestock under a taxonomy of living creatures. The hierarchy given in figure 7.3 is adapted from the combination of three different taxonomies given by Gamkrelidze and Ivanov, who include compositional features for each term (Gamkrelidze and Ivanov 1984: 471, 481 and 484).

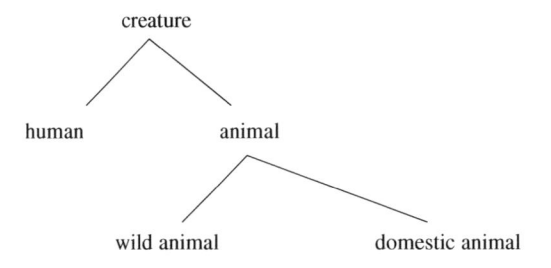

Figure 7.4   *Animal taxonomy in modern European languages*

Attractive though this taxonomy looks, it is in fact badly supported by the evidence. The superordinate term *$d^h eu$-s-*, a root meaning 'breathe', is reconstructed on the basis of a doubtful root-connection between Latin *bēstia* 'wild animal' and Germanic words (including Old English *deor* and German *Tier*) which mean 'animal' or 'wild animal'. The alternative superordinate, *anH-*, is another root meaning 'breath', reconstructed on the basis of Latin *animal* 'animal' and possible cognates in Tocharian. There are not enough data to suggest that either root formed the basis for the PIE word for 'animate creature'. More interesting is the division of *$pek\,'u$-* into quadrupeds and non-quadrupeds, since the term *$k^w etwr$-ped-* is attested in a number of daughter languages: Mycenaean Greek *qe-to-ro-po-pi* (instrumental plural), Umbrian *petur-pursus* and Sanskrit *cátuṣ-pad-*. However, as we saw above, in Sanskrit texts (and also in Umbrian) the term for 'four-footed' is in direct contrast to the term for 'two-footed', and the contrast is between men and animals, not between some forms of livestock and others. Hence, *$k^w etwr$-ped-* appears to be an equivalent to this sense of *$pek\,'u$-*, rather than a subordinate term. Note that more recently Mallory and Adams (1997: 23) have reconstructed *$k^w etwr$-ped-* as a *superordinate* to *$pek\,'u$-*, with a meaning 'animal' (apparently surviving in Albanian *shtazë* 'animal'). However, in early Latin and Umbrian, Mycenaean Greek and Sanskrit the reflexes of *$k^w etwr$-ped-* 'four-footed' refer specifically to domestic animals. Gamkrelidze and Ivanov's taxonomy does, however, share one important feature with the semantic structure recovered by Benveniste and Watkins, in that humans are associated together with domestic animals in opposition to wild creatures. If this is true, it is a valuable insight into IE vocabulary, since it means that the lexicon of PIE is structured in a different way from that of modern European languages, which in general show the semantic hierarchy of figure 7.4.

7.5   Uses of the reconstructed lexicon

In the last section we were principally interested in the *sense* relations of the reconstructed lexicon; in this section we shall consider the *denotation* of PIE lexemes. If we were able to give some idea how reconstructed lexical items were related to objects and events in the world, this would obviously be of enormous benefit to the prehistorian and help to situate the PIE linguistic community in time and space (see also section 1.5). However, the nature of the reconstructed lexicon causes more problems for the prehistorian than it does for the linguist. Together with the problem of a large number of potential lexemes, and the small number of established lexemes, which we discussed in section 7.1, there is a general problem of matching reconstructed items to real objects and practices without relying upon prior assumptions about the archaeology of the speakers of PIE. Thus, if one assumes that IE was spoken at a time when a certain artefact or cultural institution was in use, then it is often possible to come up with lexical reconstructions to support the theory, but if one assumes that the artefact or institution post-dates PIE, then these reconstructions can be explained as potential but unrealised lexemes which were created independently, or it can be argued that they originally denoted other items and were subsequently transferred in their use.

The reconstructed lexicon is also used by scholars to uncover the 'mental culture' of the speakers of PIE. We have already seen in section 7.3 some of the possible conclusions about PIE society that could be drawn from the reconstructed kinship terminology. Many scholars have also tried to use the PIE lexicon to obtain information about prehistoric religion, law and social structure. Comparison of *vocabulary* is less rewarding than might be hoped. There is no reconstructable term for 'swearing an oath', for example, although the practice is found in all early IE societies. The terms for legal or quasi-legal concepts such as 'law', 'trial', 'witness', 'guilty' and 'accuse' are all specific to different branches of IE, and, while the etymology of these terms is often revealing of prehistoric practice, it is impossible to say with any confidence what terms were used in the parent language.

Where there are apparent matches in significant cultural vocabulary, we must be careful that our eagerness to find out about PIE society does not lead us to over-interpret the linguistic evidence. In recent years, two of the most important lexical equations for the reconstruction of PIE culture have been reanalysed. The first case involves the word for 'king', reconstructed as $*h_3rēg'$-, from the following equation (Watkins 1995: 8, Beekes 1995: 39):

$*(h_3)rēg'$- 'king': Sanskrit *rā́j*-, Latin *rēx*, Old Irish *rí*

Although Sanskrit *rā́j*- means 'ruling' in compounds, such as *sva-rā́j*- 'self-ruling', and the derived form *rā́jan*- means 'king', it is more likely that the rare root-noun actually meant 'strength' or 'power', not 'king'. This sense is possible in the three attestations of the noun in the Rg-Veda and better explains the later Sanskrit formula given in example (4):

(4) *iyám te rā́ṭ*
   this-FEM.NOM.SG you-DAT.SG *rā́ṭ*-NOM.SG
   'this is your strength'

Table 7.7 *'Life' in PIE and Indo-Iranian.*

	PIE	Indo-Iranian	Sanskrit	Avestan
Nominative	*$h_2óyu$	*$áyu$	áyu	āiiū
Genitive	*$h_2yéus$	*$yáuš$	yós	yaoš

In (4) the noun *rā́ṭ* must be taken to be of feminine gender, in order to agree with the pronoun *iyám*, and hence is unlikely to refer to a masculine 'king'. The Celtic and Latin words could be explained by a metonymic change in meaning of 'strength' to 'king', in the same way that the English term 'majesty' may be used to denote the monarch, but they are more likely to have been abstracted from compounds. In Celtic, a compound such as the Gaulish name *Dumnorix* may originally have meant 'ruling the world' (cf. Sanskrit *sva-rā́j-* 'self-ruling'), but could later have been reinterpreted as 'world's ruler', leading to the back-formation of a noun *$rīg$- 'ruler'. The reconstruction of the PIE word for 'king' from the comparison of *rā́j-*, *rēx* and *rí* is consequently uncertain. This does not, however, necessarily mean that there was no PIE word for 'king', and McCone (1998) has recently argued that Sanskrit *rā́jan-* in fact continues an inherited word.

The second example of closer examinations of original texts leading to the rejection of a culturally significant etymology involves the etymology of the Latin word for 'law', *iūs*. Latin *iūs* had been compared to Sanskrit *yós* and Avestan *yaoš* both meaning 'health' or 'prosperity'. This comparison was seen by Benveniste (1969b) to be an insight into the notion of justice in prehistoric Rome. He reconstructed a term *$yous$ meaning 'l'état de régularité, de normalité qui est requis par des règles rituelles' ('the norm required by ritual rules', Benveniste (1969b: 113)). However, Szemerényi (1979) showed through analysis of the Avestan occurrences of *yaoš* that the Indo-Iranian form is not a nominative or accusative singular of an *s*-stem noun *$yew(o)s$-, as the comparison with Latin requires. In fact, the term in Avestan is clearly genitive singular to the noun *āiiū* 'life, life-force'. The original paradigms in Avestan and Sanskrit are set out in table 7.7.

The opacity of the paradigm led to the misunderstanding of the genitive *yós* in Sanskrit, and it was reinterpreted as an accusative singular neuter: the fossilised phrase *śáṃ yós*, originally meaning 'health of life', was reinterpreted as two conjoined neuter nouns 'health [and] prosperity'. The comparison between Indo-Iranian and Latin is therefore not valid, and the subtle semantic reconstructions of Benveniste must be wrong.

One area of PIE cultural vocabulary which does provide some striking correspondences is religion. The name for 'god' and the names for some of the gods can be reconstructed with confidence. Note, for example, the phrase meaning 'Father Sky' reconstructed below, the title of the chief god in the pantheon:

*$dyeu$- *ph_2ter- 'Father Sky': Sanskrit *dyáu- pitár-*, Greek *Zdeû páter*, Latin *Iūpiter*, Umbrian *Iupater*, Hittite *Sius*

In this reconstructed phrase we see the kinship term 'father' also applied to the head of the divine household, and this is no doubt significant, since other reconstructed names and titles of gods also imply a conception of a family of gods. For example, the Sanskrit goddess *Uṣás-* Dawn and her sister Night are described by the epithet *Divó duhitā́* 'daughter of the sky', which can be equated to a Greek formula *Diós thugátēr* 'daughter of Zeus' and Lithuanian *diẽvo duktė̃* 'daughter of the sky' (used of the sun, whose sister is *Aušrelė* 'Dawn'). The Sanskrit and Avestan water deity known as the 'grandchild of the waters' (Sanskrit *apā́m nápāt*) has been equated with the Latin *Neptūnus*, whose provenance includes the ocean and whose name can also be derived from the word for 'grandchild'.

These tantalising glimpses of divine names and possible mythical relationships are probably as far as linguistic comparison can take us, although there is, of course, endless scope for etymologising the names of divine or mythical figures in the different IE traditions. Beyond the realm of the purely linguistic is the so-called 'New Comparative Mythology', yet we shall briefly mention it here since it is still highly influential on the work of a number of linguists. The term 'New Comparative Mythology' is usually used in reference to the work of Georges Dumézil, the dominant figure in the twentieth century in the study of IE religion. Dumézil's scholarly output, calculated at over 17,000 pages, is enormous (see the *catalogue raisonée* compiled by Coutau-Bégarie (1998)) and full of detailed (and sometimes contradictory) discussion of numerous correspondences between different IE traditional beliefs, myths and social structures, so the label 'New Comparative Mythology' gives a misleading impression of his approach. Having started out with an etymological approach to the study of IE mythology and religion, Dumézil gradually downplayed the significance of etymology and instead looked for structural similarities between myths and the social and religious practices of different speakers of IE languages. His work is principally known for the theory of the tripartite division of IE 'ideology' between three 'functions': the sacred and sovereign function, represented in society by priests and rulers; the military, represented by warriors; and the third function, embodied by farmers and producers.

Dumézil was strongly criticised both during his lifetime and after his death in 1986 by those who saw these categories as possible divisions of any society, not just IE society; even so he himself maintained that they were specifically IE. Moreover, as Belier has shown (1991 and 1996), Dumézil was able to use the categories of the three different functions as elastic repositories for diverse material, and the criteria of falsifiability are not applicable to his findings. Although his tripartite view of IE ideology may not hold the key to IE mythology, Dumézil's work is worth reading as an enthralling adventure of the mind, and his work reveals much about the early culture of IE societies. Dumézil's own remarks about the inadequacy of linguistic comparisons where they were unmatched by research into the meaning and use of the compared terms in the IE languages provides a fitting end to this section:

Par des artifices phonétiques habiles, on ranime de vaines équations, comme celles que j'avais déjà relevées moi-même il y a un demi-siècle et que j'ai formellement restituées par la suite à leur vanité ou à leur néant. (Dumézil 1983: 8f.)

'By clever phonetic tricks, one can put life into empty comparisons, like those which I had already taken up myself over fifty years ago, and which in turn I have categorically returned to their emptiness or non-existence.'

Further reading

Most readers will first encounter the PIE lexicon through an etymological dictionary. That of Watkins (Watkins 2000) is the most accessible for English readers and is a good guide to the IE roots which have made their way into English. Rix *et al.* (1998) gives a very good survey of reconstructed verbal forms, and it is soon to be joined by two further lexica, one of reconstructed nouns and one of particles and adverbs. When these have appeared, scholars will finally be able to dispense with the much criticised work of Pokorny (1959). Mayrhofer's excellent etymological dictionary of the Indo-Aryan branch of IE gives much information and references to further work on the meaning and occurrence of a number of lexical roots and lexemes (Mayrhofer 1986–2001).

There is a great deal of current work on derivational morphology in PIE and the early IE languages, much of it deriving from the approaches of Schindler and Nussbaum, who have attempted to elucidate derivational chains and derivational processes of the parent language. Unfortunately, neither scholar has fully published his thinking on IE derivational processes, although much can be gleaned from Nussbaum (1976) (an unpublished PhD dissertation), Nussbaum (1986), Schindler (1975), Schindler (1994) and particularly from Widmer (2004), who studied with both Schindler and Nussbaum.

A different approach to the lexicon can be made through dictionaries which list the PIE equivalents to (and often archaeological information on) selected items of mental or material culture. The most useful for the linguist is probably still Buck's dictionary of selected synonyms (Buck 1949), even though this does not give PIE equivalents or systematically list Armenian, Albanian, Tocharian or Anatolian forms, it does give an illuminating overview of different semantic fields and contains brief histories of a large number of attested semantic changes. Mallory and Adams (2006) present an overview of the PIE lexicon ordered along the same lines as Buck (1949), with extensive discussion of the reconstructed vocabulary in many different semantic fields. Other encyclopaedias, such as Gamkrelidze and Ivanov (1995: 379–752) and Mallory and Adams (1997), give PIE equivalents for various areas of the lexicon. Unfortunately, the *horror vacui* sometimes leads these works to over-reconstruct and give PIE equivalents that are at best only potential lexemes of PIE and at worst not reconstructable at all, and it is advisable to use these works with caution, and to check their conclusions with etymological dictionaries such as Mayrhofer (1986–2001) or Rix *et al.* (1998).

The fullest study of the PIE lexicon of cultural institutions is the work of Benveniste (1969a and 1969b, English translation 1973), which remains a very important and challenging book. In places, however, Benveniste overstates his case or makes errors in his presentation of the evidence of the daughter languages. The scholar who has advanced Benveniste's arguments most in the years since his death is probably Calvert Watkins, whose studies on IE formulaic language often involve careful reconstruction of the conceptual universe of the speakers of PIE; his most important articles are collected in Watkins (1994), and Watkins (1995) also sheds light on a number of particular issues. There are also important collections of articles by other scholars in Meid (1987), Meid (1998) and Jasanoff *et al.* (1998).

On numerals in particular there are several monographs and collected volumes. Gvozdanović (1992) is devoted solely to numerals in IE languages, but it should be noted that many of the contributions to it were written over thirty years before it was eventually published, and several of the contributions concentrate more on the synchronic description of numerals rather than their reconstruction. The fullest work, which covers the numbers 'two' to 'five' in over 600 pages, is the unpublished habilitation of Eichner (1982). Szemerényi (1960) is devoted specifically to reconstruction, especially retracing the formation of the decads, but we have not followed his rather idiosyncratic conclusions here. Earlier works, particularly Sommer (1951) and Brugmann (1907), are also still useful, as is the collection of articles concerning numeral types and change in Gvozdanović (1999).

Kinship terms have also received monograph treatments, starting with Delbrück (1889), which remains one of the fullest and most readable accounts. Szemerényi (1977) has a very good overview of literature since Delbrück, but is itself marred by the search for etymologies for kinship terms (for example, *$b^h reh_2 ter$- 'brother' is derived from an imperative phrase meaning 'tend the fire') and a good deal of extraneous material. Since Szemerényi, accounts of the PIE kinship terms have been given by many scholars, for instance Gamkrelidze and Ivanov (1995: 658–77), Mallory and Adams (1997) and Tremblay (2003). The paper of Hettrich (1985) effectively dismisses the reconstruction of an Omaha kinship system in PIE and introduces the interesting idea that a shared change in social behaviour, i.e. the change from a nomadic to a settled system, may have led to similar changes in the use of kinship terms taking place independently.

There are many attempts to give a picture of the 'PIE world' through collections of reconstructed vocabulary, including Beekes (1995), Sergent (1995), Villar (1996), Mallory and Adams (1997), Schmitt (2000), Watkins (2000) and Fortson (2004). Raulwing (2000) gives a detailed overview of the literature relating to terms for horses and chariots, Lühr (1997a) discusses the lexical field relating to houses, Friedrich (1970) trees and Diebold (1985) fish. There are also many works that highlight the pitfalls of linguistic palaeontology (see in particular Renfrew (1987), Clackson (2000) and Raulwing (2000)). The work of Dumézil is probably best approached through the selection in Dumézil (1992). The account given by Littleton (1982) is overly partisan; a more balanced critical review of Dumézil's work is provided by Belier (1991), and a detailed criticism is given by Schlerath (1995 and 1996).

Discussion points

1. What does the study of IE linguistics have to offer the archaeologist?
2. 'The concept of the root is much more important for PIE morphology than for PIE semantics.' Discuss.
3. What does one need to know to establish whether a PIE etymology is correct?

Glossary

ablative. Case typically used to mark movement away from a location. In Latin, the label ablative is given to a case which results from the syncretism of the original ablative, locative and instrumental.

ablaut. Process of systematic vowel alternations to mark inflectional and derivational categories. In PIE, ablaut involves the alternation between the presence or absence of the vowels $*e$, $*o$, $*\bar{e}$ and $*\bar{o}$. Any root, affix or ending can undergo ablaut alternations, and the alternative forms are labelled e-grade (for example $*b^her$-, the e-grade of the root meaning 'carry'), o-grade ($*b^hor$-), lengthened $\bar{e}$-grade ($*b^h\bar{e}r$-), lengthened $\bar{o}$-grade ($*b^h\bar{o}r$-) and zero-grade, with the absence of any e or o vowel ($*b^hr$-).

absolutive. Case used in ergative languages to mark the subject of an intransitive verb and the object of a transitive verb.

accusative. Case typically used in nominative-accusative languages to mark the object of a transitive verb. In many IE languages, the accusative also functions as the case to mark movement towards a location and extent in time and space.

acrostatic. Pattern of paradigmatic ablaut variation hypothesised for PIE. In acrostatic paradigms the suffix and ending remain in zero-grade throughout the paradigm, while the root-syllable changes its ablaut vowel between strong and weak forms.

active. Verbs conjugated in the active voice typically represent the subject as the agent of the verbal action. IE languages generally oppose the active to one or more other voices: middle, medio-passive or passive.

active system. A language with an active system represents a different type of alignment pattern from nominative-accusative and ergative languages. For the purposes of case-marking and agreement, the subject of transitive verbs is grouped together with the subject of intransitive verbs where the subject is deemed to have some control over the action (as, for example, *walk* or *run*), as opposed to the subject of intransitive verbs where the subject does not have control over the action (as, for example, *rot* or *fall*), which is grouped with the object of transitive verbs. Intransitive verbs where the subject has control over the action are sometimes called active, or unergative, verbs; ones where the subject has no control are called neutral, or unaccusative, verbs.

affix. General term for any element which can combine with a root to form a derived or inflectional stem. In IE, most affixation takes place with suffixes, added at the end of the lexical root or stem, but there is also one infix, *$*n$, which is inserted within the root, normally before the final consonant.

Aktionsart. German term used to refer to the inherent aspectual character of a verb. For example, the English verb *kick* describes an action that is punctual, and so the Aktionsart of the verb *kick* is punctual, whereas the verb *remain* has a stative Aktionsart.

allomorphy. The use of different exponents to express the same morpheme.

alphabetic Greek. Stage of Ancient Greek known from inscriptions written in the Greek alphabet, dating from the eighth century BC.

amphikinetic. Pattern of paradigmatic ablaut variation hypothesised for PIE. In amphikinetic paradigms the root is in the e-grade in the strong forms, and the ending is in the e-grade in the weak forms.

Anatolian. IE sub-group comprising languages once spoken in Anatolia (modern Turkey), including Hittite, Luwian, Lycian, Lydian, Palaic and Carian.

aorist. Term taken from Ancient Greek grammar to describe a verbal stem with perfective aspect. Corresponding forms in Sanskrit and other languages are also labelled aorist, although they need not have the same aspectual meaning.

aspect. A category of the verb found in many languages which distinguishes actions and events according to how they are viewed in time, rather than when they occur in time. In English *I ran* and *I was running* both refer to actions in the past, but differ in aspect.

associative. Label given to the use of the plural or dual form of a name to refer to the name-bearer and their companions, spouses, relatives or other associates. If associative plurals were formed in English it would be possible, for example, to use the plural *Madonnas* to refer to the singer Madonna and her husband.

asyndeton, asyndetic. Two or more words or phrases which are understood to belong together but which do not have any overt conjunction, such as 'and', are said to be in asyndeton or asyndetically joined. For example, in the English sentence 'Has car, will travel' the phrases 'has car' and 'will travel' are in asyndeton.

atelic. Term used to refer to verbs which describe processes and events without reference to an end-point, opposed to telic verbs. In English the verbs *walk*, *breathe* and *think* are atelic, but *arrive*, *expire* and *decide* are telic.

athematic. Reconstructed verbal and nominal paradigms which do not include the thematic vowel are called athematic paradigms, and their inflectional endings are termed athematic endings.

Attic Greek. Dialect of Ancient Greek spoken in Athens and surrounding area in the middle of the first millennium BC. Attic Greek is the best-known and codified Greek dialect, and Attic forms are usually cited in dictionaries, handbooks and grammars.

augment. Term taken from Greco-Roman grammar for a prefix or stem-modification used to mark indicative verb forms which refer to past events. More widely used for corresponding phenomena in other IE languages and reconstructed PIE.

back-formation. Change where a more simple form is derived from a form which is morphologically more complex, but chronologically prior. The English word *phobia* is a back-formation from compounds such as *hydrophobia, claustrophobia* etc.

Baltic. IE sub-group comprising Lithuanian, Latvian and Old Prussian. Old Prussian is no longer spoken and known only from a few surviving texts.

basic vocabulary. The part of the lexicon which relates to universal human experience and natural phenomena, and for which equivalents can be found in most languages. Lists of 100 and 200 concepts which form part of the basic vocabulary were promoted by the American linguist Morris Swadesh and have been widely used in lexicostatistics.

bimoraic. Having two *morae*; in other words, consisting of two short vowels, or one long vowel, or a diphthong.

branch. Another term for a sub-group in a language family, extending the metaphor of a 'family tree'.

Brugmann's Law. Sound-change posited for the Indo-Iranian sub-group of IE, whereby an original *$*o$ develops to $\bar{a}$ in open syllables. The regularity of this sound-change, and whether it took place only in certain phonological (or morphological) environments, is still uncertain.

cardinal number. A numerical unit used in counting, for example 'four'.

Celtic. IE sub-group which comprises a number of languages spoken in the West of Europe, including the living languages Irish, Welsh, Scots Gaelic and Breton and languages no longer spoken such as Gaulish, Cornish and Manx.

centum. Term for an IE language or branch in which PIE *$*k'$ has not been palatalised. Opposed to *satem*.

cladistics. Term taken from genetics to describe the process of constructing a tree diagram for a language family.

CM. Abbreviation for the comparative method.

cognate. Genetically related. If two words, sounds or features are cognate, this means that it is hypothesised that they both continue a single word, sound or feature of the parent language.

collective. A noun which describes a plurality as a group, a class or a type, rather than as individual items. In English, the difference can be conveyed by collective nouns such as 'constellation' or 'night sky' in comparison with singular 'star' and the distributive plural 'stars'.

colon. Term taken from ancient grammar to describe a group of words shorter than a sentence which belong together as a syntactic and metrical unit.

common. Term used to describe a grammatical gender of some languages which is opposed to the neuter gender.

comparative method. The techniques used to reconstruct the parent language of a linguistic family, involving the establishment of regular and systematic correspondences between related languages.

comparative philology. An alternative term for the linguistics of language comparison and the reconstruction of proto-languages.

compensatory lengthening. Phonological change involving the lengthening of a vowel following the loss of a following consonant.

correspondence set. A set of cognate items in related languages which share the same feature.

cuneiform. Writing system used in the Ancient Near East employing wedge-shaped signs formed by pressing a stylus into wet clay. The script uses characters to represent syllables, although it also employs some characters or groups of characters to stand for whole words.

dative. Case typically used to mark the recipient or beneficiary.

daughter language. Language which is genetically descended from an earlier language (the parent). French, Italian and Spanish are daughter languages of Latin.

desinence. Another term for an inflectional ending.

disjunctive. A term for anything which divides the possibilities into two separate groups. A disjunctive question is a question that asks whether something is the case or not, and can be answered in English by yes or no. A disjunctive particle introduces a clause or sentence which contains an alternative to one already given.

distributive. A distributive plural describes a plurality as individual items. Distributive plurals are generally capable of being counted. Distributive plurals can be opposed to collective plurals.

Doric Greek. Dialect of Ancient Greek spoken in the West of Greece and in some Greek islands, and known principally from inscriptions, although Doric forms are used in some literary works. Doric Greek can be sub-divided further into local dialects.

dual. A noun or verb inflected in the dual number refers to two items or a pair of items.

e-grade. Term used to describe a particular ablaut form in PIE. For example, *$b^h er$- is the e-grade of the root meaning 'carry'.

ejective. See glottalic.

elliptical dual or **plural.** Term used in some works for associative uses of the plural or dual numbers.

ergative. Case used to mark the subject of a transitive verb, but not the subject of an intransitive verb. Languages which use different cases to mark the subjects of transitive and intransitive verbs are consequently termed ergative languages, or are said to use ergative systems.

eventive. Term for a verbal paradigm in PIE reconstructed at a stage prior to the marking of verbs as past or non-past, and prior to the separation of present and aorist stems.

exclusive. An exclusive first person plural refers to the speaker and others, excluding the addressee.

family. A group of languages which are held to derive from a single language (which is called the parent language of the family).

feminine. One of the possible genders of noun and adjectives, generally opposed to the masculine and neuter.

figura etymologica. A traditional stylistic term to describe a construction where the object of a verb shares the same lexical root as the verb. An English example would be 'to give gifts'.

fluid-S. A particular type of alignment in some active languages, in which nouns can be marked either as controlling the verbal action or not.

formula. Term used to describe recurrent phrases in oral poetry which are 'regularly employed under the same metrical considerations to express a given essential idea' (Parry 1971: 270). More widely used to describe set phrases in other contexts, not just poetry.

four-part analogy. Process whereby a new form is created through extension of an existing pattern, most frequently used in describing morphological changes. It is termed 'four-part' analogy because the newly created form functions as the fourth item in a set. Four-part analogies are normally represented in the following way (using the example of the creation of the past tense *dove* of the English verb *dive*:

drive : drove :: dive : X
X = dove.

This expresses the notion that the pattern of past tense *drove* formed from the verb *drive* is taken as the model for the formation of the past tense of the existing verb *dive*.

fronting. The process of moving one element within a sentence to the beginning of the sentence proper. In the English sentence 'What are you doing?' the interrogative *What* is fronted.

full-grade. Term used to describe any of the possible PIE ablaut forms except the zero-grade, and usually referring to either the e-grade or o-grade. Both $*b^her$- and $*b^hor$- are full-grade forms of the root meaning 'carry'.

Gathic Avestan. Avestan is an ancient Iranian language, the sacred language of the Zoroastrian religion. The earliest Avestan texts are attributed to the prophet Zoroaster himself and are called *Gathas* (Avestan *gāθā* 'hymn'), and the language of them is consequently known as Gathic Avestan.

gender. A category of nouns and adjectives in most IE languages. Different languages have different categories of gender, but many distinguish between three: masculine, feminine and neuter. There is a rough correspondence between grammatical gender and semantics: nouns denoting male animate beings are likely to be masculine, nouns denoting female animate beings are likely to be feminine and nouns denoting inanimate beings are likely to be neuter. However, there are very many exceptions to these semantic equations.

genitive. Case typically used to mark nouns which are dependent on other nouns.

Germanic. IE sub-group comprising English, Dutch, German and the Scandinavian languages, and several earlier varieties, such as Gothic, Old High German and Old Norse, which are now no longer spoken.

glottalic. A glottalic consonant is produced using air pressure made by closing the space between the vocal folds (the glottis), rather than air from the lungs. These sounds are also sometimes called ejective. The glottalic theory is the name given to the hypothesis that such sounds are to be reconstructed for PIE.

glottochronology. Term used widely to describe the work of a group of scholars in the 1950s, including Morris Swadesh, who attempted to establish the length of time separating two related languages through comparison of their basic vocabularies. Now largely discredited owing to problems in their methodology.

Grassmann's Law. Sound-change which affects both Greek and the Indic branch of the Indo-Iranian sub-group, apparently separately, whereby the first of two aspirated consonants in successive syllables loses the feature of aspiration.

Grimm's Law. Set of sound-changes posited for the Germanic branch of IE, whereby PIE voiced aspirates become originally voiced fricatives (and subsequently voiced stops in most Germanic languages), PIE voiced stops become voiceless stops, and PIE voiceless stops become voiceless fricatives.

-*hi* conjugation. One of two different verbal conjugations in the Anatolian language Hittite. The other is called the -*mi* conjugation.

hieroglyphic. Term for a writing system employing stylised pictures as characters to represent syllables or words. Hieroglyphic Luwian is the name given to a stage of the Luwian language written in such a script.

Homeric Greek. Variety of Ancient Greek used in the works attributed to Homer, including the *Iliad* and the *Odyssey*, which form the earliest extensive evidence for the Greek language.

hypotaxis. The process of combining syntactic units through explicit processes of subordination, making some clauses dependent on other ones, opposed to parataxis. In English a sentence such as 'Spare the rod and spoil the child' employs parataxis, and could be rewritten with hypotaxis as 'If you spare the rod, you will spoil the child.'

hysterokinetic. Particular pattern of paradigmatic ablaut variation hypothesised for PIE. In hysterokinetic paradigms, the suffix is in the e-grade in the strong forms, and the ending is in the e-grade in the weak forms.

IE. Abbreviation for Indo-European.

i-motion. Term for morphological phenomena in Anatolian languages, describing an alternation between forms with stem-final vowel -*i*- and forms without the vowel.

imperative. Form of the verb which is typically used to give a command.

imperfect. Term for a verbal paradigm in many different IE languages. The imperfect tense generally stands in a close semantic and formal relationship to the present tense, but refers to the past. In most languages, the imperfect encodes an ongoing action or state of affairs.

inclusive. An inclusive first person plural refers to the speaker and others, including the addressee.

indicative. Form of the verb which is generally employed in narrative or statements, and which is unmarked against, for example, the subjunctive in terms of mood.

Indo-Iranian. IE sub-group comprising the Iranian languages, the Indic languages and other languages spoken by small communities in the Hindu Kush mountains of north-east Afghanistan.

inhibitive. A prohibitive which has reference to an action which is taking place at the time of the utterance, opposed to a preventative. In English, inhibitives are often constructed with the word *stop!*, as in 'Stop writing!'

injunctive. Term for a particular verbal paradigm in the Indo-Iranian languages, formed with the endings of a past tense verb but without the augment usually present in past tense verbs. The injunctive was employed in specific contexts, including some prohibitions. By extension the label injunctive is also used for analogous formations in Ancient Greek and other languages.

innovation. Any linguistic development which replaces an earlier feature. Innovations may take place in any area of the language: sound, vocabulary, morphology or syntax. Typically, innovations take place only in some languages in a family, and separate branches will have undergone different innovations.

instrumental. Case typically used to designate the instrument or means by which an action is performed.

internal derivation. Process of deriving one lexeme from another without the addition of an extra suffix, but through change of accent or ablaut pattern.

kinetic. Class of paradigmatic ablaut variations hypothesised for PIE, in which the position of the e-grade alternates between the weak and the strong forms. The term kinetic is consequently used to describe the ablaut paradigm of root formations (where there is no suffix between the root and the inflectional endings) if the root is in e-grade in the strong forms and the ending is in the e-grade in the weak forms.

labio-velar. Name for a class of reconstructed PIE consonants hypothesised to have consisted of velar stops with concomitant lip-rounding (represented by the notation $*k^w$, $*g^w$, $*g^{wh}$). Labio-velars have diverse outcomes in different IE languages.

laryngeal. Name for any of three consonants reconstructed for PIE, in this work represented by the notation $*h_1$, $*h_2$ and $*h_3$. The reconstruction of these consonants explains aberrant patterns of vowel alternation in many IE languages and is termed 'the laryngeal theory'.

left-detachment. The syntactic process of putting extra material before the beginning of a sentence which is not essential to the content of the sentence but which expands or extends material within the sentence proper.

lengthened-grade. Term used to describe ablaut forms in PIE which contain a long vowel, either $*\bar{e}$ or $*\bar{o}$. For example, $*b^h\bar{e}r$- and $*b^h\bar{o}r$- are both lengthened-grade forms of the root $*b^her$- 'carry'.

lexicostatistics. General term to describe different ways of using mass comparison of vocabularies to determine aspects of relatedness of languages.

Linear B. Syllabic script used in Crete and mainland Greece in the second millennium BC.

locative. Case typically used to designate placement at a certain point in space or time.

masculine. One of the possible genders of nouns and adjectives, generally opposed to the feminine and the neuter.

matrilocal. System of social organisation in which a husband joins the wife's family and lives with them.

medio-passive. Term to describe a voice opposed to the active in many IE languages which combines the functions of the middle and the passive.

-*mi* conjugation. One of two different verbal conjugations in the Anatolian language Hittite. The other is called the -*hi* conjugation.

middle. Term taken from Ancient Greek grammar to refer to a set of verbal forms which are opposed both to the active and the passive in some paradigms, and more widely used to cover equivalent structures in other IE languages. Typically, the subject of a verb conjugated in the middle has some involvement in the verbal action beyond that expressed by a verb conjugated in the active. The term middle is also more loosely used to mean medio-passive.

modal formation. A verbal formation which is marked in some way for the category of mood.

mood. A category of the verb in most IE languages relating to the type of utterance in which the verb appears, and the speaker's attitude to the truth of the utterance. Typically, the indicative mood is used in statements, the imperative mood in commands and the optative (in some languages) in wishes.

mora. (Plural *morae*, adjective *moraic*.) Term for prosodic units into which syllables can be divided. In this work, it is assumed that a short vowel counts as one *mora*, a long vowel or diphthong counts as two *morae*.

Mycenaean Greek. Earliest attested form of Greek, comprising mainly short administrative texts written in the Linear B syllabary on clay tablets.

Narten ablaut. Term for a specific type of ablaut alternation hypothesised for PIE, in which the principle opposition is between the ablaut vowels $*\bar{e}$ and $*e$.

nasal infix. Another term for n-infix.

neuter. One of the possible genders of nouns and adjectives, generally opposed to the masculine and the feminine, or, in Anatolian languages, to the common gender.

neutral verb. A term used in reference to active verbal systems to describe an intransitive verb where the subject undergoes, rather than controls, the action. Also known as an unaccusative verb.

n-infix. A reconstructed affix for PIE which combines with the root in a special way, by insertion within it, normally before the final consonant of a root. The PIE root *lik^w*- 'leave' combines with the n-infix to form a present tense stem *$link^w$*- or (with the e-grade) *$linek^w$*-.

nominative. Case typically used to mark the subject of both transitive and intransitive verbs. Languages which mark the subject in opposition to the object of transitive verbs are called nominative, or nominative-accusative, languages.

nominative-accusative language. See nominative.

non-configurational. A term to describe a language where word-order is of no importance for syntax.

non-neuter. Term used to describe a nominal gender other than neuter.

non-restrictive. A non-restrictive relative adds extra information about the noun or pronoun which it refers to. In the English sentence 'The Prime Minister, who was looking tired, defended his actions' the relative clause 'who was looking tired' adds an extra fact about the Prime Minister, but does not further restrict the interpretation to a particular Prime Minister.

Nostratic. The name of a proposed linguistic phylum including IE and several other language families.

o-grade. Term used to describe a particular ablaut form in PIE. For example, *b^hor*- is the o-grade of the root meaning 'carry'.

optative. Form of the verb in Ancient Greek and the ancient Indo-Iranian languages which would typically be employed in wishes (and has many other functions). The optative is a mood marked in opposition to the indicative.

oral poetry. Poetry which is transmitted through speech alone and is not written down. The earliest surviving Greek and Sanskrit poetic texts are believed to have evolved through a long tradition of oral poetry.

Osthoff's Law. Sound-change posited originally for Greek which may also take place in other branches of IE, whereby an original long vowel is shortened before following *i *u *r *l *m *n and a consonant.

palatal. Name for a class of reconstructed PIE consonants, represented in this work by the notation *k', *g', *g'^h. In the Indo-Iranian, Slavic, Baltic and Armenian language branches, these consonants usually develop to sibilants or stops articulated further forward in the mouth than velars.

Palatals, Law of the. Sound-change affecting the Indo-Iranian branch of IE, whereby original labio-velar consonants are palatalised before the vowel *e (and subsequently may merge with the outcomes of original palatal consonants), but not before the vowel *o.

paradigm. A set of forms in complementary distribution which differ from each other only in their inflectional endings.

parataxis. The process of combining syntactic units through placing them alongside each other, without signifying any hierarchical order between them, opposed to hypotaxis. In English, a sentence such as 'Spare the rod and spoil the child' employs parataxis, and could be rewritten with hypotaxis as 'If you spare the rod, you will spoil the child.'

parent. Language from which another language (the daughter language) is genetically descended. Latin is the parent language of French, Italian and Spanish.

passive. Verbs conjugated in the passive voice typically represent the subject as the undergoer of the verbal action.

patrilocal. System of social organisation in which a wife joins her husband's family and lives with them.

perfect. The name given to various different past tenses in the IE language family. The perfect in Greek and in the early Indo-Iranian languages correspond closely and are the basis of the reconstructed perfect in PIE. The perfect in Latin partly corresponds to this, but it also contains elements from another PIE past tense.

perfecto-present. Term used to describe a group of verbs in Germanic languages which originate from PIE perfect tense formations, but which are used as present tense verbs. The English verbs *may* and *can* belong to this class.

phylogeny. Alternative term for a linguistic family tree.

phylum. A grouping of several language families into a larger genetic grouping.

PIE. Abbreviation for Proto-Indo-European.

preterite. Term used to describe the past tense in some IE languages.

preventative. A prohibitive which has reference to an action which has not yet started, opposed to an inhibitive.

primary endings. Some early IE languages have two closely related sets of verbal endings, one of which (primary endings) typically refers to events which take place in the present, and the other of which (secondary endings) typically refers to events in the past.

prohibitive. An expression which encodes a command not to do something.

proterokinetic. Particular pattern of paradigmatic ablaut variation hypothesised for PIE. In proterokinetic paradigms, the root is in the e-grade in the strong forms, and the suffix is in the e-grade in the weak forms.

prothetic vowel. Any vowel which is attached to the beginning of a word which at an earlier stage of the language did not begin with a vowel, as, for example, French *estomac* 'stomach' from Latin *stomachus*. In IE linguistics, the term is often used to refer to a historical development which took place in Greek and Armenian, whereby words which originally began with a cluster of a laryngeal followed by consonant or consonants in PIE appear with an initial sequence of vowel followed by consonant.

proto-language. A language which is hypothesised to be an earlier stage of an attested language or a group of attested languages, but is not itself attested. It is often possible to use techniques such as the comparative method to reconstruct proto-languages. The prefix *proto-* can be attached to the name of any language or language family to give the name of the proto-language for that language or family. For example, Proto-Semitic is the name of the proto-language of the Semitic language family. PIE is the reconstructed proto-language of the IE language family.

punctual. Term used to describe events or actions which can be viewed as taking place in a point in time and having no extension over time, as, for example, the English verbs *spit*, *hit* and *bite*.

reduplication. Morphological device used in IE inflection and derivation whereby the initial consonant, or in some cases the initial consonant cluster, of a lexical item is repeated. For example, in Latin the verb *canō* 'I sing' has a perfect stem *cecin-* 'sang' formed by reduplication.

resonant. Name for any of the reconstructed PIE sounds **r*, **l*, **m*, **n*, **i* or **u*. These sounds form a distinct class within PIE, since they may function both as the nucleus of a syllable, i.e. as a vowel, and as a consonant.

restrictive. A restrictive relative defines the noun or pronoun which it refers to. In the English sentence 'The woman that you met was my sister', the relative clause 'that you met' defines exactly which woman is referred to and restricts the interpretation of the noun phrase 'the woman'.

retroflex. Name for any consonant formed with the underside of the tip of the tongue in contact with the alveolar ridge (the area of the mouth immediately behind the teeth).

right-detachment. The syntactic process of including extra material after the end of a sentence which is not essential to the content of the sentence but which expands or extends material already mentioned.

Romance. IE sub-group comprising the languages derived from Latin, including French, Italian, Spanish, Portuguese and Rumanian.

root. Term applied to the basic units of the reconstructed PIE lexicon. Roots can themselves combine with inflectional endings to make full words, or they can combine with affixes to form a number of lexical stems. Most reconstructed roots have meanings which relate to verbal actions.

root-aorist. A verbal paradigm encoding the aorist tense which is formed by the combination of a root with inflectional endings and no other affix.

root-formation. A lexical stem which is made up by the root alone, which can then combine with inflectional endings to make full words.

root-noun. A noun which is formed by the combination of a root with inflectional endings, and no other affix.

root-present. A verbal paradigm encoding the present tense which is formed by the combination of a root with inflectional endings and no other affix.

RUKI rule. Sound-change affecting Indo-Iranian and Slavic, and possibly other, branches of IE, whereby an original **s* is changed when following any of the sounds **r*, **u*, **k* or **i*, and develops to a different sound from **s* in other environments. In Sanskrit, the reflex of **s* when it has undergone the sound-change is a retroflex [ṣ], conventionally written *ṣ*.

Sabellian. IE sub-group comprising languages spoken in Central and Southern Italy in the first millennium BC, and known chiefly from inscriptional remains. Sabellian languages include Oscan, Umbrian and South Picene.

sandhi. Term from Sanskrit grammar to refer to the alternation of the sounds at the edges of words determined by what follows or precedes them. For example, many speakers of British English pronounce *r* at the end of the word *far* in the phrase *far and wide*, but not in the phrase *far from*. The two alternate forms are termed sandhi variants.

Sanskrit. Name for the ancient language of India, used in this work to cover both the language of the Vedic hymns and the later stages of the language (sometimes called Classical Sanskrit).

satem. Term for an IE language or branch in which PIE *k' has been palatalised. Opposed to *centum*.

schwebeablaut. Term for a specific type of ablaut alternation hypothesised for PIE, in which the place of the ablaut vowel *e* in a root alternates between a position before and after one of the sounds *r, *l, *m, *n, *i or *u.

secondary endings. Some early IE languages have two closely related sets of verbal endings, one of which (primary endings) typically refers to events which take place in the present, and the other of which (secondary endings) typically refers to events in the past.

singulative. Term for a word referring to a single item, formed from a more basic or chronologically prior word which refers to a plurality. The closest equivalence in English is in the relationship of a noun such as *raindrop* to *rain*.

Slavic. IE sub-group comprising languages spoken in Eastern Europe, including Russian, Polish, Czech, Serbian, Croatian and Bulgarian among living languages, as well as earlier varieties such as Old Church Slavonic.

sound-law. Term applied to certain sound-changes originally in the nineteenth century (but continued in use since then). Many sound-laws are named after the scholar who first identified or described the change.

SOV. Abbreviation for Subject-Object-Verb, referring to a word-order pattern in which the verb follows the object.

Space-Time. Name given to a reconstructed model of PIE devised by the Austrian scholar Wolfgang Meid.

split-S. A particular type of alignment in some active languages, in which intransitive verbs determine how their subjects are marked.

spread zone. Term coined by the American linguist Johanna Nichols to describe a geographical area without significant natural restrictions to the movement of people and the growth of population. Languages spoken across a spread zone typically are genetically related.

static. Class of paradigmatic ablaut variations hypothesised for PIE, in which the position of the zero-grades does not alternate between the weak and the strong forms.

stative. Term used for verbs which describe states (or situations which can be viewed as states), for example English *exist*, *remain*, *have* and *know*.

stem. A lexical base which needs only the addition of inflectional endings to be a full word. In IE linguistics, a stem is normally understood to consist of a root morpheme and one or more affixes.

strong. Forms of nominal or verbal paradigms which are opposed to weak forms in patterns of paradigmatic ablaut are termed strong. The strong forms of nominal paradigms are the nominative, vocative, accusative and locative cases in the singular. The strong forms of the present paradigm of the verb are the first, second and third person singular of the active.

sub-group. A group of languages within a language family which are taken to be closely related to each other.

subjunctive. Form of the verb marked against the indicative in many IE languages, including Latin, Ancient Greek and the ancient Indo-Iranian languages. The subjunctive has many different functions, including reference to events which have not yet taken place, reference to events related by other parties and reference to events which are in some way unspecified. In very general terms, the speaker does not give the same commitment to the truth of a verbal action or state of affairs in the subjunctive as to one in the indicative.

SVO. Abbreviation for Subject-Verb-Object, referring to a word-order pattern in which the verb precedes the object.

syllabary. Writing system which represents syllables by a single character.

syllabic script. Another term for a syllabary.

syncretism. General term for the collapse of two originally distinct categories into a single category. Case syncretism refers to the merger of two or more nominal cases into a single case. For example, in Latin the original ablative, locative and instrumental cases have syncretised to give the case labelled the ablative in traditional Latin grammar.

telic. Term used to refer to verbs which describe events which are naturally bounded and can be envisaged as having an end-point, opposed to atelic verbs. In English the verbs *arrive*, *expire* and *decide* are telic, but *walk*, *breathe* and *think* are atelic.

thematic noun paradigm. The noun paradigm reconstructed for PIE with the thematic vowel before the endings. The inflectional endings are partly unique to this paradigm and therefore sometimes termed 'thematic endings'.

thematic verbal paradigm. The verbal paradigm reconstructed for PIE with the thematic vowel before the endings. The inflectional endings are partly unique to this paradigm and therefore sometimes termed 'thematic endings'.

thematic vowel. Some PIE paradigms are reconstructed with a vowel throughout the paradigm occurring before the inflectional endings. The vowel is realised either as $*e$ or $*o$. The term *thematic* is taken from the word for 'stem' in other European languages (e.g. French *thème*).

tree. A mapping of a language family showing the relations between the different languages and sub-groups.

triple reflex. Term used in reference to the development of PIE laryngeals in daughter languages. If a language has a triple reflex of the laryngeals, it means that the three laryngeals develop in different ways and do not merge together.

typology. Linguistic typology is a loose term for the study and classification of languages according to type. Consideration of a large number of known languages has led to observations that some types of linguistic structure are more common, others less so. Typology affects reconstruction inasmuch as it is argued that reconstructed languages should be consistent with the types of attested languages. Synchronic typology applies to languages as unified systems at a single point in time, and may consider factors such as possible sound-systems or word-order patterns. Diachronic typology applies to the ways languages change over time, and may consider factors such as changes in sounds or word-order patterns.

umlaut. Term used to describe a number of changes in the Germanic languages, in which a back vowel is changed to a front vowel when the following syllable has a front vowel. The plural formations of English *foot / feet, goose / geese, man / men* and others can be explained by umlaut, since at an earlier stage of English these words had a front vowel in the second syllable, **fōti* etc.

Vedic Sanskrit. The earliest stage of the Sanskrit language, attested principally in a collection of metrical texts (often called hymns), known as the Veda.

Verner's Law. Sound-change posited for the Germanic branch of IE whereby intervocalic voiceless fricatives become voiced unless the syllable which immediately precedes was accented in PIE. Verner's law explains why, for example, in German the words for 'father' *Vater* and 'brother' *Bruder* have different medial consonants, although they both derive from PIE **t.*

vocative. Case used in forms of address.

voice. A category of the verb. In many IE languages, verbs show separate paradigms which relate the subject to the verbal action in different ways. For example, in Latin the present paradigm of the active voice, *amō, amās, amat,* means 'I love', 'you love', 'he loves', but the present paradigm of the passive voice, *amor, amāris, amātur,* means 'I am loved', 'you are loved', 'he is loved'.

Wackernagel's Law. A word-order rule widely assumed for PIE and many IE languages, which states that unaccented words (called enclitics) are placed after the first word of the sentence or clause.

weak. Forms of nominal or verbal paradigms which are opposed to strong forms in patterns of paradigmatic ablaut are termed weak. The weak forms of nominal paradigms are the cases other than the nominative, vocative, accusative and locative in the singular. The weak forms of the present paradigm of the verb are the forms other than the first, second and third person singular of the active voice.

Winter's Law. Sound-change proposed for the Baltic and Slavonic sub-groups of Indo-European, whereby a vowel is lengthened if followed by an original voiced stop.

WL. Abbreviation for Wackernagel's Law.

zero-grade. Term for a particular ablaut alternative in PIE, characterised by the absence of any e or o vowel. For example, **bʰr-* is the zero-grade of the root meaning 'carry'.

References

Adams, Douglas Q. 1988. *Tocharian Historical Phonology and Morphology*. New Haven: American Oriental Society
  (ed.) 1997. *Festschrift for Eric P. Hamp. Volume I*, Journal of Indo-European Studies Monograph Series 23. Washington, DC: Institute for the Study of Man
Adams, J. N. 1994a. 'Wackernagel's Law and the Position of Unstressed Personal Pronouns in Classical Latin', *Transactions of the Philological Society* 92: 103–78
  1994b. *Wackernagel's Law and the Placement of the Copula* esse *in Classical Latin*. Cambridge: Cambridge Philological Society
Allen, W. S. 1976. 'The PIE Aspirates: Phonetic and Typological Factors in Reconstruction', in Juilland (ed.), pp. 237–47
Ammann, Hermann 1927. 'Die ältesten Formen des Prohibitivsatzes im Griechischen und Lateinischen', *Indogermanische Forschungen* 45: 328–44
Anreiter, Peter *et al.* (eds.) 1998. *Man and the Animal World: Studies in Archaeozoology, Archaeology, Anthropology and Palaeolinguistics in Memoriam Sandor Bökönyi*. Budapest: Archaeolingua
Anttila, Raimo 1969. *Proto-Indo-European Schwebeablaut*. Berkeley: University of California Press
Atkinson, Q. D., Nicholls, G., Welch, D. and Gray, R. D. 2005. 'From Words to Dates: Water into Wine, Mathemagic or Phylogenetic Inference?', *Transactions of the Philological Society* 103: 193–219
Bader, Françoise (ed.) 1997. *Les Langues indo-européennes*. New Edition. Paris: CNRS
Bammesberger, A. (ed.) 1988. *Die Laryngaltheorie*. Heidelberg: Winter
Barrack, Charles M. 2002. 'The Glottalic Theory Revisited: A Negative Appraisal', *Indogermanische Forschungen* 107: 76–98
  2003. 'The Glottalic Theory Revisited: A Negative Appraisal. Part II. The Typological Fallacy Underlying the Glottalic Theory', *Indogermanische Forschungen* 108: 1–16
Battye, Adrian and Roberts, Ian (eds.) 1995. *Clause Structure and Language Change*. New York / Oxford: Oxford University Press
Bauer, Brigitte L. M. 2000. *Archaic Syntax in Indo-European: The Spread of Transitivity in Latin and French*. Berlin: Mouton de Gruyter
Beck, Heinrich and Steuer, Heiko (eds.) 1997. *Haus und Hof in ur- und frühgeschichtlicher Zeit: Bericht über zwei Kolloquien der Kommission für die Altertumskunde Mittel- und Nordeuropas vom 24. bis 26. Mai 1990 und 20. bis 22. November 1991 (34. und 35. Arbeitstagung): Gedenkschrift für Herbert Jankuhn*. Göttingen: Vandenhoeck & Ruprecht
Beekes, R. S. P. 1990. 'Wackernagel's Explanation of the Lengthened Grade', in Eichner and Rix (eds.), pp. 33–53

1994. 'Who were the Laryngeals?', in Rasmussen (ed.), pp. 449–54

1995. *Comparative Indo-European Linguistics: An Introduction*. Amsterdam/ Philadelphia: Benjamins

Belier, Wouter 1991. *Decayed Gods: Origin and Development of Georges Dumézil's 'idéologie tripartie'*. Leiden: Brill

1996. 'The First Function: A Critical Analysis', in Polomé (ed.), pp. 37–72

Bendahman, Jadwiga 1993. *Der reduplizierte Aorist in den indogermanischen Sprachen*. Egelsbach / Cologne / New York: Hänsel-Hohenhausen

Benveniste, Émile 1935. *Origines de la formation des noms en indo-européen*. Paris: Maisonneuve

1954. 'Problèmes sémantiques de la reconstruction', *Word* 10: 251–64

1966. *Problèmes de linguistique générale*. Paris: Gallimard

1969a. *Le Vocabulaire des institutions indo-européennes: 1. économie, parenté, société*. Paris: Minuit

1969b. *Le Vocabulaire des institutions indo-européennes: 2. pouvoir, droit, religion*. Paris: Minuit

1971. *Problems in General Linguistics*. (Translation of Benveniste 1966 by M. E. Meek.) Miami: University of Miami Press

1973. *Indo-European Language and Society*. (Translation of Benveniste 1969a and 1969b by Elizabeth Palmer.) London: Faber

Bergsland, K. and Vogt, H. 1962. 'On the Validity of Glottochronology', *Current Anthropology* 3: 115–53

Blench, Roger and Spriggs, Matthew (eds.) 1997–9. *Archaeology and Language*. London: Routledge

Bomhard, Allan R. and Kerns, John C. 1994. *The Nostratic Macrofamily: A Study in Distant Language Relationship*. New York / Berlin: Mouton de Gruyter

Borgström, C. H. 1949. 'Thoughts about IE Vowel Gradation', *Norsk Tidsskrift for Sprogvidenskap* 15: 137–87

Brandenstein, Wilhelm and Mayrhofer, Manfred 1964. *Handbuch des Altpersischen*. Wiesbaden: Harrassowitz

Brogyanyí, Bela (ed.) 1979. *Studies in Diachronic, Synchronic, and Typological Linguistics: Festschrift for Oswald Szemerényi on the Occasion of his 65th Birthday*. Amsterdam: Benjamins

Brugman, Claudia and Macaulay, Monica (eds.) 1984. *Proceedings of the Tenth Annual Meeting of the Berkeley Linguistics Society, February 17–20, 1984*. Berkeley: Berkeley Linguistics Society

Brugmann, Karl 1907. *Die Distributiven und die Kollektiven Numeralia der indogermanischen Sprachen* (Abhandlung der philologisch-historischen Classe der Königl. Sächsichen Gesellschaft der Wissenschaft, Band XXV No. V). Leipzig: Teubner

Buck, Carl D. 1949. *A Dictionary of Selected Synonyms in the Principal Indo-European Languages: A Contribution to the History of Ideas*. Chicago: University of Chicago Press

Campbell, Lyle and Mithun, Marianne 1980. 'The Priorities and Pitfalls of Syntactic Reconstruction', *Folia Linguistica Historica* 1: 19–40

Cardona, George 1960. 'The Indo-European Thematic Aorists'. Unpublished PhD dissertation, Yale University

and Zide, N. H. (eds.) 1987. *Festschrift for Henry Hoenigswald*. Tübingen: Narr

Carruba, Onofrio 1998. 'Betrachtungen zu den anatolischen und indogermanischen Zahlwörtern', in Meid (ed.), pp. 505–19

Chang, S. S., Liaw, L. and Ruppenhofer, J. (eds.) 1999. *Proceedings of the Twenty-Fifth Annual Meeting of the Berkeley Linguistics Society. February 12–15, 1999*. Berkeley: Berkeley Linguistics Society

Christie, W. M. (ed.) 1976. *Current Progress in Historical Linguistics: Proceedings of the Second International Conference on Historical Linguistics, Tucson, Arizona 12–16 January 1976*. Amsterdam / New York / Oxford: North-Holland Publishing Company

Clackson, James 2000. 'Time Depth in Indo-European', in McMahon, Renfrew and Trask (eds.), pp. 441–54

Cobet, Justus, Leimbach, Rüdiger and Neschke-Hentschke, Ada B. (eds.) 1975. *Dialogos: für Harald Patzer zum 65. Geburtstag von seinen Freunden u. Schülern*. Wiesbaden: Steiner

Collinge, N. E. 1985. *The Laws of Indo-European*. Amsterdam / Philadelphia: Benjamins
    1995. 'Further Laws of Indo-European', in Winter (ed.), pp. 27–52
    1999. 'The Laws of Indo-European: The State of the Art (1998)', *Journal of Indo-European Studies* 27: 355–77

Comrie, Bernard 1993. 'Typology and Reconstruction', in Jones (ed.), pp. 74–97
    1999. 'Haruai Numerals and Their Implications for the History and Typology of Numeral Systems', in Gvozdanović (ed.), 1999 pp. 81–94
    and Corbett, Greville G. (eds.) 1993. *The Slavonic Languages*. London and New York: Routledge

Costa, Gabriele 1998. *Le origini della lingua poetica indoeuropea: voce, coscienza e transizione neolitica*. Florence: Olschki
    2000. *Sulla preistoria della tradizione poetica italica*. Florence: Olschki

Coutau-Bégarie, Hervé 1998. *L'Œuvre de Georges Dumézil*. Paris: Economica

Cowgill, Warren 1968. 'The First Person Singular Medio-Passive in Indo-Iranian', in Heesterman, Schokker and Subramoniam (eds.), pp. 24–31
    1979. 'Anatolian *hi*-Conjugation and Indo-European Perfect: Instalment II', in Meid and Neu (eds.), pp. 25–39
    1985. 'The Personal Endings of Thematic Verbs in Indo-European', in Schlerath and Rittner (eds.), pp. 99–108

Crespo, Emilio and García Ramón, José Luis (eds.) 1997. *Berthold Delbrück y la sintaxis indoeuropea hoy: Actas del Coloquio de la Indogermanische Gesellschaft, Madrid, 21–24 septiembre de 1994*. Madrid / Wiesbaden: Ediciones de la Universidad Autónoma de Madrid / Reichert

Darms, Georges 1978. *Schwäher und Schwager, Hahn und Huhn: die Vrddhi-ableitung im Germanischen*. Munich: Kitzinger

Delbrück, Berthold 1889. *Die indogermanischen Verwandtschaftsnamen: ein Beitrag zur vergleichenden Alterthumskunde* (Abhandlung der philologisch-historischen Classe der Königl. Sächsichen Gesellschaft der Wissenschaft, Band IX No. V). Leipzig: Hirzel
    1893–1900. *Vergleichende Syntax der indogermanischen Sprachen*. Strassburg: Karl J. Trübner

Devine, Andrew M. and Stephens, Laurence D. 1999. *Discontinuous Syntax: Hyperbaton in Greek*. New York / Oxford: Oxford University Press

Di Giovine, Paolo 1990–6. *Studio sul perfetto indoeuropeo*. Rome: Dipartimento di studi glottoantropoligici dell'Università di Roma 'La Sapienza'

Diebold Jr, A. Richard 1985. *The Evolution of Indo-European Nomenclature for Salmonid Fish*. Journal of Indo-European Studies Monograph Series 5. Washington, DC: Institute for the Study of Man

Dixon, R. M. W. 1994. *Ergativity*. Cambridge: Cambridge University Press

Dolgopolsky, Aharon 1998. *The Nostratic Macrofamily and Linguistic Palaeontology*. Cambridge: McDonald Institute for Archaeological Research

   1999. 'The Nostratic Macrofamily: A Short Introduction', in Renfrew and Nettle (eds.), pp. 19–44

Dressler, Wolfgang 1969. 'Eine textsyntaktische Regel der idg. Wortstellung', *Zeitschrift für vergleichende Sprachforschung* 83: 1–25

   1971. 'Über die Rekonstruktion der idg. Syntax', *Zeitschrift für vergleichende Sprachforschung* 85: 5–22

Drinka, Bridget 1995. *The Sigmatic Aorist in Indo-European: Evidence for the Space-Time Hypothesis*. Journal of Indo-European Studies Monograph Series 13. Washington, DC: Institute for the Study of Man

   1999. 'Alignment in Early Proto-Indo-European', in Justus and Polomé (eds.), pp. 464–500

Dumézil, Georges 1983. *La Courtisane et les seigneurs colorés et autres essais: vingt-cinq esquisses de mythologie*. Paris: Gallimard

   1992. *Mythes et dieux des indo-européens*. (Textes réunis et présentés par Hervé Coutau-Bégarie.) Paris: Flammarion

Dunkel, George E., Meyer, G., Scarlata, S. and Seidl, C. (eds.) 1994. *Früh-, Mittel-, Spätindogermanisch. Akten der IX. Fachtagung der Indogermanischen Gesellschaft vom 5. bis 9. Oktober 1992 in Zürich*. Wiesbaden: Reichert

Durie, Mark and Ross, Malcolm (eds.) 1996. *The Comparative Method Reviewed: Regularity and Irregularity in Language Change*. New York / Oxford: Oxford University Press

Eichner, Heiner 1971. 'Urindogermanisch $*k^w e$ "wenn" im Hethitischen', *Münchener Studien zur Sprachwissenschaft* 29: 27–46

   1975. 'Die Vorgeschichte des hethitischen Verbalsystems', in Rix (ed.), pp. 71–103

   1982. 'Studien zu den indogermanischen Numeralia.' Unpublished Habiliationschrift, Univerität Regensburg

   1985. 'Das Problem des Ansatzes eines urindogermanischen Numerus, Kollektiv' ('Komprehensiv')', in Schlerath and Rittner (eds.), pp. 134–69

   and Rix, Helmut (eds.) 1990. *Sprachwissenschaft und Philologie: Jacob Wackernagel und die Indogermanistik heute: Kolloquium der Indogermanischen Gesellschaft vom 13. bis 15. Oktober 1988 in Basel*. Wiesbaden: Reichert

Elbourne, Paul 1998. 'Proto-Indo-European Voiceless Aspirates', *Historische Sprachforschung (Zeitschrift für vergleichende Sprachforschung)* 111: 1–30

   2000. 'Plain Voiceless Stop plus Laryngeal in Indo-European', *Historische Sprachforschung (Zeitschrift für vergleichende Sprachforschung)* 113: 2–30

   2001. 'Aspiration by /s/ and Devoicing of Mediae Aspiratae', *Historische Sprachforschung (Zeitschrift für vergleichende Sprachforschung)* 114: 197–219

Etter, Annemarie 1985. *Die Fragesätze im Ṛgveda*. Berlin / New York: De Gruyter

Euler, Wolfram 1991. 'Die Frage nach der Entstehung der indogermanischen Genera im Lichte der relativen Chronologie', *Indogermanische Forschungen* 96: 36–45

1992. *Modale Aoristbildungen und ihre Relikte in den alteuropäischen Sprachen.* Innsbruck: Institut für Sprachwissenschaft der Universität Innsbruck

Finkelberg, Margalit 1986. 'Is ΚΛΕΟΣ ΑΦΘΙΤΟΝ a Homeric Formula?', *Classical Quarterly* 3: 1–5

Floyd, Edwin D. 1980. 'Kléos áphthiton: An Indo-European Perspective on Early Greek', *Glotta* 58: 133–57

Foley, John Miles (ed.) 2005. *A Companion to Ancient Epic.* Malden, Mass. / Oxford: Blackwell

Forssman, Bernhard 1985. 'Der Imperativ im urindogermanischen Verbalsystem', in Schlerath and Rittner (eds.), pp. 181–97

Forster, Peter and Renfrew, Colin (eds.) 2006. *Phylogenetic Methods and the Prehistory of Languages.* Cambridge: McDonald Institute for Archaeological Research

Fortson IV, Benjamin W. 2004. *Indo-European Language and Culture.* Oxford: Blackwell

Fox, A. 1995. *Linguistic Reconstruction.* Oxford: Oxford University Press

Francis, E. D. 1970. 'Greek Disyllabic Roots: The Aorist Formations.' Unpublished PhD dissertation, Yale University

Friedrich, Johannes 1960. *Hethitisches Elementarbuch. I Teil. Kurzgefaßte Grammatik.* Heidelberg: Carl Winter

Friedrich, Paul 1970. *Proto-Indo-European Trees. The Arborial System of a Prehistoric People.* Chicago: University of Chicago Press

1975. *Proto-Indo-European Syntax: The Order of the Meaningful Elements.* Journal of Indo-European Studies Monograph Series 1. Butte, Montana: Journal of Indo-European Studies

Fritz, Matthias 2000. 'Der urindogermanische Dual – eine Klasse für sich?', in Ofitsch and Zinko (eds.), pp. 133–37

2003. 'Untersuchungen zum indogermanischen Dual. Vom Werden und Schwinden einer grammatischen Kategorie.' Unpublished Habilitationschrift, Freie Universität Berlin

Fulk, R. D. 1986. *The Origins of Indo-European Quantitative Ablaut.* Innsbruck: Institut für Sprachwissenschaft der Universität Innsbruck

Gamkrelidze, Thomas V. and Ivanov, Vjaceslav V. 1984. *Indoevropejskij jazyk i indoevropejcy.* Tbilisi: Tbilisi University Press

1995. *Indo-European and the Indo-Europeans.* (Translation of Gamkrelidze and Ivanov 1984 by Johanna Nichols.) Berlin / New York: Mouton de Gruyter

Gates, H. P. 1971. *The Kinship Terminology of Homeric Greek.* International Journal of American Linguistics, Memoir 27. Bloomington, Indiana: Indiana University Publications in Anthropology and Linguistics

García Ramón, José Luis 1998. 'Indogermanisch *$g^{wh}en$*- "(wiederholt) schlagen", "töten"', in Jasanoff, Melchert and Oliver (eds.), pp. 139–54

Garrett, Andrew 1990. 'The Origin of NP Split Ergativity', *Language* 66: 261–96

1991. 'Indo-European Reconstruction and Historical Methodologies', *Language* 67: 790–804

1992. 'Topics in Lycian Syntax', *Historische Sprachforschung* 105: 200–12

1994. 'Relative Clause Syntax in Lycian and Hittite', *Die Sprache* 36: 29–69

1999. 'A New Model of Indo-European Sub-Grouping and Dispersal', in Chang, Liaw and Ruppenhofer (eds.), pp. 146–56

2006. 'Convergence in the Formation of Indo-European Subgroups: Phylogeny and Chronology', in Forster and Renfrew (eds.), pp. 139–51

Giannakis, Giorgios K. 1997. *Studies in the Syntax and Semantics of the Reduplicated Presents of Homeric Greek and Indo-European*. Innsbruck: Institut für Sprachwissenschaft der Universität Innsbruck

Gonda, Jan 1959. 'On Amplified Sentences and Similar Structures in the Veda', in *Four Studies in the Languages of the Veda*'s Gravenhage: Mouton

Goody, Jack 1959. 'Indo-European Society', *Past and Present* 16: 88–92, reprinted in Goody 1969, pp. 235–9

1969. *Comparative Studies in Kinship*. London: Routledge and Kegan Paul

Gray, R. D. and Atkinson, Q. D. 2003. 'Language-Tree Divergence Times Support the Anatolian Theory of Indo-European Origin', *Nature* 426: 435–9

Greenberg, Joseph H. 2000. *Indo-European and its Closest Relatives: The Eurasiatic Language Family. Volume I. Grammar*. Stanford: Stanford University Press

Gvozdanović, Jadranka (ed.) 1992. *Indo-European Numerals*. Berlin / New York: Mouton de Gruyter

1999. *Numeral Types and Changes Worldwide*. Berlin / New York: Mouton de Gruyter

Hainsworth, Bryan 1993. *The Iliad: A Commentary. Volume III Books 9–12*. Cambridge: Cambridge University Press

Hajnal, Ivo 1997. 'Definite nominale Determination im Indogermanischen', *Indogermanische Forschungen* 102: 38–72

Hale, Mark 1987a. 'Studies in the Comparative Syntax of the Oldest Indo-Iranian Languages.' Unpublished PhD thesis (Linguistics), Harvard University

1987b. 'Notes on Wackernagel's Law in the Language of the Rigveda', in Watkins (ed.), pp. 38–50

Halle, Morris 1995. 'Udarenie i akcent v indoevropejskom', *Problemy Fonetiki* 2: 135–56

1997. 'On Stress and Accent in Indo-European', *Language* 73: 275–313

and Vergnaud, J.-R. 1987. *An Essay on Stress*. Cambridge, Mass.: MIT Press

Hänsel, B. and Zimner, S. (eds.) 1994. *Die Indogermanen und das Pferd. Akten des Internazionalen interdisziplinären Kolloquiums Freie Universität Berlin, 1.-3. Juli 1992*. Budapest: Archaeolingua

Harðarson, Jón Axel 1987a. 'Zum urindogermanischen Kollektivum', *Münchener Studien zur Sprachwissenschaft* 48: 71–113

1987b. 'Das urindogermanische Wort für "Frau"', *Münchener Studien zur Sprachwissenschaft* 48: 115–37

1993. *Studien zum urindogermanischen Wurzelaorist und dessen Vertretung im Indoiranischen und Griechischen*. Innsbruck: Institut für Sprachwissenschaft der Universität Innsbruck

1994. 'Der Verlust zweier wichtiger Flexionskategorien im Uranatolischen', *Historische Sprachforschung (Zeitschrift für Vergleichende Sprachforschung)* 107: 30–4

Harris, Alice C. and Campbell, Lyle 1995. *Historical Syntax in Cross-Linguistic Perspective*. Cambridge: Cambridge University Press

Haubold, Johannes 2000. *Homer's People: Epic Poetry and Social Formation*. Cambridge: Cambridge University Press

Hawkins, J. David 2000. *Corpus of Hieroglyphic Luwian Inscriptions. Volume I*. Berlin / New York: de Gruyter

2003. 'Scripts and Texts', in Melchert (ed.) 2003, pp. 128–69

Held Jr, Warren H. 1957. *The Hittite Relative Sentence*. Language Dissertation no. 55. Baltimore: Waverly Press

Hermann, Eduard 1895. 'Gab es im Indogermanischen Nebensätze?', *Zeitschrift für vergleichende Sprachforschung* 13: 481–535

Heesterman, J. C., Schokker, G. H. and Subramoniam, V. I. (eds.) 1968. *Pratidānam. Indian, Iranian and Indo-European Studies Presented to Franciscus Bernardus Jacobus Kuiper*. The Hague: Mouton

Hettrich, Heinrich 1985. 'Indo-European Kinship Terminology in Linguistics and Anthropology', *Anthropological Linguistics* 27: 453–80

1988. *Untersuchungen zur Hypotaxe im Vedischen*. Berlin / New York: de Gruyter

1992. 'Lateinische Konditionalsätze in sprachvergleichender Sicht', in Panagl and Krisch (eds.), pp. 263–84

1997. 'Syntaktische Rekonstruktion bei Delbrück und heute: Nochmals zum lateinschen und griechischen AcI', in Crespo and García Ramón (eds.), pp. 219–38

Hewson, John and Bubeník, Vít 1997. *Tense and Aspect in Indo-European Languages: Theory, Typology, Diachrony*. Amsterdam: Benjamins

Hiersche, Rolf 1964. *Untersuchungen zur Frage der Tenues aspiratae in Indogermanischen*. Wiesbaden: Harrassowitz

Hock, Wolfgang 1993. 'Der urindogermanische Flexionsakzent und die morphologische Akzentologiekonzeption', *MSS* 53: 177–205

Hoffmann, Karl 1967. *Der Injunktiv im Veda*. Heidelberg: Winter

1970. 'Das Kategoriensysten des indogermanischen Verbums', *Münchener Studien zur Sprachwissenschaft* 28: 19–41

and Forssman, Bernhard 1996. *Avestische Laut- und Flexionslehre*. Innsbruck: Institut für Sprachwissenschaft der Universität Innsbruck

Holland, Gary B. 1984. 'Subordination and Relativization in Early Indo-European', in Brugman and Macaulay (eds.), pp. 609–22

Horrocks, Geoffrey 1996. 'Greek Voices – Indo-European Echoes. Towards a Unified Theory of the "Middle"'. Unpublished paper delivered at the Oxford meeting of the Philological Society

Huld, Martin E. 1997. '*Satəm, Centum,* and *Hokum*', in Douglas Q. Adams (ed.), pp. 115–38

Hyman, Larry (ed.) 1977. *Studies in Stress and Accent*. Los Angeles: University of Southern California

Illič-Svityč, Vladislav M. 1971–84. *Opyt sravnenija nostratičeskix jazykov*. Moscow: Nauka

Isebaert, Lambert (ed.) 1991. *Studia etymologia indoeuropaea: memoriae A. J. van Windekens (1915–1989) dicata*. Leuven: Departement Oriëntalistiek

1992. 'Spuren akrostatischer Präsensflexion im Lateinischen', in Panagl and Krisch (eds.), pp. 193–205

Jacobi, Hermann 1897. *Compositum und Nebensatz: Studien über die indogermanische Sprachentwicklung*. Bonn: Cohen

Jakobson, Roman 1958. 'Typological Studies and their Contribution to Historical Comparative Linguistics', *Proceedings of the Eighth International Congress of Linguists (Oslo 1957)* 17–35

Janko, Richard 1992. *The Iliad: A Commentary. Volume IV Books 13–16*. Cambridge: Cambridge University Press

Jasanoff, Jay H. 1977. 'The *r*-endings of the IE Middle', *Die Sprache* 23: 159–70
    1978. *Stative and Middle in Indo-European*. Innsbruck: Institut für Sprachwissenschaft der Universität Innsbruck
    1989. 'Old Irish *bé* "woman"', *Ériu* 40: 135–41
    1998. 'The thematic conjugation revisited', in Jasonoff, Melchert and Oliver (eds.), pp. 301–16
    2003. *Hittite and the Indo-European Verb*. Oxford: Oxford University Press
    Melchert, H. Craig and Oliver, Lisi (eds.) 1998. *Mír curad: Studies in Honor of Calvert Watkins*. Innsbruck: Institut für Sprachwissenschaft der Universität Innsbruck
Jeffers, Robert J. 1976. 'Syntactic Change and Syntactic Reconstruction', in Christie (ed.), pp. 1–16
Job, Michael 1989. 'Sound Change Typology and the "Ejective Model"', in Vennemann (ed.), pp. 123–36
    1995. 'Did Proto-Indo-European have Glottalized Stops?', *Diachronica* 12: 237–50
Jones, Charles (ed.) 1993. *Historical Linguistics: Problems and Prospectives*. London: Longman
Jones-Bley, Karlene, Huld, Martin E. and Della Volpe, Angela (eds.) 2000. *Proceedings of the Eleventh Annual UCLA Indo-European Conference (Los Angeles June 4–5, 1999)*. Journal of Indo-European Studies Monograph Series 35. Washington, DC: Institute for the Study of Man
Joseph, Brian D. and Janda, Richard D. (eds.) 2003. *The Handbook of Historical Linguistics*. Malden, Mass. / Oxford: Blackwell
    and Salmons, Joe (eds.) 1998. *Nostratic: Sifting the Evidence*. Amsterdam: Benjamins
Juilland, Alphonse (ed.) 1976. *Linguistic Studies Offered to Joseph Greenberg on the Occasion of his Sixtieth Birthday*. Saratoga: Anma Libri
Justus, Carol F. and Polomé, Edgar C. (eds.) 1999. *Language Change and Typological Variation: In Honor of Winfred P. Lehmann on the Occasion of His 83rd Birthday. Volume II Grammatical Universals and Typology*. Journal of Indo-European Studies Monograph Series 31. Washington, DC: Institute for the Study of Man
Kaiser, M. and Shevoroshkin, V. 1988. 'Nostratic', *Annual Review of Archaeology* 17: 309–29
Katz, Joshua T. 2000. 'Evening Dress: The Metaphorical Background of Latin *uesper* and Greek ἕσπερος', in Jones-Bley, Huld and Della Volpe (eds.), pp. 69–93
    2005. 'The Indo-European Context', in Foley (ed.), pp. 20–30
Kemmer, Suzanne 1993. *The Middle Voice*. Amsterdam / Philadelphia: Benjamins
Kerns, J. Alexander and Schwarz, Benjamin 1972. *A Sketch of the Indo-European Finite Verb*. Leiden: Brill
Kimball, Sarah E. 1987. '*H_3* in Anatolian', in Cardona and Zide (eds.), pp. 185–92
Kiparsky, Paul 1968. 'Tense and Mood in Indo-European Syntax', *Foundations of Language* 4: 30–57
    1973. 'The Inflectional Accent in Indo-European', *Language* 49: 794–849
    1995. 'Indo-European Origins of Germanic Syntax', in Battye and Roberts (eds.), pp. 140–69
    and Halle, Morris 1977. 'Towards a Reconstruction of the Indo-European Accent', in Hyman (ed.), pp. 209–38
Klaiman, M. H. 1991. *Grammatical Voice*. Cambridge: Cambridge University Press

Klein, Jared S. 1985. *Toward a Discourse Grammar of the Rigveda. Volume I: Coordinate Conjunction. Part I Introduction, ca, utá.* Heidelberg: Winter

1990. Review of Hettrich 1988, *Kratylos* 35: 86–95

Klingenschmitt, Gert 1982. *Das altarmenische Verbum.* Wiesbaden: Reichert

1994. 'Die Verwandtschaftsverhältnisse der indogermanischen Sprachen', in Rasmussen (ed.), pp. 235–51

Kloekhorst, Alwin 2004. 'The Preservation of $*h_1$ in Hieroglyphic Luwian: Two Separate *a*-Signs', *Historische Sprachforschung (Zeitschrift für Vergleichende Sprachforschung)* 117: 26–49

Koch, Harold 1996. 'Reconstruction in Morphology', in Durie and Ross (eds.), pp. 218–63

Kortlandt, Frederik 1981. 'Ist sg. middle $*-H_2$', *Indogermanische Forschungen* 86: 123–36

Krahe, Hans 1972. *Grundzüge der vergleichenden Syntax der indogermanischen Sprachen* (edited by Wolfgang Meid and Hans Schmeja). Innsbruck: Institut für Sprachwissenschaft der Universität Innsbruck

Krisch, Thomas 1990. 'Das Wackernagelsche Gesetz aus heutiger Sicht', in Eichner and Rix (eds.), pp. 64–81

1997. 'B. Delbrücks Arbeiten zur Wortstellung aus heutiger Sicht', in Crespo and García Ramón (eds.), pp. 283–309

1998. 'Zum Hyperbaton in altindogermanischen Sprachen', in Meid (ed.), pp. 351–84

Kümmel, Martin 1996. *Stativ und Passivaorist im Indoiranischen.* Göttingen: Vandenhoeck & Ruprecht

2000. *Das Perfekt im Indoiranischen.* Wiesbaden: Reichert

Kuryłowicz, Jerzy 1927. 'ə indoeuropéen et *h* hittite', in *Symbolae grammaticae in honorem Joannis Rozwadowski.* Cracow: Uniwersytet Jagiellonski

1968. *Indogermanische Grammatik. Band II: Ablaut – Akzent.* Heidelberg: Winter

Ladefoged, Peter and Maddieson, Ian 1996. *The Sounds of the World's Languages.* Oxford: Blackwell

Lamb, Sydney M. and Mitchell, E. Douglas (eds.) 1991. *Sprung from Some Common Source: Investigations into the Prehistory of Languages.* Stanford: Stanford University Press

de Lamberterie, Charles 1997. 'Milman Parry et Antoine Meillet', in Létoublon (ed.), pp. 9–22

Lehmann, Christian 1979. 'Der Relativsatz vom Indogermanischen bis zum Italienischen', *Die Sprache* 25: 1–25

1980. 'Der indogermanische $*k^w i$- / $k^w o$- Relativsatz im typologischen Vergleich', in Ramat (ed.), pp. 155–69

1984. *Der Relativsatz.* Tübingen: Narr

Lehmann, Winfred P. 1974. *Proto-Indo-European Syntax.* Austin, Texas and London: University of Texas Press

1993. *Theoretical Bases of Indo-European Linguistics.* London and New York: Routledge

Létoublon, Françoise (ed.) 1997. *Hommage à Milman Parry.* Amsterdam: Gieben

Leumann, M. 1952. 'Vokaldehnung, Dehnstufe und Vrddhi', *Indogermanische Forschungen* 61: 1–16

Lightfoot, David 1980. 'On Reconstructing a Proto-Syntax', in Ramat (ed.), pp. 27–45

Lindeman, Fredrik O. 1982. *The Triple Representation of Schwa in Greek and Some Related Problems of Indo-European Phonology.* Oslo: Universitetsforlaget

1997. *Introduction to the Laryngeal Theory*. Third Edition. Innsbruck: Institut für Sprachwissenschaft der Universität Innsbruck

Littleton, C. Scott 1982. *The New Comparative Mythology: An Anthropological Assessment of the Theories of Georges Dumézil*. Third Edition. Berkeley, Los Angeles / London: University of California Press

Lubotsky, A. M. 1988. *The System of Nominal Accentuation in Sanskrit and Proto-Indo-European*. Leiden / New York: Brill

Lühr, Rosemarie 1997a. 'Haus und Hof im Lexikon des Indogermanischen', in Beck and Steuer (eds.), pp. 26–49

1997b. 'Altgermanische Fragesätze: der Ausdruck der Antworterwartung', in Crespo and García Ramón (eds.), pp. 327–62

2000. 'Zum gebrauch des Duals in der Indogermania', in Ofitsch and Zinko (eds.), pp. 263–73

Luján Martínez, Eugenio Ramón 1999. 'The Indo-European Numerals from "1" to "10"', in Gvozdanović (ed.), 1999 pp. 199–219

Luraghi, Silvia 1990a. *Old Hittite Sentence Structure*. London / New York: Routledge

1990b. 'Note sulla legge di Wackernagel e la posizione del verbo in alcune lingue indoeuropee', in Ramat, Ramat and Conte (eds.)

McCone, Kim 1997. 'Delbrück's Model of PIE Word Order and the Celtic evidence', in Crespo and García Ramón (eds.), pp. 363–96

1998. '"King" and "Queen" in Celtic and Indo-European', *Ériu* 49: 1–12

McMahon, April (ed.) 2005. *Quantative Methods in Language Comparison*. (Special Issue of Transactions of the Philological Society 2005.2.) Oxford: Blackwell

Renfrew, Colin and Trask, Larry (eds.) 2000. *Time Depth in Historical Linguistics*. Cambridge: McDonald Institute for Archaeological Research

Mallory, James P. 1989. *In Search of the Indo-Europeans: Language, Archaeology and Myth*. London: Thames and Hudson

and Adams, Douglas Q. (eds.) 1997. *Encyclopedia of Indo-European Culture*. London: Fitzroy Dearborn

2006. *The Oxford Introduction to Proto-Indo-European and the Proto-Indo-European World*. Oxford: Oxford University Press

Malzahn, Melanie 2000. 'Die Genese des idg. Numerus Dual', in Ofitsch and Zinko (eds.), pp. 291–315

Manaster Ramer, Alexis 1993. 'On Illic-Švityč's Nostratic Theory', *Studies in Language* 17: 205–50

Matasovic, Ranko 1996. *A Theory of Textual Reconstruction in Indo-European linguistics*. Frankfurt am Main: Peter Lang

2004. *Gender in Indo-European*. Heidelberg: Winter

Mayrhofer, Manfred 1981. *Nach hundert Jahren. Ferdinand de Saussures Frühwerk und seine Rezeption durch die heutige Indogermanistik* (Sitzungsberichte der Heidelberger Akademie der Wissenschaften, Philosophisch-historische Klasse, Jahrgang 1981 Bericht 8.) Heidelberg: Winter

Mayrhofer, Manfred 1986. 'Lautlehre', in Mayrhofer, Manfred (ed.) *Indogermanisches Grammatik Band I*. Heidelberg: Winter, 1986 pp. 87–181

1986–2001. *Etymologisches Wörterbuch des Altindoarischen*. Heidelberg: Winter

Meid, Wolfgang 1975. 'Probleme der räumlichen und zeitlichen Gliederung des Indogermanischen', in Rix (ed.), pp. 204–19 (ed.) 1987. *Studien zum indogermanischen Wortschatz*. Innsbruck: Institut für Sprachwissenschaft der Universität Innsbruck

1994. 'Die Terminologie von Pferd und Wagen im Indogermanischen', in Hänsel and Zimmer (eds.), pp. 53–65

(ed.) 1998. *Sprache und Kultur der Indogermanen: Akten der X. Fachtagung der Indogermanischen Gesellschaft, Innsbruck, 22.–28. September 1996*. Innsbruck: Institut für Sprachwissenschaft der Universität Innsbruck

and Neu, Erich (eds.) 1979. *Hethitisch und Indogermanisch, vergleichende Studien zur historischen Grammatik und zur dialektgeographischen Stellung der indogermanischen Sprachgruppe Altkleinasiens*. Innsbruck: Institut für Sprachwissenschaft der Universität Innsbruck

Meier-Brügger, Michael 2003. *Indo-European Linguistics*. Berlin: de Gruyter

Meillet, Antoine 1964. *Introduction à l'étude comparatif des langues indo-européennes*. University of Alabama: Alabama University Press

Meiser, Gerhard 1992. 'Syncretism in Indo-European Languages – Motives, Process and Results', *Transactions of the Philological Society* 90: 187–218

1993. 'Zur Funktion des Nasalpräsens im Urindogermanischen', in Gerhard Meiser (ed.), pp. 280–313

(ed.) 1993. *Indogermanica et Italica: Festschrift für Helmut Rix zum 65. Geburtstag*. Innsbruck: Institut für Sprachwissenschaft der Universität Innsbruck

1998. *Historische Laut- und Formenlehre der lateinischen Sprache*. Darmstadt: Wissenschaftliche Buchgesellschaft

Melchert, H. Craig 1994a. *Anatolian Historical Phonology*. Amsterdam / Atlanta, Ga.: Rodopi

1994b. 'The Feminine Gender in Anatolian', in Dunkel, Meyer, Scarlata and Seidl (eds.), pp. 231–44

(ed.) 2003. *The Luwians*. (Handbook of Oriental Studies / Handbuch der Orientalistik. Section 1. Volume LXVIII.) Leiden / Boston: Brill

(ed.) 2004. *A Dictionary of the Lycian Language*. Ann Arbor / New York: Beech Stave Press

de Melo, Wolfgang David Cirilo 2004. 'Gab es im Uritalischen einen *a*-Präventiv?', *Historische Sprachforschung* (*Zeitschrift für vergleichende Sprachforschung*) 117: 249–68

Nagy, Gregory 1990. *Greek Mythology and Poetics*. Ithaca, New York / London: Cornell University Press

Narten, Johanna 1968. 'Zum "proterodynamischen" Wurzelpräsens', in Heesterman, Schokker and Subramoniam (eds.), pp. 9–19

Neu, Erich 1985. 'Das frühindogermanische Diathesensystem. Funktion und Geschichte', in Schlerath and Rittner (eds.), pp. 275–95

Nichols, Johanna 1992. *Linguistic Diversity in Space and Time*. Chicago / London: University of Chicago Press

1996. 'The Comparative Method as Heuristic', in Durie and Ross (eds.), pp. 39–71

Niepokuj, Mary 1997. *The Development of Verbal Reduplication in Indo-European*, Journal of Indo-European Studies Monograph Series 24. Washington, DC: Institute for the Study of Man

Noyer, R. 1997. 'Attic Greek Accentuation and Intermediate Derivational Representations', in Roca (ed.), pp. 501–27

Nussbaum, Alan J. 1976. 'Caland's "Law" and the Caland System.' Unpublished PhD thesis, Harvard University

1986. *Head and Horn in Indo-European*. Berlin / New York: de Gruyter

1998. *Two Studies in Greek and Homeric Linguistics*. Göttingen: Vandenhoeck & Ruprecht

Oettinger, Norbert 1976. 'Der indogermanische Stativ', *Münchener Studien zur Sprachwissenschaft* 34: 109–49

1979. *Die Stammbildung des hethitischen Verbums*. Nuremberg: Carl

Ofitsch, Michaela and Zinko, Christian (eds.) 2000. *125 Jahre Indo-Germanistik in Graz: Festband anlässlich des 125jährigen Bestehens der Forschungseinrichtung 'Indogermanistik' an der Karl-Franzens-Universität Graz*. Graz: Leykam

Panagl, Oswald, and Krisch, Thomas (eds.) 1992. *Latein und Indogermanisch. Akten des Kolloquiums der Indogermanischen Gesellschaft, Salzburg, 23.–26. September 1986*. Innsbruck: Institut für Sprachwissenschaft der Universität Innsbruck

Parry, Milman 1971. *The Making of Homeric Verse: The Collected Papers of Milman Parry*. Oxford: Oxford University Press

Penney, John 2000. Review of Crespo and García Ramón (eds.) 1997, *Kratylos* 45: 29–35

Pinault, Georges-Jean 1989. 'Introduction an tokharien', *Lalies. Actes des sessions de linguistique et de littérature* 7: 1–224

Polomé, Edgar C. (ed.) 1996. *Indo-European Religion after Dumézil*. Journal of Indo-European Studies Monograph Series 16. Washington, DC: Institute for the Study of Man

Pokorny, Julius 1959. *Indogermanisches etymologisches Wörterbuch*. Bern / Stuttgart: Francke

Probert, Philomen 2006. 'Clause Boundaries in Old Hittite Relative Sentences', *Transactions of the Philological Society* 104: 17–83

Ramat, Paolo (ed.) 1980. *Linguistic Reconstruction and Indo-European Syntax: Proceedings of the Colloquium of the 'Indogermanische Gesellschaft', University of Pavia, 6–7 September 1979*. Amsterdam: Benjamins

Ramat, Anna Garcialone and Conte, M. E. (eds.) 1990. *Dimensioni della linguistica*. Milan: Franco Angeli

Ramat, Anna Giacalone and Ramat, Paolo (eds.) 1997. *The Indo-European Languages*. New York: Routledge

Rasmussen, Jens Elmegård 1989. *Studien zur Morphophonemik der indogermanischen Grundsprache*. Innsbruck: Institut für Sprachwissenschaft der Universität Innsbruck

(ed.) 1994. *In Honorem Holger Pedersen: Kolloquium der indogermanischen Gesellschaft vom 25. bis 28. März 1993 in Kopenhagen*. Wiesbaden: Reichert

Rauch, Irmengard 2003. *The Gothic Language: Grammar, Genetic Provenance and Typology, Readings*. New York: Peter Lang

Raulwing, Peter 2000. *Horses, Chariots and Indo-Europeans: Foundations and Methods of Chariotry Research from the Viewpoint of Comparative Indo-European Linguistics*. Budapest: Archaeolingua

Renfrew, Colin 1987. *Archaeology and Language*. Cambridge: Cambridge University Press

and Nettle, Daniel (eds.) 1999. *Nostratic: Examining a Linguistic Macrofamily*. Cambridge: McDonald Institute for Archaeological Research

Rieken, Elisabeth 1999. *Untersuchungen zur nominalen Stammbildung des Hethitischen.* Wiesbaden: Harrassowitz

Ringe, Donald A. 1988–90. 'Evidence for the Position of Tocharian in the Indo-European Family?', *Die Sprache* 34: 59–123

   1992. *On Calculating the Factor of Chance in Language Comparison.* Philadelphia: American Philosophical Society

   1995. 'Nostratic and the Factor of Chance', *Diachronica* 12: 55–74

   1999. 'How Hard is it to Match CVC- Roots?', *Transactions of the Philological Society* 97: 213–44

   2000. 'Tocharian Class II Presents and Subjunctives and the Reconstruction of the Proto-Indo-European Verb', *Tocharian and Indo-European Studies* 9: 121–41

   2002. Review of Greenberg 2000, *Journal of Linguistics* 38: 415–20

   Warnow, T. and Taylor, A. 2002. 'Indo-European and Computational Cladistics', *Transactions of the Philological Society* 100: 59–129

Risch, Ernst 1985. 'Die Entwicklung der verbalen Kategorien im Indogermanischen', in Schlerath and Rittner (eds.), pp. 400–10

Rix, Helmut (ed.) 1975. *Flexion und Wortbildung: Akten der V. Fachtagung der indogermanischen Gesellschaft. Regensburg, 9.–14. September 1973.* Wiesbaden: Reichert

   1976. *Historische Grammatik des griechischen Laut- und Formenlehre.* Darmstadt: Wissenschaftliche Buchgesellschaft

   1979. 'Abstrakte Komplemente im Urindogermanischen', in Brogyanyí (ed.) Part II. pp. 725–47

   1986. *Zur Entstehung des urindogermanischen Modussystems.* Innsbruck: Institut für Sprachwissenschaft der Universität Innsbruck

   1988. 'The Proto-Indo-European Middle: Content, Forms and Origin', *Münchener Studien zur Sprachwissenschaft* 49: 101–9

   1991. 'Uridg. **gheslo*-in den südidg. Ausdrücken für "1000"', in Isebaert (ed.), pp. 225–31

   1998. 'Eine neue frühsabellische Inschrift und der altitalische Präventiv', *Historische Sprachforschung (Zeitschrift für vergleichende Sprachforschung)* 111: 247–69

   Kümmel, Martin, Zehnder, Thomas, Lipp, Reiner and Schirmer, Brigitte 1998. *Lexikon der indogermanischen Verben: die Wurzeln und ihre Primärstammbildungen.* Wiesbaden: Reichert (2nd, corrected edn. 2001)

Roca, Iggy (ed.) 1997. *Derivations and Constraints in Phonology.* Oxford: Clarendon Press

Rowenchuk, K. 1992. 'Why Aren't Americans Interested in Nostratics?', in Shevoroshkin (ed.), pp. 84–92

Ruijgh, C. J. 1971. *Autour de "τε épique": Études sur la syntaxe grecque.* Amsterdam: Hakkert

   1990. 'La place des enclitiques dans l'ordre des mots chez Homère d'après la loi de Wackernagel', in Eichner and Rix (eds.), pp. 213–33

Rumsey, Alan 1987a. 'Was Proto-Indo-European an Ergative Language?', *Journal of Indo-European Studies* 15: 19–37

   1987b. 'The Chimera of Proto-Indo-European Ergativity', *Lingua* 71: 297–318

Salmons, Joseph C. 1992. *The Glottalic Theory: Survey and Synthesis,* Journal of Indo-European Studies Monograph Series 10. McLean, Va.: Institute for the Study of Man

Saussure, Ferdinand de 1879. *Mémoire sur le système primatif des voyelles dans les langues indo-européennes.* Leipzig: Teubner

Schindler, Jochem 1966. 'Bemerkungen zum idg. Wort für "Schlaf"', *Die Sprache* 12: 67–76

1970. Review of Anttila 1969, *Kratylos* 15: 146–52

1975. 'Zum ablaut der neutralen *s*-Stämme des Indogermanischen', in Rix (ed.), pp. 259–67

1977a. 'A thorny problem', *Die Sprache* 23: 25–35

1977b. 'Notizen zum Sieversschen Gesetz', *Die Sprache* 23: 56–65

1994. 'Alte und neue Fragen zum indogermanischen Nomen', in Rasmussen (ed.), pp. 397–400

Schlerath, Bernfried 1987. 'On the Reality and Status of a Reconstructed Language', *Journal of Indo-European Studies* 15: 41–6

1995. 'G. Dumézil und die Rekonstruktion der indogermanischen Kultur, 1. Teil', *Kratylos* 40: 1–48

1996. 'G. Dumézil und die Rekonstruktion der indogermanischen Kultur, 2. Teil', *Kratylos* 41: 1–67

and Rittner, Veronica (eds.) 1985. *Grammatische Kategorien, Funktion und Geschichte: Akten der VII. Fachtagung der indogermanischen Gesellschaft, Berlin, 20.–25. Februar 1983*. Wiesbaden: Reichert

Schmidt, Karl H. 1999. 'On Congruence in Languages of Active Typology', in Justus and Polomé (eds.), pp. 528–36

Schmitt, Rüdiger 1967. *Dichtung und Dichtersprache in indogermanischer Zeit*. Wiesbaden: Harrassowitz

1981. *Grammatik des Klassisch-Armenischen mit sprachvergleichenden Erläuterungen*. Innsbruck: Institut für Sprachwissenschaft der Universität Innsbruck

2000. 'Indogermanische Altertumskunde', in *Reallexikon der germanischen Altertumskunde*, Second Edition. Berlin: de Gruyter. Volume XV: 384–402

Schmitt-Brandt, Robert 1967. *Die Entwicklung des idg. Vokalsystems*. Heidelberg: Julius Groos

Schrijver, Peter 1991. *The Reflexes of the PIE Laryngeals in Latin*. Amsterdam / Atlanta, Ga.: Rodopi

Schwink, F. 2004. *The Third Gender: Studies in the Origin and History of Germanic Grammatical Gender*. Heidelberg: Winter

Sergent, Bernard 1995. *Les Indo-Européens: Histoire, langues, mythes*. Paris: Payot

Shevoroshkin, Vitalij V. (ed.) 1992. *Nostratic, Dene-Caucasian, Austric and Amerind: Materials from the First International Interdisciplinary Symposium on Language and Prehistory, Ann Arbor, 8–12 November, 1988*. Bochum: Brockmeyer

and Manaster Ramer, Alexis 1991. 'Some Recent Work on the Remote Relations of Languages', in Lamb and Mitchell (eds.), pp. 178–99

and Markey, Thomas L. 1986. *Typology, Relationship and Time: A Collection of Papers on Language Change and Relationship by Soviet Linguists*. Ann Arbor: Karoma

Shields, Kenneth C. 1992. *A History of Indo-European Verb Morphology*. Amsterdam / Philadelphia: John Benjamins

Sihler, Andrew L. 1995. *New Comparative Grammar of Greek and Latin*. New York / Oxford: Oxford University Press

Sommer, Ferdinand 1951. *Zum Zahlwort*. (Sitzungsberichte der Bayerischen Akademie der Wissenschaften. Philosophisch-Historische Klasse; Jg. 1950, Heft 7.) Munich: Bayerische Akademie der Wissenschaften

Starke, Frank 1990. *Untersuchung zur Stammbildung des keilschrift-luwischen Nomens.* Wiesbaden: Harrassowitz

Steever, Sanford B., Walker, C. A. and Mufwene, Salikoko S. (eds.) 1976. *Papers from the Parasession on Diachronic Syntax, April 22, 1976.* Chicago: Chicago Linguistic Society

Stempel, Reinhard 1996. *Die Diathese im Indogermanischen: Formen und Funktionen des Mediums und ihre sprachhistorischen Grundlagen.* Innsbruck: Institut für Sprachwissenschaft der Universität Innsbruck

Strunk, Klaus 1967. *Nasalpräsentien und Aoriste. Ein Beitrag zur Morphologie des Verbums im Indo-Iranischen und Griechischen.* Heidelberg: Winter

   1983. *Typische Merkmale von Fragesätzen und die altindische Pluti.* (Sitzungsberichte der Bayerischen Akademie der Wissenschaften. Philosophisch-Historische Klasse: Jg. 1983, Heft 8.) Munich: Bayerische Akademie der Wissenschaften

   'Further evidence for diachronic selection: Ved. *ráṣṭi*, Latin *regit* etc.,' in Cardona and Zide (eds.), pp. 385–92

   1994. 'Relative Chronology and the Indo-European Verb-System: The Case of the Present- and Aorist-Stems', *Journal of Indo-European Studies* 22: 417–33

Szemerényi, Oswald 1960. *Studies in the Indo-European System of Numerals.* Heidelberg: Winter

   1973. 'La théorie des laryngales de Saussure à Kurylowicz et à Benveniste. Essai de réévaluation', *Bulletin de la Société de Linguistique de Paris* 68: 1–25

   1977. *Studies in the Kinship Terminology of the Indo-European Languages.* Leiden: Brill

   1979. 'Vedic *šam, šaṃ yoh* and *šaṃ(ča) yošča*', *Incontri Linguistici* 4: 159–84

   1996. *Introduction to Indo-European Linguistics.* Oxford: Clarendon Press

Thomas, Werner 1975. 'Zum Problem des Prohibitivs im Indogermanischen', in Cobet, Leimbach and Neschke-Hentschke (eds.), pp. 307–25

Tichy, Eva 1993. 'Kollektiva, Genus femininum und relative Chronologie im Indogermanischen', *Historische Sprachforschung (Zeitschrift für Vergleichende Sprachforschung)* 106: 1–19

Trask, Robert Lawrence 1996. *Historical Linguistics.* London: Arnold

Tremblay, Xavier 2003. *La déclinaison des noms de parenté indo-européens en -ter-.* Innsbruck: Institut für Sprachwissenschaft der Universität Innsbruck

Trubetzkoy, N. S. 1939. 'Gedanken über das Indogermanenproblem', *Acta Linguistica* 1: 81–9

Uhlenbeck, C. C. 1901. 'Agens und Patiens im Kasussystem der indogermanischen Sprachen', *Indogermanische Forschungen* 12: 170–1

Untermann, Jürgen 1997. *Monumenta Linguarum Hispanicarum. Vol. IV Die tartessischen, keltiberischen und lusitanischen Inschriften.* Wiesbaden: Reichelt

   2000. *Wörterbuch des Oskisch-Umbrischen.* Heidelberg: Winter

van Valin Jr, Robert D. and LaPolla, Randy J. 1997. *Syntax: Structure, Meaning and Function.* Cambridge: Cambridge University Press

Vaux, Bert 1998. *The Phonology of Armenian.* Oxford: Clarendon Press

Vennemann, Theo (ed.) 1989. *The New Sound of Indo-European. Essays in Phonological Reconstruction.* Berlin: Mouton de Gruyter

Villar, Francisco 1984. 'Ergativity and Animate/Inanimate Gender in Indo-European', *Zeitschrift für Vergleichende Sprachforschung* 97: 167–96

1996. *Los indoeuropeos y los orígenes de Europa. Lenguaje e historia*. Second Edition. Madrid: Gredos

Wachter, Rudolf 1998. 'Wortschatzrekonstruktion auf der Basis von Ersatzbildungen', in Meid (ed.) 1998, pp. 199–207

Wackernagel, Jacob 1896. *Altindische Grammatik. Lautlehre*. Göttingen: Vandenhoeck & Ruprecht

1910. 'Indoiranica', *Zeitschrift für vergleichende Sprachforschung* 43: 277–98

1942. 'Indogermanisch -*que* als alte nebensatzeinleitende Konjunktion', *Zeitschrift für vergleichende Sprachforschung* 67: 1–5

1953. *Kleine Schriften. I*. Göttingen: Vandenhoeck & Ruprecht

Watkins, Calvert 1962. *Indo-European Origins of the Celtic Verb I. The Sigmatic Aorist*. Dublin: Dublin Institute for Advanced Studies

1964. 'Preliminaries to the Reconstruction of Indo-European Sentence Structure', *Proceedings of the Ninth International Congress (1962) of Linguistics*, pp. 1035–42

1969. *Formenlehre. Teil I. Geschichte der indogermanischen Verbalflexion*, in Kuryłowicz (ed.) *Indogermanische Grammatik*. Heidelberg: Winter

1976. 'Towards Proto-Indo-European Syntax: Problems and Pseudo-Problems', in Steever, Walker and Mufwene (eds.), pp. 305–26

1979. 'NAM.RA GUD UDU in Hittite: Indo-European Poetic Language and the Folk Taxonomy of Wealth', in Meid and Neu (eds.), pp. 269–87

(ed.) 1987. *Studies in Memory of Warren Cowgill. Papers from the fourth East Coast Indo-European Conference. Cornell University June 6–9 1985*. Berlin / New York: de Gruyter

1994. *Selected Writings*. Innsbruck: Institut für Sprachwissenschaft der Universität Innsbruck

1995. *How to Kill a Dragon: Aspects of Indo-European Poetics*. New York / Oxford: Oxford University Press

2000. *The American Heritage Dictionary of Indo-European Roots*. Second Edition. Boston: Houghton Mifflin

Werba, Chlodwig H. 1997. *Verba Indoarica: die primären und sekundären Wurzeln der Sanskrit-Sprache*. Vienna: Verlag der Österreichischen Akademie der Wissenschaften

West, Martin L. 1988. 'The Rise of the Greek Epic', *Journal of Hellenic Studies* 108: 151–72

Widmer, Paul 2004. *Das Korn des weiten Feldes. Interne Derivation, Derivationskette und Flexionsklassenhierarchie: Aspekte der nominalen Wortbildung im Urindogermanischen*. Innsbruck: Institut für Sprachwissenschaft der Universität Innsbruck

Winter, Werner (ed.) 1965. *Evidence for Laryngeals*. London / The Hague / Paris: Mouton

(ed.) 1995. *On Languages and Language*. Berlin / New York: Mouton de Gruyter

Woodard, Roger (ed.) 2004. *The Encyclopedia of the World's Ancient Languages*. Cambridge: Cambridge University Press

Yoshida, Kazuhiko 1990. *The Hittite Mediopassive Endings in -ri*. Berlin: De Gruyter

Zerdin, Jason R. 1999. 'Studies in the Ancient Greek Verbs in -sko.' Unpublished DPhil dissertation, Oxford University

Word index

Language index

Person index

Subject index

acrostatic paradigm 80
active alignment 178
a-declension in Lycian 109
alignment change 176–80
amphikinetic paradigm 80
aspect 133–6
atelic roots 134
augment 123

Balkan sub-group of Indo-European 7
basic vocabulary list 10–12, 18
Brugmann's Law 32, 61

centum languages 49
cladistics 9–15

e-grade 65, 75
elliptical dual 101, 184
ergative 177
etymological dictionaries 187
Eurasiatic 20, 24

family tree 5, 10–13
full-grade 71, 72

gender, in nouns 91
    in Anatolian 104
glottochronology 18
glottalic model 45–8
Grassmann's Law 32, 49
Greco-Aryan model of the reconstructed verb
        115–29
Grimm's Law 32
-*hi* conjugation in Hittite 129, 138–42, 179

hypotaxis, diachronic relation with parataxis 171
hysterokinetic paradigm 80

i-motion in Anatolian 108–10
Indo-European language family (*see also*
        Proto-Indo-European) 2
    criteria for membership 2–4
    spread of 7–9, 17, 18
    sub-families of 5–6
injunctive 130–2, 162

kinetic paradigm 80
Kurgan theory 18

labio-velar stops 49
laryngeals 53–61
    hiatus caused by in Indo-Iranian 58–59
    loss of in IE languages 59–60
    phonetic nature of 57
    initial vowel form in Greek and Armenian 58
    triple reflex of in Greek 58–9
language shift 8–9
lengthened grade 72, 79
limitation of accent in Greek 75, 76

-*mi* conjugation in Hittite 129, 179
mora 76
movable **s* 67

Narten ablaut 83–4
nasal infix, present stem formed by 153–4
neuter nouns 177
    agreement patterns of 101
New Comparative Mythology 212
non-syllabic resonant
Nostratic 20–3

o-grade 75
optative *see* modal formations
Osthoff's Law 32

palatals, law of 32
parataxis, diachronic relation with hypotaxis 171
phylogeny *see* family tree
proterokinetic paradigm 80
Proto-Indo-European (*see also* Indo-European
        language family)
    ablative singular case marker 97
    ablaut 54, 64, 71–4
    accent 75–8
    athematic noun declension 92–5
        replaced by thematic 99
    athematic verb conjugation 123–5
    *b as reconstructed phoneme 33, 40, 46
    centum / satem dialectal division in 51
    collective 101–3, 107–8

UNIVERSITY OF WINCHESTER
LIBRARY

UNIVERSITY OF WINCHESTER
LIBRARY

21885865R00158

Printed in Great Britain
by Amazon